The Origins of Language

Contributors

Robbins Burling
Department of Anthropology, University of Michigan

Iain Davidson
School of Human and Environmental Studies
University of New England (Australia)

Kathleen Gibson
Department of Basic Sciences
University of Texas Health Science Center

Stephen Jessee
Department of Basic Sciences
University of Texas Health Science Center

Barbara J. King
Department of Anthropology, College of William and Mary

Dario Maestripieri
Human Development Committee, University of Chicago

Lorraine McCune
Department of Educational Psychology, Rutgers University

Sue Savage-Rumbaugh
Language Research Center, Georgia State University

Charles Snowdon
Department of Psychology, University of Wisconsin

Sherman Wilcox
Department of Linguistics, University of New Mexico

The Origins of Language

What Nonhuman Primates Can Tell Us

Edited by Barbara J. King

School of American Research Press
Santa Fe, New Mexico

School of American Research Press
Post Office Box 2188
Santa Fe, New Mexico, 87504-2188

Director of Publications: Joan K. O'Donnell
Copy Editor: Jane Kepp
Designer: Context, Inc.
Indexer: Andrew L. Christianson
Typographer: Jim Mafchir, Western Edge Press

Library of Congress Cataloging-in-Publication Data:
The origins of language : what nonhuman primates can tell us / edited by Barbara J. King.
p. cm. — (School of American Research advanced seminar series)
Includes bibliographical references and index.
ISBN 0-933452-59-4 (Cloth). — ISBN 0-933452-60-8 (Pbk.)
1. Language and languages—Origin. 2. Animal communication. 3. Primates.
I. King, Barbara J., 1956 – . II. Series.
P116.O75 1999
401—dc21   99-28268
                                                                             CIP

Cover photograph: A subadult male cotton-top tamarin "long-calling."
Copyright © Carla Y. Boe. Cover design by Context, Inc.

Contents

Illustrations

Tables

Preface

During the five years since the publication of my first book with the School of American Research (SAR) Press—*The Information Continuum* (1994)—my views on communication have evolved considerably. For many years I had accepted the typical linear view of communication: one individual produces signals that may be sent to a second individual, who may then respond. The conventional emphasis is on the production of vocal signals by single individuals. In the terms of my 1994 book, information is often donated from a more experienced member of society to a less experienced member, whether the society is a human one or one composed of monkeys or apes.

More recently, influenced by thinkers from a variety of disciplines, I have come to see communication (including language) as dynamic—as about use and interaction rather than about some static set of features. Communication involves comprehension as well as production. It is a distributed process, such that the object of study should not be the calls or words produced by single individuals but rather the communication, vocal and nonvocal, that occurs within a whole social unit (for example, the dyad or the subgroup). Communication is emergent, and it emerges anew every time participants act together.

During the time that my views about communication were evolving in this way, I became progressively disenchanted with the typical procedure by which information is imparted within the anthropological community. Conferences were the venue of choice, and I was a regular participant. Dutifully, I would show up at some hotel crowded with hundreds or thousands of anthropologists. I would attend paper sessions in chilly conference rooms, listen to other speakers offer their ideas in the 15- to 20-minute time slots available, present my own research in the same length of time, and hope for a brief exchange of views at the conclusion of the session.

These situations left little opportunity for true discussion of ideas. During one such frustrating experience, I began to recall images from my year in Santa Fe as a resident scholar at SAR. I had observed small groups of anthropologists and scholars from related disciplines arriving at SAR for week-long advanced seminars. The groups' intensity of focus and purpose and their evident sustained energy over five seminar days stayed in my mind. And on a crisp fall morning in October 1996, I found myself back at SAR, joining nine other scholars whom I had invited to an advanced seminar of our own, in order to discuss primatology and language origins. All nine had had a profound influence on my thinking and writing over the years. They had been flown in from Australia and Wisconsin and everywhere in between. Many of us had never met in person. Could anything meaningful possibly emerge from this group in less than a week?

The answer was yes, as I believe this seminar volume amply demonstrates. It was a privilege to work with these scholars—the chapter authors represented here plus my valued colleague Talbot Taylor from the College of William and Mary, who acted brilliantly in the role of discussant.

Without the vision of Douglas Schwartz, president of SAR, advanced seminars would not succeed as they do. It is one thing to collect 10 people in a room and quite another to ensure that they interact productively. Doug achieved this by setting just the right tone with a mix of structure and freedom-from-structure. Cecile Stein and Sarah Wimett made the week in Santa Fe a delightful experience, having arranged everything for us from easy transportation to delicious meals.

At SAR Press, Joan O'Donnell and her staff provided superb assistance at every stage in the publication of this book. A special word must be said about Jane Kepp, who, by editing this volume so intelligently, enabled the emergence of our clearest, best writing.

For years of superb discussions about anthropology, primatology, the evolution of language, and the process of writing, I have many people to thank. In addition to Talbot Taylor and the contributors to this book, these include Joanne Bowen, Deborah Forster, Grey Gundaker, Christine Johnson, Janette Wallis, and Anne Zeller. To Sherman Wilcox, Willow Powers, Danielle Moretti Langholtz, and Stephen Wood, a special thanks for many years of particularly intense and valuable talks.

During the advanced seminar, Sue Savage-Rumbaugh invited me to study bonobo communication at the Language Research Center (LRC) at Georgia State University. It would be impossible to overestimate the importance to my understanding of language origins of either Savage-Rumbaugh's own work or my opportunity to carry out research at the LRC. Her faith in me has meant a great deal. Duane Rumbaugh, director of the LRC, facilitated my work there in many important ways. Without Dan Rice's participation in my research, the project would have suffered enormous gaps; I thank him both for collecting data and for understanding the goals of the project so well. Data have also been collected during two summers by two exceptionally skilled students, Erin Selner and Heather Bond, both of whom studied anthropology with me at the College of William and Mary.

My colleagues in the Department of Anthropology at the College of William and Mary provide a collegial and stimulating environment in which to work. Over the years, the mentoring of Virginia Kerns, Vinson Sutlive, and Mary Voigt has been invaluable. Willam and Mary has supported my research financially through a series of research grants, for which I am grateful.

Stuart Shanker has, through his research, his generosity in sharing ideas, and his continual guidance, enormously affected not only what I think but also how I think. Stuart's steady friendship and constant kindnesses have meant more to me than he knows.

The meaning in my work comes from my interaction with my family. To my mother, Elizabeth King, and to my late father, Walter King, I owe so much. The life I share with Charlie and Sarah Hogg means everything to me. And Charlie, only you know how much this book owes to you.

The Origins of Language

1

Introduction

Primatological Perspectives on Language

Barbara J. King

At the close of one long, productive day, those of us participating in the School of American Research advanced seminar on primatology and language origins, held in October 1996, accomplished what we hadn't done, or even aimed to do, all day. We reached a consensus. It has become impossible, we agreed, for anyone interested in the origins and evolution of language to keep up with the recent explosion of books and articles on the topic. New theories and reviews of evidence appear monthly in fields as diverse as linguistics, anthropology, philosophy, psychology, cognitive science, and neuroscience. If there is a drawback to working interdisciplinarily—indeed, in an area Gómez (1997) characterizes as having second-order interdisciplinarity because so many of its constituent fields are themselves interdisciplinary—it is the risk of information overload.

Yet the variety of approaches evident in this burst of publishing is not so great as one might expect. One or two perspectives dominate, whereas others are found only in an occasional article or book. Indeed, a driving force behind my proposal in 1994 to organize the seminar was the recognition that a strong corpus of work is needed from within primatology and paleoanthropology—a perspective that is absolutely crucial to understanding language origins and evolution.

Currently in vogue is a view that emphasizes the uniqueness of human language in comparison with all other systems of communication in the animal world. Essential, qualitative differences are believed to set human language apart from other animal communication, and it is held that few or no meaningful precursors to human language inhere in animal communication. Although some theories allow a significant role for the social shaping of language skills during childhood, the most fashionable view is the innatist or nativist one, in which language is seen as an instinct—as an innate biological system with features that are unique to our species.

This idea can be traced back centuries, but in modern times the strong nativist perspective gained prominence with the work of Chomsky. As most readers of this book will know, Chomsky's (1965) view is that language is an innate, rule-based system existing in the brain of the developing child. Language unfolds according to a set of inborn rules, or a "universal grammar," derived from a genetic specialization in the human brain. The essential task is to study these rules. Chomskian theory is concerned primarily with syntax; it is not concerned with conceptual or pragmatic aspects of language comprehension and use (Tomasello 1995). Furthermore, in the Chomskian view, nothing meaningful can be gained by studying language from an evolutionary perspective.

Since the publication of Chomsky's initial theories, most linguists have been responding to him, whether positively or negatively, explicitly or implicitly: "Every modern linguist carries, involuntarily and sometimes unfairly, a vest-pocket vita summarizing his life's work as pro-Chomskian or anti-Chomskian" (Rymer 1993:28). And the Chomskian influence extends far beyond linguistics to other fields that study language acquisition and the evolution of language. When strict innatist views are challenged by those who see human linguistic uniqueness as stemming primarily from social interaction, the research issues still derive, very often, from a Chomskian framework (see Reed 1995). Even one of the most cited and discussed versions of how language evolved in our ancestors—Pinker and Bloom's theory of gradual evolution through natural selection in the hominid lineage (Pinker and Bloom 1990; Pinker 1994)—is a modification of Chomskian theory. Indeed, by arguing that language is a "specialized biological system" that evolved through natural selection, Pinker and Bloom (1990:726) have broadened the audience for innatists' views by drawing in some of those who were uncomfortable with Chomsky's complete dismissal of an evolutionary perspective (see King, chapter 2, this volume).

The popularity of assertions about the innateness of language is an intriguing phenomenon in its own right. Alternative frameworks suggest interpretations of how language develops that are quite different from Pinker and Bloom's. Yet even the most compelling alternative approaches seem to garner less attention. These alternatives include cognitive and functional approaches that derive language universals from cognitive and social universals rather than from inborn grammatical rules (see Tomasello 1995; Wilcox, this volume), as well as developmental approaches that show modifiability of communication or language based on social parameters (see Snowdon, this volume).

A parallel example of the attraction of innatist thinking comes from the "grammar gene" controversy. This debate centers on the idea that human grammatical capacity is determined by a specific gene. When a report in a scientific publication described a genetic cause of aggrammatism in one family, academics, science writers, and even the public responded with extreme interest. When rebuttals were published, scant attention was paid (Elman et al. 1996:377–78). Why should this be the case? "There seems to be a deep-rooted desire to believe that humans are not only unique (every species is, after all) but that our uniqueness arises from a quantum leap in evolution" (Elman et al. 1996:378). Yet the data ably counter other nativist claims—for example, that grammar function is localized within the human brain or that critical periods for language acquisition are compatible only with a view of language as innate (see Elman et al. 1996 for accounts that challenge these claims).

A major flaw in many accounts of human uniqueness, whatever their emphasis, is their failure to incorporate information about nonhuman primates. If such data are used at all, the tendency is to focus on a few examples—perhaps a few captive nonhuman primates or a few "famous" populations of free-ranging monkeys or apes (often the Gombe chimpanzees or the Amboseli vervets)—without any understanding of the breadth and complexity of nonhuman primate behavior (Wiener 1984:255–56; King, chapter 2, this volume). Anthropology, given its dependence on cross-cultural variation and the role of learning through social interaction, tends to be skeptical of strongly innatist scenarios but is itself far from immune to the neglect of data from nonhuman primates. Even where the four-field approach is practiced—integrating cultural anthropology, biological anthropology, archaeology, and linguistic anthropology—as it is in many colleges and universities in the United States, many anthropologists are reluctant to embrace a view that is cross-species as well as cross-cultural. And some anthropologists reject outright the worth of a focus on our evolutionary past. Consider what a former editor of *Current Anthropology*, the major international journal in anthropology, had to say:

> Human beings today live very differently from even their ancestors of a thousand years ago. We should not then expect to learn very much about our present nature from a study of remote ancestors scratching a living some forty thousand years ago, let alone from the primates who were contemporary with Australopithecus some four to five million years ago. If ultimate origins are supposed to explain the essence of what we are, we might just as well go back to the first insects that spread over the world, or forward to the origins of capitalism. (Kuper 1994:100–101)

The assumptions expressed in this quotation are fascinating, starting with the idea that hominids whom we know to have been capable of complex social behavior can be described as scratching a living. Also significant is the thought that evolutionary analysis cannot explain our essence. Primatologists would reply—at least this one would—that we cannot understand our essence without looking at other species, particularly humans' closest living relatives, the monkeys and apes (see Shephard 1996).

Many other anthropologists do accept the worth of the perspective that Kuper rejects, but they focus on nonbehavioral research issues or else study (or reconstruct) behavior but exclude monkeys and apes from their analyses. Biological anthropologists have tended to emphasize either fossil or artifactual analysis. Methods of choice involve reconstructing skulls and vocal tracts (e.g., Lieberman 1991), relating degree of encephalization to language (e.g., Tobias 1987), and evaluating whether behavioral products such as stone tools reflect linguistic skills (e.g., Gibson and Ingold 1993). When the emergence of language is considered, questions often focus on controversies concerning hominids alone, such as whether Neandertals had language.

Although these approaches from biological anthropology can yield valuable insights into the origins and evolution of language, they cannot address questions of central importance to the topic. What aspects of language or language use in hominids or humans evolved before the split between African apes and hominids? What does language have in common with the communication systems of nonhuman primates and even with their nonlinguistic behavior? How is language different? Surely only by approaching these questions with data from behavioral primatology can we even know the full range of questions to ask about language evolution. As Taylor (1996) has said, if it can be shown convincingly that the behavior of nonhuman primates indicates no "language gap" between monkeys and apes, on the one hand, and hominids and/or modern humans, on the other, then there is no need to create theories capable of explaining how "the language gap" was bridged.

To be sure, some language theorists do integrate the nonhuman primate behavioral data into their analyses. Some conclude that nonhuman primate behavior is significantly languagelike or shows language precursors, either in the wild (Boehm 1992; Savage-Rumbaugh et al. 1996; see King 1994a) or in captivity (Savage-Rumbaugh et al. 1993). Precursors can include simpler versions of so-called language properties such as syntax or displacement or wholly different behaviors that nonetheless contain some essential features of the property in question (and could thus have evolved over time into that property). Other language theorists maintain that despite some basic evolutionary commonalities, there is a fundamental discontinuity between nonhuman primate communication and human language (Noble and Davidson 1996). Some theorists broaden the search for selection pressures to include those operating on nonhuman primates (Dunbar 1993, 1996). What is missing, however, is a comprehensive attempt to pull together the nonhuman primate data and discuss their implications for language origins and evolution. Such an endeavor is less likely to come from a single scholar or research team than from a tightly focused, cross-disciplinary group. The SAR advanced seminar provided a chance for just such a group to write about and discuss the relevant issues at length.

SOME QUESTIONS AND SOME ANSWERS

During our advanced seminar we explored a host of issues, including these: Are there (or were there) linguistic and/or behavioral precursors to language in nonhuman primates, including the hominids? How can they best be sought? To what degree does primate vocal and gestural communication unfold in a flexible manner, according to experience and interaction, instead of unfolding according to prespecified, biologically determined structures or processes? How do events during ontogeny contribute to the development of language? What specific processes contributed to the emergence of language both ontogenetically and phylogenetically and to the subsequent evolution of language over time? How can the future study of nonhuman primate communication and cognition advance our understanding of language origins?

The chapters in this book reflect the significant headway we made during the seminar in answering these questions. In the next chapter, I lay groundwork for what is to come later in the book by analyzing some recent language-origins theories. I ask not only how language-origins theorists interpret the data from primatology but also why they need to arrive at such interpretations. Although the oft-used terms "continuity theory" and "discontinuity theory" are too simplistic, a continuum of theories can be identified by analyzing each theory in terms of the questions it asks (and does not ask), the definitions it uses (and rejects), the assumptions it makes (and does not make), and the evidence it reviews (and ignores). Sorting out such differences across theories should clear the ground for more productive dialogue across the disciplines involved in the study of language origins and evolution.

Next come three chapters by primatologists who provide data on primate communication and insights into how these data can aid in understanding the origins of language. In chapter 3, Dario Maestripieri compares the gestural repertoires of three species of macaque monkeys in order to evaluate the hypothesis that sophisticated communication is most likely to develop in societies that are more egalitarian and individualistic than dominance-oriented. His data support the suggestion that when flexible individual strategies and coordination of behavior are at a premium, the size of the gestural repertoire will be greater. Maestripieri's research provides a window into the dynamic interaction between primate social life and the evolution of communication and into the broader question of evolutionary trends in primate communication.

In chapter 4, Charles Snowdon discusses his research with marmosets and tamarins, monkeys from the New World, and reviews evidence from a number of other primate species to demonstrate that vocal communication and language are socially constructed. Hard data point to continuity between nonhuman communication and human language and to the importance of social experience in the development and expression of primate vocalizations. Claims that critical periods tightly constrain development in primates and that vocal learning is absent in nonhuman primates—which, if correct, would render suspect the notion of an evolutionary continuum in language—are greatly weakened by Snowdon's data.

Through allegory and imagined dialogue between an animal-language researcher and a skeptic of claims from animal language work, Sue Savage-Rumbaugh shows in chapter 5 how primatologists must adopt a new starting point if they hope to fully understand nonhuman primate communication. Merely counting types of vocalizations produced and assigning function to calls depending on the events immediately following them will not give us insights into the rich communication of monkeys and apes. Currently, it is unacceptable in the scientific community to assume even that nonhuman primates actually mean to communicate, much less that they purposefully coordinate their complex behavior. Yet, Savage-Rumbaugh says, these are exactly the things we must assume before we can start to understand primate communication. She elaborates on this point by discussing her research with enculturated apes.

The next trio of papers broadens the scope of the book to consider hominids. In chapter 6, Kathleen Gibson and Stephen Jessee review the comparative anatomy, brain structure, and behavior of humans and great apes in order to suggest that quantitative changes in the brain during evolution—not the appearance of unique organs in the brain—enabled humans to construct more hierarchically complex schema, both in language and in other behavioral arenas, than other animals can construct. They discuss evidence in support of their suggestions that by the time of *Homo erectus,* hominids were using language to coordinate action and that Neandertals and anatomically modern humans were cognitively indistinguishable.

In counterpoint to Gibson and Jessee, Iain Davidson argues in chapter 7 that Neandertals and modern humans were fundamentally distinct in their use of language. For Davidson, the essence of language is symbol production, which he sees as uniquely human. But there is a twist to Davidson's discussion of the discontinuity he sees between modern humans and all other creatures, for he emphasizes that language itself fosters this discontinuity. Humans can name events, objects, and people, and in doing so can change their perception of their world. Davidson, like Gibson and Jessee, analyzes changes in brains during human evolution, but he understands and discusses this evolutionary change in the context of human development. He emphasizes the uniquely human process of joint attention between caretaker and child in children's acquisition of language and also in language origins.

Data on children's behavior and possible patterns in primate ontogeny are discussed by Lorraine McCune in her developmental, comparativist account in chapter 8. McCune's previous research had demonstrated that one type of children's grunt vocalization—the final grunt to develop in a sequence of three—reliably predicted the child's first use of language referentially. The child's own experience of her grunt apparently facilitates recognition of the correspondence between sound and meaning in adult communication. McCune suggests that grunts may function similarly in other primates: monkey and ape grunts may help their producers establish a correspondence between sound and meaning and may act as a bridge to use of the species-specific communicative repertoire.

Two concluding chapters ask about processes involved in language emergence. In chapter 9, Robbins Burling suggests a special role in the evolution of language for motivated signs. Motivated signs are those that are not arbitrary but instead depend on an individual's ability to recognize similarities between a sign and the thing it stands for. Burling points out some continuities between human and ape use of motivated signs, noting that apes alone among animals have demonstrated productive iconicity. Building on this fact, Burling constructs a stagelike model by which a species without language might evolve into a species with language.

In the final chapter, Sherman Wilcox sees even broader continuities across species and asks whether general cognitive abilities account for the emergence of language. He contrasts Cartesian approaches to language evolution, which emphasize grammar as structure, with cognitive-functional views, which see grammar as emerging from cognitive abilities. Building on the cognitive-functional view, which requires no special human abilities in order for language to emerge, Wilcox argues for a catalytic role for visible gesture as a raw material in the evolution of language through ritualization. Ritualization involves repetition, and so gestures can become, over time, indexical of the act they perform. Eventually they can become signs for, and then symbols of, the act itself.

This volume begins, then, with a general overview of language-origins theories and moves on to reports of empirical research on monkeys, apes, hominids, and humans. It concludes by considering how we can use these data to fashion more reliable and rigorous theories of language origins and evolution. The brief chapter summaries just concluded are meant to invite readers to delve into each author's rich treatment of language-origins issues. The authors themselves frequently cite each other's chapters, drawing the reader into a closely interconnected network of ideas. In the remainder of this chapter, I hope to provide a framework for those connections by discussing different views of what language is and how the primatological perspective can inform them.

WHAT IS LANGUAGE, ANYWAY?

Rule-based grammatical systems, as I mentioned earlier, have assumed a monumental presence in modern linguistic theory, such that most theorists—including but not limited to the innatists—define language through syntax. It thus becomes significant to ask whether syntax has any precursors in nonhuman primates. Testing hypotheses along these lines is difficult at present, because we have so little knowledge about units of perception and communication in other species (Hauser 1996). Building up such knowledge, however, is a better alternative than equating syntax with word order, which is far too simplistic a reduction of a system that involves complexities such as phrases embedded within other phrases.

In aiming for a comparative investigation of syntactic capabilities, we might ask, Do other animals have precursors to syntax in their behavior, either vocal or nonvocal? Can a plausible account be offered for the incremental development of syntax? Several recent papers address the first question. Snowdon (this volume) and Wiener (1984) review attempts to identify precursors to syntax in the way units are structured in utterances of monkeys and apes, finding some plausible examples. Ujhelyi (1996), in asking whether there is any intermediate stage between animal communication and language, considers what she calls "naturally occurring syntax." Based on a literature review, she concludes that certain types of nonhuman primate calls, such as the songs of gibbons, titi monkeys, tamarins, and indris, fit the criteria of a "minimal language." She justifies this conclusion by noting that "it can be shown that a given call is built up from a limited number of elements, which form complex, acoustically different sound lines. . . . The call variants resulting from combination of available elements not only express the actual emotional states of an animal but [also] contain some representational meaning by signaling individual identity" (Ujhelyi 1996:73–74).

Ujhelyi sees language as composed of subsystems, some of which emerged earlier evolutionarily than others. She stresses that structural reorganization at the subsystem level can lead to the emergence of an entirely new system (see also Elman et al. 1996 for a discussion of this kind of nonlinear change), a perspective that allows human language to be unique while also having evolutionary precursors (see also King 1994a).

Looking for syntax or its precursors outside of vocal behavior is also possible. When monkeys or apes show that they understand relationships across complex patterns of social behavior, we might infer, if arguably, that they are displaying cognitive precursors to some syntactic capability (King 1996). An example in which monkeys likely are understanding such relationships among patterns—not just relationships among objects—is when vervets, in forming alliances with unrelated conspecifics, choose as allies those monkeys who have groomed them at the highest rates in the past (Cheney and Seyfarth 1990). De Winter (1988:257; see also Peters 1972:37; Fischer 1988) goes even further, suggesting that syntactic rules of language "are derived from the syntactic rules which govern all flexible behavior." This suggestion is made because flexible behavior can be broken down into parts and recombined to form "new functionally complete sequences, following strict rules of recombination," thus producing a "striking" analogy to language (de Winter 1988:256).

Yet each of these analyses of syntax remains vulnerable to charges of reductionism—to being judged to significantly underestimate the complexity and generative nature of syntax. More robust analyses await more data. Meanwhile, a strong response to claims for the innateness of syntax comes from an evolutionary scenario put forth by Armstrong, Stokoe, and Wilcox (1995) in which syntax is derived incrementally in the hominid lineage. Edelman's (1987) idea of neuronal group selection provides the mechanism for the process being described, in which gesture is seen as containing the seeds of syntax, and sorting words into categories is enhanced by the experience of gesturing (Wilcox, this volume). Growing attention to the topic of communicative gestures by apes, broadly defined to include movements of the body, limbs, and hands as well as facial expressions, shows that ape gesture may be an important raw material for natural selection in a way that nicely supports the "seeds of syntax" view as developed by Armstrong, Stokoe, and Wilcox (see Savage-Rumbaugh, Wilkerson, and Bakeman 1977; Goodall 1986; Tomasello, Gust, and Frost 1989; Tomasello et al. 1994; Tanner and Byrne 1996; King n.d.). The most detailed studies of ape gesture have been carried out on animals in captivity, although field studies show that communicative gestures occur in wild populations as well (for a review see Tomasello and Camaioni 1997; King n.d.).

Many language theorists, of course, see language not just as a system of universal grammar but as a collection of various unique features or properties. Influenced by Hockett's (1960) analysis of 16 of the design features of language, primatologists have asked which of these language features are uniquely human and which are more widely distributed in animals. Only a few features appear to be unique to humans (Weiner 1984; Boehm 1992; McCune, this volume; Snowdon, this volume; but see Noble and Davidson 1996 for a different view). Even what looks like displacement, or at least a precursor to it, has been tentatively identified in the nonvocal behavior of wild bonobos, who flatten vegetation to indicate the direction of group travel across time and space (Savage-Rumbaugh et al. 1996).

Another common view is that language is representational—that is, words "stand for" or represent real things in the world. Language thus encodes or reflects something real and can transfer information or ideas from mind to mind. The units of language and the information they contain encode meaning. Alternatives do exist to these mentalistic ways of thinking about language, as when language is seen as interaction, with the meaning residing in the interaction. In this view, meaning is negotiated dynamically by participants in ongoing interactions. The linguist Halliday, for example, thought about language in ways quite opposed to Chomsky's:

> Halliday's theory of language is part of an overall theory of social interaction, and from such a perspective it is obvious that a language must be seen as more than a set of sentences, as it is for Chomsky. Rather, language will be seen as a text, or discourse—the exchange of meanings in interpersonal contexts. The creativity of language is situated in this exchange. A Hallidayan grammar is therefore a grammar of meaningful choices rather than of formal rules. (Malmkjaer 1991:160)

When language is viewed as use and interaction, wholly different methods for studying its origins and evolution emerge. In these methods, there is little value in parsing sentences or searching for the meaning in words and units. What is meaningful in language is not static in structure but constructed in use. If we accept that meaning is constructed socially and does not reside in an innate ruled-based system, then the most valuable places in which to look for linguistic precursors are social behavior, social interaction, and the comprehension and coordination of activities—perhaps in developmental contexts most critically of all. Particularly valuable will be data collected in naturalistic contexts where the responses of the subjects under study are not tightly constrained. In these contexts, the effects of social interaction on the acquisition of linguistic skills can be well understood, as they cannot be in studies where subjects' acquisition skills are examined in isolation.

Richman (1997:21–22) points out a potentially fruitful direction to take in studying the evolutionary roots of language from the perspective of interaction:

> I'm going to suggest that human beings and some highly social primates both use in their social lives a wide variety of meaning-producing symbols that we could call presentational gestures. Presentational gestures are multi-media complexes of intentional movements of different parts of the body that develop over a course of time and which produce meanings and demand responses from others. . . .
>
> Because presentational gestures are actions that develop over the course of time, because they enact life and emotions (not represent static substitutions), [and] because they demand participation by others, their meanings are public, out in the open, and interactive. So the story of meaning for them is not just one about how meaning is produced by individual actors, but also how it is reproduced by others in their responses.

Here we are back to an emphasis on gesture, but with the focus broadened to include not just apes but other nonhuman primates as well. Hamadryas baboons "vote" on the direction of group travel by using specific facial expressions and orienting their bodies in a certain direction, near certain conspecifics (Kummer 1968). By doing so they affect what others will do, just as what others already did has affected their own bodily movement, in a way that likely involves Richman's presentational gestures. Not only behavioral outcomes but also meanings are negotiated as action unfolds.

What one might do in studying such interactional gestures is not to carry out spectographic analyses of vocalizations or apply a trait-list approach to properties in vocal or gestural behavior or even use an initiator-response linear framework for studying communication. Rather, one might ask, How do subgroups coordinate their fission-fusion patterns on a daily basis (see Maestripieri, this volume)? How do individuals coordinate their movements during a hunt? How do caretakers and very young infants coordinate their behavior and communication right from birth (Parker 1985; Borchert and Zihlman 1990; King n.d.; McCune, this volume; see Trevarthen 1979)?

These questions might be thought about in a systems, or coordinated-action, perspective. Much better established in the human than in the nonhuman primate literature (e.g., Eckerman 1993; Hutchens 1995; Markova, Graumann, and Foppa 1995; but see Strum, Forster, and Hutchens 1997 for an example from primatology), this view considers behavior and cognition to be processes in which two or more participants coordinate their actions on a subtle level. The communication and meaning emerge from the system rather than flowing in a linear fashion from an initiator to a recipient. This can be most easily seen, perhaps, in mother-infant pairs, where the pair is the system, where eye and limb movements are coordinated right from birth, and where signals of mutual understanding are developed gradually from those movements, vocalizations, and facial expressions.

Of course a systems perspective does not preclude wanting to know whether vocalizations have syntax, displaced reference, or other structural properties. Yet the underlying assumptions of the various conceptions of language explored here differ enough that the questions of origins and continuity emphasized by each will differ also. Those who see meaning in interaction and not in the utterances themselves are less likely to do structural or design-feature analysis of the utterances. Those who want to know whether strings of calls or gestures have design features may not pay close attention to the dynamics of negotiated meaning. Only when researchers begin to make explicit how they think about language will the reasons for the questions asked and not asked become clear in the language-origins literature (Taylor 1996; Savage-Rumbaugh, Shanker, and Taylor 1998; King, chapter 2, this volume).

THE FUTURE OF LANGUAGE-ORIGINS RESEARCH

No matter what view of language is taken, the primatological perspective suggests that language has a long evolutionary history. Most of us in the seminar agreed with this statement. We found precursors to language properties and features as well as precursors to the construction and negotiation of meaning, and we saw commonalities across species in how ontogenetic patterns affect both comprehension and production. Still, it would be misleading to overestimate our agreement about continuities. Some participants saw vast differences between the productive and symbolic capacities of human language and the capacities of other primates' communication systems (Burling, this volume; Davidson, this volume). All of us, nonetheless, saw both continuities and discontinuities—a duality that forms the heart of Davidson's chapter.

Stemming from this basic split in opinion, perhaps, was another divergence in our viewpoints. We differed over an issue of critical importance to the future of studies relevant to language origins. That is, should we try to set out, as clearly as possible, what is unique about human language? Is it important to be precise about ways in which we see human language as different from all other animal communication, even if only as a first step toward searching for these very features of human language in other species? Or is this attempt misguided, likely to result only in "top down" analyses in which we seek syntax in some human form or referential communication in some human form, to the neglect of finding out what monkeys and apes really do? Would Savage-Rumbaugh and her colleagues (1996) have suggested that wild bonobos flatten vegetation to indicate the direction of group travel— and thus appear to have a form of displacement in their communication—if they had looked solely for mirror reflections of human linguistic skills? Does it even make sense to ask which species have language? Wouldn't it be better to look not at "language" as a package but instead at each type of linguistic skill—whether verbal, vocal, or nonvocal behavioral—on its own? Should we throw out the trait lists altogether and build understanding of the units of primate communication from the bottom up (see Kuczaj and Kirkpatrick 1993)?

We did agree that specific proposals about the uniqueness of human language will be most useful when they are grounded in reliable data on what primates can do and in a broad conception of language as both comprehensive and productive, both gestural and vocal. We were prodded toward this broad view by, in particular, Burling, Maestripieri, Wilcox, and Savage-Rumbaugh, each of whom urged us, in a different way, not to focus exclusively on vocal capacities. Through Burling's discussion of motivated signs, Maestripieri's of the relationship between gesture and social organization, and Wilcox's of the catalytic role of visible gesture, and through Savage-Rumbaugh's insistence that we recognize the theoretical and practical significance of comprehension in communication, we found a host of ways in which to explore both continuities and discontinuities outside the vocal realm.

Taken together, the chapters in this book make a powerful case against the fashionable position that language is an innate biological system unique to humans. That language is, in significant part, socially constructed emerges as a theme of the book. The importance of social interaction during development for an animal's communicational competence is highlighted again and again. In writing our chapters, we have used data from both children and nonhuman primates to demonstrate the role of social experience and learning in acquiring communication and language skills. In doing so, we do not aim to deny any role for innate processes or to polarize "innate" versus "learned" processes, which surely interact during language acquisition (and evolution) just as they do in the acquisition (and evolution) of other behavioral systems. We do aim to reject a view of language that is, in our opinion, too narrow in its dismissal of the role of social interaction and social construction. Our chapters further suggest that many aspects of language, under all but the most anthropocentric of definitions, likely have a long evolutionary history. In the opinion of many of us, that history extends back beyond hominids to encompass our closest living relatives in the animal world.

Human language may have emerged gradually via general cognitive capacities (Ragir 1992; Gibson and Jessee, this volume; Wilcox, this volume). It may have emerged in a mosaic fashion, so that certain elements have a longer evolutionary history than others (Ujhelyi 1996). Alternatively, there may have been a system-level reintegration leading to the spontaneous emergence of language as a system from its component parts—a system that is more than the sum of its parts (see Elman et al. 1996). And with this alternative, we return to questions of naming, to concerns with what is language and what is not (see Davidson, this volume), and to a recognition that continuities and discontinuities can both occur in the same evolutionary process (Davidson, this volume; King, chapter 2, this volume).

We may never be able to determine which of these alternatives best characterizes what happened in evolutionary history, but we can give them prominence as frameworks to guide our thinking and analysis—prominence equal to that of the innatist framework that now commands so much attention. From a primatological perspective that begins with new questions in new frameworks, new answers are sure to emerge.

2

Viewed from Up Close

Monkeys, Apes, and Language-Origins Theories

Barbara J. King

The linguist Bickerton (1995:35) despairs over the "syndrome" afflicting nonlinguists who write about language origins. Such people view language "as if from some mountaintop," a vantage point from which language "is but a misty blur, deprived of the knotty peculiarities with which we linguists have to wrestle in our daily toil." He has a point: the subtle but elegant complexities of syntax, for example, are too often overlooked by those who do not study them. Equating syntax with simple word order contributes to an underestimation of the complexities of human language that does not well serve an understanding of how language evolved.

Yet for those struggling to understand language origins and evolution, other challenges loom as large as the need to comprehend features of human language. As this volume attests, questions of language origins are necessarily interdisciplinary; an examination of present-day language alone is insufficient. For a full evolutionary picture to emerge, the skills and behaviors of both extinct hominids and extant primates must be closely analyzed. Without doing so, we cannot know which communicational abilities evolved only in the hominid lineage and which have longer evolutionary histories. A blurry report from this mountaintop is surely as great a concern as Bickerton's.

Some interpretations of the primate evidence that appear in language–origins theories can, of course, be more "right" than others. It is simply wrong to claim that wild nonhuman primates can communicate about their emotional states but not about specific features of the environment, or to say that non-emotional, referential communication occurs but then to label it exceptional (see data in Steklis 1985; Gouzoules, Gouzoules, and Ashley 1995). Other statements are open to honest disagreement. Wild apes may communicate about things distant in time and space, but we currently have few data with which even to begin to address this issue (Savage-Rumbaugh et al. 1996). If enough effort is put into developing appropriate methodologies, however, primatology will address it. After all, despite postmodern skepticism on the point, there is a real world out there. Primatologists can get closer and closer to understanding it, whether through the scientific method (Cartmill 1994) or through adopting new frameworks for interpretation (Savage-Rumbaugh, this volume).

Yet it would be a mistake to think that the only task standing between us and a good understanding of the evolution of language is to bring language theorists down from the mountaintop—that is, to achieve a state in which the characteristics of all primates' communication systems are brought into sharp focus. Even so desirable a state as this will not be enough. This is because the questions being asked by language-origins theorists—and the definitions, assumptions, and criteria used for admitting evidence into their theories—vary widely. Different theories ask different questions and thus have different requirements for types of data appropriate to address them (Taylor 1996; King and Shanker 1997). Owing to these unacknowledged yet fundamental differences, language-origins theorists frequently talk past one another, trapped in a cycle of claim and counterclaim.

That different language theories address different sets of questions, each set derived from the theorist's own conceptual lens, is an underappreciated point. As Taylor puts it:

[Most theorists] address the problem of language origins as if it were not different in kind from a problem like "How did the human eye evolve?" or "When did our ancestors first leave the African continent?"...However, when one looks closer, the problem of language-origins reveals itself as a conceptually derivative issue: as a problem which is generated by the theorists' overarching conception of the nature of language and the mind. (Taylor 1996:72)

When evaluating language-origins theories, then, it is important to work at two levels. First, the rigor of the data used and the interpretations based on those data should be assessed. Second, it must also be clarified—as I attempt to do in this chapter for a subset of these theories—what questions are being asked, what definitions are employed, what assumptions are made, and what criteria are used for evaluating the evidence. As a first step, consider in the paired claims that follow the broad contrasts in how monkey and ape abilities are assessed.

Pair A, about ape cognition:
[Apes'] behavior, complex as it is, seems unreflective, concrete, and situation-bound. Even their uses of signing and their social behavior are immediate, short-term responses to the environment....Their lives are lived entirely in the present. (Donald 1991:149)

A number of great-ape achievements can all be viewed as flowing from the ability to plan: deceiving intentionally and forestalling the deceptive intention of others; selecting or making an appropriate tool for the job, in advance of attempting the task; organizing several familiar processes into a new programme for a new goal; anticipation of future outcomes of current actions; and taking account of knowledge gaps in infants (teaching) and of the problems and plans of other individuals. (Byrne 1995:225)

Pair B, about animal languages in the wild:
[Animal languages], with few apparent exceptions, and perhaps

no real exceptions,...indicate how the animal feels or what the animal wants, but not what the animal knows. (Bickerton 1995:12)

[T]he calls of some primates and at least one bird convey information about objects and events in the environment, although at present it is difficult to say anything more precise about their meaning. The functional significance of a referential system is that individuals can understand what the caller is yapping about without having to see what is going on. (Hauser 1996:647–48)

Pair C, about ape language in captivity:
Kanzi...learned to bang on visual symbols on a portable tablet. Kanzi is said to have learned his graphic symbols without having been laboriously trained on them—but he was at his mother's side watching while she was laboriously trained on them (unsuccessfully)....A human would surely do no better if trained to hoot and shriek like a chimp, a symmetrical project that makes about as much scientific sense. (Pinker 1994:341–42)

Kanzi's ability to understand complex speech and to use written symbols spontaneously suggests that present-day apes possess the capacity for a simple language system and thus that our common ancestor was capable of some sort of symbolic communication. (Savage-Rumbaugh et al. 1993:106)

Nonhuman primates are viewed strikingly differently in the first and second quotations of each pair. In the first, animals respond only to immediate environmental stimuli. Their calls report only their feelings rather than information about the external world. Apes may be capable of learning some clever languagelike tricks in the laboratory, but they cannot produce or understand any aspects of language. In the second quotation of each pair, the same animals can refer to concrete aspects of the physical or social environment. They can plan for and anticipate the future. When given enriched surroundings in the laboratory, they can communicate symbolically and with true understanding. These divergent descriptions are not, of course, ends in themselves; they permit very different conclusions about how and when language originated and developed.

By virtue of its special properties and special use, human language is, for some theorists, different in kind from all other communication systems. These theorists focus on the origins of language's special features, locating them entirely within the hominid line or even as recently as 60,000 years ago, after modern humans emerged. Other theorists see precursors to features of human language in the social-communicational behaviors of monkeys and apes. They extend the roots of language deeper in evolutionary time, before the split between African apes and hominids, or in some cases they abandon the search for origins entirely (see Taylor 1996). In these theories, differences between human language and animal communication systems are differences of degree only. During hominid evolution, according to this view, communicational and cognitive abilities expanded from the base already present in monkeys and apes. Consequently, no moment of language "emergence" can be identified.

Typically, writers dichotomize these types of theories as strict opposites that compete for the "best" interpretation of the evolution of language. Each new theory is assigned (whether by the authors themselves or by reviewers of the theories) to one camp or the other. Students of language origins rarely borrow ideas approvingly from both or take lessons from both (but see Hauser 1996). Applying neat labels to the two types of theories makes it easy to see them not as just two important types but as the only two types of theories—as dichotomized types that represent the full range of variation in current language-origins thinking. Human uniqueness theories are labeled "discontinuity" or "essentialist" theories, and the others are labeled "continuity" or "evolutionist" theories.

Language theories do vary, of course, but in a more complex way than these labels suggest. Explaining more fully why the perceived dichotomy is incorrect and offering a more accurate account of the variation across theories is my first goal in this chapter. Next I take a step toward breaking the cycle of claim and counterclaim in current language-origins theories by bringing to the foreground the usually unacknowledged differences in perspective that the theories subsume. This can be accomplished by asking the following questions about each one: Which data about nonhuman primate skills and behaviors are presented, and which omitted, in each theory? How are these data interpreted within a language-origins framework? What assumptions are made and what definitions are used as part of that framework? For example, how is language understood and described by each theorist? And perhaps most critically, why should the data be interpreted so differently according to the nature of the theorizing? That is, do the authors of language-origins theories need to interpret the primate data in certain ways in order to support their theories?

DITCHING THE DICHOTOMY

Considering that the continuity-discontinuity labels (and other, comparable pairs) are widely employed—so much so that I myself used them in my earlier work (e.g., King 1994a, 1994b)—my wish to abandon them requires justification.[1] These terms carry a great deal of baggage that retards progress in interdisciplinary dialogue about language origins. Certain expectations seem to accompany their use, not only in publications but also in less formal contexts such as conference discussions and manuscript reviewing. My experience is that primatologists are thought to be continuity theorists, likely to find language or its precursors in nonhuman primates and to admit no special features or unique aspects of language in humans. Linguists, in contrast, are labeled discontinuity theorists, likely to focus too much on syntax or other abstracted properties of language and to admit no continuity between language and the communication of other animals. Such extreme viewpoints are uncommon, however, and some theorists resist being pigeonholed by either label.

Further, continuity theory is commonly equated with a view of gradual, incremental change over time, and discontinuity theory with large leaps at certain intervals. But continuity theory need not imply step-by-step gradualism (Wilcox, this volume). As Bates and colleagues have discussed in a different context, scientists are gaining an appreciation for the fact that "complex, surprising and apparently discontinuous outcomes can arise from small quantitative changes along a single dimension" (Bates et al. 1996:2). So-called continuity theories can incorporate fairly major shifts, and discontinuity theories may recognize long periods of slight shifts or stasis.

The trick is to get away from simple labels and to analyze each theory's elements and conclusions using a clear set of questions. For ease of comparison, my discussion is divided into two sections, the first primarily involving treatment by language-origins theorists of data from wild primates, and the second, their treatment of data from captive primates.

PRIMATES IN THE WILD

Some published theories give readers surprisingly little opportunity to quibble about the interpretation of data from nonhuman primates in the wild: wild primates are scarcely mentioned. The focus is on a few "famous" species from "famous" wild sites, or on enculturated apes instead.

Pinker, for instance, is unimpressed with the cognitive or communicational abilities of free-ranging nonhuman primates or their relevance for understanding how language evolved. He sees chimpanzees as "strong, vicious wild animals" (1994:335) that "hoot and shriek" (1994:342). Nowhere in his article with Bloom (1990) or in his book chapter (1994) about language origins (entitled "The Big Bang") does Pinker describe or analyze wild chimpanzee vocal or gestural signals.

Pinker's stance is that language developed gradually via natural selection, but entirely within the hominid lineage. This view requires him to find chimps "languageless" (1994:345) so he can argue that language evolved gradually during the five to seven million years after the ape-hominid split. As Pinker says (1994:346), "an ancestral ape with nothing but hoots and grunts is unlikely to have given birth to a baby who could learn English or Kivunjo. But it did not have to; there was a chain of several hundred thousand generations of grandchildren in which such abilities could gradually blossom."

Why doesn't Pinker consider how wild chimpanzees use communicative signals, whether vocal or gestural, and why doesn't he ask about the features of such signals? Why doesn't he take a hard look at the apes' natural communicational behavior—the behavior that undergoes natural selection, which is the very agency he says produced language in the hominid line? He could then look at how meaning is conveyed by chimpanzees, whether by precursors to reference, syntax, and other features critical to language or by species-specific methods entirely unlike anything found in language. Pinker says he is uninterested in the "fruitless and boring" (1994:347) debate over what constitutes true language. He is equally indifferent to trait lists of language features. What he wants is to discover which traits are homologous by comparing species: "To check for homology, one would have to find some signature trait that reliably emerges both in ape symbol systems and in human language and that is not so indispensable to communication that it was likely to have emerged twice, once in the course of human evolution and once in the lab meetings of the psychologists as they contrived the system to teach their apes" (1994:348).

For Pinker, then, the comparison of interest is that between natural human language and enculturated ape language. Why? In order to understand his choice, we must look more closely at the nature of language. For Pinker, the essence of language is grammar, the elegant rules of sentence construction that are deeply seated in the human brain. Language is not a shaper of thought (1994:19); it is not the zenith of human intelligence (1994:20). Rather, it is a biological instinct, a specialized human skill that develops spontaneously in children without conscious effort or formal instruction (1994:18). Being so specialized, so tied to grammar—which is uniquely human—this skill is "distinct from more general abilities to process information or behave intelligently" (Pinker 1994:18).

By combining the notion of language-as-grammar with that of the gradual development of language within the hominid lineage, Pinker shields the innatist position (see King, chapter 1, this volume) from the complaint that it implausibly ignores the role of natural selection in shaping human behavior.[2] In Pinker's version of the innatist theory, we still have a uniquely human instinct, but one that nevertheless develops gradually within the hominid line. Even though he denies language to prehominid primates, Pinker calls himself a gradualist. Indeed, he is rightly considered one when compared with other theorists to be discussed later. He might with equal justification, however, be called a discontinuity theorist by those who do see precursors to language, or language itself, in nonhuman primates. The terms applied depend, as does all else, on one's starting point.

Pinker's decision to concentrate on enculturated apes allows him to evaluate—as he could not do for wild apes, given the scarce data— whether or not our closest living relatives communicate using syntax, that all-important element of language. That is, he asks whether enculturated apes can do what humans do. Pinker might have pointed out one of the greatest gaps in the primatological data: very little is known about the communicational behavior, either vocal or gestural, of wild apes. Some primatologists emphasize that the right observations and experiments for assessing the flexible vocal production and response skills—or syntactic skills—of apes have not yet been done (Savage-Rumbaugh et al. 1996). Others (Snowdon 1993a, Mitani 1996) conclude that apes do not communicate vocally with any great precision or sophistication—or with syntax. This latter conclusion might strengthen Pinker's case, for the lack of known syntax in vocal communication by wild monkeys and apes could be seen to confirm the gap he envisions between those creatures and hominids (but see the review in chapter 1 for a different conclusion about primate syntax; see also Burling, this volume, and King n.d. for discussions of the important role of ape non-vocal behavior).

Bickerton (1995, 1990) also makes a case for the biological nature of syntax in humans. Syntax is not an invention but "something quite mechanical: the unconscious, mindless cranking out of formal syntactic patterns" and the "mechanism that underlies all distinctively human behavior" (1995:139). Like Pinker, Bickerton dismisses the claim that there is grammar in enculturated apes' symbolic production (and he does the same for all so-called protolanguages, including the language of young children). He concentrates his challenge to the nonhuman primate data elsewhere. Making broader statements about nonhuman primate communicational abilities than Pinker does, Bickerton insists that animal signals indicate only what the animal feels or wants. Other animals, upon hearing these signals, may infer meaning from them, but "there is a world of difference between inferred meaning and intended meaning" (1995:12), and "one cannot conclude that the alarm calls of vervets (or of any other species) convey factual information."

Bickerton spends much time considering the alarm calls of the Amboseli vervet monkeys. Discovered by Struhsaker (1967) and thoroughly researched by Cheney, Seyfarth, and colleagues (reviewed in

Cheney and Seyfarth 1990), these alarm calls differ acoustically according to predator type. If a vervet manages to infer meaning from an alarm call, says Bickerton, that is one thing, but the range of possible intended meanings is limited to the emotional. Bickerton offers a possible paraphrase of such an alarm call: "I am alarmed by a predator approaching and I feel you should share my alarm." This paraphrase is consistent with his overall point, but he then offers a second possibility: "I am alarmed by a terrestrial predator and you too should be alarmed." Why labeling a predator "terrestrial," apparently as opposed to "aerial," does not count as conveying information—perhaps in addition to conveying feeling—Bickerton does not say.

At issue is whether the alarm calls are referential signals, defined as signals that convey more than just emotion. In focusing on vervet alarm calls (although not exclusively—he does mention a few other primates such as the cotton-top tamarin), Bickerton omits primatological data relevant to his argument. A wide variety of primate species produce referential signals (Steklis 1985; see review in Gouzoules, Gouzoules, and Ashley 1995). At a minimum these signals are referential in a functional sense, but intriguing hints speak to the heart of Bickerton's definition—hints that the signals are intentionally referential in that their production is altered according to the producer's context or audience (for an interesting discussion of the type and significance of reference in vervet alarm calls, see Deacon 1997:54–68).

The strongest argument that primate signals are produced referentially and not just emotionally comes again from vervet monkeys, not from the alarm-call data themselves but from data arising from so-called habituation-dishabituation experiments (Cheney and Seyfarth 1990; see Hauser 1996 for a review). The idea behind these experiments is to discover whether vervets categorize vocalizations on the basis of their acoustic similarities or, alternatively, on the basis of their semantic similarities. One test was carried out with vervet vocalizations that are acoustically different—wrrs and chutters. Both are produced during intergroup encounters, but chutters are produced during more aggressive interactions. If vervets assess similarity on the basis of acoustic structure only, it was reasoned, then the animals' response to wrrs should stabilize as they habituate to the sounds of wrrs, but this habituation should be followed by an altered response (dishabituation) when chutters are heard instead. Similarly, habituation to chutters should be followed by dishabituation to wrrs if acoustic structure is the salient variable. If, however, vervets assess similarity in call type according to call meaning, then the switch from one call type to the other should not alter the state of habituation (Hauser 1996:527). Results showed that when a monkey's calls were played back to its group, habituation in the response of other vervets to the calls was maintained, even following a switch from one call type to the other. This finding suggests that the responders paid attention to call meaning, and it strengthens the case for true referentiality or semanticity in vervet alarms.

For Bickerton, a second important feature of communication systems found among wild animals is the invariant nature of responses to calls. In animal call systems, "if one species member utters a certain type of call, other members will react [in] a predictable way—by running up trees, retreating, trying to mate, or whatever" (1995:54). Bickerton considers the predictable nature of the response to be under neurological control. But primatological accounts suggest otherwise. The developmental literature indicates, for instance, that the response to some calls is variable and learned. Immature primates need considerable social experience before they respond correctly to calls ranging from predator alarms to social calls (Seyfarth and Cheney 1997). As adults, nonhuman primates can respond to the same call in different ways when it comes from different individuals. For example, a call announcing the discovery of choice food might be responded to differently when it comes from a dominant rather than a subordinate animal. Adult nonhuman primates can also respond to the same individual differently in different contexts—for example, in the initiation of group travel versus the announcement of a food discovery.

Why does Bickerton so emphasize lack of intended meaning, except for emotional meaning, and lack of variable response? It is because both serve to separate the cognitive base of animal communication from that of human language, and separating the two is crucial for Bickerton because he sees language not as primarily communicational, as Pinker does, but as primarily representational. Animals can transmit information, but that is all they can do in their communication. Language, by contrast, shapes and even transforms our very thought processes.

Bickerton's reason for dichotomizing animal and human cognitive abilities is foreshadowed in his discussion of communication in wild primates: "If one envisages language as no more than a skill used to express and communicate the products of human thought, it becomes ipso facto impossible to regard language as the Rubicon that divides us from other species" (1995:9). But because language is representational, its status as the Rubicon to be crossed remains intact. Indeed, Bickerton locates the emergence of language far closer to the present than Pinker does; he limits language to modern human beings. Bickerton, like Pinker, dismisses claims for languagelike features in free-ranging nonhuman primates, but he sees evidence for so-called protolanguage in enculturated apes and some hominids. Protolanguage, which differs in five specific ways from true language (see Bickerton 1990:122ff.), "had to be transformed into true language through the emergence of grammatical items and syntactic structures" (Bickerton 1990:163).

Noble and Davidson (1996; see Davidson, this volume) reject Bickerton's notion of intermediate steps in the evolution of language and Pinker's view that language emerged gradually in hominids. As they see it, "if something is not thus language as we (actually or potentially) know it then it is misleading to refer to it as language at all" (1996:8). After reviewing research results from primatological studies of nonhuman communication and from paleoanthropological analyses of hominids, they argue for the emergence of language by about 60,000 years ago. For them, the key features of language are use of symbols and awareness of the production of meaning. Not only do monkeys and apes lack the ability to communicate with semanticity, arbitrariness, duality of patterning, displacement, and other features of language, write Noble and Davidson, but they also lack awareness that the signals they do produce carry meaning. Further, "the operation of concepts is language-dependent" (1996:61): language and mind emerged together. This perspective enables, and perhaps forces, Noble and

Davidson to conclude—since no languagelike communication is found in nonhuman primates—that monkeys and apes do not have minds in any meaningful sense of the term.

One might argue with some of these conclusions by introducing evidence from primatology that Noble and Davidson ignored. Some characteristics of monkey and ape communication do show precursors to language or features of language (King and Shanker 1997; Snowdon, this volume). Data on planning and memory do give evidence of nonhuman primate minds at work (Byrne 1995; King and Shanker 1997). Yet it is clear that Noble and Davidson's conclusions are driven as much by their starting point regarding primate social life—by the questions they are willing to ask—as by analysis of the evidence. They state that mind is socially distributed and that understanding is an interpersonal achievement (1996:105); their emphasis on the social construction of meaning and mind in humans is welcome. Their assumptions about the evolution of sociality, however, lead them to deny to other primates the very sociality that enables construction of meaning:

> Ingold (1989) properly draws a distinction between definitions of "society" either as emphasising interactions between individual animals (applicable to any animals), or as essentially concerned with rules and relationships (and applicable only to humans). Whilst (with Ingold) we recognise that there must be some continuities of patterns of inter-individual interaction during the course of evolution, we also recognise (with Ingold) the fundamental importance of language in defining rules. In a discussion that seeks to understand the evolutionary emergence of language, we find it most convenient to limit the word "social" to humans, lest we slither from one understanding to another and trick ourselves into seeing social rules where there were none. (Noble and Davidson 1996:53–54)

Thus, participation in a community is "a critical constraint on any attempt to explain the origin of symbol use" (Noble and Davidson 1996:82).

Yet a very different starting point and different questions emerge from doing primatology in the field. Long-term field studies have shown that monkeys and apes are social in the sense of having relationships—not only patterns of interactions but full-blown, recurring relationships based on past interactional histories (e.g., Goodall 1986; see Hinde 1987). Within this framework, it is perfectly logical (as it was not for Noble and Davidson) to ask whether nonhuman primates have rules—that is, whether rule-following evolved before language—and to posit possible examples of rule-following in nonhuman primates (King and Shanker 1997).

In short, if primates are indeed social—if they participate in a community marked by long-term social relationships—then meanings might be shared and symbols constructed, and monkeys and apes might be aware of the meanings they produce. Tomasello (1993), for example, recognizes awareness of meaning in the gestural signals produced by some chimpanzees, as will be discussed later. Savage-Rumbaugh and colleagues (1996) have suggested that wild bonobos use symbols, which, if accurate, would by definition imply that the apes are aware of produced meaning. Interestingly, neither example involves vocal production.

Noble and Davidson's central points about how language differs from nonhuman primate communication are quite useful to evolutionary thinking about language. Noble and Davidson say that if chimpanzees do have symbols (they never entirely rule out this possibility), then those symbols evolved separately from the symbols that make up human language, so that the two sets of symbols are evolutionarily independent. Indeed, we must ask open-ended questions about the distribution of symbol use and awareness of meaning in primates, and we must work to understand selection pressures for them if they do exist. It may be that these aspects of language use, even if not unique to humans, combine with other human behaviors to form an elaborated suite of abilities that is in fact species-specific to humans.

Noble and Davidson insist that their theory couples aspects of "continuity" and "discontinuity" views. Although they reject gradual stages in the development of language, they "are also arguing in an evolutionary framework, so we assume that distinctively modern behaviour came to dominate the world of hominids by natural selection from a range of behaviours exhibited by them" (1996:174). Noble and Davidson work squarely within a framework that embraces developmental factors. They give particular weight to the discovery of meaning through social interaction by children and by enculturated apes in the present and by hominids in the past; they reject innate causes for the representational function of language.

Wallman, too, mixes elements of what he calls continuity and discontinuity theory in his book *Aping Language* (1992). He opens his chapter devoted to free-ranging primates ("Primate Communication in Nature") by noting that the data on wild primate communication provide much more support for the discontinuity position than for the continuity position (1992:128). Yet his subsequent statements vary in the degree to which they support this conclusion. In reviewing the data on referential signaling in primates, Wallman discusses the alarm calls of a variety of species, calling these vocalizations plausible precursors of words (p. 134). He goes on (p. 137) to acknowledge the need for "a continuum model of signaling, ranging from the more referential to the more affective, rather than a dichotomous contrast between mutually exclusive characteristics." Later, however, when Wallman sums up the differences between animal and human communication (p. 152), this notion of a continuum is gone, replaced by a dichotomy: "[O]ther primates, with a few exceptions, [do not] evince language-like principles in their natural systems of communication. Ours, dispensing with qualifications, is cortical, while theirs is limbic; our symbols are learned, while their calls are inborn; our language is referential, their communication affective." Wallman, then, places some languagelike elements on a continuum, and others, he does not. How, then, does he arrive at the conclusion that these data support the notion of a uniquely human language?

First, he contrasts referential vocalizations with words in order to show how the two differ. Referentiality may be present in some cases but is not robustly continuous with what humans do. Echoing Bickerton, Wallman gives us a laundry list of what alarm calls are not: they are not given in a state of equanimity or in the absence of the referent, and there is no possibility of variant response to them. I have already discussed these claims in the section about Bickerton.

Second, like Noble and Davidson, Wallman relies heavily on the supposed lack of languagelike features in nonhuman primate communication, including duality of patterning and vocal learning. One may respond again with an alternative reporting of the evidence (King and Shanker 1997; Snowdon, this volume). We now know, for instance, that vocal learning does occur in monkeys and apes. (These data were available in the 1980s, but they have been shaped into a coherent argument largely since Wallman's book appeared.)

Call production does seem to be largely of non-neocortical origin in nonhuman primates (Hauser 1996:210). Yet there seems to be some plasticity in primate vocal production, albeit limited. For example, the structure of the trill call produced by the pygmy marmoset, a New World monkey, is modified during the course of development (Snowdon and Elowson 1992; Snowdon, this volume). Further, calls can be suppressed under certain circumstances, as when chimpanzees silently patrol the borders of their communities (Goodall 1986) or when vervets vary their rate of calling according to the composition of their audience (Cheney and Seyfarth 1990). Evidence such as this "audience effect" in vervets does not completely rule out alternative interpretations—for example, that social factors act as additional stimuli that could help control an involuntary response.[3] But it is a reasonable interpretation to use such evidence in support of claims for voluntary production, especially when it is considered together with information about ape gestural behavior.

That apes produce gestures intentionally is quite clear (Savage-Rumbaugh, Wilkerson, and Bakeman 1977; Tomasello, Gust, and Frost 1989; Tomasello et al. 1994; Tanner and Byrne 1996; Savage-Rumbaugh, Shanker, and Taylor 1998; King n.d.). After they produce gestures, the captive chimpanzees studied by Tomasello and colleagues, for example, either wait, suggesting that they expect a response from a fellow chimpanzee, or alternate their gaze between their goal and a fellow ape whose help they need to attain that goal, indicating an awareness of that need. Chimpanzees also use the same gestures toward different ends and different gestures toward the same end, which similarly indicates intentionality. My own study of a captive bonobo family reaches similar conclusions. The mother and older sib-lings direct movements of their heads, limbs, and whole bodies toward the very young infant in ways that are clearly communicative. The apes use the same movements over time, but with variations on the basic pat-tern depending on the context and the infant's own movements and responses. They direct these movements—"patterned interac-tions," in my terminology—to the infant when the infant is attending, thus establishing the meaning of certain signals over time while also enhancing behavioral coordination with the infant. By the time of her first birthday, the infant regularly uses gesture and touch in commu-nicative ways. The infant and her family thus *co-construct* her gestures.

A focus on call production in nonhuman primates omits two other facets of vocal development: call usage and call response. Vocal usage and especially vocal response appear to be innately controlled to a lesser degree than is vocal production (Gouzoules and Gouzoules 1989; Seyfarth and Cheney 1997). Vocal usage depends on social expe-rience in that immature primates conform only gradually to the use of calls in correct contexts. Vocal response is even more flexible, as is shown most clearly in a series of cross-fostering studies in which macaques of one species were reared with macaques of another. The cross-fostered monkeys gave correct responses to the "strange" calls of the "strange" species after a period of learning. Statements based on studies of call production alone, then, exaggerate differences between animal and human communication systems (Seyfarth and Cheney 1997).

Wallman avoids explicit claims about the features distinctive to language. Yet as we will see later, when Wallman discusses ape language projects, he zeroes in on the issue of whether ape communication can be said to contain units that are like our words or sentences? He asks the very same question of wild primates: do homologues to words and sentences exist in their communication? Interestingly, he recognizes precursors of these units in some nonhuman primate communication. Wallman's main goal—like Pinker's—is to reject the idea that encultur-ated apes show anything resembling true linguistic ability, but he treats the data on free-ranging primates in greater depth than does Pinker. Still, he cannot push the gradual approach too far without endanger-ing the uniqueness of words and sentences; he must be particularly careful when considering precursors of traits such as voluntary open production, duality of patterning, and syntax.

The theorists considered so far tend to use standards for assessing the presence of language in nonhuman species that are derived from human linguistic production—words, sentences with syntax, or symbols created with awareness of meaning. In asking whether monkeys and apes meet these standards, the theories are in one sense limited, as any anthropocentric approach to other species is limited. Yet they also do the study of the evolution of language a great favor, for surely the aspects on which these theories concentrate—whether or not they in fact set language apart from other communication—are elaborated differently or more highly in human language than in communication by other species. By going beyond an accounting of similarities to ask how human language is different from other communication systems, we can prevent the study of language origins from succumbing to Bickerton's "mountaintop syndrome," in which the very phenomenon we wish to understand is blurred.

All of these theories situate the origins of language within the hominid lineage or within the time span following the appearance of modern humans. But it is possible to take another look at nonhuman primates—a hard look at their day-to-day behavior, not just at facets of their linguistic production—and come to very different conclusions about their communicational abilities and indeed about the origins of language. One approach searches for behaviors of monkeys and apes that, although different from human ones in form, might be meaningful precursors to some human abilities (Cartmill 1990; King 1994b). A related method asks to what degree human skills and abilities might be found in nonhuman behaviors (Gibson 1993a). This method involves a move away from asking whether skills and abilities are "present" or "absent" in an all-or-nothing manner.

Primatologists may start with close description of some behavior of a particular species and then draw parallels with human activity without assuming, or even looking for, identical forms of the two species' activities. One potentially productive avenue is to create rich, detailed descriptions of how apes use their bodies, heads, and limbs communicatively (King n.d.). Yet vocalizations and gestures are not the only possible subjects for productive study. Observing wild bonobos at Wamba in Congo (the former Zaire), Savage-Rumbaugh and colleagues (1996) noticed that when the apes traveled, they sometimes appeared to flatten the vegetation purposefully. Deliberately flattened leaves and broken branches differed in appearance from those that were bent or minimally disturbed in the normal course of travel. Criteria developed in the field, rather than argument by analogy with humans, were used to say that the vegetation was flattened intentionally by the apes. For example, flattening was more likely to occur at trail junctions, digging sites, and rest areas; it rarely occurred where the trail was clear and easy to follow. These characteristics were hard to recon cile with an argument that the vegetation was flattened by accident. In this case, a natural, nonvocal behavior might well indicate capacities for symbolism and even displacement by wild bonobos, since the flattening might communicate across time and space. Savage-Rumbaugh and colleagues (1996) speak of this behavior as potentially "bridging the gap" between the context-independent system of language and those systems dependent on the here and now.

Another example of an innovative approach to nonhuman primate communication involves conversational turn-taking. Recent experimental data permitted Hauser (1996:487) to conclude that "countercalling, either in the form of one-on-one interactions or vocal choruses, is common among nonhuman animals." Some of these vocal exchanges indicate conversational ability because the animals seem to seek information in a turn-taking format akin to human question-and-answer sessions (Snowdon and Cleveland 1984; Symmes and Biben 1988). Here, as in the foregoing example from wild bonobos, the aim of the research was not to start with some linguistic trait and then go out and find the identical trait in nonhuman primate communication. Rather, the goal was to describe some behavior fully in order to help primatologists understand the scope of monkey or ape communication. Only then did the appropriateness of comparisons with human language emerge from the description (see also Hauser 1996:97). The different starting point is not trivial. Abandoning human standards at the outset allows researchers to see what monkeys and apes really do without the constraints imposed by using some standard of human behavior as an indicator of what to seek.

Other theories describe nonhuman primate behavior but assess not so much different forms of behavior as different degrees of elaboration of some behavior—or they perhaps forge some combination of the two approaches. Gibson (1990, 1993a, 1994; Gibson and Jessee, this volume) suggests that monkeys and apes are only quantitatively different from humans in both communicational skills and the brain mechanisms underlying them. She integrates behavioral and neurological data from a variety of species in order to argue that there is no convincing evidence for qualitative differences across primates. Rather, the unique level of human intelligence and language can be explained by "brain-mediated–expansions of mental constructional skills" (1990:98). Monkeys can, for instance, combine two vocal calls, and different call combinations lead to different meanings (1994:102, citing the research of Snowdon). Captive apes can use single gestural symbols and some three-gesture combinations, and they even have simple grammar. Humans go further by making "highly varied, hierarchically organized sentences containing embedded clauses and phrases" (1990:98). Thus, what is for theorists like Pinker and Bickerton a uniquely hominid/human instinct—generative syntax—is for Gibson an expansion of traits found in other primates.

Gibson discusses other features of human language, including voluntary control of vocal production, and concludes that rudimentary forms exist in nonhuman species. Why is it important to Gibson to find evidence of multiple languagelike abilities in other species, rather than just one or two essential features? For her, language is essentially hierarchical, "an emergent property" (1994:101) built out of components; there is no unique feature of human language. Apes may not have all the components and abilities associated with human language, but they have some significant ones. What is distinctive about human language does not transform it into a unique system.

From Gibson's work we see again that simple labels cannot be effectively applied to language-origins theories. She does not claim that there are only similarities and no differences between the communication systems of different species, just as the theories by others already discussed do not insist upon complete discontinuity between the communication of modern humans and that of other primates. Gibson (1993a:7–8) takes care not only to emphasize that humans reach higher levels of accomplishment in every domain—vocal, gestural, imitative, technical, and social—but also to point out that other species do not "combine social, technical, and linguistic behaviors into a rich, interactive and self-propelling cognitive complex." Here Gibson echoes Bates and colleagues' (1996) point that comparing each skill, one by one, across species is insufficient, because it is possible and even likely that elements can combine to produce emergent phenomena.

Yet Gibson embraces the continuum concept and seeks precursors to human traits in other primates (see also Cartmill 1990). Other theorists (e.g., Bickerton 1995) respond to her approach by denying that any known nonhuman primate behavior is related to the specialized, inborn system that we call syntax (see also Pinker 1994 and the discussion in chapter 1). Gibson's approach, highly elaborated and clear when discussing the subtleties of primate behavior and of brain structure, is less detailed when considering the hierarchical organization of human language.

The key claim in Gibson's theory is that small neurological changes (described in detail in Gibson 1990) can explain the incremental changes in communicational (and cognitive) abilities across primates. Language is thus represented as a mosaic of features rather than as any one essential thing. The success of this theory depends on its ability to demonstrate that early hominids possessed no major brain structures or behaviors that are absent in apes. Whereas the theorists discussed previously had to pay close attention to—one might even say they had to preserve—the ape-hominid boundary in order to argue convincingly for hominid or human uniqueness, Gibson must show the boundary to be a false one. This goal could potentially be met by analyzing data about communication by wild apes, but these are scarce. We do not even have solid evidence for referential signaling by great apes in the wild. For now, Gibson must plug this potential hole in the primate continuum by citing data from enculturated apes. She must also downplay any sharp breaks across the primate continuum, even at the ape-hominid boundary and even in such sophisticated skills as syntactic abilities.

Gibson is less interested in pinpointing the emergence of language than in supporting the idea that primates differ from one another only quantitatively, not qualitatively, in terms of both communication and behavior. This orientation, which differs so much from, say, Noble and Davidson's desire to come up with an explicit date for the emergence of language, is characteristic, too, of other theories to be considered in what follows. These theories turn their back on the language gap question. If there is no gap, but only a continuum, then there is no need to posit factors that might jump the gap (Taylor 1996).

My own work (King 1994a, 1994b, 1996) has been significantly influenced by Gibson's. On the basis of my own research and a literature review, I argued in previous publications that precursors to features of language and language use can be found in nonhuman primate vocal behavior (see also Snowdon 1993a:122, and this volume). Referentiality, vocal control, precursors for syntax, and precursors for conversational turn-taking are present in monkey communication, whereas some apes (perhaps wild bonobos and enculturated apes) show evidence for symbol usage and comprehension. Therefore, references to "language origins in the hominid lineage" seem to be based on an essential misunderstanding, both because the roots for language skills exist in nonhuman primates and because there is no single essential factor that marked the emergence of language at a specific point in time.

In my work I have sought, more than Gibson has, different forms of human species-specific behaviors in order to map out the primate continuum. Just as New World monkeys produce patterned vocal exchanges that might represent a form of conversational turn-taking, monkeys and apes may indicate through nonvocal behaviors the ability to produce and understand syntactic relationships even if they do not produce humanlike syntactic constructions (King 1996). Looking primarily at single utterances as the only meaningful unit in animal communication has constrained our research for too long.

I have written of language as a species-specific form of social information donation. Social information donation, as I originally formulated it, refers to instances in which one animal guides the behavior of another via demonstration of skills, intervention in behavior, or directed sending of messages (see King 1994a for details). Nonhuman primates often donate information to others nonvocally, particularly to immatures, as when a monkey mother teaches her offspring to walk by altering her own movements or when a chimpanzee aunt intervenes in her niece's food choice. Humans use language in addition to nonverbal demonstration in donating information. Over the course of primate evolution, environmental shifts selected for enhanced verbal information donation in the context of apprenticeshiplike situations involving adults and immatures (Parker and Gibson 1979; Parker 1985; Borchert and Zihlman 1990; King 1994a; Wilcox 1996; Wilcox, this volume).

One problem with the term "social information donation" is its implication that information is neatly packaged and can be transferred from one animal to another just as a piece of food can be transferred. I now believe that communication is too dynamic a process to be reduced to such a simple, linear operation. An approach that focuses on the communicative act itself as the unit of analysis, rather than on the supposed initiator or recipient of that act, is preferable because it emphasizes the interactional, distributed nature of communication (Markova et al. 1995; Savage-Rumbaugh, Shanker, and Taylor 1998; King n.d.). Further, in viewing language as a type of information transfer, I have neglected other uses of language. Presumably, for theorists such as Bickerton, this aspect of my writing about language has been impoverished on two counts. Not only are the details of the structure of language left out, as they are in Gibson's work as well, but also a representational role for language is ignored. Nonhumans may well store and represent information, but testing hypotheses to prove or disprove that possibility is beyond the scope of my research (see Tomasello and Call 1997).

One issue comes up repeatedly in theories of language origins and evolution—that of whether precusors to syntax exist in primate communication. Armstrong, Stokoe, and Wilcox (1995; see Wilcox, this volume) discuss the evolution of syntax by emphasizing that continuity may have existed in the gestural-optical channel as well as in the vocal-auditory one. They contend that visible gestures promoted an understanding of sequential actions such that the ability to produce syntax might have evolved via a brain feedback loop and neuronal group selection. Visible gestures differ from speech in one critical feature:

they demonstrate visibly and concretely the structure of a minimal sentence (for instance, the subject-verb-object structure so familiar to speakers of English), in which something does something to something else. Thus a manual gesture—let us say the gesture representing a raptor seizing a prey animal, to use the authors' example—involves an active hand, a target or object hand, and an action itself. For hominids to have understood the relationship among these components "would have resulted in an explosive multiplication of the lexicon of gestural words, and because of the syntactic pattern in the gesture, the visible words in it would already be effectively divided into nouns and verbs" (Armstrong, Stokoe, and Wilcox 1995:185).

Armstrong, Stokoe, and Wilcox make it clear that apes had (and have) motor and cognitive preadaptations for the gradual process underlying the development of syntax. They situate the evolutionary "action" in the hominid line, but nowhere do they state that apes lack certain abilities necessary for such action. This lack of interest in drawing a line between apes and hominids sets their theory apart from the "discontinuity" theories reviewed earlier, which critically depend on apes' lacking certain abilities. Indeed, their theory critically depends upon certain abilities being present in apes, and the roots for those abilities may extend even farther back in primate evolutionary history than the authors claim (King 1996).

But why do Armstrong, Stokoe, and Wilcox need to grant manual and cognitive skills to apes rather than to hominids alone? For them, all language, whether spoken or signed, is gesture. They are suspicious of dichotomies and discontinuities. They try to avoid using them when discussing spoken and signed languages, and they certainly do not want to introduce them when comparing animal and human communication systems. Yet they want to explain something that is uniquely developed in human language—syntax—and they need a brain-based and gradual way to get there. Armstrong, Stokoe, and Wilcox must explain how the comparatively primitive gesturing of apes in the wild might have given rise to the semantic and syntactic gesturing of hominids. For them, hominids cannot be the starting place for explaining the origins of syntax, for they accept Gibson's view that no major new cognitive structures or behaviors separate early hominids from apes. Instead, they explain increased language abilities in hominids in terms of selective pressures associated with a social structure based increasingly on fluid, fission-fusion compositional changes. This step in their argument is problematic because apes themselves show complex fission-fusion patterns. Yet the theory as a whole succeeds. It does so because it derives syntax incrementally without diminishing the linguistic meaning of the term.

In short, some language-origins theorists who discuss the behavior of nonhuman primates in the wild consider what monkeys and apes really do by looking at the full range of social-communicative behaviors shown by the animals. Other theorists emphasize vocal production in considering only whether these animals can do what humans do. Some search for the point of origin of language, on the assumption that the emergence of language can be pinpointed in time (a time that could theoretically predate the ape-hominid split).[4] Others characterize the notion of a "language gap"—and any need to search for the origins of language—as a "conceptual illusion" (Taylor 1996:75).

In discussing the evidence from wild primates, I have made brief references to research with enculturated apes. This source of data deserves consideration in its own right, and I turn to this topic now.

ENCULTURATED APES

Orangutans, gorillas, chimpanzees, and bonobos have been studied in enriched environments by researchers who want to know whether these apes can communicate using human symbols. The symbols may be taught to the apes as part of some version of American Sign Language (ASL) or may be learned spontaneously by the apes as "lexigrams," which are abstract notations on a keyboard (for reviews and analyses of these projects, see Wallman 1992; Savage-Rumbaugh et al. 1993; Savage-Rumbaugh, Shanker, and Taylor 1998). Considering that enculturated apes live in a human environment and use and respond to human symbols, it is unsurprising that most studies of their abilities are designed to ask whether the apes can do what humans do. But even within this framework, different approaches can be identified.

The structured daily regimens the apes undergo are in some cases credited for whatever linguistic success the apes attain. Kanzi, the bonobo studied by Savage-Rumbaugh and colleagues for his comprehension of spoken English as well as his lexigram production, is described by Pinker as the equivalent of a trained bear in the Moscow circus (Johnson 1995; Pinker also calls signing chimps "highly trained animal acts" [1994:339]). Other critics use the term "interaction" rather than "training" but still maintain that human tutors are responsible for any success the apes achieve in working with symbols. For these theorists, ape symboling can have no relevance to our understanding of language origins because "in the evolutionary origin of...symbol use there can have been no equivalent tutor" (Noble and Davidson 1991:134). If the capacity for grammar is considered to be inborn, it is possible to argue that when enculturation drives language acquisition, the resulting communicational system must be qualitatively different from human language. The claim that ape language, unlike human language, is derived entirely from enculturation renders the two systems so incomparable that achievements by apes can have no meaning for understanding of the origins of language.

Many early ape language projects did rely heavily on rewards that humans gave apes for correct answers during drills. For example, an ape received an apple when the animal produced the correct sign (or used the correct symbol of whatever type) for apple. Savage-Rumbaugh and her colleagues (e.g., Savage-Rumbaugh et al. 1993) rejected this method. They recognized that when apes were rewarded with the very objects they signed about, it became impossible to know whether the apes really understood the symbols they produced. They might be expressing merely a simple learned association. Savage-Rumbaugh points out that Kanzi, unlike all previous ape pupils, was never intended to be the subject of a research project on language. By his own choice, he observed the teaching sessions aimed at his mother. He spontaneously began to use lexigrams in communicating with humans and to demonstrate understanding of spoken English. Pinker (1994) counters that Kanzi, nevertheless, was at his mother's side while she was being trained. Pinker is unwilling to concede to Kanzi the spontaneous acquisition of languagelike skills.

Pinker's criticism is worth considering. When results from the Kanzi project are discussed in print, "freedom from rewards" is frequently mentioned as a significant aspect of the methodology used. This phrase seems to mean "freedom from edible rewards" (Sundberg 1996:482). Kanzi was not drilled during structured question-answer sessions or given food as a reward for answering test questions. But many things besides food, including positive social interaction with preferred associates, can reinforce and reward behavior. It is unlikely that Kanzi was free of all potential reinforcers or completely free of what might reasonably be called "training." In an analysis of Kanzi's interactions with human associates, Sundberg (1996:484) found "verbal prompts, praise, and reprimands in the shaping of successive approximations to receptive discriminations." Considering that such behaviors are likely used with human children during the early years of language acquisition, social rewards and social "training" do not bias the results of the ape-child comparisons in these research projects. But for anyone wanting to use apes to represent a baseline point from which to model the evolution of language within the hominid lineage, effective use of these data might be precluded, a consideration that has not gone unnoticed by ape-language researchers themselves (Miles and Harper 1994; but see Savage-Rumbaugh, Shanker, and Taylor 1998).

Aside from the issues of training and enculturation, how are the achievements of enculturated apes evaluated? Certain points must be conceded by almost everyone, as is the case with some of the results from Savage-Rumbaugh's work with Kanzi. Noble and Davidson accept, for example, that Kanzi uses and understands symbols, even while they emphasize the learning-interactional context for this behavior (Noble and Davidson 1996). Wallman, who concludes that enculturated apes do not have languagelike elements in their communication, nonetheless admits that Kanzi uses his lexigram keyboard to comment, without prompting, on ongoing events and to state his intended actions (1992:25). Wallman says the evidence for Kanzi's production is the best claim so far for reference in the ape language work: "The fact that he acquired his lexigrams without training, his untutored ability to press the corresponding lexigram when shown an object, and the reportedly significant frequency of noninstrumental lexigram presses all suggest that Kanzi was functionally aware that lexigrams are names for things" (1992:36).

Given this statement of Wallman's, how does he conclude that apes' abilities are being overinterpreted? First, he emphasizes the high rate of "instrumental utterances" given by all the apes, including Kanzi. These utterances are requests meant "almost exclusively to acquire things or to induce their human companions to do things" (1992:75). According to Wallman, Savage-Rumbaugh thought this high rate weakened the claims of the earlier ape language studies, even those that produced anecdotal evidence of noninstrumental utterances. Wallman writes: "Yet such anecdotes did not impress critics, such as Savage-Rumbaugh herself, sufficiently to keep them from dismissing these projects for having failed to produce referential use of language, presumably because, as with Kanzi, the overwhelming majority of usages were instrumental in nature." Yet Savage-Rumbaugh explains her dissatisfaction with the earlier studies in a different way: those studies could not discover whether the apes were capable of truly understanding the meaning of their utterances (Savage-Rumbaugh and Lewin 1994).

Second, Wallman expresses even greater skepticism about claims coming out of projects other than Savage-Rumbaugh's. He dismisses many reports about impressive rates of vocabulary acquisition by apes taught a version of ASL. These reports inflate the apes' accomplishments, Wallman says, because natural ape gestures were included in the tallies made of the artificial gestures acquired. He points out, as does Pinker (1994), that the symbol system learned by the enculturated apes was not ASL. ASL is a full language, and no ape has acquired it or any other language. But to my knowledge no ape-language researcher has reported that apes acquired ASL, nor has any linguist sympathetic to the continuity position done so (e.g., Stokoe 1983). Wallman's point is, nonetheless, a useful reminder for those ape-language researchers who lapse into shorthand when describing the skills that apes acquire. Miles and Harper (1994:256) write about "the natural language approach [that] utilized American Sign Language for the deaf" and then go on to report that "sign language was used to communicate with all three of the great apes." In fact, a simplified version of sign language—or perhaps more properly, English put into manual signs—was used (Stokoe 1983).

Some theorists go much further in dismissing what the ASL apes have been reported to do. They see no strong evidence for truly referential behavior, for grammar- or rule-ordered production, or for spontaneity and inventiveness in production. Donald (1991:152) characterizes ape signing behavior as follows: "[It] is restricted to situations in which the eliciting stimulus, and the reward, are clearly specified and present, or at least very close to the ape at the time of signing." But Donald never discusses the data that show evidence for spontaneous initiation of conversations, the ability to produce novel combinations, and the ability for displacement, all of which have been reported for an orangutan (Miles 1990; Miles and Harper 1994) and for at least some of the other signing apes. (Wallman discusses Miles's data too briefly as well.)

Data on ape communication are valuable currency in the debate over language origins. As we have seen, these data are scarce from wild populations, a situation that only heightens the significance of information from enculturated apes. Those who situate language origins in the hominid lineage alone have a vested interest in preventing the gap between apes and hominids from being convincingly "filled in" by data on communicative behavior in enculturated apes. They can also, or alternatively, argue that the enculturation process itself negates the significance of those data for understanding language origins.

Those who study ape language themselves (Savage-Rumbaugh et al. 1993; Savage-Rumbaugh and Rumbaugh 1993; Miles 1990; Miles and Harper 1994; Savage-Rumbaugh, this volume) construct a picture different from the one created by those who restrict language to the hominid lineage. Nonetheless, these ape-language researchers do explicitly compare ape linguistic skills with those of children. One case study compared the performance of an eight-year-old bonobo (Kanzi) with that of a two-year-old girl. Both subjects could "comprehend both the semantics and the syntactic structure of quite unusual English sentences....The lack of contingent reward, the novel nature of the requests, the absence of previous training to perform these specific requests, and the unique nature of each trial countermand simple explanations that depend on the conditioning of responses independently of semantic and syntactic comprehension" (Savage-Rumbaugh et al. 1993:98).

Savage-Rumbaugh has found evidence that when apes use lexigrams to produce utterances, they sometimes initiate conversations spontaneously (as Wallman pointed out) and that the utterances have protogrammatical structure. Yet for Savage-Rumbaugh, language is about comprehension: "[I]t is not the ability to 'name' different exemplars that is critical to language but rather the ability to understand that a word such as ball has a common meaning whether one says 'It's my ball,' 'Go hide the ball,' or 'Where did you leave the ball?'" (Savage-Rumbaugh et al. 1993:15).

Her focus on comprehension rather than production enables Savage-Rumbaugh to look in ape communication for the criterial element for language. Given that apes' vocal tract configuration constrains their vocal production, ape production cannot be measured as reliably as comprehension (see also Sundberg 1996). Why then, given her view that comprehension is at the heart of language, does Savage-Rumbaugh make repeated claims for protogrammatical rules in production (e.g., Greenfield and Savage-Rumbaugh 1990)? She interprets Kanzi's tendencies to place the lexigram first in lexigram-gesture combinations and to put certain action lexigrams in first and others in second position as rule-governed behavior: "The nature of these particular rules suggests that the evolutionary origin of grammar lies in rules for sequencing actions" (Greenfield and Savage-Rumbaugh 1990:568).

Savage-Rumbaugh is searching for precursors to the syntactic ability inherent in the use of human language. She must do this if her work is to be taken seriously by linguists who consider syntax to be of paramount importance in deciding what is language (see Bickerton 1990:544). (Savage-Rumbaugh evidently prefers to avoid this anthropocentrism; see Greenfield and Savage-Rumbaugh 1990:544; Savage-Rumbaugh et al. 1996; Savage-Rumbaugh, this volume). To some degree, then, when assessing the abilities of enculturated apes, language-origins theorists converge on what characteristics of language it is key to look for, if not on how the results of such searches are to be interpreted.

Savage-Rumbaugh also emphasizes that physiological constraints, rather than cognitive ones, inhibit capacities for full language use in enculturated apes. When those constraints were removed—that is, when selection pressures forced reorganization of the skull and vocal tract in human evolution—the lexicon increased. Additional changes were also set in motion: "Kanzi's ability to decode human sounds as well as syntactic constructions using combinations of these sounds suggests that ancestral Homo had developed a primitive linguistic skill that was awaiting the proper articulatory system" (Savage-Rumbaugh et al. 1993:109). Once this system was in place and "early hominids could produce a greater variety of easily discriminable distinct sound units than they could form previously" (1993:109), language evolution really took off. At first glance this might be read as a return to questions about the timing of language emergence. Yet ape-language researchers are mostly interested in showing that language did not originate with hominids. This, rather than deciding which particular species first developed language, is their major concern.

CONCLUSION, WITH AN EYE TO FUTURE THEORIZING

Few of the theories I have assessed here should be labeled "continuity" or "discontinuity." In the ways in which they define language and in the evidence they use to discuss the origins of language, they differ too widely to be easily categorized. Theories that are heavily grounded in data compiled by primatologists on free-ranging monkeys and apes often focus on what these animals do in a broad behavioral sense, rather than in the narrow sense of vocal production alone. They also expend little effort on pinpointing a time at which language originated in prehistory or on highlighting the complexities of syntax and symbol production in human language. Instead, they tend to minimize differences across species. Behaviors that others might judge to be totally distinct are frequently classed as merely "different forms" of the same basic behavior. Yet it often is left unclear what evidence would be sufficient to differentiate some specific feature of human language from its supposed precursor or "different form" in other species. Among the questions that are grappled with too rarely in these theories are these: When do the rudimentary syntax, symbol use, or protogrammatical behavior of free-ranging monkeys and apes differ so greatly from human syntax, symbol use, or grammar that the first cannot reasonably be called precursors or "different forms" of the second? When are suggestions of continuity in referential or semantic signaling based on data that are too scanty or too ambiguous to be convincing?

By contrast, those who endeavor to support the idea that human language differs qualitatively from ape communication would benefit by addressing another set of questions: What evidence would be sufficient to conclude that nonhuman primate communication has elements or features of language or language use? Can ape or monkey behavior—communicative or otherwise—be found that meets these criteria? These questions are aimed at finding out whether anything short of linguistic units arranged in sentencelike syntactic strings counts as language in other species. These theories rarely indicate what kind of data would falsify a claim for qualitative differences between nonhuman primate communication and human language.

Attention, then, needs to be paid not only to unacknowledged differences across theories but also to what evidence would support or falsify the ideas at the core of the theories. Doing so will allow us to view up close both language itself and the origins of linguistic behavior in other primates.

A NOTE ON PRIMATE COGNITION

A separate chapter could be written asking questions about theories of comparative cognitive abilities analogous to those just posed about theories of comparative communicational abilities. The data on monkey and ape cognition are treated in ways no less variable than are the data on communication. This is an important point, because conclusions about comparative cognitive skills are frequently used to bolster specific points in language-origins theories.

Let me return to Bickerton for a good example. For him, animals are "on-line" thinkers. Only humans can think both on-line and offline. He explains the difference between the two types of thinking in this way: "[O]n-line thinking involves computations carried out only in terms of neural responses elicited by the presence of external objects, while off-line thinking involves computations carried out on more lasting internal representations of those objects. Such computations need not be initiated by external causes, nor need they initiate an immediate motor response" (1995:90). Animals, including monkeys and apes, can react only to stimuli in the present. This level of cognitive response constrains the animals' level of communicative response. Indeed, these cognitive limitations are lifted only when language appears on the scene: "[L]anguage is the only thing that could have provided us with the means to free our thoughts from the exigencies of the moment and to structure them into complex wholes" (1995:100). (On this point, Noble and Davidson [1996] come close to Bickerton's views.)

Similarly, Donald labels ape cognition "episodic," in contrast to the higher forms developed by hominids and humans. Episodic cognitive culture severely limits what apes can do: "[Apes'] lives are lived entirely in the present, as a series of concrete episodes, and the highest elements in their system of memory representation seem to be at the level of event representation. Where humans have abstract symbolic memory representation, apes are bound to the concrete situation or episode" (1991:149). Donald's view of impoverished ape communication, then, derives from his view of ape cognition.

It is easy to see that Bickerton's and Donald's language-origins scenarios require these types of ideas about how animals think. If robust cognitive powers were accorded to nonhumans, it would be much harder to argue for qualitative distinctions between animal communication and human language. If, on the contrary, monkeys and apes have impoverished cognitive faculties in comparison with humans, it becomes easier to see nonhuman communicational abilities as impoverished in comparison with language.

This portrait of monkeys and apes as bound to react only to present stimuli and unable to either remember or plan ahead is unrecognizable to many primatologists (King and Shanker 1997). Both qualitative and quantitative data show that monkeys and apes from wild and captive populations do remember the past and do plan ahead (see, e.g., Cheney and Seyfarth 1990; Rumbaugh, Savage-Rumbaugh, and Washburn 1994; Tomasello and Call 1994, 1997; Byrne 1995; de Waal 1996). Two kinds of evidence are particularly persuasive in this regard. First, a variety of monkeys and apes navigate between distant feeding sites over optimal trajectories, indicating that foraging paths are planned in advance. In addition, when foraging, some apes fashion tools well before performing the actual tool-using task. Second, monkeys and apes frequently redirect aggression to previously uninvolved parties after significant delays, indicating that they remember past social interactions. Vervets and macaques, for instance, attack the kin of an animal perceived to have wronged them earlier.

Often, then, what is said about the relationship of nonhuman primate communication to human language is grounded in what is said about the relationship of animal to human cognition. The two sets of claims are intertwined and should be addressed together.

Notes

1. Even in the version of this chapter circulated before the Santa Fe seminar I retained the use of the terms "continuity" and "discontinuity." When I use these terms here, however, it is only because the theorists themselves have done so. It is a measure of our seminar's impact on my thinking that I have changed my view so much.

2. Thanks to Talbot Taylor for helping me to understand this.

3. Thanks to Rob Burling for helping me see this. I hasten to add that Burling makes no strong claim that the behavior in question is likely to be involuntary; he is simply searching for a rigorous interpretation of the data.

4. I appreciate Stuart Shanker's making this point clear to me.

3

Primate Social Organization, Gestural Repertoire Size, and Communication Dynamics
A Comparative Study of Macaques

Dario Maestripieri

In recent years there has been considerable debate over the usefulness of a comparative approach to the study of language evolution (Premack 1986; Bickerton 1990; Snowdon 1990; Kendon 1991; Noble and Davidson 1991; Burling 1993; Schepartz 1993; King 1994a, 1994b, chapter 2 this volume). This debate is ultimately rooted in a controversy over the definition of language, its fundamental function, and the selective pressures that were responsible for its evolution. Proponents of the comparative approach view language as a system of cognition and communication that is adapted primarily to the social environment (e.g., Dunbar 1993; Armstrong, Stokoe, and Wilcox 1995). From this perspective, the comparative method can provide insights into the evolution of language because it enhances our understanding of how pressures from the social environment influence the cognitive abilities and communication systems of primates (see Tooby and DeVore 1987 for an application of "strategic" modeling to the study of human evolution).

To date, the most systematic attempt to extrapolate an evolutionary trend from primate social behavior to human language has been made by Dunbar (1991, 1992, 1993, 1995; Aiello and Dunbar 1993). Building on a correlation across Old World monkeys and apes between group size, neocortex size, and amount of time devoted to grooming, Dunbar suggested that an increase in group size, driven by ecological factors, selected for primate encephalization. At some point during the course of human evolution, this increase in group size and neocortex size precipitated the evolution of language, because a social bonding mechanism more efficient than grooming was required to maintain social relationships.

Although Dunbar's application of the comparative method to the question of language evolution was generally well received, some authors criticized his use of the neocortical ratio (the ratio of neocortex size to the rest of the brain) as a measure of cognitive capacity (Gibson and Jessee, this volume) and the criteria by which he assessed group size in several primate species and in humans (Davidson, this volume). Dunbar's model was also criticized for its emphasis on grooming rather than on communication patterns and for identifying the social pressures for the evolution of cognition and language as an increase in the number of social relationships rather than as an increase in their complexity (see commentaries in Dunbar 1993). Nonhuman primates possess specifically adapted signals such as gestures and vocalizations that help maintain a stable group structure and facilitate intragroup cooperation. Therefore, an obvious extension of Dunbar's hypothesis would be to investigate whether there is a relationship between group size, encephalization, and the size and complexity of the communicative repertoire across extant primate species.

In searching for an evolutionary relationship between primate social organization and communication, sources of social complexity other than group size should also be investigated. Some authors have suggested that social characteristics such as frequent polyadic interactions, alliance formation, and intergroup transfer may select for advanced cognitive and communicative abilities in primates (Harcourt 1993; Whiten 1993). Here I propose that a reduced influence of dominance and kinship on intraspecific social dynamics in primates could, along with group size, select for a wider repertoire of social signals and more complex communicative interactions.

Among primates, the influence of dominance and the influence of kinship on intraspecific social dynamics often covary along a continuum, with "despotic-nepotistic" societies at one extreme and "egalitarian-individualistic" societies at the other (Thierry 1990). In despotic-nepotistic primate societies, the distribution of affiliative interactions (e.g., grooming) and agonistic interactions (aggression and coalitionary support) is strongly influenced by a linear dominance hierarchy and by kinship. In contrast, in egalitarian-individualistic societies, a strict dominance hierarchy is usually absent, strong bonds between kin are limited to those between mothers and their immature offspring, and physical and social skills play an important role in defining the individual's position in the social group.

It may be argued that in a social system in which relationships are strongly influenced by differences in dominance and in which cooperation occurs mainly within clusters of kin—that is, between individuals who are very familiar with each other—there may be little pressure to develop a sophisticated system of communication. Maintenance of group structure and coordination of behavior between individuals can be effectively achieved if a few unequivocal indicators of dominance rank are recognized and if unrelated or distantly ranked individuals simply avoid each other. In societies that are more egalitarian and individualistic, flexible individual strategies will be favored, which may include, for example, the formation of temporary alliances with unrelated and less familiar individuals. Under these circumstances there may be selective pressure to develop complex patterns of affiliative communication and bonding that allow coordination of behavior and facilitate interactions between relatively unfamiliar individuals. An increase in group size resulting from the need to protect the group from predators or from the need to compete with other groups could lead to further interaction between unfamiliar individuals and to more complex communication dynamics.

Variation in primate social organization along the dominance-kinship gradient could ultimately be accounted for by ecological factors such as the nature and intensity of food competition (Vehrencamp 1983; van Schaik 1989). The dominance-kinship gradient, however, accounts for only part of the variation in primate social and mating systems. Not all primate species live in groups, and not all group-living species have systems of intragroup cooperation or competition based on dominance hierarchies or alliances. Therefore, the proposed relationship between dominance, kinship, and size and sophistication of the communicative repertoire may apply only to a subset of primate species, notably those with a frugivorous or omnivorous diet and social systems characterized by dominance hierarchies and alliance formation. Interestingly, these characteristics are shared by most Old World monkeys and apes—that is, the primates most closely related to humans—and by humans themselves.

Macaques (genus *Macaca*) could be a good model for investigating the proposed evolutionary relationship between primate social organization and communication. The genus *Macaca* consists of 19 extant species (Fooden 1980) that vary considerably in terms of the relative influence of dominance hierarchy and kinship on social dynamics (de Waal 1989; Thierry 1990). Although we have few or no comparative data on vocal communication in macaques, a number of studies have reported considerable variation in visual and tactile communication patterns across macaque species (Andrew 1964; van Hooff 1967; Bernstein 1970; Redican 1975; Maestripieri n.d.). This variation is less pronounced in agonistic displays (e.g., threats) but is found especially in displays of affiliation and bonding (van Hooff 1967; Petit and Thierry 1992; Thierry et al. 1989; Maestripieri 1997).

Rhesus (*Macaca mulatta*), pigtail (*Macaca nemestrina*), and stumptail macaques (*Macaca arctoides*) belong to three different phyletic groups within the genus *Macaca* (Fooden 1980) and are characterized by some important differences in social organization. Rhesus macaques are a good example of a despotic-nepotistic society. Among rhesus macaques, intragroup cooperation, in the form of grooming and agonistic support, occurs primarily between matrilineal kin and/or adjacently ranked individuals (Sade 1972; Kaplan 1977; Bernstein and Ehardt 1985a; Maestripieri and Scucchi 1989). The frequency of spatial avoidance is higher and the frequency of postconflict reconciliation is lower than in pigtails and stumptails (Bernstein and Ehardt 1985b; de Waal and Ren 1988; Judge 1991; Maestripieri 1994). Social cohesion is evident only within clusters of kin, and individuals at the extremes of the dominance hierarchy rarely, if ever, interact with each other.

The social dynamics of pigtail macaques are quite similar to those of rhesus macaques in that agonistic support and grooming occur mostly between matrilineally related and/or adjacently ranked females (Massey 1977; Defler 1978; Wade 1979; Bernstein, Williams, and Ramsay 1983; Caldecott 1987; Boccia 1989; Oi 1990). The lower levels of spatial avoidance, the higher reconciliation frequency, and the higher rates of approaches and grooming between pigtail females relative to rhesus macaques (Maestripieri 1994) suggest, however, that pigtail macaque society is more cohesive and conciliatory than rhesus society. Aggression rates have been reported as similar in pigtails and rhesus (Maestripieri 1994) or lower in the pigtails (Bernstein, Williams, and Ramsay 1983). Aggression, however, more frequently involves the participation of third individuals among pigtails than among rhesus (Bernstein, Williams, and Ramsay 1983), and postconflict reconciliation is also frequently extended to the opponent's kin and allies (Judge 1991).

Stumptail macaques exhibit higher rates of proximity, contact, huddling, and grooming than do rhesus and pigtails, suggesting that they have the most cohesive society of the three species (Bernstein 1980; de Waal and Ren 1988; Butovskaya 1993a; Maestripieri 1994). The frequency of aggression in stumptails has been reported as higher than in rhesus and pigtails (Weigel 1980; de Waal and Ren 1988; Butovskaya 1993a, 1993b), although stumptail aggression is often bidirectional and only rarely escalates to serious biting (e.g., aggression often involves mutual slapping [de Waal and Ren 1988]; but see Bernstein 1980; Ruchlmann et al. 1988). Stumptail macaques possess a linear dominance hierarchy (Bertrand 1969; Estrada, Estrada, and Ervin 1977; Bernstein 1980; Nieuwenhuijsen, Slob, and van der Werff ten Bosch 1988; Rhine, Cox, and Costello 1989), but matrilineal kinship plays a smaller role in the distribution of agonistic support and grooming in stumptails than in rhesus (Butovskaya 1993a, 1993b). For example, stumptail juveniles receive agonistic aid from adult males more than from their mothers or other female relatives (Bernstein 1980), and they easily maintain their dominance rank in the absence of their mothers (Estrada, Estrada, and Ervin 1977).

The present study investigated the size of the gestural communicative repertoire (facial expressions, body postures, and tactile inter-actions) and the intragroup communication dynamics in rhesus, pig-tail, and stumptail macaques. Specifically, I compared the frequency of occurrence and contextual usage of the most prominent gestures of dominance, submission, affiliation, and bonding in these species. The hypothesis being tested is that pigtail macaques and especially stump-tail macaques have a wider repertoire of gestures than rhesus macaques. The contextual usage of gestures and their information content are also expected to be more complex in the first two species than in the last.

METHODS

This study was conducted at the field station of the Yerkes Regional Primate Research Center in Lawrenceville, Georgia (USA). The Yerkes field station is a 117-acre facility located in a wooded area and devoted to the breeding and use of nonhuman primates for behav-ioral and biomedical research. It currently houses about 1,200 macaques in addition to other monkeys and apes. Most of the macaques live in social groups in large (35 m^2) outdoor compounds with attached indoor quarters. Group sizes and composition approxi-mate those found in the wild. In the wild, macaque groups range in size from more than 10 to fewer than 100 individuals, with a constant aver-age across the genus of about 18–32 individuals and an adult sex ratio skewed toward females (Lindburg 1991). The groups are composed of clusters of related females (matrilines) with their offspring and unre-lated adult males. Females typically spend their entire life in their natal group, whereas males leave their group at puberty and immigrate into a new group after a brief period of solitary life (Lindburg 1991).

This study was conducted with three social groups—one each of rhesus, pigtail, and stumptail macaques. The rhesus group consisted of 2 adult males and 26 adult females, the pigtail group of 5 adult males and 28 adult females, and the stumptail group of 8 adult males and 17 adult females, all with their respective subadult, juvenile, and infant offspring. Each group had the matrilineal structure and dominance hierarchy typical of that macaque species in the wild.

Each group was observed for 100 hours between September 1994 and April 1995. Data were collected during 30-minute observation sessions randomly distributed between 0800 and 1900 hours. Data were collected with the behavior sampling method (Martin and Bateson 1986), which involves watching the whole group and recording every occurrence of a particular type of behavior, together with other related behaviors and the identities of the individuals involved. Particular effort was made to avoid sampling specific individuals or classes of individuals preferentially because of their conspicuous physical appearance or activity patterns. Because data collected with the behavior sampling method would be inappropriate for use in estimating the rate at which specific individuals participated in specific communicative interactions, the analyses described in this chapter focus primarily on comparisons between sex-rank classes of individuals.

Observations were focused on 15 facial expressions, body postures, and tactile interactions (collectively referred to as gestures; see table 3.1 for definitions). As assessed on the basis of preliminary observations and information available in the literature, these gestures are the most prominent signals of dominance, submission, affiliation, and bonding in rhesus, pigtail, and stumptail macaques, although not all gestures are present in each species. Threat and play displays such as the "staring open-mouth face" and the "relaxed open-mouth face" (van Hooff 1967) were not considered in this study because they are remarkably similar in structure and contextual usage among the three species (Maestripieri 1997).

Behavioral sequences involving the gestures were recorded only when the behavior preceding the signal (e.g., approach or aggression) was actually observed. In those cases the behavioral sequence was followed until the end (e.g., when two individuals were more than 5 m apart from one another and did not further interact for 10–20 seconds). The occurrence of any interaction between the sender and the receiver of the signal, as well as the behavior of any other individuals participating in the interaction, was recorded. The following behaviors were considered: approaches and departures (when one individual moved within arm's reach of another without making contact, or moved away from it), bodily contact (when two individuals touched each other with their hands or bodies for more than 5 seconds),

TABLE 3.1

Behavioral Definitions of Gestures

Behavior and Code	Definition
Lip-Smack (LS)	Rapid opening and closing of the mouth and lips such that when the lips close they make an audible smacking sound.
Pucker (PC)	The lips are compressed and protruded; the eyebrows, forehead, and ears are retracted.
Teeth-Chatter (TC)	The mouth is rapidly opened and closed and the lips are retracted, exposing the teeth.
Bared-Teeth (BT)	The mouth is closed and the lips and lip corners are retracted so that the teeth are exposed in a white band.
Eye-Brows (EB)	The scalp and brow are retracted and the mouth is open.
Touch-Face (TF)	One hand is extended to touch the face of another individual while standing or sitting in front of it.
Touch-Genitals (TG)	Manipulation of the genitals of another individual without olfactory inspection. The tail is raised to expose the genitals.
Present (PR)	The tail is raised to expose the genitals.
Hip-Touch (HT)	Brief touch of the hindquarters of another individual with one or both hands without putting arms around.
Hip-Clasp (HC)	The hindquarters of another individual are clasped with both arms, usually in the sitting position.
Mount (MT)	Mount with or without foot-clasp but with no intromission or thrusts.
Present-Arm (PA)	One arm or hand is extended across the face of another individual to be bitten.
Mock-Bite (MB)	Gripping another individual's skin with the teeth, slowly, without roughness, for several seconds.
Face-Inspection (FI)	Close inspection of the face of another individual, usually staring into its eyes for several seconds while the other individual freezes (not recorded during feeding).
Embrace (EM)	Ventral embrace with both arms around the torso of another individual, in the sitting position and kneading the partner's fur or flesh.

grooming (when one individual picked or stroked the fur or skin of another with its hands), aggression (with threats, bites, or chases), avoidance (when one individual withdrew from another in response to an approach), vocalizations (screams and grunts), social play (e.g., rough-and-tumble or chase play), and infant handling (when one individual briefly touched, held, or carried a young infant).

Data on unidirectional agonistic encounters recorded during preliminary observations were used to establish a dominance hierarchy among all individuals within each group. Unidirectional agonistic scores required an act of aggression (e.g., threat or bite) from one individual followed by a clear submissive response from another. These data were then ordered in a matrix to minimize the number of scores falling below the diagonal when winners were listed in the columns and losers in the rows.

Interspecific comparisons of the frequency of gestures were conducted with Friedman's analysis of variance followed by post-hoc tests. Comparisons of the contexts of occurrence of gestures were conducted with two-way Analysis of Variance (ANOVA) for repeated measures, as recommended by Kramer and Schmidhammer (1992) when dealing with dependent observations. Bonferroni-Dunn tests were used as post-hocs. All statistical tests were two-tailed. Although the statistical analyses of the contextual usage of gestures used data points for all individuals, data are presented in terms of percentage scores.

RESULTS
Size of the Gestural Repertoire in the Three Species
Figure 3.1 shows the number of observed gestures per individual in the three species. The five most frequent gestures across the three species were Present (PR), Teeth-Chatter (TC), and Bared-Teeth (BT) in stumptail macaques and Pucker (PC) and Lip-Smack (LS) in pigtail macaques.

In rhesus macaques, only 4 gestures (Bared-Teeth, Present, Mount, and Lip-Smack) were displayed with a frequency equal to or greater than one event per individual, compared with 8 gestures in pigtail macaques and 12 in stumptail macaques. The frequency of gestures

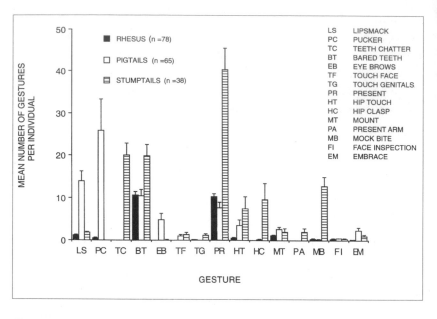

FIGURE 3.1

Mean number of gestures (+ standard error of mean) per individual in the three macaque species. Data refer to the occurrence of each of the 15 selected gestures during the entire study period.

per individual was significantly different in the three species ($\chi^2 = 8.0$, df = 2, $p = .01$; fig. 3.2) and was higher for pigtails and stumptails than for rhesus ($p < .05$). Thus, pigtail macaques and especially stumptail macaques have a wider repertoire of gestures of dominance-submission and affiliation than do rhesus macaques, and they use these gestures with higher frequency.

The contexts of occurrence of the most frequent gestures (frequency > one event per individual) were compared within each species. The following sections summarize the main findings of these analyses to illustrate the most salient features of communication dynamics in rhesus, pigtail, and stumptail macaques. All statistical tests, along with a multivariate analysis of the occurrence of signals in each species, have been presented elsewhere (Maestripieri 1996a, 1996b; Maestripieri and Wallen 1997).

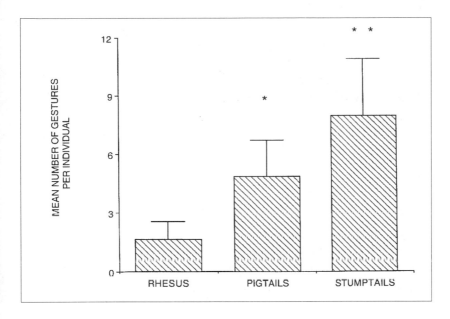

FIGURE 3.2

Mean number of gestures (+ standard error of mean) per individual in the three macaque species. Data refer to all the gestures combined over the entire study period.

Communication Dynamics in Rhesus Macaques

Bared-Teeth (BT) and Present (PR) were by far the two most common gestures observed in rhesus macaques, accounting for 43 percent and 41 percent, respectively, of all observed signals. The vast majority of these gestures were displayed by subordinate individuals to dominants (BT, 97%; PR, 91%) in situations involving risk of aggression, such as immediately after receiving an attack or after being approached by a dominant individual. The most striking difference between the contextual occurrences of Bared-Teeth and Present was that the former occurred primarily after an approach from the front and the latter after an approach from the rear. Only a small proportion of these signals was followed by an affiliative interaction involving contact, grooming, or play (BT, 2%; PR, 3%). Bared-Teeth and Present appear to be functionally equivalent signals whose meaning may be "I am afraid" or "Do not attack me" or a combination of the two (Maestripieri 1996c). By simultaneously baring their teeth and presenting in response to aggression or during a chase, rhesus macaques may reduce the risk of further aggression from different directions.

Lip-Smack was much less frequent than Bared-Teeth and Present. Among adults, 80 percent of Lip-Smacks were displayed by subordinates to dominants. When compared with Bared-Teeth and Present, Lip-Smack between adults was most likely and Bared-Teeth least likely to occur in conjunction with a spontaneous approach by one individual to another. Lip-Smack was more likely (> 50% of occurrences) to be followed by affiliative behavior than was Bared-Teeth or Present. Specifically, Lip-Smack was used by both dominants and subordinates to initiate grooming interactions and by mothers to retrieve their infants. Therefore, although Lip-Smack has a submissive component similar to that of Bared-Teeth and Present, this signal also communicates the intention to establish contact and engage in friendly interaction.

The fourth gesture that occurred with a frequency greater than one event per individual was Mount. As defined in table 3.1, this gesture included only mounts without intromission and thrusting. About 70 percent of Mounts occurred between males, and intermale mounting was initiated by both subordinates and dominants. Mounts often occurred during alliance formation and during play. Mounts were immediately preceded by an exchange of signals such as Bared-Teeth, Present, and Lip-Smack (69%) or by a spontaneous approach (18%). About 30 percent of Mounts were followed by contact, grooming, or play. The evidence available suggests that Mount functions as a signal that results in bonding between males.

Communication Dynamics in Pigtail Macaques

Pucker, Lip-Smack, and Bared-Teeth were the three most common gestures observed among pigtail macaques, accounting for 35 percent, 19 percent, and 14 percent, respectively, of all observed signals. As in rhesus macaques, Bared-Teeth, Lip-Smack, and Present were mostly displayed by subordinates to dominants (BT, 97%; PR, 91%; LS, 94%). Pucker, however, was performed by both dominants (63%) and subordinates (37%) and was therefore analyzed separately from the other three signals.

Bared-Teeth, Lip-Smack, and Present differed significantly from one another in their context of occurrence. Bared-Teeth was more likely to occur in response to aggression or to an approach than was Present or Lip-Smack. Present was most likely and Bared-Teeth least likely to be displayed in conjunction with a spontaneous approach to another individual. Present and Lip-Smack were more likely to be followed by affiliation (contact, grooming, or play) than was Bared-Teeth. Lip-Smack was more likely to be followed by other gestures such as Pucker, Bared-Teeth, Embrace (EM), Present, Hip-Touch (HT), or another Lip-Smack than was Bared Teeth or Present. Therefore, whereas Lip-Smack and Present were sometimes followed by affiliation or other gestures, Bared-Teeth was rarely followed by any other social interaction. Based on these findings, Bared-Teeth appears to be a reactive response elicited by the behavior of another individual and to commu nicate fear and submission in situations of high risk of aggression. Present is used by subordinates to appease dominants even in the absence of an overt risk of aggression, whereas Lip-Smack communicates both submission and intention to initiate friendly interactions.

Because of the possibility that female and male pigtail macaques use Pucker in different contexts (Christopher and Gelini 1977), females' and males' Puckers were first analyzed separately and then compared. Females used Pucker in some contexts common to Lip-Smack, but there were some important differences between the two gestures. Lip-Smack was more likely to occur in response to aggression or to an approach than was Pucker, whereas Pucker was more likely to precede affiliation and infant handling than was Lip-Smack. Females' Puckers often occurred in response to another Pucker, whereas Lip-Smack was more likely to be followed by other facial expressions and gestures.

Females often displayed Pucker while approaching another female: in 50 percent of cases, the signaler proceeded to make contact and initiate grooming immediately after the display of the signal, whereas in 33 percent of cases, she initiated affiliation after the second female responded with Pucker. Pucker was also displayed by a female who was sitting at some distance from another female (from 1–2 m up to 20–25 m away) or when a female turned around and moved away from another female. In 83 percent of cases in which Pucker was displayed by a female sitting at a distance or turning around and moving away (n = 178), the receiver of the signal immediately approached or followed the signaler—in 34 percent of cases after having displayed Pucker herself—and groomed or embraced the signaler.

Although there were some differences in the contextual usage of Pucker by males and females, the meaning of the signal appeared to be the same for both sexes. Males displayed most Puckers (96%) toward females, and Pucker was often accompanied by Hip-Touch and Mount. Like females, males puckered from a distance or while moving away from a female. Females were more likely to approach and groom a male than to present if the male puckered while sitting at a distance (sitting, groom = 86%; present = 21%), and more likely to approach and present than to groom if the male puckered while walking away from them (walking away, groom = 14%; present = 79%). Therefore, Pucker while sitting functioned as a request by a male for grooming, and Pucker while moving away functioned as a request for a female to follow and present. The main difference in the usage of Pucker by males and females was that females used it to facilitate affiliative interactions with other females, whereas males used it to facilitate mating. Individuals of both sexes used Pucker to coordinate their behavior in complex sequences of interactions, including the manifestation of preferences for sites in the compound where grooming could take place and attempts to recruit agonistic support from high-ranking individuals. By turning their head and pointing their lips, pigtail macaques used Pucker to ask another individual to move in a specific direction.

Mount (MT) was displayed by both males and females, and in 75 percent of cases by the dominant individual in the dyad. Mount occurred in various contexts such as after one individual spontaneously approached another, in conjunction with other gestures, and after aggression. In most cases, Mount was followed either by no interaction or by grooming. The effect of dominance rank on Mount suggests that this behavior functions to assert dominance over another individual without resorting to aggression.

Embrace occurred almost exclusively between females and was often mutual. Embracing was mostly preceded by Pucker by one or both females (82%) and was followed by grooming (72%). Embrace clearly resulted in bonding between females and facilitated the occurrence of affiliative interactions such as grooming and infant handling.

Eye-Brows (EB) was shown by both dominants and subordinates and was especially common between adult males. Eye-Brows was commonly displayed by an individual while spontaneously approaching another and in response to another Eye-Brows, with or without other gestures. The exchange of Eye-Brows between adult males was frequently accompanied by approach-retreat interactions, Hip-Touch, and brief bouts of play. It occurred in some specific contexts such as immediately before or after agonistic support, the reintroduction of individuals to the group after a brief removal, the aftermath of episodes of female mobbing of high-ranking males, and the group's reaction to an external threat or disturbance. Eye-Brows appears to function to request agonistic support or protection and to resolve dominance relationships when these are uncertain or challenged.

Communication Dynamics in Stumptail Macaques

Present, Teeth-Chatter, and Bared-Teeth were the three most common gestures observed among stumptail macaques, accounting for 34 percent, 17 percent, and 17 percent, respectively, of all observed signals. Bared-Teeth, Present-Arm (PA), Lip-Smack, Present, Teeth-Chatter, and Touch-Face (TF) were mostly displayed by subordinates (BT, 98%; PA, 93%; LS, 78%; PR, 98%; TC, 73%; TF, 71%). In contrast, Mount, Mock-Bite (MB), Hip-Clasp (HC), and Hip-Touch were mostly displayed by dominants (MT, 72%; MB, 77%; HC, 92%; HT, 87%). Most Embraces (71%) occurred between females and were initiated by both dominants and subordinates. In contrast, most Touch-Genitals (TG) (79%) occurred between males and were often performed by dominants (74%).

There were some important differences in the contextual usages and meanings of the different submissive signals. Bared-Teeth was primarily a reactive response elicited by risk of aggression and infrequently followed by affiliation. As in the other species, it probably reflects a combination of fear and submission. Present-Arm was mostly elicited by squabbling, a form of aggression in which two individuals sat opposite each other, threatening and slapping each other. This signal appears to communicate submission in a conflict without necessarily reflecting fear. Present was primarily an appeasement gesture used by subordinates even in the absence of an impending risk of aggression. Subordinates repeatedly approached and presented to dominants without any previous or further interaction. Lip-Smack was also spontaneous but was often followed by affiliation; this signal communicated submission as well as intention to engage in a friendly interaction. Teeth-Chatter was used in contexts common to both Bared-Teeth and Lip-Smack; this signal has a meaning similar to that of Lip-Smack but apparently a stronger emotional component, which ranges from fear to excitement.

Mount, Hip-Clasp, and Hip-Touch did not differ significantly in their most common contexts of occurrence, namely, in response to Present, in response to approach, after spontaneously approaching another individual, in conjunction with Teeth-Chatter, and before contact, grooming, or play. Hip-Clasp, however, was mostly used by adults when interacting with juveniles. Mount, Hip-Clasp, and Hip-Touch also occurred during postconflict reconciliation, when adult males disrupted fights between juveniles, and in conjunction with extragroup disturbance. Typically, in response to an external threat or disturbance, juveniles ran toward adult males, presented their hindquarters, and screamed while receiving Hip-Clasp. Mount had a higher assertive component than did Hip-Clasp or Hip-Touch. Although Hip-Clasp and Hip-Touch may serve a specific reconciliatory function after conflicts, they also communicate reassurance, protection, or bonding in other contexts.

Mock-Bite was displayed in aggressive contexts (58%), notably squabbling, and was a common response to Present-Arm. In other words, when two individuals were threatening and slapping each other, one or both of them displayed Mock-Bite. Mock-Bite appears to be a ritualized aggressive behavior pattern that stumptail macaques use to resolve their dominance relationships when these are uncertain or challenged. Embrace between females was mutual in 55 percent of cases, often accompanied by Teeth-Chatter and screams and followed by huddling or grooming. As in the pigtails, Embrace resulted in bonding between females and facilitated friendly interactions between them. Touch-Genitals occurred in contexts similar to those of Mount, Hip-Clasp, and Hip-Touch and was most frequent between males.

DISCUSSION

Social Organization and Communication in Macaques

This study revealed marked differences in the gestural repertoires and communication dynamics of rhesus, pigtail, and stumptail macaques. As predicted, pigtail macaques and especially stumptail macaques have a wider repertoire of nonaggressive gestures than do rhesus macaques. A richer repertoire of signals in the former species is accompanied by more sophisticated communicative interactions.

Aside from threats and play displays, which were not considered in this study, rhesus macaques have a relatively poor repertoire of gestures. It consists mainly of two submissive signals—the bared teeth display and the hindquarter presentation. Thus, most gestural communication in rhesus macaques has to do with the regulation of dominance relationships and with minimizing the risk of aggression. Affiliative signals that facilitate contact and grooming are infrequent and limited to particular classes of individuals such as mothers and infants, or males. The overall frequency of occurrence of affiliative gestures is low compared with that of submissive signals in the same species or of affiliative signals in the other two species.

Affiliative facial expressions such as the pucker and lip-smacking are most frequent among pigtail macaques. Although lip-smacking seems to have a stronger submissive component among pigtails than among rhesus and stumptails, the pucker is a true affiliative signal, used to coordinate movements and facilitate cooperation between individuals (see also Jensen and Gordon 1970; Maestripieri 1996d). The complexity of the contextual usage of the pucker, which often involves "conversational" exchanges of the signal (Maestripieri 1996a), has no parallel in the social communication of rhesus and stumptail macaques. Pigtail macaques also exhibit ventro-ventral embracing between females and the eye-brows display, which is mostly exchanged between males.

Bonding patterns are especially conspicuous among stumptail

macaques; in this species, affiliative gestures are frequently exchanged between all sex and age classes of individuals. Visual and tactile bonding patterns similar to those observed in pigtails and stumptails have been described in other monkeys and apes and are often referred to as "greetings" (Pelaez 1982; Thierry 1984; Colmenares 1990; Smuts and Watanabe 1990). Greetings have been hypothesized to serve several functions, including reduction of tension and negotiation of alliances between individuals. In addition to bonding patterns, stumptail macaques have a complex and almost redundant system of assertive and submissive signals. Unlike the interactions of pigtail macaques, therefore, most of the communicative interactions observed in stumptail macaques do not occur in the context of coordination of behavior or affiliation but appear to be aimed at the regulation of aggression and the enhancement of intragroup cohesion and bonding.

The differences found in the size of the gestural repertoire and in the communication dynamics of rhesus, pigtail, and stumptail macaques are generally consistent with the characteristics of their social organization. The despotic and nepotistic features of rhesus society leave little room for complex patterns of affiliative communication and bonding. Intense affiliative communication and bonding patterns in pigtail macaques appear to have coevolved with complex dynamics of intragroup cooperation and with considerable social tolerance. Although stumptail macaques have a rich communicative repertoire, the communication dynamics observed in this species do not support the view of stumptail macaques as an example of egalitarian society (e.g., de Waal 1989). In contrast, the variety of assertive and submissive signals observed in stumptail macaques suggests a great potential for intraspecific conflict in this species. Communication of dominance and submission, however, is also accompanied by conspicuous expressions of reassurance and bonding, suggesting a need for high intragroup cohesion, perhaps for competition with other groups or protection from predators. In this case, it seems that the need for cooperation between unrelated individuals, rather than a relaxation of the dominance hierarchy, might have selected for the development of complex communication dynamics (see Maestripieri 1996b for further discussion).

The hypothesized relationship between social organization and communication dynamics in rhesus, pigtail, and stumptail macaques would be strengthened if comparison of the vocal signals of these species produced results similar to those obtained for gestures. Unfortunately, no direct comparisons of the vocal repertoires or of the complexity of vocal exchanges in rhesus, pigtail, and stumptail macaques have yet been made. Several authors, however, have noticed that stumptail macaques have an extremely rich vocal repertoire relative to other macaque species (e.g., Bertrand 1969; Bernstein 1980). Thus it seems likely that differences in vocal communication among macaque species are parallel rather than complementary to those found for their gestural communication.

Social Organization and Communication in Anthropoid and Human Evolution

The results of this study are only a first attempt at understanding the relationship between social organization and communication systems in primates. The hypothesized relationship between dominance-nepotism and complexity of communication dynamics should be further tested with other primate species. Other intriguing hints that the lack of strict dominance hierarchies, the need to cooperate with unrelated individuals, and increased group size may select for complex communication dynamics come from a comparison of the great apes that are phylogenetically and behaviorally closest to humans—chimpanzees (Pan troglodytes) and bonobos (*Pan paniscus*).

The social organization of bonobos differs from that of chimpanzees in several important respects. First, bonobo society is more egalitarian and cohesive than chimpanzee society (Nishida and Hiraiwa-Hasegawa 1987; Kano 1992). Second, whereas in chimpanzees strong bonds are formed between natal males, among bonobos it is migratory females who bond strongly with same-sex strangers later in life (Nishida and Hiraiwa-Hasegawa 1987; Kano 1992). And third, bonobos live in larger groups than do chimpanzees (Chapman, White, and Wrangham 1994). Interestingly, bonobos possess a wider and more complex communicative repertoire than chimpanzees, including more frequent eye contact and more frequent and more elaborate gestures and vocalizations (Savage-Rumbaugh, Wilkerson, and Bakeman 1977;

Savage-Rumbaugh and Wilkerson 1978; de Waal 1988). Moreover, bonobos appear to be more proficient in the acquisition and communicative use of symbols than chimpanzees and the other apes seem to be (Savage-Rumbaugh, Rumbaugh, and McDonald 1985; Savage-Rumbaugh and Lewin 1994). Further comparative studies of social organization and communication in chimpanzees, bonobos, and the other apes are needed in order to better understand the role of the social environment in the evolution of the communicative skills of anthropoid primates. The comparative data, along with archaeological data documenting changes in brain size and vocal tract (Davidson, this volume; Gibson and Jessee, this volume), could provide some insight into the evolution of complex communication systems in the hominid and human line.

Dominance hierarchies and nepotistic behavior have probably been a constant presence in human evolution and are still conspicuous in most contemporary human societies. In the initial stages of hominid evolution, however, an increase in group size resulting from direct intergroup competition might have intensified intragroup competition and in turn enhanced the need to recruit allies from beyond the boundaries of an individual's kin group or dominance class (Alexander 1974). Complex social competition and cooperation within groups, in their own turn, might have played an important role in the evolution of human cognitive and communicative abilities (e.g., Humphrey 1976).

Interestingly, it has recently been suggested that the long hunter-gatherer phase of human evolution might have been characterized by a relatively individualistic and egalitarian lifestyle (Knauft 1991; Boehm 1993; Erdal and Whiten 1994). The psychological dispositions underlying this lifestyle, including the tendencies both to dominate and to resist domination, to share and to be opportunistically selfish, and to pursue flexible and short-term strategies of cooperation with different individuals according to the circumstances, could have been important factors in molding the early human mind. They might even have played a causal role in the encephalization process that took place during this phase of human evolution (Erdal and Whiten 1994, 1996). This argument shares some similarities with the hypothesis presented here, for it might be argued that a number of specific communicative skills probably coevolved with a complex social intelligence.

The Primate Precursors of Language: Gestures or Vocalizations?

The search for evolutionary precursors of language among primate communicative patterns has often been accompanied by the debate over the importance of vocal versus nonvocal signals (e.g., Hewes 1973; Burling 1993). Because human language is often equated with speech (but see Armstrong, Stokoe, and Wilcox 1995), it has appeared natural to look for language precursors in the vocalizations of nonhuman primates and not in their gestural signals. For example, great emphasis has been placed on the finding that vervet monkeys (*Cercopithecus aethiops*) possess different alarm calls for aerial and terrestrial predators and are therefore capable of semantic communication (Struhsaker 1967; Cheney and Seyfarth 1990; Gouzoules, Gouzoules, and Ashley 1995). It is now recognized, however, that this ability is shared by a number of birds and other mammals (Macedonia and Evans 1993; Hauser 1996).

There is reason to believe that selective pressures for propositional communication were more likely to arise in the context of communication about social behavior and conspecifics than in the context of communication about external referents such as food (Dittus 1984) or predators (Macedonia and Evans 1993). This is because the problems faced by most primates during foraging or escaping predators are simply no different in complexity from those faced by most other animal species. Therefore, it is difficult to argue that these activities posed a special pressure to evolve higher cognitive or communicative abilities. In contrast, the strategies of intragroup cooperation and competiton employed by nonhuman primates have no parallel in the animal world, and there is a clear trend in the increasing complexity and flexibility of these strategies from the prosimians to the group-living apes (Tomasello and Call 1997).

The agonistic screams of macaques appear to elicit different responses from other group members in relation to opponents' characteristics, such as their dominance rank (Gouzoules, Gouzoules, and Marler 1984), and representational signaling in the context of recruitment of agonistic support is an ability that might have been strongly selected for in the social environment of group-living primates. Vocalizations that are emitted in order to coordinate the behavior of group members during travel or to facilitate affiliative and bonding interactions are an even more promising area of investigation because, unlike antipredator calls and recruitment screams, these signals are not obviously associated with states of high arousal. Contact vocalizations that facilitate coordination of group movements and close-range interactions are particularly well developed in arboreal species such as New World monkeys (Snowdon 1989; Boinski 1993). The complexity of vocal structure and vocal sequences in New World monkeys, however, is likely to be the result of the pressures of an arboreal life rather than those of social variables (Snowdon 1993b).

Although Old World monkeys and apes utter grunts and other calls in specific social circumstances, much of their communication at close range relies on visual and tactile signals. In the Cercopithecidae and in the great apes there is a clear increase in the role played by facial expressions (associated with the development of complex facial musculature) relative to body postures and vocalizations. Moreover, in the great apes there is an involvement of the arms and hands in making social gestures to a degree that is not observed in other nonhuman primates or other animals (Kortlandt 1962; Goodall 1968, 1986; Hewes 1973; McGrew and Tutin 1978; Plooij 1978, 1979; Nishida 1980; Berdecio and Nash 1981; Tomasello et al. 1985, 1994; de Waal 1988; Tomasello, Gust, and Frost 1989; Bard 1992; Maestripieri and Call 1996). Chimpanzee gestures are acquired through processes of individual and social learning, are produced intentionally, are often idiosyncratic, and are flexibly adjusted to various communicative circumstances including the attentional state of the recipient (Plooij 1978, 1979; Tomasello et al. 1985, 1994; Tomasello, Gust, and Frost 1989).

Thus, if any evolutionary trends are apparent in primate communication, they are (1) the preponderance of vocal signals in arboreal species versus the preponderance of gestural (visual and tactile) signals in terrestrial species, and (2) the increasing complexity of gestural signals from the prosimians to the great apes. It might be speculated that life in the open savannas after departure from the forests selected for the physical characteristics, especially bipedalism, found in Australopithecines and later species, as well as for a further enhancement of the use of gestural communication. Furthermore, bipedalism probably had a more profound influence in freeing the hands for communication than in altering the vocal repertoire (Hewes 1973; Corballis 1992). The patterns of gestural communication observed in extant species of primates, like the macaques of this study, suggest that gestures could have been used initially to communicate information about social actions and requests and commands for action on the part of others, and subsequently about aspects of the external environment such as food, predators, and tools. The emancipation of gestures from their instrumental function to that of symbols might have been accompanied by a gradual shift from the visual to the acoustic modality without requiring the appearance of new cognitive skills or a major reorganization of the structure of gestural communication (Armstrong, Stokoe, and Wilcox 1995; Wilcox, this volume).

Note

This work was supported by grants from the Biomedical Resources Foundation (Houston, Texas) and from NIH (MH56328) and in part by NIH grant RR-00165 to the Yerkes Regional Primate Research Center. The Yerkes Center is fully accredited by the American Association for Accreditation of Laboratory Animal Care. I thank Robin Dunbar, Mike Tomasello, Kim Wallen, and all the participants in the SAR seminar on the evolution of language for comments on the manuscript and helpful discussion.

4

An Empiricist View of Language Evolution and Development

Charles T. Snowdon

How should one approach the study of language and its origins—as a psychologist, a biologist, an anthropologist, or a linguist? Each discipline makes distinctive claims for the best approach. I am a biological psychologist, and my views are shaped by those two disciplines. The biologist in me thinks it natural to find broad continuities across diverse species while accepting that there are also species-specific adaptations. As a biologist I am more interested in studying the "natural languages" of nonhuman species than in imposing a human form of language on them. As a psychologist I hold a strong empiricist view with respect to both the importance of experience in the acquisition of behavior and the value of good empirical data for supporting theoretical views. I take on both aspects of the empiricist view in this chapter, presenting first some ideas and data in support of continuities between human and nonhuman species in languagelike phenomena and then discussing an empiricist view of language acquisition that counters some of the currently popular nativist views. Next I present some work from our laboratory at the University of Wisconsin on vocal development in nonhuman primates that I think suggests continuities in developmental processes between human and nonhuman primates. Finally I present a scenario based on the principles discussed here under which human language might have evolved.

DESIGN FEATURES OF LANGUAGE

Hockett (1963) described 16 design features of language that provide a model for evaluating the similarities between human language and the communication systems of nonhuman species. Although the model has been criticized for failing to specify the functional significance of language (Hauser 1996), Hockett's framework is one of only a few that attempt to define precisely what language is. Many of the design criteria are easily met by all species that use vocal communication. One of these is an auditory vocal channel, although note that an auditory channel is not necessary for language (see Wilcox, this volume, on signed language) or complex communication (see Savage-Rumbaugh et al. 1993 on the visual symbols used by bonobos). Others are broadcast transmission and directional reception, rapid fading, interchangeability (all users can produce sounds they comprehend), complete feedback (communicator perceives the signals he or she produces), specialization (the energetic costs of signals are trivial; only the triggering effects are important), semanticity (signals are associated with objects and events in the environment; signals have denotations), arbitrariness (signals are not iconic or onomatopoetic; the denotation is independent of any physical or geometric resemblance to the signal), discreteness (units can be individually differentiated and do not intergrade with each other—e.g., call notes, phonemes), and tradition (signals can be transmitted to others by teaching or learning).

It is easy to find examples of birds or mammals in which all of these features can be observed. For example, the oft-cited alarm calls of vervet monkeys (*Cercopithecus aethiops*) (Cheney and Seyfarth 1990) are auditory with broadcast transmission, rapid fading, interchangeability, complete feedback, specialization, semanticity, arbitrariness, and discreteness. At present it is an open question whether the production of calls is transmitted through learning, but vervets' appropriate usage and response to calls does fit the definition of tradition (Seyfarth and Cheney 1997).

The remaining criteria are more problematical, but evidence for them can be found in nonhuman species. Displacement involves referring to things remote in space or time. The waggle dance of honeybees (*Apis mellifera*) provides one of the best nonhuman examples of displacement. It has been difficult to find many more good examples of displacement in nonhuman animals, but Hockett notes that many language utterances do not show displacement.

Openness refers to the ability to coin new utterances both by blending or transforming utterances through grammatical patterning and by assigning new semantic values to new or old elements. Simple syntaxes (the orderly or predictable sequencing of single elements into a longer utterance) have been reported for a variety of nonhuman primate species—by Cleveland and Snowdon (1982) for cotton-top tamarins (*Saguinus oedipus*), by Pola and Snowdon (1975) for pygmy marmosets (*Cebuella pygmaea*), by Robinson (1984) for capuchin monkeys (*Cebus olivaceus*), and by Hauser and Fowler (1991) for rhesus macaques (*Macaca mulatta*). None of these examples, however, appears to be more than a phrase-structure grammar lacking the capacity to generate an infinite number of combinations. The best example of generative grammar in a nonhuman species comes from a most unlikely source, the black-capped chickadee (*Parus atricapillus*). Hailman, Ficken, and Ficken (1985) report that the chickadee call is composed of four notes that occur in either of two sequences—(A) (D) or (B) (C) (D)—where the note in parentheses can be repeated any number of times, thus creating a generative grammar. Although the structural description of the chickadee grammar is elegant, there are no data suggesting that each separate structure has a distinct meaning. This is perhaps an unfair complaint, however, since Chomsky's famous example "Colorless green ideas sleep furiously" illustrates the working of grammar in the absence of functional meaning.

Hockett's next design feature, prevarication (conscious lying or deceit), has until recently been difficult to document in nonhuman animals, but recent data summarized by Whiten and Byrne (1988) show that great apes are capable of deliberate deception. (It seems to me a bit shaky to construct a definition of language on a foundation that includes prevarication, but perhaps this is no different from the dye mark or rouge test for self-awareness and self-consciousness in apes [Gallup 1970, 1982], which requires vanity as the evolutionary precursor of self-awareness.)

Learnability refers to the ability of speakers of one language to learn other languages. In songbirds with dialects, there is abundant evidence that a bird can learn the dialect of another population or even learn to sing the song of a different species with which it has social contact (Baptista and Gaunt 1997). The mothers of cross-fostered rhesus macaques or Japanese macaques (*Macaca fuscata*) can learn to respond to the calls of their foster offspring (Seyfarth and Cheney 1997). Vervet monkeys can learn to respond to the alarm calls of superb starlings (*Sprea superbus*) (Hauser 1988), and ring-tailed lemurs (*Lemur catta*) can respond appropriately to the aerial and terrestrial alarm calls given by Verraux's sifakas (*Propithecus v. verrauxi*) (Oba and Masataka 1996). Domestic animals respond to human commands as well. This evidence of cross-species learning goes well beyond within-species learnability.

Reflexiveness is the ability to communicate about communicating. I find it difficult to imagine how one might discover whether nonhuman animals are communicating about their communication system. There are some examples of metacommunication, however, that suggest signals can be used to comment about relationships. Smith, Newman, and Symmes (1982) found that "chuck" calls were exchanged between female squirrel monkeys (*Saimiri sciureus*) that had strong social affiliations with each other. The authors hypothesized that the chuck calls were "comments" on the social relationship. The play signals used by a variety of species communicate about the lack of seriousness in subsequent interactions. The sharing of song motifs by birds that are close socially (see, e.g., Hausberger et al. 1995) may be another form of communication about relationships. Although these examples clearly are not communications about communicating, they seem to represent a higher level of abstraction than communicating about emotional state or making reference to predators or food.

Hockett's remaining criterion is duality of patterning, or the ability to combine morphemes into more complex units such as phonemes, phonemes into words, and words into sentences in order to have different meanings (such as "god" and "dog," or "boy", "bit", and "dog" to form "The boy bit the dog" and "the dog bit the boy"). Weiner (1984) argued that combination of individual elements or calls into sequences that retained the meaning of the individual elements was observed in cotton-top tamarins (Cleveland and Snowdon 1982) and cebus monkeys (Robinson 1984), which thus represent examples of duality of patterning in nonhuman primates. The monkey calls that Weiner cited, however, always occur in a fixed sequence (e.g., A B C), and thus we do not know whether the elements ordered A B C would be semantically different from the sequence C B A or whether the monkeys would interpret both orders equivalently. Those working with enculturated dolphins and great apes have found that their subjects can respond appropriately to reversed word order such as "take the ball to the chair" and "take the chair to the ball" and to sequences they have never been exposed to or explicitly trained with (see Savage-Rumbaugh et al. 1993). Matsuzawa's (1996) chimpanzee Ai is able to select the features that make up the lexigrams she uses for communication, using the same component with different other components to create labels for different objects. Thus, nonhuman animals display some capacity for duality of patterning, even if it only rarely comes "naturally." However weak these examples may be, Armstrong, Stokoe, and Wilcox (1995) have argued that duality of patterning is not part of signed languages and thus is not a good trait to be considered a design feature for language.

I know of no single nonhuman species that incorporates all of Hockett's criteria in its communication system, but it should be evident that each of the criteria can be found either realized or as a potential capacity in some nonhuman species. If one accepts Hockett's design features as sufficient criteria for language, then clear continuities exist between humans and nonhuman animals (see King, chapter 2, this volume).

PRODUCTION AND PERCEPTION

Humans are thought to be unique with respect to speech in both production and perception. Lieberman (1975) has shown that chimpanzees (*Pan troglodytes*), Neandertals, and infants differ from modern adult humans anatomically in that only modern adults have the anatomical structures necessary for the full range of human speech. The placement of the larynx relatively low in the throat in humans creates a two-tube supralaryngeal resonator that is important in producing the point vowels [I], [a], and [u]. The higher placement of the larynx in chimpanzees would preclude them from producing these particular vowels but should not prevent them from producing many other vowel sounds. Lieberman (1975) argues that chimpanzees should be capable of voicing stop consonants with dental, bilabial, and glottal stops, nasals, fricatives, and many other sounds. It might be difficult for chimpanzees to produce [g] and [k].

Although Lieberman views chimpanzees' deficiencies in terms of production as severe, an alternative view is that there are remarkable similarities in the vocal production abilities of chimpanzees and human beings. Considering that some languages have very few phonemes (11 each—3 vowels and 8 consonants—in the Rotokas and Mura languages [Maddieson 1984; cf. Kluender 1994]), it should be possible for chimpanzees to create a spoken language that would be recognizable to humans. The surprise is that chimpanzees do not speak, given their strong anatomical parallels to humans. The failure of chimpanzees to speak must be explained in terms of the motor control system or the motivational system and not just in terms of articulatory structures (see also Gibson and Jessee, this volume). It is possible that an elaborate gestural-visual communication system suffices for chimpanzees (Armstrong, Stokoe, and Wilcox 1995).

A second point of uniqueness claimed for humans is the ability to perceive speech sounds as speech. It has been difficult to find acoustic invariants in the structure of phonemes that would provide unequivocal cues for phoneme classification, because of the extensive coarticulation between a consonant and its preceding or following vowel. For example, as the consonant-vowel cluster /dv/ is varied from /dI/ through /da/ to /du/, there is no common acoustical feature to indicate the initial consonant [d] unambiguously. It was thought that one had to be a speaker of a language in order to be able to extract its invariant features (Liberman et al. 1967). A special type of perception, "categorical perception," was invoked. In experiments, synthetic speech sounds were varied across a continuum of voice onset times or second format onset frequencies, and human subjects labeled these sounds into a limited number of categories. They failed to discriminate tokens of sounds from within categories, but sounds varying by the same degree physically that were parts of separate categories were readily discriminated (Liberman et al. 1967). Thus, two different sounds varying in voice onset time that were from the same phonetic category, /ba/, could not be discriminated, whereas two other sounds with the same difference in voice onset time but representing a /ba/ and a /pa/ could be discriminated readily.

A series of studies over the past 25 years, however, has undermined the view that categorical perception is unique to humans because they can produce speech sounds. First, it was found that infants could discriminate speech sounds categorically even before they could produce the sounds (Eimas et al. 1971). Then several studies showed that some nonhuman species could display categorical perception (chinchillas, Kuhl and Miller 1975; rhesus macaques, Morse and Snowdon 1975; Waters and Wilson 1976). Thus, the ability to perceive sounds was not a function of the ability to produce those sounds. Kluender, Diehl, and Killeen (1987) trained Japanese quail (*Coturnix japonica*) to learn a concept of [d] by training them with the vowels [dI], [da], and [du] and showing generalization to [d] with eight novel vowels. Kluender (1994) also trained quail to make complex discriminations involving the gender of the human speaker, voiced versus unvoiced stops, and front versus high vowels. Birds trained on syllables representing two of the three features learned to discriminate these from syllables representing only one feature. They readily generalized to novel tokens and responded well to prototypes contrasting all three features. All of these studies together suggest that the ability to discriminate human speech is evolutionarily very conservative. Because it is unlikely that species such as quail, chinchillas, and rhesus macaques have ever been under significant selection pressure to discriminate human speech, the more likely explanation is that humans have exploited long-standing, highly conservative perceptual capacities in constructing a spoken language (Kluender 1994).

Several studies have also demonstrated that nonhuman species can categorically perceive their own sounds. Ehret (1987) showed that house mice (*Mus musculus*) categorically discriminated ultrasounds from their pups. Masataka (1983) demonstrated categorical labeling of alarm calls in Goeldi's monkey (*Callimico goeldi*), and Nelson and Marler (1989) demonstrated categorical discrimination of note duration in the swamp sparrow (*Melospiza georgiana*).

Green (1975), using careful acoustic analysis, found that Japanese macaques had seven different variants of coo vocalizations that were used in different contexts. Subsequent studies by Zoloth and colleagues (1979) showed that two variants of these coos were discriminated more readily by Japanese macaques than by other species, and May, Moody, and Stebbins (1989) demonstrated categorical perception of the coo types. Cleveland and Snowdon (1982) documented eight variants of chirp vocalizations used by cotton-top tamarins in different contexts, and Bauers and Snowdon (1990) showed that tamarins could readily discriminate between the two most similar of the chirp variants. These studies show that nonhuman primates have subtle variations in calls that might not be readily discriminable to human ears, that these variants are associated with different contexts, and that the primates segment the calls into discrete categories, providing evidence of a discrete communication system (see also Owren, Seyfarth, and Hopp 1992).

Snowdon and Pola (1978) reported that pygmy marmosets (*Cebuella pygmaea*) categorically labeled their synthetic trill vocalizations on the basis of call duration. Later we reported that these monkeys showed within-category discrimination if they were presented with synthesized calls that represented familiar individuals (Snowdon 1987). That is, monkeys would respond most to a short-duration call if it was synthesized to represent a familiar individual that typically produced short-duration calls; they responded more to long-duration calls that were synthesized to represent individuals with typically long-duration calls. Thus, whether one finds categorical labeling or within-category discrimination depends on the demands of the experiment. Studies with human subjects and speech sounds have also reported good within-category discrimination when the demand characteristics of the experiment favored it, either by reducing memory demands on the subjects or by presenting adjacent stimuli in sequence rather than at random (Pisoni and Lazarus 1974; Pisoni 1977).

Upon reflection, the idea of categorical perception appears to be odd. Essentially, listeners are ignoring much of the acoustic information in a signal (e.g., intonation contours and information on age, sex, and individual) when they perceive categorically. Why should listeners ignore this additional information? From a naturalistic perspective there is, I think, a clear answer. Listeners must attend to the linguistic content of a signal, but since communication is a social transaction, other, nonlinguistic information of potential importance is also encoded in a signal: gender, individual identity, geographical origin, emotional state (see also Armstrong, Stokoe, and Wilcox 1995). Whether or not this nonlinguistic information is useful depends upon the context of communication. If I am in a dark theater and someone yells "fire," it is probably best to focus my attention on the linguistic aspects of the signal. But if in the same theater I hear the phrase "Kiss me! I love you," it is probably insufficient to respond to the linguistic input alone. It is important that I identify the sex and individual identity of the speaker and the direction from which the sound is coming before I respond. Different social contexts demand that different degrees of information be processed from the input.

If we then apply these demand characteristics back to the original studies of categorical perception, it appears that synthesized speech stimuli containing only phonetic information would lead to clear categorization of phonemes. With more information about the individuality or gender of the speaker, as is encoded in natural speech, more fine-grained discrimination is possible if the experimental task requires it (Snowdon 1987). A parallel in color discrimination would be whether an experiment required the response "red" as sufficient or whether a distinction between cerise and burgundy was required. The point is that we do not need to invoke "special" perceptual modes for human speech; there is nothing "special" about speech perception. It utilizes phylogenetically old perceptual contrasts, and the form of perception is similar to that found in other modalities.

AN EMPIRICIST VIEW OF LANGUAGE ACQUISITION

Language development is an important area that has been relatively neglected in arguments concerning the evolution of language. As

Davidson (this volume) notes, language emerges from developmental processes, and an understanding of the development of language and of communication in nonhuman animals will provide important data for understanding the evolutionary origins of language.

Are There Universals in Language Development?

Many linguists and psychologists speak of language as an "instinct" or as a phenomenon that has a strong biological basis (e.g., Lenneberg 1967; Pinker 1994). Although there clearly is a necessary biological basis to language, the relative importance of biological versus environmental factors is an empirical question. Environmental influences on language learning may be more important than several recent popular books would allow (e.g., Bickerton 1990; Pinker 1994). In favor of this argument there is, first, the tremendous diversity evident in human languages, which suggests that a universal biological explanation is inadequate. Kluender (1994) summarizes results from the UCLA Phonological Segment Inventory Data Base showing that human languages use a total of 558 consonants, 260 vowels, and 51 diphthongs. Obviously, no one language uses all of these phones (!Xu uses a mere 141), but the fact that there are 869 phones in use in modern spoken languages suggests the necessity of great flexibility in the learning of speech.

Second, there is an apparent absence of language universals, contrary to what might be expected if language were entirely instinctive. There are, however, some near universals. All languages use stop consonants, and most use three places of articulation: bilabial, alveolar, and velar. All use voicing as a contrast, and regardless of the number of vowels in a language, most languages seem to space vowels to provide the maximum discriminability among vowels. Jakobson and Halle (1956) have described the similarities of phonetic ontogeny across languages.

On the other hand, Bates and Marchman (1988) have argued against *grammatical* universals in the development of language. Although they do not deny that children are predisposed to communicate with others and to learn language (perhaps just as birds are predisposed to learn song), they find little evidence of a universal sequence of grammatical development that follows a fixed time scale. They present four types of cross-language evidence to argue against universals of grammatical development (Bates and Marchman 1988). First, children do not move from single words to ordered, uninflected word combinations and then to word combinations with grammatical inflection. Children who are learning an inflected language (in which word endings rather than word order indicate grammatical units) such as Turkish acquire inflections as early as 14 months and master case morphology by 24 months. English-speaking children, for whom word order is an important part of grammar, learn word order sooner than inflections. Thus, the acquisition of word order and inflection appears to be related to the structure of the language to be learned.

Second, children do not always omit verbs from their first multi-word utterances. Verbs are said to be morphologically more complex than nouns and to express more complex semantic relationships. But Italian children learn verbs sooner than do English-speaking children, despite the fact that verb forms are more complex in Italian (six forms for each tense rather than the one or two in English). In Italian, word order can be flexible and subjects are frequently omitted. Therefore, to understand Italian, it may be more important to understand verbs than nouns.

Third, semantic cues leading to agent-object relations are not always acquired before word-order cues. English-speaking children focus on word-order cues first, whereas semantic cues are the first to be noticed by Italian children. Word order is important in English, and semantics are more important than word order in Italian. Young children follow the demands of their own language.

Fourth, word-order cues for agent-object relations are not always acquired before grammatical morphology. Again, Turkish children, as well as Hungarian and Polish children, learn case inflections well before they learn word order. In all of these examples the supposed universals are based on an Anglocentric view of language. Once children from other languages are examined, many apparent universals disappear. (There is even variation in the consequences of brain damage for language. Italian and German Broca aphasics—those with damage to the part of the cerebral cortex involved in speech production—retain more control over grammatical morphology in both production and comprehension than do English aphasics [Bates and Marchman 1988]).

Even among English speakers, Bates and Marchman (1988) argue, there is no universal pattern of language development. Children vary in terms of whether they first develop global features of phonology or local features and in whether they learn nouns first or develop noun phrases at the same time. The onset of production of words, phrases, and so forth is highly variable and seems not to be related to any major neurological markers of development.

There are, however, some general trends in childhood language development: rare and difficult-to-produce phones tend to appear later in development, and cognitively more complicated grammatical skills (negatives, passives, subjunctives) arise late. But the timing of these phonetic and grammatical aspects can be explained as much by difficulty in learning, by relative lack of models, or by relative lack of practice—that is, according to empiricist principles—as by nativist or biological factors.

Another line of evidence favoring the importance of environmental factors in language development is that infants are highly successful in identifying statistical regularities in speech input and might use these statistical properties rather than requiring innate brain structures to learn language. Saffran, Aslin, and Newport (1996) demonstrated that eight-month-old infants presented with a two-minute string of nonsense syllables could learn to recognize which triads of nonsense syllables had high transitional probabilities between them (that is, the infants recognized triads of nonsense syllables that co-occurred 50% or 70% of the time as patterned "words," in contrast with syllable triads that rarely occurred together in the speech string). If infants can learn to recognize "words" by extracting statistical transitional probabilities from two-minute sequences of nonsense syllables, how much more might they be learning through normal exposure to speech accompanied by social reinforcement?

The nature and degree of parental input also appear to be factors in the progress of language development. De Boysson-Bardies and colleagues (1992) found that the babbling of 10-month-old children could be readily identified according to the language of their parents.

Huttenlocher and colleagues (1991) showed that the amount of input a child received had an influence on the rate of language development. Locke and Snow (1997) argued that the intensity of interaction with a parent may govern the rate of acquisition. They summarized studies claiming that children who were abused actually scored somewhat above normal age levels in language production, whereas neglected children were several months behind their age norms. A recent study of one set of twins in France by Jouanjean-l'Antoene (1997) found consistent differences between twins reared together. One twin had a preferred attachment to her father, the other to her mother. Each twin showed a high degree of reciprocal imitations with the preferred parent. The father was in contact with both twins much less than was the mother, but he nonetheless influenced the vocal development of the daughter who preferred him. The production of words rather than nonverbal vocalizations appeared sooner in the twin who interacted with the mother. There were also differences in interactional style, with the more "distant" child acquiring language mastery sooner than the more "social" child. The striking differences in the rate of language development in twins reared under identical conditions and their differences in emotional style and choice of preferred parent suggest that social influences are important in vocal development.

Social environments can influence language performance at all ages. Poplack (1987a, 1987b) studied bilingual communities in the Ottawa-Hull region on the Ontario-Quebec border and reported that the number of English intrusions into the French speech of native French speakers was directly related to the social environment of the speakers. Those living in a predominantly English-speaking community showed many more English intrusions when they spoke French than did those living in a predominantly French-speaking community. Goodwin (1990, 1997) showed how children alter language styles such that distinct male- and female-typical patterns are evident but each child is able to communicate in either mode. In these studies, the local social environment played an important role in, respectively, the degree of bilingualism shown and the ability of children to adopt male-like or femalelike modes of communicating.

There are some important counterexamples to these studies.

Goldin-Meadow (1997) and her colleagues have been studying deaf children born to speaking parents who have not allowed their children to be trained in sign language. The deaf children do develop spontaneous gestures that have a clear morphology and a clear syntax, and they develop more complex gestures than their parents use toward them. A comparison of deaf children in the United States, where mothers provide relatively little input, and in China, where mothers provide a high degree of input, showed no clear cross-cultural differences in the structural complexity of signing by the infants. There is even a community of deaf people in Nicaragua (Kegl, Senghas, and Coppola 1996) that has created its own unique sign language in the absence of any other input (a finding similar to that for Zebra finches, *Taeniopygia guttata*, where young birds housed together develop a species-appropriate song [Volman and Khanna 1995]). Goldin-Meadow argues that these data imply that language is highly resilient to disruptions of input. The notion of resilience in the face of disrupted input is compatible, I think, with the idea that the nature, quality, and quantity of early language experience have an important influence on vocal development. The deaf children are strongly motivated to communicate with others, and they appear to learn quickly how to develop effective gestural signals.

Critical Periods

It is often argued that there are critical or sensitive periods for vocal development, with puberty representing the cut-off for language learning. Sources of data are children who had brain damage at different ages and children who were deprived of language contact until close to puberty (Lenneberg 1967; Lane 1976; Rymer 1992a, 1992b; Candland 1993). These examples are not ideal because the isolated or brain-damaged child may have suffered retardation or autism that prevented subsequent language learning, or the mere fact of social isolation may have prevented the acquisition of social skills that are necessary prerequisites for language learning (Lane 1976; Rymer 1992a, 1992b; Candland 1993).

An alternative methodology has been to look at bilingualism. A brilliantly designed study by Johnson and Newport (1989) looked at

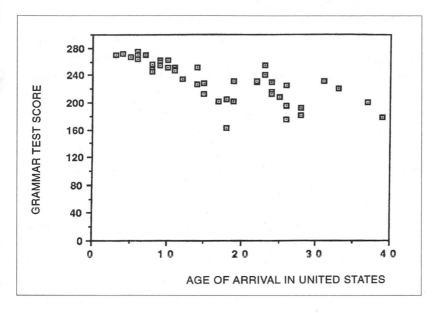

FIGURE 4.1

Performance on a test of English grammar by native speakers of Chinese and Korean as a function of when they were first extensively exposed to English (plotted from data in Johnson and Newport 1989).

native Chinese and Korean speakers who had moved to the United States at various ages. At the time of testing all had been speaking English for at least five years and had been resident in the United States for at least three years. The subjects were given a test of English grammar, and the distribution of scores provided support for a critical-period hypothesis. Those who started learning English before age eight had scores equal to native English speakers. There was a progressive decrease in performance with increasing age of first exposure to English. The worst performance, however, was still at the 75-percent level, far different from the completely disrupted performance of song-birds deprived of input during their sensitive period. There was also a great deal of individual variation, and some individuals with late exposure to English performed quite well (fig. 4.1). Johnson and Newport (1989) concluded that their study supported the idea of critical periods in first language learning and extended the results to second language learning.

93

In contrast to these results are findings by Sorensen (1967) for a population in the northwest Amazon where, owing to highly localized languages and a high degree of exogamy, each individual knows two, four, or more languages. Minimally, a child starts off learning its mother's and father's separate languages, but because of the presence of people from several language groups in a village, the child may learn many more. A young adult seeking a mate may be lucky enough to find a partner who speaks a maternal or paternal language, but often new mates must learn each other's languages. The languages in the area come from more than four language families, and thus many of them are quite distinct from one another. Learning one or two languages does not automatically ensure fluency in other languages. Sorensen (1967) did not measure grammatical skill, as Johnson and Newport (1989) did, nor did he measure oral fluency, so we cannot evaluate the competency of his informants in each of the languages they use.

There are alternative explanations for the critical-period effects. Marchman (1993) has used neural-network methods to simulate learning the past tense for English verbs, a system used by Pinker (1991) in support of modularity of language subsystems and critical-period effects. The neural network simulations showed rapid acquisition of the rules for forming the past tense. Then Marchman selectively "damaged" varying proportions of hidden layer units of the neural network models at different stages of acquisition. She found that these damaged neural networks could acquire the rules for past tense if sufficient learning time was allowed after the "lesion." Marchman concluded that what appear to be critical-period effects in the language of children who are brain damaged could be explained more parsimoniously in terms of time available for learning after the damage. Thus, critical-period effects need not derive from endogenously determined maturational change but might result from learning history. The study also compared learning of regular and irregular forms of the past tense and found more severe deficits with damage to the neural network in acquiring regular forms of past tense due to interference with the irregular past tense forms. This suggests that selective dissociations can result from general damage in systems that are not modularized. Thus, one need not invoke separate innate modules for regular and irregular forms of verbs (Pinker 1991).

Returning to Johnson and Newport's native Chinese and Korean subjects, I might offer a more personal argument to explain the English-language deficits they displayed. I first learned German in college, Spanish when I was in my thirties, and Portuguese in my mid-forties. I am fluent enough to be understood when I lecture and to find my way around a country in each of these languages, but I am far from perfect. German, which I studied daily for two years at the youngest age, is the most fluent, especially in social conversation. But I learned German as a college student with a relatively large amount of time available and through specific instruction and correction. I had to learn Spanish and Portuguese for research-related purposes in the midst of a busy professional life. I was probably less tolerant of critical feedback then than I was as a college student, and others were probably less inclined to give me feedback at my more advanced age. My lack of fluency in Spanish and Portuguese compared with German could be due to my very different modes of learning these languages. For Spanish and Portuguese I had less practice, less consistent feedback, and less time to do rote drills. Even as a college student learning German, I was cognitively "time-sharing" much more than I would have been as an eight-year-old learning a language. Thus, what appears to be a critical-period effect might be explained as an artifact of different cognitive styles applied to language learning at different ages and of different demands placed on learners under different circumstances. We learn enough of a new language to "get by" but not enough to be completely fluent. Results from studies of language-deprived or brain-damaged children and of the age of learning second languages cited in support of an innate modular determination of language might be accounted for instead by basic differences in the amount and quality of learning experienced and by social motivation and social environment.

VOCAL DEVELOPMENT IN NONHUMAN PRIMATES

Studies of nonhuman primates are fascinating because of the high level of social and cognitive complexity that primates display in foraging, interacting with social companions, rearing infants, and defending against predators. In contrast to many other nonhuman species, in which instinctive or genetically determined processes appear to control behavior, monkeys and apes appear to be highly flexible in behavioral responses, sensitive to subtle changes in their social and physical environment, and able to develop novel solutions to problems. In short, they seem almost human, with apes showing much greater cognitive competence than monkeys (Byrne 1995).

The most glaring exception to the idea of nonhuman primates as highly intelligent and flexible animals has been in the development of their communication skills. There has been little evidence of a role for learning in primate communication, and this contrasts sharply with data from songbirds. We have extensive evidence from studies of bird song that young birds must be exposed to the song of adult tutors during a critical period of development, and subsequent practice prior to a male bird's first breeding season is necessary for a male bird to develop normal song. After this practice period (of subsong and plastic song), song becomes "crystallized," and further modification in song is unlikely (Marler 1970; Marler and Peters 1982). A similar argument has been made that children must be exposed to the sounds of language early in life, and infants must "babble" to practice the phonemes and words of their language (Locke 1993).

In nonhuman primates, several species produce calls that are the functional equivalent of bird songs. Because most research on the development of bird song has been done in the northern temperate zone, where song is produced mainly by males under the control of testosterone, one important parallel has been the "loud calls" of Cercopithecine primates, which are given only by males. These calls have been assumed to be genetically fixed (Gautier and Gautier-Hion 1977). There are also many examples of primate species in which duetting is common (titi monkeys [Callicebus], Robinson 1979; gibbons, Brockelmann and Schilling 1984; Tenaza 1985) or in which both sexes equally produce long calls (Callitrichids, Snowdon 1993c). In gibbons there is strong evidence from studies of hybrids that song is under genetic control, and I have suggested (Snowdon 1993c) that the conservative structure of Callitrichid long calls can be used in taxonomy.

Other studies that involved the deafening of infant monkeys, especially squirrel monkeys (Saimiri sciureus), or rearing them in acoustic isolation (Talmage-Riggs et al. 1972; Lieblich et al. 1980; Herzog and Hopf 1984) have suggested that vocal structures are innately determined in monkeys. Newman and Symmes (1982) showed that offspring of hybrid squirrel monkeys acquired the isolation peep structure of their mothers. Studies of isolation-reared rhesus monkeys documented some minor differences in vocal structure compared with normal controls, but the deficits were considerably less profound than those found in songbirds reared in isolation or deafened.

Thus, this evidence from monkeys suggested that with respect to vocal development, monkeys were profoundly different from songbirds and humans. This work, however, focused exclusively on vocal production, whereas a communication system really involves three distinct components: production of signals with appropriate structure, use of these signals in appropriate circumstances, and response to the signals of others (comprehension). Recently, Seyfarth and Cheney (1997) have argued that the production of vocal signals is quite conservative across primates (human and nonhuman alike), with the possibility of modification within constraints. They find greater flexibility in the ontogeny of usage of vocal signals and a high degree of flexibility in how monkeys respond to vocal signals. In short, they suggest that strong parallels in vocal development do exist between human and nonhuman primates.

There are several possible reasons for the failure to find evidence of plasticity in primate vocal development. First, many of the calls that have been studied most intensively are used in contexts where flexibility would be maladaptive. The long calls or loud calls used in territory defense or to maintain a group against intruders are highly species-specific and thus should be conservative (Snowdon 1993c). Other calls that have been studied are those given by infants when separated from their caretakers (Newman 1995), another call type that should not be plastic or flexible. Still other studies have looked at alarm calls. In life-or-death situations involving separated infants or predators, highly stereotyped calls would be much more useful than highly variable calls.

In birds there is increasing evidence that the structure of songs and other vocalizations can be influenced by interaction with social companions. Thus, European starlings (*Sturnus vulgaris*) share the song structure of close social companions, and when social companions change, the birds change the songs they produce to match those of their new companions (Hausberger et al. 1995). In budgerigars (*Melopsittacus undulatus*), birds in the same social groups share calls with one another (Farabaugh, Linzenbold, and Dooling 1994). Black-capped chickadees (*Parus atricapillus*) live in territories part of the year but form social flocks to survive winters in the Northern Hemisphere. These birds showed convergence in the structure of their call notes within a week after flocks are formed in late autumn (Nowicki 1989). The American goldfinch (*Spinus tristis*) has a variety of call notes that are used, and when a male and female mate, each gives up some of its own vocalizations and acquires some of the calls of the new mate (Mundinger 1970). Each of these species lives in year-round social associations with other animals, in contrast to the territorial and seasonal associations found in the birds that have been studied most extensively.

Because monkeys, too, live in year-round social groups, the most likely place to find evidence of vocal plasticity is in vocalizations used to communicate about social relationships, especially when there is a change of some sort in those relationships. Thus, rather than look at predator alarm calls or infant separation calls, it may be more profitable to study calls that are used to maintain affiliative relationships among social companions. As noted by Armstrong, Stokoe, and Wilcox (1995), language evolved to serve social functions and develops within a social context, so studies on affiliative social communication in non-human primates might be the most productive place to find parallels to language.

AFFILIATIVE VOCALIZATIONS IN MARMOSETS AND TAMARINS

With my colleagues A. Margaret Elowson, Rebecca S. Roush, and Cristina Lazaro-Perea, I have been studying three phenomena in pygmy marmosets (*Cebuella pygmaea*) and cotton-top tamarins (*Saguinus oedipus*) that we think provide promising evidence of vocal plasticity in monkeys and illustrate the importance of affiliative social interactions in the study of vocal development, as well as demonstrating potential parallels to human language learning.

Trill Vocalizations of Pygmy Marmosets

We have extensively studied the trill vocalizations of pygmy marmosets. These are high-pitched, frequency-modulated calls that are used within groups of captive and wild marmosets to communicate with each other throughout the day (Pola and Snowdon 1975). We have documented that there are individual-specific features to these calls that allow other group members to recognize familiar individuals. Monkeys take turns in calling, so that frequently each group member gets a chance to call before any other calls a second time. There is also a regular order of turn-taking (Snowdon and Cleveland 1984). In the field, pygmy marmosets shift the acoustic structure of the calls to increase the number of cues used for sound localization as individuals get farther away from other group members (Snowdon and Hodun 1981). Thus, the calls are not simply reflexive or automatic; the monkeys can use them in appropriate sequences and can alter the structure of calls to make them more cryptic or more easily localized. The calls are individually distinct, and by using them continuously throughout the day, pygmy marmosets have a social "map" of their group, always knowing who is in earshot and where in the habitat each individual is located.

We completed a longitudinal study of the ontogeny of these trill vocalizations from birth through the second year of life, using as our subjects nine infant monkeys from five litters living in groups housed under seminatural captive conditions (Elowson, Sweet, and Snowdon 1992). We used the results to evaluate each of four models of vocal development in animals (Snowdon and Elowson 1992). First, acoustic structure can be fixed at birth and subjected to only minimal subsequent modification. Second, vocal development may be an artifact of physical maturation. As an organism gets larger, its vocal chords increase in length and the pitch of the voice decreases. With physical maturation comes the ability to control breathing better and so to produce longer utterances, and there may be improved fine motor control. The third mechanism is that vocal learning may occur within a limited time period during development, and after sufficient practice the vocalizations become fixed and stereotyped with no subsequent modification. This is the model that is most often applied to bird song and human language learning. Finally, vocal learning may be completely flexible throughout an animal's life, with totally new vocalizations learnable at any age. A few extraordinary birds, such as parrots, appear to show this high degree of vocal flexibility (Pepperberg 1997).

Our results showed that call structure changed with age, so there was no support for a model of genetically determined calls. Although some of the monkeys showed the lower pitch and increased duration of calls that would be predicted by a maturation model, other monkeys actually showed an increased pitch and decreased duration of calls with increasing age. Thus, vocal changes could not be related to simple physical maturation. We examined the variability of call structure over development and found that throughout the first two years of life, there was little evidence that monkeys were developing increased stereotypy in vocal structure, as the model of bird-song learning requires. There did not appear to be evidence of a critical period after which vocalizations were highly stereotyped. The possibility remained that our pygmy marmosets, like goldfinches, starlings, chickadees, and many other birds, had the ability to alter their vocal structure throughout their lives.

On the basis of work done on birds, we hypothesized that we would find evidence of vocal plasticity in monkeys related to changes in their social environment. We have completed two studies that provide evidence of plasticity. In the first study, we were offered a colony of pygmy marmosets from the U.S. National Institutes of Health. These groups of monkeys were completely unrelated to our colony, and there had been no previous exchange of animals between colonies. During the quarantine period, we made recordings of trill vocalizations from our own colony of monkeys and from the new groups. During quarantine the new monkeys were housed in social groups in the same type of cages as our own animals but in a different part of the building, where neither colony could hear the vocalizations of the other. Then we housed both colonies of monkeys in the same large room and made systematic recordings over the next 10 weeks. We found that the trill structure of all of the monkeys changed, regardless of the colony of origin. Monkeys increased the peak frequency of their trills and the bandwidth of their calls. There was no difference in the degree of plasticity shown as a function of age; young infants and breeding adults were equivalent in the flexibility of their vocal structure. These changes in structure were maintained for as long as we continued to record the monkeys (Elowson and Snowdon 1994).

In another study, we recorded trills for several weeks from four male and four female monkeys while they were living in their family groups. Then we formed four breeding pairs from these animals, with the male and female of each pair both unrelated to and unfamiliar with each other. We continued to record vocalizations for the first six weeks after pairing, and then we returned to record six of the eight animals three years after they were paired. We measured four acoustic parameters in the trill vocalizations of each individual. Prior to pairing, there was little change in the structure of trills over a two-month recording period. Three of the four newly mated pairs changed acoustic parameters of trill structure to produce trills that were more homogeneous between mates than were trills prior to pairing. Pairs that differed the most in trill structure prior to pairing showed the greatest amount of convergence. These changes were highly stable. When we examined two of the pairs three years after initial pairing we found no differences in the trill structure of pair mates. Thus, when pygmy marmosets acquired a new mate, they rapidly shifted the structure of their trills, and subsequently these altered trill structures remained quite stable.

I should note that marmoset and tamarin species are reproductively inhibited while living in a subordinate role in family groups, and reproductive physiology becomes activated with a change in social environment. We have recently found, however, that some female pygmy marmosets begin ovulating while in their natal group (Carlson, Ziegler, and Snowdon 1997) and that subadult males are hormonally identical to breeding adults, so the changes in vocal structure cannot be related to the onset of reproductive hormonal activity.

Other studies have reported similar results in nonprimate species. As noted earlier, Mundinger (1970) found that goldfinches, when paired, altered the distribution of their call notes so that each of the mates acquired some of the notes of the new mate. Hausberger and colleagues (1995) found that European starlings changed the song types they used when the social structure of groups was changed. Outside of the breeding season, starlings tended to affiliate with members of their own sex, and individuals exchanged the same song types with their preferred companions. Kangaroo rats (*Dipodomys spectabilis*) in the desert of the southwestern United States have a unique form of seismic communication in which they drum with their hind legs on the ground in an individual-specific pattern. Randall (1995) has found that kangaroo rats will modify their foot-drumming signatures to avoid overlap in rhythm with nearby neighbors. Boughman (1997, 1998) has found that greater spear-nosed bats (*Phyllostomus hastatus*) have group-distinctive calls. Because females within a group are unrelated, the group-distinctive calls must be learned by individuals joining the group. Tyack and Sayigh (1997) have described how dolphins (*Tursiops truncatus*) acquire signature whistles from each other when they have a close social relationship. Finally, in prosimians, Stanger (1993) found that dwarf mouse lemurs (*Cheirogaleus medius*) changed the pitch of their whistle calls when their social groups were changed and animals were housed with new companions.

A parallel set of studies of human beings shows how we modify our language when joining a new social group (Giles and Smith 1979). This has been called "optimal convergence," and it has been found in humans of all ages, from young children through adults. We speak in different ways to children than to other adults, and many social groups mark themselves by special words or phrases, a form of social "badge." (The jargon used by scientists in each subdiscipline is a good example of such a social badge.) When we join a new social group, we can indicate our interest in being part of it by altering how we speak, but although we modify our speech to indicate solidarity, we maintain our individual distinctiveness as well. Fowler (1995) reported the case of a native speaker of Portuguese from Brazil attending university in the United States whose pattern of production of the voiceless stops /t/ and /p/ shifted between Portuguese and English voice onset times as a function of how recently she had been in a Portuguese versus an English linguistic environment. Each of the examples of birds, kangaroo rats, dolphins, dwarf mouse lemurs, marmosets, and humans I have described represents a type of "optimal convergence" and suggests that this plasticity in vocalization has a long phylogenetic history.

Babbling in Pygmy Marmosets

As I noted earlier, babbling is thought to play an important role in helping human infants to develop language skills. The closest equivalent to babbling that has been reported in a nonhuman species has been the subsong and plastic song of birds. Marler and Peters (1982) reported that some songbirds, having been exposed to models of species-specific song early in life, will begin to produce a large number of highly imperfect versions of song near the start of the breeding season the following spring. Over a short period of time, the calls become increasingly more organized and approximate adult song more closely, until a stage of crystallized song appears just about the time that male birds must compete for territories and mates. Although this song practice phase has been often compared to babbling in human infants, there are some major differences. In songbirds in the northern temperate zone, it is generally males, not females, that sing, and the "babbling" period corresponds with puberty. Furthermore, song represents only one of a large number of vocalizations in a bird's repertoire.

In children, babbling begins early, is completed long before puberty is reached, is not specific to males alone, and includes a large number of phonemes that are used in speech (Locke 1993). My colleagues and I have been looking for a nonhuman primate model for this babbling. We noticed that infant pygmy marmosets were extremely vocal during the early weeks of life, when long sequences of calls lasting several minutes were common. We have completed a longitudinal study of babbling in eight infant pygmy marmosets through the first 20 weeks of life (Elowson, Lazaro-Perea, and Snowdon 1998a, 1998b). We found several parallels between babbling in human infants (as described by Locke 1993) and in pygmy marmosets.

First, babbling is universal in both species. Even deaf children show manual babbling (Petitto and Martentette 1991). Second, babbling begins early in life. Human infants start babbling by seven months of age, and we found that pygmy marmosets begin to babble as early as the first week of life, with all infants babbling by the fourth week. Third, babbling is rhythmical and repetitive. The same sound is repeated several times before a human infant switches to a different sound. We found this in pygmy marmosets as well. Fourth, babbling uses a subset of adult sounds. Typically, human infants use only about 50–70 percent of the phones in their parents' language, and we found that pygmy marmosets used 14 of the 24 call types we had documented in adults (Pola and Snowdon 1975).

Fifth, human infants produce sounds that are recognizable as phonemes from speech. Of the more than 21,000 calls we have analyzed from infant pygmy marmosets, 71 percent were adultlike and 19 percent were recognizable as variants of adult vocalizations. Only 10 percent of the calls were not obviously related to adult calls. Sixth, babbling has no obvious referent. That is, human infants produce sounds that have no clear relationship to objects or events in the environment. Pygmy marmoset babbling consists of a large number of different call types produced in close juxtaposition: an alarm call might be followed by a threat vocalization and then by an affiliative call. An average of 10 different call types was produced in each bout of pygmy marmoset babbling.

Finally, babbling is a social act for human infants. Caretakers often respond to infants when they babble, and this provides reinforcement for still more babbling. We have found that caregivers are highly responsive to pygmy marmoset infants when they are babbling, and we found significantly higher rates of approach to the infant, grooming or contact behavior, and carrying of infants when they were babbling compared with control periods when infants were not babbling. Thus, each of the seven major features of babbling in human infants has a parallel in the vocalizations of infant pygmy marmosets.

This babbling is not unique to captive pygmy marmosets but is also found in wild pygmy marmosets (S. de la Torre, personal communication) and is represented in the genus *Callithrix*, with similar findings reported by B. Stumpf and C. Lazaro-Perea (personal communication) for common marmosets (*Callithrix jacchus*) and by Omedes (1985) for the silvery marmoset (*Callithrix argentata*). Interestingly, we have found nothing similar to babbling in *Saguinus* species. We can now begin to examine the timing of caregivers' response to infants when they are babbling to see whether social reinforcement leads to changes in the structure of calls. We are also finding evidence that the structure of calls improves with age, suggesting some possibility that pygmy marmosets learn how to vocalize through the practice gained by babbling.

Ontogeny of Food-Associated Calls

Many primate species have calls that are specific to feeding situations. We have been studying food-associated calls in cotton-top tamarins. Adult cotton-top tamarins have two types of short, frequency-modulated calls (C-chirps and D-chirps; see Cleveland and Snowdon 1982), that are used primarily in feeding contexts. We recorded vocalizations after we presented adult tamarins with a variety of different foods as well as nonfood, manipulable objects such as pen caps and paper clips, and we also recorded when no food or manipulable objects were present. More than 97 percent of C- and D-chirps were given only when food was present. C-chirps were given primarily as animals approached the food dish and sorted through the food items, and D-chirps were given when animals picked up a food item and moved away from the dish to eat. We evaluated the individual food preference rankings of each of the monkeys and found a positive correlation between the preference ranking and the number of chirps the monkey gave to a particular item (Elowson, Tannenbaum, and Snowdon 1991). Thus, tamarins communicate honestly about their food preferences, suggesting that food-associated calls not only refer to a specific type of object in the environment (food) but also provide information about the monkey's arousal level.

A subsequent study by Roush (1996) separated monkeys from their mates and presented food to one monkey both with and without visual contact with the mate. In both cases the monkey discovering the food gave high rates of food-associated calls whether or not the mate could also see the food, and the mate responded with food-associated calls whether or not it could see the food. The response of the listener—giving food-associated calls when it could not see the food but could only hear the calls of its mate—indicates that the calls do convey representational information about the presence of food.

We also tested immature tamarins ranging in age from 4 months to 28 months. Puberty occurs at about 18 months of age, but female tamarins are reproductively suppressed while they live in their family groups (Ziegler, Snowdon, and Uno 1990). Roush and Snowdon (1994) presented immature tamarins with different types of food as well as nonfood, manipulable objects and recorded the vocalizations given in these contexts. We also tested immature tamarins for their food preferences. We found several differences in the results from those obtained with adults. Immature tamarins produced most of their food-associated calls in the presence of food, but they also overgeneralized and produced a significant number of chirps to manipulable objects as well. Compared with adults they produced a high proportion of calls that were variants of adult calls (C-like and D-like chirps) as well as a high proportion of calls that were not food associated. We were surprised to find no correlation between the age of the immature monkey and the probability of producing adult vocal structures. A monkey at 28 months was as likely as a monkey of 4 months to produce a variant of an adult call or a different type of call. This finding extended to the usage of calls and to food preferences. Immature monkeys, regardless of age, showed a high number of tied food-preference ranks and violations of transitivity in food preference tests, and they failed to show a correlation between food preferences and chirp rate. Roush and Snowdon (1994) hypothesized that social status was more important than age in governing the production and usage of these vocalizations and that it might be an advantage for tamarins to act like infants even after puberty to signal their subordinate status to adults.

The strongest test of this hypothesis is to study the same animals while they are subordinate members of a family group and then immediately after a change in social status when they are paired with a novel mate and become reproductively active. Roush and Snowdon (n.d.) studied 15 monkeys first in a subordinate status in the family group and then immediately after pairing. The immature monkeys in this study behaved the same way as immature monkeys in the previous study, but immediately after pairing there was a rapid decline in the number of non-food-associated calls given (fig. 4.2). The rate of decline within a pair was directly correlated with the degree of affiliative behavior displayed. The greater the affiliative behavior within a pair, the more rapid the transition to adult vocalizations. Changes toward adult forms of C- and D-chirps also occurred (fig. 4.2), but more slowly, and they were unrelated to the nature of the social interactions, suggesting a different form of developmental process. Thus, social environments have an important influence on vocal development

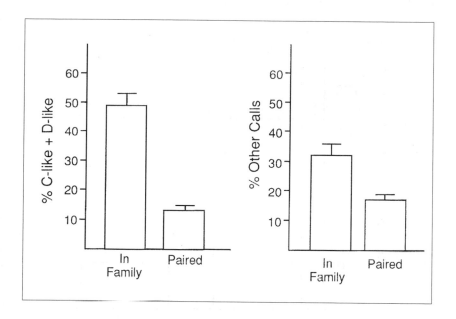

FIGURE 4.2.

Changes in the frequency of C-like and D-like chirps and other calls during feeding in cotton-top tamarins while living first in their natal family groups and then after being paired with a new mate. C-like and D-like chirps are calls that are recognizably like adult calls but are imperfectly formed. Other vocalizations are calls that are not typically observed in adults during feeding.

both to facilitate development and, in subordinate tamarins, to inhibit development.

One final study of food-associated calls looked at the food-sharing behavior that is common to tamarins at the time of weaning. Typically, adult males offer food to an infant, and the adults usually produce a long sequence of D-chirps as they offer the food. Roush (1996) found that infants had a high probability of receiving food if the adults were vocalizing but rarely received food if the adults did not vocalize (fig. 4.3). Furthermore, in about 15 percent of the observations, other group members oriented toward the adult with the food and emitted vocalizations as well, creating a situation in which infants could easily learn what was appropriate food and what were the appropriate vocal-

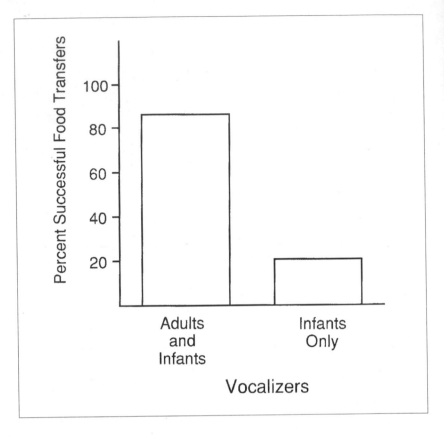

FIGURE 4.3

Successful food transfers from tamarin adults to infants as a function of whether infants alone vocalize or both adults and infants vocalize. Food transfers are generally successful only when adults provide models of food-associated calls.

izations to be given when feeding. There was a significant correlation between the age of the infant when adults began transferring food to it and the time at which infants began to eat independently on their own ($R_S = 0.99$, n = 10, $p < 0.004$). There was also a correlation between the age of first independent feeding and the rate of other vocalizations produced ($R_S = 0.69$, n = 10, $p < 0.02$). This vocalizing during food sharing

appears almost to be a form of "teaching" or social information donation (King 1994a) on the part of the adults that facilitates infants' early
feeding and appropriate use of food-associated calls.

MECHANISMS OF SOCIAL INFLUENCE

So far I have described several phenomena that illustrate how
social companions influence development and change in vocal structure and usage in marmosets and tamarins. But it is insufficient just to
demonstrate that the phenomena exist; we also need to begin examining potential mechanisms. There are three potential mechanisms by
which a social companion can influence vocal communication. First,
social interactions usually provide information in several modalities.
Most of us hate to make telephone calls when traveling in another
country where we are using a second language. It is much easier to
understand someone if we have simultaneous visual and vocal cues.
Thus, organisms might learn faster when presented with cues in multiple modalities. Engaging multiple sensory modalities may enhance language acquisition.

Second, social interactions provide a focus of attention. An organism is more likely to focus on the behavior of a social companion than
on an inanimate object, and so a social companion can direct the
learner's attention to the relationship between the sound and the
object. This is what the adult male tamarin does when vocalizing as he
offers a piece of food to an infant (see also McCune, this volume, and
Savage-Rumbaugh, this volume, on the role of joint attention in human
children and bonobos, respectively).

Finally, social companions provide reinforcement, either directly,
as in the case of the male tamarin sharing food with an infant, or indi-
rectly, by providing praise or social attention. The example of cotton-
top tamarins' sharing food while vocalizing illustrates all three
mechanisms operating at the same time. These hypothesized mechanisms mesh closely with the ideas of Locke and Snow (1997) on the role
of social interaction and positive affective behavior in human language
development. Future research should establish the importance of each
of these social mechanisms.

CHARLES T. SNOWDON

HOW DID WE GET HERE FROM THERE?

The major issue confronting any attempt to understand the evolution of human language is how we get from animal communication systems to the complex language that humans use in a way that is consistent with evolutionary principles. It seems to me that we must rule out creationist or semicreationist explanations that posit humans as fundamentally different from other species without specifying exactly how they are different and how they became different (Lenneberg 1967; Pinker 1994). I think we must also rule out a single gene mutation (Bickerton 1990) as sufficient to lead to language, because so many factors are involved in language: production, perception, comprehension, usage, and cognition.

There are several points that seem to lead to a coherent model for the evolution of language. First, as I have illustrated here, there is evidence for each of Hockett's design features of language in at least some nonhuman species. I have tried to provide evidence for developmental parallels between humans and other animals as well. Furthermore, work on chimpanzees and bonobos shows that both species use complex cognitive processes in their natural environments. Matsuzawa (1996) provides a hierarchical analysis of chimpanzee tool use that has many similarities to models of tool making by early hominids (Davidson, this volume), as well as to the diagrams used to illustrate syntactic relationships in language. At least some chimpanzees operate on a three-level hierarchical system in their tool making (equivalent to noun, verb, adjective + [another] noun in a grammar diagram), which Matsuzawa interprets as indicating a high degree of cognition. The finding of Savage-Rumbaugh and colleagues (1996) that bonobos deliberately create trail markers by bending or flattening vegetation and moving branches suggests the operation of symbolic communication. These trail markers must have a socially shared meaning if they are used successfully by bonobo parties to find the rest of their community.

Matsuzawa's field studies of tool-use acquisition and his and Savage-Rumbaugh's laboratory work demonstrate that basic learning principles can be used by apes to acquire complex cognitive and communicative ability. The work I have presented on food-sharing as an environment for learning communication skills in cotton-top tamarins and on the social reinforcement of babbling in pygmy marmosets, along with research on grunts as a precursor to language by McCune and colleagues (1996; McCune, this volume), provides good empiricist mechanisms for the ways in which communication signals are learned and shaped into adult modes of production, usage, and comprehension. Just as Hemelrijk (1996) has shown that complex processes such as reciprocal altruism and social organization can be explained parsimoniously as a side effect of self-reinforcing social interactions among animals—that is, they can be explained according to a bottom-up principle—so it seems to me that complex communication and language could have emerged in the same way.

Burling (1986) argues cogently that language evolution is likely to have been driven by social purposes. Those who could communicate most effectively about the location of food or shelter or about predators and how to avoid them would have had greater reproductive success, both by being viewed as better mates and therefore obtaining more matings and by leaving behind more offspring that would survive to reproductive maturity. It is probably not accidental that the best examples of complex communication in nonhuman species discussed here have been those related to communication about food, predators, and monitoring of the social group. The adaptive value of social life leads to communication skills that go beyond mere gossip in order to manage social relationships.

There are some apparent inconsistencies in the data available for evaluating this scenario. Mitani (1996) has argued that there is little evidence in great apes for humanlike developmental processes and for the complex vocal communication with referential signaling that is found in some other nonhuman primates (but see Savage-Rumbaugh, this volume). Both Maestripieri (this volume) and Wilcox (this volume) have argued for the importance of gestural and visual communication, and Savage-Rumbaugh and colleagues (1996) found that wild bonobos used visual symbols for trail marking. Vocalizations were rare. Visual symbols have the advantage of greater permanence than auditory signals, and studies of signing indicate a much more rapid rate of information transfer than is possible by vocal means (Wilcox, this volume). Therefore, we might expect greater efficiency and complexity of communication to have developed first in the gestural-visual modality. Yet one can pose good arguments counter to this expectation.

Because great apes and humans have highly overlapping binocular fields of vision, we lose the ability to detect visual or gestural signals that are more than 70–80 degrees to each side. We also have a small vertical range of vision. Although the auditory modality is limited because signals fade quickly and information channels are narrow-band in comparison with vision, auditory-vocal communication offers many advantages. We can communicate with companions who are out of sight. We need not relax visual attention toward a predator, a prey animal, or a valued social partner in order to perceive vocal signals and respond to them. We can free our limbs for locomotion and for carrying objects while still communicating. And we can extend our activities beyond daylight into the night. Thus, although terrestrial Old World primates and great apes may use gestural-visual communication to a much greater degree than auditory-vocal systems, those of our human ancestors who could exploit the evolutionarily conservative features of the auditory system to create a complex vocal language would have moved an important step beyond other primates. A rapid expansion of vocal communication might have led to more complex social and cognitive interactions with a greater number of individuals, which in turn might have driven increased cranial size and a more complex neocortex (see Davidson, this volume; Gibson and Jessee, this volume).

Thus, I think the data from nonhuman animals support a bottom-up, empiricist approach to language origins that establishes language as one point on a continuum of communication abilities. It is unnecessary to hypothesize special perceptual abilities, special cognitive abilities, or special brain structures to support language; rather, it is more parsimonious and more consistent with an empiricist point of view to see these as resulting from the increased communication abilities, including language, that have emerged in human evolution.

CONCLUSION

In this chapter I have tried to make three interrelated points. First, it is very difficult to find explicit criteria that differentiate human language from the vocal communicative capacities of other species, yet it is clear that something is different about language. This difference might lie in the combination of all the design features in the human species, in the greater neurological complexity that quantitatively increases the communicative ability of humans, or in the increased social responsiveness and social dependence that provided motivation for a complex language. Human languages have developed to exploit sensory and perceptual processes that are phylogenetically ancient, and some related species such as chimpanzees should have the anatomical ability to produce at least a rudimentary spoken language, even though they do not. It appears difficult to specify precisely what is special or unique about language.

Second, many of the data that support the innateness of language learning, such as universals of development and critical periods, may be accounted for by learning and motivational processes. Language learners are very responsive to their environments, both linguistic and social, and they acquire first the sounds and grammatical features that are important to their first language. In addition, language learning is extremely resilient. There are many different developmental routes to the same outcome of fluent language, and although the quantity and quality of input do influence the rate of language learning, children also can compensate for inadequacies of input. Language learning may not be age-limited; it should be viewed as a life-long possibility in which the degree of fluency we achieve in late language learning is determined by motivation and by cognitive and learning variables rather than by "hard-wired" neuroanatomical modules. The processes of vocal accommodation in humans, monkeys, and birds suggest a degree of vocal plasticity that enables individuals to adapt readily to changes in the social environment.

Third, data on how changed social environments affect trill structure in marmosets, along with the demonstration of clear parallels between the babbling of pygmy marmosets and human infants and the potential teaching of food-associated calls in cotton-top tamarins, provide experimental models for understanding processes of the ontogeny of vocal production, usage, and response. The results we have obtained to date with marmosets and tamarins support similar findings in other primates, other mammals, birds, and children to suggest that similar developmental processes are involved across a wide range of species (Snowdon and Hausberger 1997). Just as perceptual processes appear to be highly conserved phylogenetically, so ontogenetic processes may be similarly conservative.

Finally, an underlying theme in this chapter is that language (or vocal communication) is socially constructed. The functions and modifiability of language (and calls) are best observed in social contexts and when significant changes occur in social environments. The ontogeny of language (or vocal communication) arises from a rich social environment. It is in this environment that animals and children are motivated to learn the structure, usage, and responses of their vocalizations.

Note

This research was supported by United States Public Health Service Grants MH 29,775 and MH 00,177. I am grateful to A. Margaret Elowson, Rebecca S. Roush, and Cristina Lazaro-Perea for their collaboration in the work presented here, and to Keith Kluender and Barbara J. King for their critical review of the chapter. I am grateful to all the participants in the School of American Research seminar for their input.

5

Ape Language

Between a Rock and a Hard Place

Sue Savage-Rumbaugh

This chapter is about questioning the means available within primate behavioral research to do Science. (I use the capital *s* to distinguish between the accepted Scientific methods of our time and science as an inevitable endeavor of the human spirit, the methods of which differ across time and across societies.) A seminar such as the one that generated this volume is one of the few places where such a discussion can begin to take root. Journals are adequate for presenting data, and invited presentations offer forums for laying out research frameworks, findings, and conclusions. But where does one find a setting in which to question the processes and definitions of how one is to do the Science of primate behavior? Few forums exist for discussing the limitations that one's indoctrination into the halls of Science imposes upon what it is that one is permitted to do in the name of research.

Many things are deemed to be beyond the bounds of Science—such areas are, in the case of humans, typically left to the domain of religion, metaphysics, or superstition (Alcock 1996; Gross, Levitt, and Lewis 1996). But when one studies the great apes and comes up against the workings of a conscious nonhuman mind, should one stop doing Science and leave one's questions on the doorstep of religion? Suggestions have been made that apes possess religion and superstition (Yerkes 1925; Goodall 1986), so perhaps this is an option. Even to contemplate the contents of ape minds is a sort of Scientific heresy, because the contents of "mind" are assumed to be revealed only through self-report, and only *Homo sapiens* is deemed capable of "saying what he thinks."

Science, as it is currently practiced, is poorly prepared to address questions about the contents of individual minds—about consciousness, plans, intentions, goals, purposes, reason, or intuition—in any species, including humans (Baars and Bernard 1996). Some researchers are addressing the issue of whether or not animals even have minds (Whiten 1991; Povenilli, Rulf, and Bierschwale 1994). Others grant them minds and are inquiring into the nature and structure of different sorts of animal minds (Bekoff and Jamieson 1996). But no scientists, other than those in animal language research, deal with the moment-by-moment, fleeting and changing contents of those minds, for such thoughts, if they exist, can be probed only with language.

What should a scientist who finds himself or herself face-to-face with issues of mind contents in nonhuman beings elect to do? According to current wisdom, one has to prove that the capacities for purpose, goals, consciousness, beliefs, intuitions, and insights exist before studying them in any nonhuman species. The problem with this task is that we have not proved the existence of such capacities in ourselves, and so we have developed no accepted methodology for proving the existence of intangible states of mind. We simply accept that such conditions exist in the minds of humans. Studies of ourselves proceed on the assumption that our minds generally exist in some state of consciousness, with some intent and purpose. Such assumptions are different from "proof" and cannot readily be subjected to proof. By requiring "proof" of animal minds but not of human minds, we deliberately set a double standard that is completely arbitrary. We grant complete overlap between the biology and anatomy of humans and apes—it is only the "mind" that we say contains a fundamental difference.

The study of ape language has been severely, if not irreparably, limited by the accepted norms of "doing Science" in the field of primate behavior. Language is too complex to be interpreted by traditional statistical methods. Yet because such methods are de rigueur for the study of animal communication, students of ape language must "count utterances" and do cross-checks between externally constructed categories in order to prove that language exists. Counting utterances and looking at syntax would be a rather curious way to go about proving that a human being knew what it was saying.

In a recent book entitled *The Flight from Reason and Science* (Gross, Levitt, and Lewis 1996), members of the New York Academy of Science warn of the many perils of rejecting the Scientific method. Surely it would be folly to reject Science entirely. Still, to make progress in the arena called "mind," we must begin to search for methods of science and reason that do not treat the social world as reducible to a series of replicable, countable, linear events. We must develop methods that acknowledge that the social world is a reflection of the mental world, and the mental world is constantly manifesting itself by recreating a social world in which the mental world can verify its constructs—and this phenomenon is happening not only in humans but in apes as well, and perhaps in other species. We call this process "culture" in humans, but we ask for proof of "culture" in other species (Tomasello, Kruger, and Ratner 1993).

The problems I have encountered by trying to confine my Science to the currently accepted methods are difficult ones to explain. This is because many of the "caveats" of our indoctrination into the Scientific method function to define what one can and cannot consider appropriate to mention. Even the suggestion that something cannot be understood when it is studied through normal Scientific means is quickly labeled "charlatanism" by those who view the current Scientific method as the only route to true knowledge (Bunge 1996).

Typically, any suggestions I have proffered about the need for new methods to study behavior have been met by others with patient explanations of the Scientific method—as if the real problem is that I do not understand how to do Science correctly, because if I did, the difficulties I raise would vanish from my field of vision. Yet those who would patiently explain the methods of Science to me have no grasp of the true nature of the phenomena with which I deal on a daily basis. I cannot even describe these phenomena without having my descriptions tossed out of Scientific court as inappropriate or anthropomorphic. Accurate description is the first requirement for any proper scientific investigation, yet the things I wish to describe are themselves required to be "proved" in order for my description not to be thrown out at the outset. So I must underreport the things I observe apes to do. There are some things in Science that one is simply not permitted to discover.

Thus, in the interest of describing the problem more palatably, I offer a chapter that is part allegory, part satire, part self-revelation, part descriptive account, and part philosophy. Its goal is to clarify the problem faced in ape language research or in any language work with a nonhuman species. For many readers, the purpose of my doing this may remain unclear, and you may suggest that I would have been better off presenting "hard data." To those who take this view, I can say only that it is in the nature of mind that its true contents are transient and ephemeral. One can structure data collection techniques to make minds appear to behave like machines. One can count and classify and lump, but one learns little by making a mind appear to fit the current mold of Science.

In the future, a "new methodology" must be developed if humans are ever to grasp the true nature of the relationship between their own behavior and that of their closest living relatives. Attempts to elucidate ape behavior on the basis of ecological explanations or reinforcement principles alone will explain no more about apes than such techniques explain why any of us do what we do from day to day.

Currently "hot" questions, such as why there is a fundamental difference between humans and apes in their flexibility of behavior and ability to use symbols (Davidson and Noble 1993a), are misguided. These questions take as their starting point the presupposition of a human-ape linguistic gulf, which is at base groundless. Until scientists attempt to grapple with ape behavior in all its complexity, speculations about our evolutionary history and how far we have moved from an "apelike" intelligence to our present glorious state have little meaning (Gibson and Ingold 1993). All of these speculations are based upon an unrealistic view of the apelike creatures from which we are said to have arisen.

PECULIARITIES OF THE THING WE LIKE TO CALL "LANGUAGE"

Readers who have attended academic conferences know that language is a rather strange sort of thing. Have you ever been in a room full of people, talking to them for a long time about many things, only to come away feeling that much more has transpired or been communicated among you than words can convey? Those who have attended such conferences know that published volumes rarely come close to catching the essence of the conference, even when a tape recorder is going and the transcriber tries to capture the critical portions of what has been said. This is why we bother to attend conferences rather than correspond in writing—it would certainly be less expensive and less disruptive of our lives to hold "written conferences," and we are all clearly skilled at written communication. Why is no one interested in attending a "written conference?" Might it be that there is more to communication than we can put into written language? Might it be that we convey information to one another in a way that we have not yet learned to translate into written form? Certainly we produce glances and handshakes and postures that are supposed to tell others how we feel about them and ourselves, but we can do that with written words as well—sometimes quite incisively. Are there communications that we cannot put into words as we know them?

From an evolutionary perspective, it should not seem strange that a primate that has spent most of its evolutionary history in social groups has evolved multiple sophisticated means of communication, many of which rely on being in the presence of others (Smith 1996). For many aspects of the way in which we conduct our current business of culture, the written word is adequate—but not all cultures have found a need for written communication. Sound and vision are certainly basic forms of primate communication, but there are others as well. Olfaction and alternations in the organism's electromagnetic state may contribute to communication in ways that are currently difficult to discern. In addition, our present understanding of the vocalizations of animals seems only vaguely related to the true complexity of information that is transmitted between them (Zimmerman, Newman, and Jurgens 1995).

Any scientist who has observed a group of primates for any length of time recognizes that much more information passes quickly between group members than the scientist is able to comprehend. If such a scientist were suddenly thrown into the body of one of the animals he or she had been observing for years, but with no special knowledge of the communication system beyond that acquired by watching the animals, he or she would be at a severe social disadvantage. Indeed, the scientist would most likely become a social outcast quickly, because of failure to coordinate appropriately and effectively with other members of the group. Given such complexity in communication, is it any surprise that our many scientific efforts to search for "words" in the vocalizations of other primates have met with limited success (Gouzoules, Gouzoules, and Ashley 1995)?

Surely, if nonhuman primates communicate only about positive and negative feelings—as has been suggested (Bickerton 1990)—it should not be so difficult to learn to understand all that is going on in a group. Why would the animals need such complex and diverse vocalizations to communicate feelings as simple as "I like, or don't like, what you are doing," "I might, or might not, attack you," or "I am, or am not, afraid of you"? Why do we find ourselves so often surprised and puzzled about what individuals do? If nonhuman primates' "calls" are so simple, then why do we, as Scientists, with all our sonogram charts and statistical categories, remain more or less at a loss in our attempts to explain what they are saying to each other? Why, after years of effort, are we restricted to conclusions such as "females seem to give loud calls for the same reasons as males....Regarding function, loud calls are thought to facilitate communication between different groups" (Hohmann and Fruth 1995). Have we no way to learn what is being communicated?

Could the problem possibly be that we have been too focused on language as words, especially words as discrete units that have a packaged meaning that can be printed in a dictionary? Could we be too certain that we know what language is—that it is composed of discrete units that mean something apart from what the speaker imbues them with in the act of producing them? Could we possibly be too certain that our treasured distinction between language and communication, and thus between animals and humans, is accurate?

THE STORY

I would like to tell a story about a young child who was brought into the world with the most caring and loving of parents. All the child's needs were met with tenderness, gentleness, and love. When the child was hungry, good food was offered; when the child was tired, a comfortable, soothing place for sleep was provided; when the child was scared by a loud noise or sudden change in light, it was comforted. The child was carried and caressed all through the day, and it grew and came to understand the world as a beautiful and wondrous place filled with a fantastic array of sights and sounds and smells and feelings, each interesting in its own way. The child then began to become dimly aware that people around it were "talking," or rather, they were making melodious noises with their mouths while they gazed at the child and others. When these melodious noises came out of their mouths they also produced colors that hung briefly in the air and made the melody of the sound evident to the eye as well as the ear. It seemed to be a beautiful act, and the child began to watch closely so that it, too, could engage in this wondrous activity.

These sounds and noises did not tell the child anything special about how the people felt or what they wanted it to do; it already seemed to know that. So the child did not realize that people were using these sounds to give information of some sort to one another. Yet people seemed very happy when they engaged in these actions with one another, just as they did when they touched one another. The child guessed that they seemed somehow to use this special ability to resonate about the ideas they were exchanging—ideas that they jointly understood and that the child understood as well. It never occurred to the child to ask itself how these ideas were understood—they just seemed to be apparent to all who were in a room together, and since everyone knew, no explanation was needed.

The child simply thought that this behavior was a wondrous thing, just as touching and loving were wondrous things, and so the child practiced and practiced until sounds and colors began to flow from its mouth as well. In its joy and happiness, the child directed these emissions toward others, to show them its accomplishment. They were most pleased and responded to the child in kind. The child was delighted with its newfound ability, because now it no longer needed to wait until the people around it decided to produce these melodious sounds and colors; instead, it could get them to do so simply by directing its own sounds and colors toward them, and they would instantly respond in kind.

The child worked at making some of the same melodious sounds that it heard others make and found that the same colors came out of its mouth. It also found that certain ideas in its mind always seemed to come with some of the sounds and colors, but it did not occur to the child that people were using these sounds to communicate the ideas. It was as if the sounds and colors were manifestations of the ideas, and people elected to make the sounds and colors because they were beautiful, just as they elected to hug and caress the child as expressions of their love. The idea of love was not in the hug or transmitted by the hug; the hug was simply an expression of an idea that was felt and shared at some common level.

One day the child commented to its mother on the particular joy and beauty of the colors it experienced when it heard a new sound that was the name of someone who had visited for the first time that day. The child wanted to know if the mother liked this new color they were using as much as it did. The mother had a great deal of difficulty understanding what the child was asking, but she could see that the question was a real one and that the child was looking for an answer, so she encouraged the child to try and ask again.

The child was very, very puzzled that the mother could not grasp the idea of the question, because it had never experienced this problem before—it thought everyone always understood everyone else. The child tried again to think the question, and again words and colors came out of its mouth and it said/thought/spoke/projected the new color again to remind its mother. The child then became aware that it had never really tried to remind its mother of things before; they had always just been thinking about things as they happened. Now the child was thinking about something that had happened in the past, remembering its beauty and wanting to share the remembrance of that beauty with its mother. That was why it had felt the question.

The child then felt its mother ignore the color and focus her mind closely on the child's sounds. Then the mother explained to the child that she could not understand the question because there were no colors; the sounds that people made were "words," and people used these "words" to tell others things, just as the child was learning to do. The child was puzzled and at first could not understand why its mother was saying that there were no colors, that words did not produce colors, and that words were things.

The next morning when the child awoke, it noticed that when its mother spoke, the colors had vanished and the wonderful sounds had taken on a dull and monotonous tone. To hear the different parts of this tone, the child now had to work to listen, because the tones varied little. The child became very sad that the colors were gone, and it now felt very small compared with all the big people around it. Before, it had not realized that it was so small. Now, when the child tried to make the monotonous sounds without colors, it found this hard, and it also found it hard to tell what people were saying to each other when they spoke these sounds so rapidly.

The child could still talk to its mother by thinking and feeling and finding that sounds come from its mouth, and the child could talk to its father the same way, but it was very difficult to talk to anyone else. And when its mother and father talked to other large people who came to their home, the child could no longer understand what they said to each other.

The child thus talked only to its mother and father and to other small people like itself. It did not like to talk to other big people, for they made it feel very small and very weak, since it could not tell what it was they said to each other. They seemed to talk without any feelings coming out of their mouths, in a very monotone and rapid manner. These big people also never liked to play; they spent all of their time just talking.

PROVING THE STORY

The story I have just told is true. I know it is true because I was that child. For a long time, I never told this story to anyone because I thought there had been something wrong with me. Later, when I grew up and began to study psychology, I learned that there is a real phenomenon called synesthesia, and people who have this capacity undergo visual experiences when exposed to sounds, generally musical sounds but sometimes other sounds as well. At once I knew that this was what I had done and what I had ceased to do when I was told that it was not the way people were to function.

Before one knows that one is supposed to be of limited capacity, one does not stop oneself. But now I can no longer recreate the experience—I can only recall vividly that I had it, that it was entirely natural, and that I assumed everyone else had it. I assumed that colors and sounds were all linked to communication and that communication was the intentional extension of one's ideas to another accompanied by beautiful sounds and colors. I can also recall the pain I felt upon learning that what I was doing was unacceptable—it was the first rejection of me and how I functioned that I had experienced. It was the first time I was told to do something some other way. I never considered not following the path that was suggested to me; I only puzzled that I was to do so, since the world was so monotonous and flat when one did that.

What if I had been investigated by a child psychologist attempting to prove the existence of synesthesia in young children? How could he or she have done so? By wondering about my abilities and questioning them, the psychologist might have caused them to cease to exist just as my mother did, even though she was loving and had no idea what was happening to me. How could I have proved to the psychologist that I saw these colors if I had wanted to do so? Because the psychologist did not see them, he would have had only my word for it—even if he, too, had seen such colors when he was younger but had lost the memory of it. Nothing I could have done would have helped him to understand what I was experiencing unless he could join me in a common appreciation of what was happening. Before I realized that I was not to see these colors, I thought others saw them all the time, because they often looked as if they were watching them as I did.

Of course a psychologist interviewing me now might conclude that I had invented this memory, since others do not report similar accounts, or he might conclude that I was unique. If enough others read my account, however, someone would turn out to have a similar memory, perhaps even more detailed than mine. Then the psychologist would have to determine whether my memory influenced other accounts or whether the fact that similar accounts came forward meant that other people had experienced the same phenomenon I did.

Basically, the psychologist has no means of validating this phenomenon except that of consensual validity, and consensual validity itself acts upon the perception of individual group members to push them toward the norm. Indeed, phenomena such as mystical healing and witchcraft in other cultures are said not really to exist but to occur only because all the people practicing them believe in them. It is the belief itself that causes the healing or the ailment, much as a placebo helps a third of the subjects who receive it to improve.

Similarly, people generally have no means of assuming that animals know what they are saying, and so they treat them as if they do not. They may continue to "talk" to their animals, but they do not treat them as if they are comprehending. Had my colleagues and I not treated the apes we have worked with as if they understood our language, it is unlikely that they would have come to do so. It was the treating them "as if" the possibility existed that made the emergence of language possible.

THE BOUNDARIES OF BELIEF

In behavioral Science as we know it, the belief of a subject has no place. Scientists elect not to study the accuracy of beliefs because currently there is no means of proving that a belief is true or false; it is simply "a state of mind." And because we have no agreement on what "mind" consists of, we cannot possibly study its various states with any degree of precision or certainty. But if beliefs can make us well, without the side effects of drugs or surgery, should we not be attempting to understand the role of belief better? Even though "beliefs" do not currently effect healing for everyone, perhaps if we better understood what happens to us as we form perceptions/understandings/beliefs about our world, our own abilities to perceive ourselves as healthy could be utilized. Any drug that reliably cured 30 percent of the population of a large number of diseases would be carefully studied.

We hold beliefs not only about ourselves, our abilities, and our health but also about other humans and their capacities and about all nonhuman creatures and their abilities. We commonly accept that animals are incapable of holding beliefs of their own and therefore of communicating any beliefs to others. Any "language" that an animal may acquire from humans, we assume from the outset, must be limited to the expression of immediate desires or needs. Because of this assumption, anyone listening to an animal interprets all utterances produced within such a framework.

The degree to which our current opinions regarding the capacity of animals to hold beliefs affect the way in which reports of apes with language are received has not been fully recognized within the academic community (but see Taylor 1994; King, chapter 2, this volume). This community assumes that if apes do have language, then the current boundaries of the scientific endeavor are sufficient to enable proof (or disproof) of the phenomenon. This assumption is inadequate. Current scientific boundaries, while taking us partway, are incapable of permitting "proof" that apes or any other animals are capable of language, even if they in fact are.

Discussions of why current scientific boundaries operate in such a manner are difficult and inevitably pedantic. Moreover, analysis of a problem does not necessarily lead to recognition of concrete examples of that problem when it actually occurs. For that reason, I have elected to present the problem in the form of a satire—an imaginary debate between myself and a skeptic of ape language. The goal is a dual one. First, I attempt to illustrate the unfolding and elliptical nature of the sort of thinking that arises when beliefs about the capacities of mind are treated as scientifically verifiable data within the current domain of measurable behavioral phenomena. Second, I attempt to suggest ways out of this dilemma—different ways of thinking about the problems of mind and Scientific proof in the domain of behavior, about the nature and domain of patterns of behavior, and about why the role of the observer or participant within interactions cannot and should not be "factored out" of behavioral data.

INTERVIEW WITH A LINGUIST AND AN
APE-LANGUAGE RESEARCHER

"Wally," the critic, is an invention. He is a completely fictitious character whose views represent those of an amalgamation of many critics who have responded to animal language research (ALR). No resemblance to any specific living person is intended. I invented him in order to permit myself to say things that cannot be said in the conventional academic format without becoming embedded in the pedantic mode of explanation.

Some of the arguments leveled by Wally can be found in the works of Bickerton (1990), Pinker (1994), Sebeok and Rosenthal (1981), Seidenberg and Pettito (1979), Terrace and colleagues (1979), and Wallman (1992), but others are not found in scholarly critique. The battle of animal language work is a strange one in that much of it has been waged in the press, over the airwaves, and in the comments of journal reviewers and editors. Many times articles are rejected, even without review, on the basis of comments such as those found in the following pages. To reject an article without review, one does not need to publish a critique; one needs only to have a philosophy that does not include minds for animals.

Much of the criticism that animal language work has received has taken a derisive and sarcastic bent. In part this reflects a lack of understanding of the phenomenon itself, but it also reflects a deep personal rejection of or revulsion toward the very idea of "animal talk"—as if the entire endeavor were a bad joke on Science, something like the Piltdown fossil. This "tone" of the ALR criticism is reflected in Wally's comments not to deride the critic but to make manifest the depth of the personal-intellectual conflict that undergirds much of the current ambivalence regarding all ALR work. The format for this "invention" is that of a talk show interview about my work.

Narrator: Hello, Dr. Tycouth, how are you?
Wally: Fine, Bob, just fine, and how have you been? You've had a really first-rate, hard-hitting show lately.
Narrator: Thank you, Dr. Tycouth. (To the audience:) I

would like to introduce Dr. Walter Tycouth. Dr. Tycouth is a widely respected linguist and cognitive psychologist who has studied language patterns in both children and adults in English as well as in French, German, and Italian. He has also published several thorough critiques of ape language research and is well known and highly regarded as an outspoken skeptic.

Dr. Tycouth has accepted an invitation to go one-on-one with Dr. Sue Savage-Rumbaugh, one of the more controversial figures in the field. Dr. Savage-Rumbaugh is a well-known researcher in the field of ape language research. She has published several books describing her experiences with an amazing chimpanzee named Kanzi.

(To me:) Hello, Dr. Savage-Rumbaugh, how are you and Kanzi? Did Kanzi decide to come per chance? You know he was invited.

Me: No, he declined—actually, he wanted to come, but he isn't permitted to leave the research facility. If he ever were to go someplace like this he would probably be scared to death. I must admit, I am a little nervous myself.

Narrator: Well, give Kanzi my regards and I'm sure that once we get going you will plow right in.

Dr. Tycouth, why don't you start things off by asking the first question.

Wally: Right-o, thank you, Bob.

Well, hello Sue, I'm so glad to have this opportunity to chat with you, as I have heard about your work, of course—who hasn't? I mean a chimp that talks makes news and is something everyone wants to hear more about. Well, let's start with the latest—are there any new things that Kanzi is doing lately, any really startling new findings after these many years of working with him that we haven't yet heard about?

Me: Well, uh, thank you Wally, I have heard about your work as well and find it interesting that there are these similar patterns in languages all over the world, though I don't think, of course, that similarity is necessarily indicative of innateness, but I guess we can talk about that later. Well, yes, Kanzi is doing some interesting things, he always does new and interesting things every day that I interact with him, and so are Panbanisha and Tamuli and Matata and Neema. Many of the things that are of great interest to me often don't seem equally fascinating to others, though.

Wally: Perhaps you could give us a few examples? You have to realize that the rest of us don't have the opportunity to talk to apes much, so we have to rely on you to tell us what they say. Has Kanzi, for example, talked about how he feels about the recent Monkey Wars battle that is going on between scientists and animal rightists? I assume that he is on the side of the monkeys, of course.

Me: No, I'm afraid he hasn't actually discussed this with me, and if he did, I don't know which side he would be on as he hasn't seen many monkeys and he hasn't had a chance to make friends with any.

Wally: Ha, ha, ha, ha—forgive me for laughing, the way you talk is so, well, unusual sometimes—Kanzi doesn't have any monkeys as friends...he, he, he. You must realize that sounds odd to those of us who tend to think of Kanzi as a monkey.

Of course, I understand that you love him and that he is not "just a monkey to you," but could he really now, I mean really have a conversation with you about the topics in the book *Monkey Wars* [Blum 1994]? I mean he couldn't really discuss something like the "treatment of monkeys" with you, could he? The best I can tell from reading your work is that Kanzi doesn't have anything like "real" conversations with you—the most he does is type out his needs and wants on the computer.

Me: It is difficult to explain to other people what Kanzi can and can't do, since other people lack experiences similar to mine with bonobos. However, most of what I try to say is very simple and straightforward. It is so hard to get across even the most obvious things that Kanzi does that I rarely even try to describe something that might reflect the real limit of Kanzi's abilities—or those of the other bonobos for that matter. You know, there are other bonobos at the Language Research Center—we have five bonobos and five common chimpanzees as well. Research has been going on there since 1972, or over twenty-five years now, so when I reach a conclusion regarding some capacity that apes have, it is generally not based just on Kanzi.

Wally: Oh, now, Sue, you don't need to get defensive of ALR already. Of course we know that the Language Center has put out a lot of material on apes ever since Duane first began that early work with Lana.

Me: No, Kanzi does not read books like *Monkey Wars* and discuss them with me, much less Lana. However, he is capable of discerning mistreatment of other bonobos or chimpanzees when he sees it, and he takes immediate exception to it. If someone has done something to him that he does not like, he will complain to me if I am there and sometimes even later.

Wally: What! You mean to tell me that Kanzi is now talking about past events and is even telling on people who have been mean to him? Well now, that's very interesting— exactly how does Kanzi do this? Do you have words for the past tense on the keyboard now?

Me: Well, no, we don't. That's a great oversight. Had I known how easily Kanzi would learn language I would have tried to put some sort of method of expressing the past tense into the lexigram system, but then there are a lot of things that I would have done differently if I had known the outcome before I began working with Kanzi.

One example we have of bonobos referring to the past is that Panbanisha has told people about a fire that happened outside the play-yard. One of the kerosene heaters that we had placed outdoors to warm up the bonobos' outdoor enclosure caught fire one day. The bonobos weren't in any danger, since the heater was outside their yard, not in it, but it was rather frightening, and many people at the lab were talking and running about trying to put it out. At the time of the actual fire, Panbanisha was inside and did not see it herself. But after all the excitement was over she asked to be taken to the "play-yard," which is near where the fire occurred. Once there, she walked over to the blackened and burned heater and looked it over very carefully. That afternoon, when Jeannine came in to work with her, she said "fire" and took Jeannine to the play-yard and showed her the burned-out heater. Jeannine had not heard about the fire but realized what must have happened once she saw the heater. So in this case, not only was Panbanisha talking about a previous event, but the event was one she had not seen for herself but had only heard others describing. Nonetheless, she elected to pass this information along to Jeannine, who had not known about the fire.

Of course, you could say that she wasn't really telling Jeannine about the fire—that she was just saying "fire" at the keyboard because she wanted to go and look again at the place were the heater was burned. And the fact that she watched Jeannine's reaction when they arrived was just coincidental, or a function of the fact that Jeannine displayed surprise. You could argue that she really wasn't talking about the past at all. You see, that's the trouble with presenting any given instance or "anecdote," as people call it—you can always take a reductionist view and explain the event in some trivial manner.

It is only when one is presented with the hundreds of different incidents that make up the stuff of daily life with bonobos that one concludes that it is folly to explain everything away as mindless chance events. When one is constantly on the receiving end of communicative interactions as well as initiating them and waiting to see if they are understood, one's impression of the competencies of the bonobos is shaped by one's overall experiences, not by any one incident. Unfortunately, it is impossible to publish hundreds of individual accounts in a journal. Science is all about lumping things together.

Wally: Well, that's all well and good, but of course one's individual experiences and one's reaction to them are not science. How am I to know that my experiences with the bonobos would be at all like yours? I might interpret things very differently from you—after all, I have to admit that I don't hold them in the same sort of affectionate regard that you do, and I surely couldn't imagine having one of them in my home and feeding it with a bottle as you described in one of your articles—my wife wouldn't permit it if I tried! Ha, ha, ha. Seriously, though, I don't think I could feel right about all the responsibility of being a parent to an ape, not to mention the fact that I might be screwing it up just by doing all those human things to it. Doesn't this ever worry you? I mean, don't you ever think about the fact that you might be screwing up these animals' concept of who they are and about what right you have to do that?

Me: One of the reasons our lab has grown so large is that we care about raising apes who are comfortable with other apes. That is why we have worked to provide the facilities to house and care for social groups of both species that we have studied.

Apes are not as prejudiced as most human beings. They do not treat us differently just because we look different to them. They do treat us differently as a function of how we behave, and consequently their reactions to one person are very unlike their reactions to any other person.

It is important to note that humans exist in many different cultures and even in many different environments within a given culture. Often we assert that we are screwing up children by raising them in tenement housing where their only "successful" role models are drug pushers. Others suggest that we are screwing up children by raising them in special elite schools where they are taught mainly social graces and how to manage the interest on large sums of money [Greenfield 1997]. But the rearing of either group is equally far from the natural condition.

Of course, one could always argue that Kanzi, Matata, Panbanisha, Tamuli, and Neema would be better off in the wild, undisturbed by human experimenters. The clear answer to that question right now is that life in the wild for bonobos is very precarious. They may enjoy it while they have it, but they are likely to end up as dinner on someone's supper table—their numbers are decreasing dramatically in the Congo.

Wally: Yes, it is a pity, so many endangered animals. Man isn't taking care of the planet as he should. But to get back to the matters of scholarly concern at hand—so given that you rear these animals and try to teach them how to get along with apes and with people, it must be a pretty big job. I mean it must take a lot of time and dedication and commitment to the animals, and certainly this is bound to influence your view of them, doesn't it?

Me: I guess I wouldn't be human if it didn't.

Wally: Of course, but now how can we, I mean the rest of us, be sure that what you see in these apes is really there? After all, it is impossible for parents to be objective about their own children—how can other scientists reasonably expect you to be objective about apes that you have raised?

Me: Well, I haven't exactly raised these apes as children. I have helped to raise them, to be sure, but a lot of other people as well as other apes have helped to raise them as well.

Wally: Well, however you have done it, you are regarded as a central figure by these apes, are you not?

Me: Yes.

Wally: So how can the rest of us, as scientists, trust your judgment, your reports, as valid? How can we be sure that you are not just seeing and hearing things that are colored by how you feel about these animals?

Me: Well, you know, Wally, another part of the research effort has dealt with children who are retarded, children who have been unable to develop any sort of normal language system even though they have been reared by loving and caring parents who would not be inhibited by Morgan's Canon, or the view that one must always strive for the simplest explanation of behavior. Yet try as they do, they cannot make their child "normal" just by reading things into its behavior that are not there. It is not as easy to determine the line between cueing and scaffolding as you suggest.

Wally: Yes, I have read a little about the work you are doing with retarded children, and I see your point—you can't read just anything you want to into behavior. However, I don't believe that this is really the issue here. Let me be a bit more specific. You say somewhere in one of your articles that on one occasion a bonobo named Tamuli, is that right...?

Me: Yes, we have a bonobo named Tamuli. She hasn't learned to use the keyboard, because she stayed with her mother while Kanzi and Panbanisha came out during the day to be with people and to use the keyboard.

Wally: Yes, yes, and one day Tamuli had your keys and wouldn't give them back to you, and so you told Kanzi to tell her to give you your keys back and she did. Do I have it right?

Me: Yes, that is pretty much what happened.

Wally: Well, I'd like to go into this in a bit more detail. Just how did you ask Kanzi to tell this to Tamuli—is that her name?

Me: Yes, Tamuli—it is Swahili for thoughtfulness.

Wally: Okay, how did you ask Kanzi to tell Tamuli about your keys?

Me: I just said to him in English, "Kanzi, I can't open the door unless I have my keys," and I pointed to the door. I

said, "Tamuli has my keys," and I might have pointed to
Tamuli—I can't recall if I did or not. I said, "You need to
get Tamuli to give me my keys back, so that I can open
the door."

You see, Kanzi had asked me to open the door
between his cage and Tamuli's, and I had to have my keys
to unlock the padlock on the door so I could let him go in
and be with Tamuli. That was the reason he told her to
give me my keys back. He understood that I would open
the door if I had my keys. Otherwise, if he had not wanted
that door opened, he probably would not have bothered
to tell Tamuli anything at all about the keys, since he
would not have cared whether she gave me back my keys
or not.

Wally: I see…okay…well, uh, let's go on to the next part—
now exactly how was it that Kanzi told Tamuli to give you
your keys back?

Me: Well, he climbed up to the top of the cage so he could
get eye contact with her—there is a concrete block wall
between the cages in the low portion, but a mesh wire in
the upper portion. Tamuli saw Kanzi and realized he was
looking at her and vocalizing to her in a sort of pleading
manner, with his stomach pressed against the mesh, which
he does only when he is in a suppliant mood. Tamuli went
up to the top of the mesh and pressed her stomach up
against Kanzi's, something like the bonobo version of two
people attempting to hug while separated by a wire fence.
Kanzi then looked right at Tamuli and vocalized using
about three or four separate sounds that would be difficult to imitate. Tamuli listened to Kanzi, then dropped
down to the floor and walked to the door of the cage and
handed me my keys. Kanzi then vocalized and pointed
expectantly to the lock, and I opened the door and let
him visit Tamuli.

Wally: Well, to be perfectly honest, I find it difficult to
accept your description of these events, but since I wasn't

there I can't offer a counter one. Nonetheless, if I were there, I feel certain that I would not have described the events as you did. Why should I accept your description? Don't you realize that you are attributing all of these things to these animals without any basis or justification?

For example, you say you told Kanzi in English to tell Tamuli to give you your keys. But what proof do you have that Kanzi understood what you said? It is one thing to practice sentences like "Put the apple in the bowl," and to teach Kanzi to do so in reply, but quite a jump of logic from that to thinking that he really understands sentences such as "Tell Tamuli to give me my keys."

Don't you realize that by making such leaps of logic without offering proof that Kanzi has a concept of a verb such as "to tell," you undermine the credibility of your other claims for Kanzi?

Me: Well, uh, if you put it that way, yes, I can see how it might make some people wonder whether or not Kanzi is doing everything that I say he is doing. However, it is the case that one can design carefully controlled studies only to prove something that one already knows or suspects to be so. With Kanzi, and with all apes really, a great deal of what goes on should properly go under the name "discovery." Many people don't realize it, but it is awfully difficult to fake a true discovery. The most likely thing is that you will miss it because you do not expect it and you are not looking for it—but it really is the fun of science, you know.

Sorry, I digressed there. Well, yes, I can't prove that Kanzi understood the verb "to tell," but then why did he go and tell Tamuli to give me my keys back? Surely it must count for something that he did this after I asked him to do so using the verb "tell," doesn't it?

Wally: Perhaps you cued him in some manner. You were standing right there in front of him, weren't you? And you were looking at Tamuli. Maybe he looked at her because you did, and then maybe she handed you the keys because you were staring at her.

Me: I look at these bonobos all the time. I was looking at Kanzi and Tamuli before this happened and after it happened, and all the time I was there. If there was something so special about how I looked at them just at the moment that caused all this to happen, I would certainly like to know what it was—I could put it to use.

Wally: Sorry, I didn't mean to get you on the defensive, I was just trying to determine explicitly how it was that you knew your interpretation of events was accurate.

Me: Let me try again. While one is in the midst of an activity, one doesn't know exactly what is happening or how things will or should turn out, or that one will cite this later as an anecdote or try to "prove" anything that happened, or even that it actually happened. I really wasn't thinking about any of this at the time—I just needed my keys and wasn't having any luck getting them from Tamuli and so I solicited Kanzi's assistance. I didn't know for sure if he would understand what I said, or, even if he did, whether he would or even could help. I just didn't know what else to do at that point. When he vocalized so quickly to Tamuli and when she gave me my keys right away, I was surprised. I don't think her behavior was cued by my intent. If my "intent" caused her to give me the keys, why did it not work before I requested Kanzi's help? I think it was his intent.

If you were there instead of me, and you were not placing the same sort of interpretive lens on the situation, you would never have decided to ask Kanzi to tell Tamuli to give you your keys back—you might have decided to try something like trading M&Ms for your keys and gotten them back. You would then have concluded that bonobos need to be paid for favors, and maybe even that they are different from human beings in that regard.

You see, the "interpretation" is not just an "interpretation"—it influences, indeed even guides and directs the flow of events. Therefore, different people do have different views of bonobos—and the critical thing is that these different views produce different sorts of bonobos. Do you understand what I am trying to say?

Wally: Well, you do argue a convincing case for your interpretation in this instance, but more to the point is not how convincing Sue Savage-Rumbaugh can be, but rather what it is legitimate to conclude, scientifically, based on hard evidence. Anytime a discipline falls prey to the fact that different people can come up with different interpretations, it has moved out of the realm of science and into the realm of opinion. Now, I understand that you have opinions that are based on experience, and you can argue strongly for your opinions, but it is precisely this sort of argument that science attempts to take us beyond. How can you be doing apes or anyone a favor by perpetuating the idea that all we need to do to understand ALR claims is simply to have different people describe what they think apes are doing? That is not science, it is just glorified anecdotes, made to sound scientific because they are described by scientists—is it not?

Me: Well, no. That is not actually what I am trying to do. I only discussed this because you asked me about this example. We really have collected a lot of very straightforward data regarding the language capacities of Kanzi, Lana, Sherman, Austin, and Panbanisha, as well as data on the lack of these skills in Matata, Tamuli, and Mercury.

Wally: Yes, of course, perhaps we should focus a bit more on that body of data, which, as you say, is large. You have, I believe, presented a corpus of Kanzi's multiword utterances in an article written by yourself and Patricia Greenfield. In that article you argue that Kanzi follows simple syntactical rules and that he even makes up his own rules. Very interesting collaboration indeed between you and Greenfield. In that article you list many two-word combinations by Kanzi but note that only 10 percent of his utterances were two-word combinations. Doesn't the fact that most of Kanzi's utterances are limited to a single word raise questions as to why he isn't able to say more complex sorts of things?

Me: Yes, you could say that, but you see there are both advantages and disadvantages to the keyboard. I'll skip over the decided advantages right now, even though they are pivotal for language acquisition in apes, and simply point out that when you have to physically find the keyboard and then find the words you want to use every time you wish to speak, it sort of puts a damper on fluency, and one ends up tending to be rather elliptic and to use as few words as possible. One of our analyses of adult human speakers revealed a mean utterance length at the keyboard of two words.

Then of course there is the problem of the words that are on the keyboard—they may or may not be the ones you need or wish to use, yet they are all you have. Consequently, you have be very innovative in your use of even single words. Sometimes, figuring out how to combine a single word with the appropriate contextual situation to convey your intent can be more difficult than trying to figure out how to string a number of words together. For example, when Kanzi says "peanut hide" and looks at your pocket, he is asking you if you have peanuts. If he says "peanut hide" and drops some peanuts on the ground into a clump of grass, he is talking about what he is doing—hiding peanuts. And if he says "peanut hide" and takes you to the staff office and points to the cabinets, he is trying to tell you that he wants some of the peanuts that he knows are kept there.

Each of these two-word sentences has a very different meaning, depending upon what else is occurring at the time of utterance. One-word sentences are the same way—their meanings vary considerably from one instance to the next. Kanzi and Panbanisha often come up with a completely new meaning for a well-worn word, simply as a function of how they use it. One day Panbanisha called a visitor "mushroom." At first I thought she was asking for mushrooms, but she didn't want any. Then I thought she was confusing mushroom with something else, but she insisted on using it when I tried to correct her. Finally I realized that the visitor had a very unusual hairdo that in fact looked like a mushroom. I exclaimed, "Oh, you are calling X 'mushroom.'" Panbanisha vocalized an excited reply of agreement, then continued to use "mushroom" to refer to the visitor, and we had no more miscommunication on this topic.

Wally: That example seems to fall into the same category as Lucy's "cry radish hurt" or Washoe's "water-bird" [Fouts 1975]—yet you have criticized these instances, saying that Washoe and Lucy were just responding to the experimenters' requests for signs....It seems that ALR folks don't trust anyone's data but their own.

Me: No, I don't think that is so. Remember that I worked with Lucy and I observed many signing sessions with Washoe. Lucy and Washoe differ from Sherman and Austin in many ways, and Sherman and Austin differ from Kanzi. It is an oversimplification to assume that apes who have been exposed to very different rearing experiences, very different linguistic systems, and very different training paradigms should all be judged together. Any organism whose behavior is so flexible as to permit it to learn a good deal of the language of another species is definitely going to be profoundly influenced by its rearing experiences.

Of course, Panbanisha, Washoe, and Lucy all use symbols in novel ways at times. Some have called these errors and others have termed them innovations. Actually, both are correct. They are errors by any normative standard of language, and language is and must be a normative activity, as your work with different language patterns clearly shows. However, they are innovative by the individual standard, in that lacking the proper word, these apes nonetheless figured out a way to say what they wished by using in a novel way words already at their disposal. This open-endedness is, as you know, one of the defining characteristics of language.

One way in which Panbanisha differs is that the use of "mushroom" was not preceded by a "what's this" question. Washoe and Lucy, in the examples you just gave, were both presented with things for which they had no name, and a response was demanded of them. They did the best they could, but whether they would have elected to name such things if left to their own devices is difficult to say.

Panbanisha was not asked to name the visitor. She heard people using the visitor's real name, but it wasn't on her keyboard. However, she could easily gesture toward the visitor to indicate her. The fact that Panbanisha elected to assign the visitor a name was very surprising. I was not ready to recognize her usage of the word "mushroom" in this way. Indeed, she used the word several times throughout the morning and each time I was puzzled as to why she said mushroom.

Wally: Well, that's all very interesting, but it seems to me that basically what you have is an example of one of the main problems of ALR, that of rich interpretation or over-interpretation. Of course, you can interpret Panbanisha's use of "mushroom" in the rich way that you have, but you really have no data to prove that Panbanisha intended the word to function as you describe.

As a science, the field of animal language leaves one on a slippery slope of overinterpretation. But what bothers me most of all is that "intent" is assigned to the ape's behavior whenever it seems appropriate. There is really no basis, other than your own intuition and that of a few other animal-language people, with whom you disagree, to conclude that apes "intend" to say anything, much less to label a person a mushroom because of her hairdo.

Surely, if psychology and linguistics are going to continue to progress as sciences, it isn't going to be on the basis of the intuition of the animal-language people.

Me: Intent is a key issue all right. Descartes brought us to believe that only humans have minds and only minds can have intentions and engage in self-reflection, and thus animals, lacking minds, can have only responses or reflexes but not intentions. Psychology has been on a slippery slope ever since, for by such thinking we separated ourselves needlessly from all the other creatures from which we evolved and with whom we share nearly all our genetic heritage.

Wally: So you are satisfied that animals have minds and engage in self-reflective thought, are you?

Me: Cogito ergo sum. Well, as I understand it—though I must admit I am not very well versed in philosophy—Descartes was simply stating the obvious. We cannot really experience thinking in other humans in the manner that we experience it in ourselves. We know that we plan and think ahead and have reasons and intentions for our actions because we experience these thoughts directly, so to speak. That is, they seem to be a part of our experiential existence, like seeing or hearing. We don't know that others have a similar experiential existence, but we assume that they do because they appear to. But more importantly, they are human beings like ourselves, so we reason from ourselves to them. However, since Descartes, "science" has decided not to extend similar reason to non-human beings. Instead, under the guise of parsimony, we have elected to assume that they do not have minds. Isn't that pretty much how the argument goes?

Wally: Precisely. After all, parsimony is one of the great principles of science. If it weren't for parsimony, people could and would invent all sorts of magical explanations for everything. We would still be thinking that Atlas carried the world around on his shoulders and that "animal spirits" were carried by our neurons.

You know, it wasn't until after Descartes that people began to realize that the brain had to construct the world from the effects on nerves and that the nature of the world was not just "given" to us but rather constructed by us.
Me: Yes, and not only do we have to construct our worlds, but animals must construct theirs as well. But more importantly, the way any creature "constructs" its mental world is a function of its experience. And I suspect that the larger the brain, the more construction is possible. You know, apes that are raised in isolation for the first two years of life can't even construct normal social interchanges with other apes—that is to say, they can't read the expressed intentions of others from their facial expressions.
Wally: Come on, now. Are you really saying that apes "intend" to make facial expressions?
Me: Well, we intend to make facial expressions, don't we?
Wally: You continue to reason from yourself to animals as if there were no difference at all. Descartes was right: attributing every human emotion, thought, or ability to animals is downright folly, and there is no end to the sheer nonsense such an approach can generate. It is quite well known that the facial expressions and calls of animals are innate. Even you yourself point out that Kanzi cannot speak as we do because of the construction of his vocal tract. Certainly his vocal tract is not an "experiential" construction, nor, may I say, are the sounds that go along with it.
Me: The real issue is, which aspects of behavior are under what we like to call "voluntary control" and which, if any, are not? Even more fundamentally, one might say, the real issue is, what is this thing called voluntary control?
Wally: Do you mean consciousness? Are you asking, "What is consciousness?"?
Me: Well, you could interpret my comments that way, I guess.
Wally: Of course, these are new and upcoming research

areas, animal consciousness and animal mind. Scientists studying these are doing a much better job of framing the issues, if I may say so, than the animal-language enthusiasts. It is much more to the point to ask what sort of mind an animal has than to ask the murky questions that ALR thought it was answering.

Me: Yes, I have read much of that work.

Wally: Well, good, maybe you will try some of it in your own lab with your animals—after all, they would be ideal candidates for such experiments, you know. I mean, if any apes do possess something like beliefs about the intentions of others, it should be language-competent apes, right?

Me: No, not really. You see, the so-called theory-of-mind question is really not a question about whether children believe that others have minds—it is really a developmental linguistic question. When do children become able to properly answer a question such as "What will Johnny think?"?

Many psychologists have made the mistake of confusing the ability to verbally express or understand a linguistic concept with the existence, in any shape or form, of the concept itself. What they fail to realize is that labels—take "belief," for example—are just that—labels. They are names applied to behaviors that have a certain pattern or regularity. When the pattern or regularity in behavior is identified, it is given a "name." The problem is that the psychologist then assumes that the name represents some underlying process. Once this step is taken, careers can then be devoted to trying to determine the location, structure, developmental sequence, etc., of that underlying process—which is given existence by the fact that it has a name. The problem is that the name was given originally only because there was some pattern of behavior that evoked a perception of regularity or commonality across diverse instances, and so it was given a name, a shorthand way of referring to lots of different instances. That is all a "concept" is, nothing more and nothing less—and looking for the location of concepts or their underlying structure in the brain is not nearly as productive an activity as simply looking at the behavior itself and deciding when most people would be willing to give it the label "belief." The idea that the "belief" is inside the person rather than in the decision to apply a label is, it seems to me, somewhat ludicrous.

Wally: Uhh-hmmm, it seems a bit odd to me that someone such as yourself should be saying that concepts are not in people—I seem to recall that you have frequently attributed some pretty esoteric concepts even to apes. Weren't you just telling me that Kanzi understands the concept "to tell"? Well, just exactly where is that understanding if it isn't inside Kanzi's head?

Me: Oh, it is inside Kanzi's head, just not in the way you might think.

Wally: For the first time, I believe we are starting to agree on something here.

Me: You see, what I am trying to say is that language is really just a lot of word and phrase usage rules—we think that these things called words really help us to think—but they don't, they really don't at all. It is, in fact, amazing that we can think so well sometimes in spite of being in the grip of all these words. Words are not for thinking, they are for telling someone else something. And when we think in words all we really do is think about how to use them to tell someone else something—we don't think up the "something" itself.

Wally: Well, uh, I guess I will have to admit that I was wrong. We weren't starting to agree—I guess it was just an illusion.

Me: Yeah, I know what you mean, words do that sometimes, don't they?

Wally: Perhaps they do when you talk to Kanzi, or more

properly, I should say, perhaps they do when he talks to you. But most of the time, between human beings, language is much more than a zero-sum affair. We are apparently able to tell each other very complex sorts of thoughts if we elect to do so—witness the civilization of man as contrasted with the life of an ape.

Apes differ little from monkeys or any other of God's creatures, if I may say so. Clever enough at finding food in the forest, yes, and surprisingly adept at nonverbal social interaction, but quite unable to convey even something as simple as the name of the man who shot them for dinner. Whether one believes in the Bible or not, it is a simple fact that man has dominion over animals, for better or for worse.

You know as well as I that when Seyfarth and Cheney tested the idea that monkeys know what it is they are saying to each other under natural circumstances, they found that the monkeys failed. It seems that monkeys can communicate, but they don't know they are communicating. But you not only insist that Kanzi knows he is communicating but even that he can do such things as choose to purposefully tell another bonobo something—or choose not to tell. In addition, you say he does this not by means of lexigrams but by actually talking in some sort of bonobo squeals.

Now, I have a good friend, a musician, who insists that his cat talks to him as well. It tells him when it wants to go out, when it wants to be fed, and when it wants to get up on the bed—it has a different sort of purring sound for each activity. The trouble is, no one else can understand this cat.

It seems to me that there is a lot of common ground between Kanzi and my friend's cat. Each of them has learned how to get some things it wants. Both of them have probably tried a whole raft of different noises and found some that work—some that get my friend to put down the food dish and some that get you to give Kanzi a banana. The trouble is, who has conditioned whom in this case? Has the cat conditioned my friend to give him food? Has Kanzi conditioned you to give him a banana? Or has my friend conditioned the cat to make a particular noise and you have conditioned Kanzi to touch the banana symbol? Perhaps both things have happened, perhaps each has conditioned the other, but the problem is that no one recognizes what has happened because no one was wittingly setting about to make it happen—it just happened.

I am not trying to say that animals are machines, or even that they are simple or that their behavior is simple or anything like that. To the contrary, it is exceedingly complex and subtle. So subtle in fact that sometimes relationships can be shaped between humans and animals of which neither is aware.

This is where science permits us to escape the philosophical trap. We don't have to forever debate about whether animals really know things, for example. We can turn to experiments for the answers.

Me: Now it's my turn to say, "For the first time I believe we are starting to agree on something."

Wally: What do you mean?

Me: I mean experiments can begin to tell us when the behaviors we are talking about are subtle forms of what you would like to call conditioning and when they are not. But it is not just the experiments themselves that tell us things, it is how we agree to talk about them—that is what permits them to tell us things. We have to be willing to listen to our own experiments—that is, we cannot assume that we know the conclusions in advance. We also cannot assume that there is any one critical experiment that can definitively answer a specific question—and we must be far more careful about everything we do in the experiment than has typically been the case, say, in those sorts of studies of animal communication where one plays a tape-recording of some vocalization and then tries to determine whether the animals who heard it, heard it as a word.

Wally: Well, just how would one know if they heard a sound as a word?

Me: How do you know when I am using words to speak to you, Wally?

Wally: Surely you don't expect me to take that question seriously.

Me: What I am trying to say is that the act of referring is an interindividual behavior—that is, it cannot be said to reside precisely in the listener or in the speaker, but rather is to be located solely in the nature of the exchange between them.

Wally: Oh, I see—sort of like when Panbanisha tells you that she is calling someone a mushroom and you agree with her? Is that it?

Me: No, in that case, reference was not occurring because, at least at first, I did not know what she was doing and I could not agree with her.

Wally: But then you somehow managed to accomplish that feat, by leap of intuition or faith or whatever you wish to call it, and suddenly reference leapt into existence—is that what you are saying?

Me: Sort of.

Wally: Well, in that case I'm afraid I have to simply say that there wouldn't be any reference here without the human mind's putting itself in the situation. Maybe "mushroom" refers to a person's hairdo for you, but somehow there seems to be paltry evidence that it refers to anything for Panbanisha. The human mind and the animal mind are not the same, no matter how much you or anyone else wishes to equate them and regardless of where it is you would prefer to locate the phenomenon of reference.

In this case, it is clear that it is in your head, and it is rather questionable what is in Panbanisha's head. Maybe her finger is touching a symbol for mushroom, but it is a giant leap from that to concluding that she is thinking about mushrooms at all, much less about using this word as a name for a person because of her hairdo.

I fear that I simply do not understand how anyone, other than a layperson who is taken in by the charm of the chimp, can conclude that the referents for words are in the minds of these animals.

Me: I didn't say that the referent for "mushroom" was in Panbanisha's mind. It is in the interchange between us. It is manufactured from and by that interchange. If I do not treat "mushroom" as a referent for the person, then it is not one, regardless of what Panbanisha might or might not have thought. Similarly, if she did not use the word as a referent for the person, I could not have treated it as such no matter what I did or did not wish to do. That is to say, if she had been wanting to eat a mushroom as she spoke, and if I had treated it as a referent for the person with the unusual hairdo, it just wouldn't have worked—there would have been no reference.

Wally: Well, if this is the type of thing you are referring to when you say we can do experiments to objectively determine whether animals know when they are using words or not, I'm afraid I can't buy it, and I doubt many others will either.

Me: I didn't say this was an experiment.

Wally: You know, it is the whole process of trying to grapple with these issues in a scientific manner that is simply totally lacking in anecdotes such as these. Why don't you and the other animal-language people—at least that faction of researchers who profess ALR to be a scientific endeavor—feel a real and pressing need to come to a firm experimental grip on this phenomenon?

Let us grant for a moment that chimpanzees really were using language—doesn't it behoove you to do your very best, for the sake of all the rest of us who are trying to understand exactly what it is that these animals are doing, to provide us with something more than anecdotes or contrived tests in which the responses are so thoroughly trained that the ape always succeeds in naming everything you show him? Don't you ever feel that you owe science more than this?

Me: Yes, I feel that all the time. How, in your view, should I go about doing that?

Wally: This is the point at which I have to turn it over to you, Sue. At this juncture the ball is in your court, as I have been trying to convey in the articles I have written on ALR issues. The linguist can provide a method for analyzing the data, but the ape must provide the data. And you see, that is what has simply not been forthcoming, and that is why, even though my regard for your work is keen, as I said in the beginning, it simply can't be concluded that apes have language.

Me: Wally, do you think there could really be data that would convince a critic such as yourself?

Wally: Of course, of course there could. Furthermore, it is quite probable that with more than thirty years of animal language work now in the journals, if that data were there to be had, I most likely would already have seen some flashes of it.

Narrator: Well, uh, excuse me. Perhaps as an interested bystander I could interject a word here.

Wally: Yes, Bob, after all, it is important that other people understand these issues, because otherwise, it's all too easy to conclude that bonobos are just miniature human beings in fur suits.

Narrator: Well, I have the good fortune to have a two-and-a-half-year-old son at home, and he is just going through that phase kids go through when they have just begun to talk but they don't always know the meaning of everything they say. Now, the other night he said to me, "Daddy I's loves you," and then walked out of the room. I should mention that this was not long after I had become angry with him for pushing down his younger brother, who is just learning to take his first steps at one year. When I asked him why he did that, he didn't answer me, and so I sent him to his room. Then he came out with that statement I told you about.

Now, of course I was happy that he loved me, but he should have been sorry for what he did to his brother. Was he just trying to please me by saying that when he knew I was mad, or did he really mean it? And do bonobos ever do anything like this? For it seems to me that in addition to the grammatical issues, there are some very basic things that we humans do with language, and it is these sorts of things that we do when we talk to each other that make us feel as if we know that what we are hearing is language. After all, I doubt that a machine could ever really feel sorry, could it?

Wally: Well, Sue, that's a fair question. Do bonobos ever say they are sorry? And if they do, do they mean it?

Me: This is kind of like the past tense problem, Wally. I neglected to put the word "sorry" on their keyboard, so they can't say it, but they can feel it, I guess, just as Bob's son could have been feeling sorry without saying that he was sorry.

Wally: Well, how would we know that if it were the case?

Me: We wouldn't know it. Bob doesn't know whether or not that's the case with his son.

Wally: Yes, but Bob isn't studying his son, and you are studying Kanzi.

Narrator: I'm afraid I have to interject here. I do feel as if I am studying my son. In fact, I feel that I am studying both my sons. I know I don't take regular data on them, but I do study them.

Me: Anyone who is trying hard to be a good parent does.

Wally: Yes, of course, good parents study their children and learn a great deal from them. Some of them also take data and it is from such parents, like Patricia Greenfield and Mike Tomasello, that we learn a great deal about the patterns of language usage shown by children acquiring their native tongue.

But Sue, permit me to take the initiative just one more time, if I may—

Me: Of course, Wally, please do.

Wally: Well, I'd like to get this discussion back onto a lighter note and away from the area of controversy. Perhaps I have been too dogmatic and insisted on too strong a criterion for proof. Let me be the first to lay down my sword and my pen and listen with open ears to what you would like to try and tell us about Kanzi.

Me: Thank you, Wally. Well, I suppose the first thing I would like to say is that I think this idea that language is a vehicle that permits thought is all wrong. Also, I would like to say that the intentions and thoughts of animals, as well as people, can be conveyed as readily through what are traditionally called nonverbal channels as they can through verbal ones, and the line that separates the two is an artificial line, constructed by humans in our need to glorify our own form of communication relative to that of other creatures—

Wally: (Interrupting) That's quite a mouthful you have there, Sue.

Me: I wasn't finished.

Wally: Well, let's start with this—you know, if you go too fast I just might get lost.

Me: I'm sorry, Wally.

Wally: I am frankly puzzled by your assertion that there is really no difference between verbal and nonverbal communication. Do you mean to say that there is no fundamental difference, for example, between the display of a male Siamese fighting fish when it is placed in the same bowl with another male fish and the kind of dialogue that human males typically engage in when they meet one another?

Me: No. I was only trying to convey the idea that the level of communication, or the degree of understanding of intentionality and reference, that is possible is not a function of any particular medium or set of constructions or rules for conveying information, but rather of the competencies the individuals bring to the exchange. That's why Marcel Marceau can communicate so well through mime, for example. It's also why deaf children in a study by Goldin-Meadow [Goldin-Meadow and Mylander 1983] were able to invent their own so-called language. When apes wish to communicate, even though they cannot produce the same sorts of sounds that we can, they have, as we do, many other means at their disposal. It is only because we have analyzed and objectified certain of our means and called them "sign language" or "English" and restricted our study of referential communication to those arenas that we have become blind to the vast array of referential communication we are using in many other domains, sometimes with awareness and sometimes without awareness.

Wally: Pardon me, but I still don't see what this has to do with nonverbal communication in apes or other animals. When an ape gives a pant-hoot and open-mouth bared-teeth facial expression, you mean it is referencing something?

Me: Sure, it is referencing something about how it feels, but from that one tiny bit of action alone you can tell nothing it is as if I showed you a snapshot of me smiling at some time in the past. Would you know why I was smiling? Was I smiling for the photographer or because I was happy about something I had just learned or who I was with? Had I just heard a joke?

Wally: Okay, you got me. Why were you happy?

Me: That's not the point. The point is that apes use what we call nonverbal behavior to tell each other things, in a referential sense, all the time—constantly, in fact—at least while they are awake. Most people don't see this because they look at each act as an isolated instance rather than looking at the patterns that exist between the acts themselves, as well as the interplay between the actions of various apes and how this is embedded in the overall contextual situation.

Have you ever tried watching a soap opera on television with the sound turned down?

Wally: Generally, I don't watch soap operas, but if I did, I think they would be even more painstakingly boring with the sound turned down.

Me: Try it some time. I bet you will find that you don't really need the sound at all to figure out the main outline of the plot, the relationship between the characters, who is lying to whom, who is cheating on whom, who is jealous of whom, who is in love with whom, who is plotting against whom, and even, in many cases, a first-order approximation of what they are saying to one another—even if you come in at the middle of an episode. It's truly amazing how much is communicated—and we don't need language to understand it.

Apes can communicate all these sorts of things to each other and to you as well, once you learn how to interpret their facial expressions and body postures. Of course, you'll need to take the context into account as well and have knowledge of the current ways of speaking in the group you observe, since these things are important to apes as well as to humans.

Wally: But how can we ask such questions experimentally? Do I just walk up to Kanzi, or to the dolphin Aka-kami, for example, and say, "Hello, what are your feelings about your cagemates or tankmates today?"

Me: The problem lies in the way we have constructed the domains we call the science of behavior and its stepchild, the science of behavioral cognition. We have it all wrong. We assume that behavior is replicable in the same way a chemistry experiment is replicable.

In fact, regarding behavioral data, nothing really qualifies as data unless you can count it. That is, the only type of behavioral datum of import is the kind that occurs sufficiently often and with sufficient invariability to be counted as a token or instance of X. Once we have identified a sufficient number of Xs, we first make sure that interobserver reliability is achieved—that is, that a second person can count instances of X_{1-y} in a manner that is virtually identical to the way I do so.

Then we set about to collect instances of X_{1-y} and look at relationships among them or between them or to find similar behavioral instances that have been gathered for another researcher. The real problem is this: Behavior does not, except in the laboratory, repeat itself. And certainly, complex interindividual behavior such as referential communication and the subset of this phenomenon that we call "language" does not repeat itself. If it did, the world would be a boring and totally predictable, if complex, place, something like a videotape that you had seen before. But instead, life is new each day.

It is only patterns that are recognizable, in some sense, as alterations on themes that do repeat themselves. But the individual things we treat as "measurable units" within those patterns don't repeat themselves in the same order and for the same purpose every time—at least not so long as behavior reflects an interaction between the social environment and the individual.

When an individual withdraws completely unto himself, behavior begins to lose its reference point—unless, of course, the person bifurcates and creates, in his mind, his own social world, just as I have created you, Wally.
Wally: What do you mean, you created me? The presumption of ALR people is sometimes downright insufferable.
Me: I mean that the human mind can talk to itself, prepare its own creations, and react to them as though they

were in fact the work of another, when it knows this not to be the case. I don't believe the ape mind is capable of such bifurcation.

Wally: I see. Well, it is exactly that capacity for bifurcation that renders us conscious and therefore different from animals.

Me: Yes, Wally, we are different from animals. But what does that mean?

Wally: It means that we can reason, we can think, we can make laws, we can construct civilizations, we can feel guilt, we can feel empathy, we can be held responsible for our mistakes, we can create art, we can paint, we can create music, we can devise religions, we can use language, we can deceive, and, most importantly of all, we are aware that other human minds can do these things as well.

Me: And do you believe that animals can do none of these things?

Wally: Well, certainly not in the way man does—but even if they could, of what relevance should it be? After all, Kanzi and Panbanisha's languagelike communications would be nothing without you. But who was there to drag us early hominids up from the depths of stupidity? Certainly not you.

Me: No, not me, thank goodness. Not you either.

Wally: No one carried around a keyboard and pointed at words for us. However you look at it, figuring out language all by yourself is vastly different from what Kanzi and Panbanisha have done.

Me: Well, how do you suppose we did it, Wally?

Wally: Something happened to us to enable us to order the world hierarchically and representationally, something very different from anything that has happened to other animals. This shaped our brains in a unique way and permitted language to flower as result.

Me: That's a great story. But what was it that happened?

Wally: Well, no one is really certain, but it definitely has something to do with our large brains, our ability to make tools, the shape of our hands and feet, and our bipedal gait—all those things that make us so different from apes.

Me: Maybe we are just building on a skill that was already there. Maybe some apes already have language in the field.

Wally: That's highly unlikely. Hundreds of thousands of hours have been spent studying apes in the field and no one has seen anything like language.

Me: But how would they know what to look for unless it looked like human language? I mean, what if it was not like human language—what if the sounds were completely different and the topics not like ours at all?

Wally: Well, that is pretty unlikely. For a language to be of any value, it must surely be something akin to our own. It must have recombinable phonemes of some sort, it must have something akin to words, and since words can't convey anything of significance without a grammatical basis, it must have that as well, or it would be just a hodgepodge of emotional sounds—which is precisely what we hear when we listen to animals—screams, shrieks, groans, and bellows, a hodgepodge of sound. Such sounds may carry feeling, but they lack sufficient structure to carry real information.

Me: Maybe bonobos need to talk about things like where they will make their nests at night and who is sleeping with whom. Maybe they don't have words for ball, shirt, car, or other things that they learn in the laboratory. Maybe we think they don't have language because they don't point at objects and purposefully label them. Maybe they leave messages for each other in the vegetation, by the manner in which they break off branches and place them on the ground—or by the type of vegetation they elect to place somewhere as a "note" for those who happen along the trail later.

Wally: Certainly there is no evidence for such behavior. If apes were capable of intentionally leaving such messages, they would have to be able to realize that the mind of the ape who later saw the message was different from their own, that it held "different contents." It has not even been demonstrated that the minds of apes have content, much less that they realize that the contents of different minds are dissimilar. And how could they possibly know that an ape coming later along a trail would need information?

Me: They do leave messages along the trail for friends and relatives who will come along later and need to know what direction to take and perhaps other things as well. I have seen bonobos at Wamba in the Congo intentionally break off vegetation and place it deliberately on the trail, pointing in the direction of travel where the trail splits, so that individuals coming along later will know which fork in the trail to follow [Savage-Rumbaugh et al. 1996].

Wally: And I suppose you interviewed these wild bonobos using the lexigram keyboard that you have, and they told you hidden meanings behind all such signs, so that you and you alone can now reveal to the world their secrets.

Me: I took no keyboard with me to the Congo. I did take a high opinion of the intelligence of these apes, an eye trained for twenty-five years to observe the smallest details of their behavior, and an ear tutored as long to listen for meaning in a confluence of their sounds.

But I had no experience with jungles, and it took months before I began to learn how to see even the most obvious changes in vegetation. But the native trackers pointed out that the bonobos altered the vegetation in a deliberate way and that if you took the guidance they offered, you could quickly determine their travel route. Lacking such guidance, one quickly lost them in the forest.

Wally: It seems that not only do bonobos talk to you in your lab in ways that are unheard of elsewhere but that they talk for you in the field in ways that are also unheard of by others. Doesn't it strike you as odd that other scientists aren't out there attempting to replicate your work in droves?

Me: Now that you mention it, it does seem a little odd. But replication is something that is discouraged in the field of primate behavior these days.

Wally: I don't wish to seem rude, but have you ever considered the possibility that perhaps you tend to read just a bit more into the facts than others do?

Me: Of course I've considered that possibility. That's what any sleuth or detective does—reads more into the set of available facts than others do. That's precisely why we all love Sherlock Holmes. But of course, in the end, once Holmes explains the facts to the rest of us, we can all see that what appeared mysterious at the time was really a simple reading of some rather obvious circumstances.

Wally: So you fancy yourself to be the Sherlock Holmes of ape language, is that it?

Me: Well, no. The message I bring from the apes is simple. Wake up, wake up, look with your eyes and your ears, rather than your word-blinded minds. Animals are conscious and they are trying their best to tell us so. If we don't learn how to listen—if we continue to patronize them, fear them, or just ignore them—we ourselves will fall into an even deeper slumber, a slumber from which we may never, never awake.

Wally: Uh, don't you think it would be good if we all stopped for a cup a tea? And maybe then we can attempt to focus on the science of how to determine what, if anything, is in the minds of other creatures.

WALLY'S FALLACIES

If you identify with Wally and are a critic of ape language studies, perhaps you find yourself puzzled and feel that my answers have not responded adequately to Wally's assertions. Perhaps you wonder why I do not really seem to recognize that my answers are either evasions or incomplete. The important message is not in my answers alone or in Wally's position as a "critic" but in the way the dialogue proceeds as the topics shift between us. It is also in the way Wally mixes common sense, logic, and humor to develop in the mind of the listener a platform of reality that cannot legitimately include a "talking ape."

If you did not identify with Wally, perhaps you have already recognized the fallacies embedded in his dialogue. At the risk of making clear points obtuse, I next attempt to take a few of Wally's comments and explain straightforwardly the messages they and my answers were intended to convey.

Fallacy A

Wally begins with a comment, disguised as humor, about why the ape is not there doing the talking instead of me. The comment is not ostensibly intended to be a serious query; it is employed in a light-hearted and therefore "unobjectionable" manner to emphasize that there is a distinct difference between Kanzi and me. I must speak for Kanzi—he clearly cannot be there speaking for himself. Because this message is delivered in a humorous and subtle way, it functions at the outset of the interview to undermine the validity of any account of Kanzi's linguistic competencies before it can be presented.

Kanzi could "speak" for himself, but to gain that capacity he must be treated as a competent member of the linguistic community to which he is speaking. He is not treated in this way except by a few people—and with them, he does speak for himself. Fallacy A is to require that Kanzi behave as a competent linguistic human would behave before he can be treated as competent. We human beings gain our competencies because of the way we treat each other, not because we are human. Were Kanzi's behaviors, including his glances, his postures, and his vocalizations, treated as fully meaningful in the same way we treat such actions as fully meaningful in human beings, then Kanzi could easily speak for himself. By denying his actions such credibility— by not hearing him unless he literally speaks the king's English and behaves like a modern-day American—we take away his capacity to speak for himself by refusing to be comprehending listeners.

The standards applied to Kanzi under fallacy A are not applied to human beings. Except in extreme cases, all human beings treat other individuals as human; they do not have to prove they are human before they are permitted to learn to speak. Thus we are granted, by birthright, the very quality or capability to which we attribute our humanness. But we deny this same capability to other animals—instead, they must prove that they have it.

Fallacy B

Fallacy B is that of constantly requiring new evidence or proof without evaluating prior evidence or proof. Most critics of ape language have evaluated experimental studies superficially, in a manner designed to discredit rather to constructively critique. They have refused to study videotapes or to attempt to determine whether their classification of events as "anecdotal" is reasonable.

By always requesting new information before evaluating extant information, critics diminish the value of what has already been learned. There are no accepted grounds within Science that permit acceptance of a cognitive skill such as language in a nonhuman species. Since no agreement can be achieved about the very existence of the phenomenon under investigation, past evidence is discounted on definitional rather than procedural grounds, while "new" evidence is constantly demanded.

Fallacy C

This fallacy states that the "feelings" of the researcher must get in the way of the collection, interpretation, and presentation of scientific data. Science is supposed to an objective enterprise wherein the experiences of one party can be verified by the experiences of another. Feelings are acknowledged to be inherently private and personal, so the idea of a researcher interacting with the subjects rather than observing them is considered objectionable in Scientific procedure. No two parties can engage in precisely the same sorts of interaction with the subjects, and thus no two individuals can have precisely the same sorts of interpretations of those experiences.

The real difficulty here is that living organisms do normally interact, and the "observer" stance is not the same as the "participant" stance. We cannot treat primates like particles of matter, for which the mixing and treatment procedures of one chemist can be replicated by those of another. Primates have memory, and the history of one's past

interactions determines the nature of future interactions. One participant is not equal to another because their histories are not equal. And
an observer is not equal to a participant because an observer stands outside.

In the arena of language acquisition, to stand outside is to assure
that no language acquisition takes place. In the arena of ape language,
the participants are also the researchers. There are no other
"observers" standing by observing the participants. But even if there
were, the interpretation of the ape's behaviors would be made by the
participants, not by the observers. Thus, if I interpret a particular sort
of glance with stiffened shoulders to mean that Kanzi is concerned
about a noise he has just heard and is wondering what it means, and
I explain that the noise means someone is hiding in the woods, then I
have changed Kanzi's perception of the woods. Observers, by themselves, cannot change Kanzi's perception of the woods, nor can Kanzi's
behavior change their perceptions. Thus a true observer would never
encounter the effect of language.

By the current standards of Science, I must have an observer of all
my actions and all Kanzi's actions in order to validate any report.
(Actually, I must have two observers who agree on nearly everything
they see, as well as a video record, with excellent camera shots, of all
events.) Kanzi and I, however, are not like vials of sodium and chloride
waiting to interact, unaffected by whatever means is used to join us or
watch us. We are constantly interacting, and the nature of our interaction is affected by the observer. Moreover, each observer affects the
nature of that interaction differently. To pretend that this not so is folly.
Indeed, to be observed without any goal of interacting is an unnatural
situation for all primates. We humans observe others intimately only
when we watch television, and television performances are generally
planned for such observance.

Thus Science, as currently structured, will not take the participant's account and does not recognize as real the effect of the observer.
The situation is even more complicated, however, in that the participant's account is accepted in all human linguistic interactions. If I go to
someone and say, "John told me he wants to go outdoors and look for
pine cones," my report is perfectly acceptable. I can report what
another human said to me, but I cannot report what an ape has said.

Even if I film the ape saying something, there is suspicion that if it were not for my presence to "cue" the ape, nothing would have been said.

The "data" of ape utterances, then, produced under all types of circumstances, are unacceptable, according to current standards of Science, because the participant observer cannot effectively serve as a reporter of the events, which in turn is because the participant observer has "feelings." If we were to acknowledge these data, they could provide us with a great deal of information about what apes think and how they perceive situations. Would Science be in danger of accepting as facts the perspective of the participant observer? Of course, but different participant observers can report their perspectives, and from different independent reports some commonly shared perceptions can be distilled.

All scientists experience feelings about their work, regardless of the domain. And of course these feelings will affect how they elect to collect, classify, analyze, interpret, and report their findings. Whether or not ape language is really different, and whether or not scientists in this field should be excluded from self-report, is the question.

Fallacy D

This is the fallacy of equating unique observations with anecdotes. In most areas of Science, observed events are termed "data" once the scientist becomes trained to distinguish the events of interest in that field. Yet ape-language researchers are not permitted to group independent observations into something called "data." Instead, each observation, even though it is made by a trained person familiar with the ape, will be labeled an "anecdote" by the critic. And multiple "anecdotes" will not be addressed as "data."

Most primatologists note what animals do in the wild by taking behavioral data on a check sheet, giving due regard to things such as unbiased sampling. But a different standard is required for animal language research. An animal-language researcher taking similar data is said to be potentially "cueing the animals." Even setting cueing aside, any interesting example of an utterance with sentient linguistic content will be labeled an "anecdotal account" because it is a single observation of an unusual, nonreplicable incident.

By labeling each interesting example reported in ALR an "anecdote," the critic makes it impossible for animal-language researchers to group such observations into what would normally be termed "data." The critic insists that the animal-language researcher present multiple instances of each event. But interesting and unusual events do not, by the nature of language, lend themselves to meaningful repetition. Rarely do people, or apes, find themselves in the same situation saying precisely what they said before. If it were necessary to verify human language by observing people repeat each conversation multiple times—in order to prove that what was said was not uttered "by chance"—then it is unlikely that conversations would ever be repeated often enough to "prove" the existence of language in our species.

Certainly some situations, such as "greeting routines," "food-ordering routines," and other "routinized actions," are repetitive, and apes do engage in these types of routines. But the critic asserts that routine conversations are not of interest because the "schema" may be memorized and thus cannot reflect real linguistic competency. The critic calls for novel or unusual behavior that reflects true inner intelligence, as opposed to something that might be an "imitation" of a human statement. Yet when such examples are presented, they are dismissed with the label "anecdotal" because they are single-case examples. Even though different examples abound, the critic finds them not to be acceptable data points and requests "real data."

This is viewed as a "legitimate criticism." Since shortly after the publication of Romanes's (1882) treatise on animal intelligence, nearly all examples of animals' behaving in an intelligent manner have been classified as anecdotes. Romanes included stories about the behavior of animals that were produced by persons who knew little about the animal they were describing. Often, the described behavior had been seen during a chance encounter with the animal. Consequently, some of these stories were later proved erroneous, though the majority remain well founded. That some examples were incorrect has been used to ban the method of reporting any single event as data.

Not only are the "utterances" of apes relegated to the anecdote dustbin, but interesting and important single events in the lives of many primate groups also go unreported because of a general Scientific aversion to reporting any event that has been observed only once. However, we have but to read the daily newspaper regarding what humans do on a given day to find that no two days are alike. No two murders or rapes will be the same, no two heroic actions identical. Either sort of event may actually be observed by no one or by only one person. It will still be taken for granted that the event indeed happened, that it was reported reasonably accurately, and that it was important in the overall life of humans—that is, it made enough of a difference to merit being selected as news. It is surely true for animals as well as for ourselves that many, many events happen only once in their lives, yet these events are no less important than things that may occur repeatedly.

The problem with the critic's requirement is that it imposes an impossible double standard on the events of interest, namely, those of symbolic communication. What passes for symbolic communication between people cannot be accepted as communication of a similar nature if it occurs between a human being and ape, or between two apes.

The critic of ape language has no difficulty accepting interpretations of the meaning of the utterances or actions of other human beings, even though these utterances or actions occur only once. The critic freely ascribes intent to the utterances or actions of human beings and takes at face value a person's expression of intent. When an ape reveals its intent, however, the critic dismisses the event as an anecdote. Few people question the propriety of such an action on the part of the critic, so ingrained is the double-standard view of animals and people (Taylor 1994).

Thus, being human, I can say, "I am using the word 'mushroom' as a name for a person," and the statement is accepted simply because I make it. Yet if I say to Panbanisha, "Are you using 'mushroom' as a name for a person?" and she answers yes, the critic will insist upon an array of proofs before even considering the answer. He or she will require that two people see the answer and report it independently. At least one of these persons must not know what the question is at the time he or she determines the answer. This means that a spontaneous and unplanned conversation must be videotaped, and the camera must have a clear view of Panbanisha's answer. And Panbanisha must be shown, independently of the conversation, to understand the meaning of each of the words in the question and the meaning of her answer.

Demonstrations of comprehension must be made using tests that control for any knowledge of the question on the part of the persons testing Panbanisha, and the tests must be replicable by different parties. This must be done with a number of similar conversations. If all these things are done, then the methods employed will themselves be subject to extensive critique. If, in the end, the critic accepts these findings, then he or she is likely to assert that Panbanisha has employed only a single word, "yes," rather than a complete sentence—and thus this utterance cannot be presumed to address the issue of syntax and should be held in "abeyance" until Panbanisha can be shown competent to utilize full human syntax.

Since the critic has already established that such activity requires specifically human genes, there is really no chance at all that an ape can do this. If it does, it can only be that the data are flawed, and it will be intimated that the researcher should readdress the data and find the flaw.

There are also those who would conclude that the "human" behavior of the ape is only a product of the enculturated environment and so not anything we really have to take into account. But to do so belittles the whole of enculturation and its ability to instill language in our own species. If it is culture that makes us "human," and if culture can be acquired by an ape—at least acquired sufficiently to produce language—then it is something we cannot afford to ignore in any discussion of evolution.

Fallacy E

This fallacy assumes that all ape utterances can be explained as conditioned behaviors designed to elicit rewards. Because this assumption is an underlying premise rather than a hypothesis, only explanations that fulfill the constraints of the assumption are permitted to stand as "proper explanations" for any given observation.

Consequently, if Kanzi is said to "tell" another bonobo something, the critic must question how, in fact, Kanzi can "tell" another bonobo anything. If Kanzi is truly "telling" Tamuli something upon my request, then his behavior cannot be interpreted, under the assumption that apes use language only for their own ends or for a "reward." That is, if Kanzi can "tell" Tamuli things that I request, it implies that he fully understands the function and value of language and that he uses language to pass ideas from the mind of one party (himself) to another, his sister Tamuli. There can be no other viable explanation for why Kanzi can tell Tamuli something. But since, under fallacy E, this cannot happen, the credibility of the individual reporting the event must be questioned. Having dismissed all examples as "anecdotes" under fallacy D, it now becomes possible for the critic to question how it is that I know my interpretation of this "anecdote" is accurate.

There is really little to "interpret" about the fact that Kanzi vocalized to Tamuli and Tamuli gave me my keys. One can "interpret" this only in one of two ways. Either it is a chance set of events or else Kanzi told Tamuli to give me my keys. Whether we conclude that apes have language or not is really a matter of what we choose to accept as an instance of data. By setting the criterion for apes higher than that we set for ourselves, the critic can remain certain that apes and other animals do not possess language.

Fallacy F

This fallacy asserts that because ape-language researchers disagree about the abilities of apes, apes must not be capable of true language. In taking this stance, the critic disregards the fact that scientists in all fields often honestly and openly disagree about findings. Indeed, honest disagreement is offered as the process by which Science itself advances. In the field of ape language, however, critics have used the existence of disagreements as reason to abandon the endeavor completely. They characterize ape-language researchers as "attacking" each other. By calling disagreements "attacks" rather than acknowledging that they are part of the scientific process, the critic avoids the need to seriously consider the points of agreement that have been reached by researchers in this field.

The critic employs this tactic to move important findings out of focus and dismiss them, along with the validity of the entire field. This maneuver has been aided by the fact that animal-language researchers compete for extremely limited funds and thus begin to view the inevitable disagreements among themselves as threatening the survival of their projects and the very lives of their research "subjects." After talking with an ape for many years, it becomes difficult to view it as a "subject," and one feels obligated to ensure it a meaningful existence.

Fallacy G

This fallacy is the accusation of anthropomorphism. When researchers reason from their own interpretation of a situation to that of the ape, they are said to commit the error of anthropomorphism. Thus, my concluding that Panbanisha used the word "mushroom" to refer to a person with a hairdo like a mushroom cannot be taken seriously because it is something I myself might do, and thus I am being "anthropomorphic."

The reason this is a fallacy is that the only means we have of understanding what any other person is saying to us is by relating to that party as if we were able, at least in part, to take his or her perspective. There really is no other means of understanding what another individual is saying.

When a critic denies to the animal-language researcher the right to assume that he or she can assess the ape's utterances, it becomes impossible for the researcher to impute meaning to any conversation with an ape. And if meaning cannot be imputed, conversations cannot take place. Therefore, there is no way the animal-language researcher can talk with an animal and not engage in what is called anthropomorphism.

Fallacy H

This fallacy assumes that it is impossible for apes to recall or communicate about past events because no test of such an activity can be validly set forth. In part this fallacy derives from fallacy E, because if apes can communicate only for rewards, it follows logically that they cannot discuss past events, for no immediate reward could ensue upon the mention of a past event.

Acceptance of this fallacy means that no action on the part of the ape can be interpreted as a reference to a past event unless it can be proved that the ape is thinking about and referring to the past event at the time of the utterance. The nature of the thought behind an utterance can never be proved, for human or animal. All that is available to another mind is the utterance itself, unless we assume that thought transference is a real possibility.

Like many of the other fallacies, this one makes an assumption that, if accepted, blinds the critic to any interpretation of the data other than the one deemed acceptable prior to data collection. That is, fallacies such as this ensure that the nature of the data about animal language will have no effect upon the conclusions that are to be drawn.

Fallacy I

This fallacy asserts that if an ape is raised in a manner that permits it to acquire something like language, its normal "ape behavior" will not be permitted to flower and it will become a psychologically devastated animal. Generally, this fallacy assumes that any ape exposed to a human language will become abnormal as a direct result of the exposure. It is true that the first ape "subjects," Washoe, Lana, and Sarah, were not permitted to be around other apes, and so the view developed that it was impossible to learn to communicate with normal human beings and be an ape as well. It is not necessary, however, that an ape be isolated from other apes or that it forgo normal ape behavior in order to learn a human communication system. Kanzi and Panbanisha have lived in social groups throughout their lives.

It is also not the case that exposure to human beings renders apes into totally unnatural creatures. This depends upon the nature of their interactions with people. Apes, like humans, can exist in a wide variety of environments and remain "apes." Similarly, human beings can exist in rural Congo or Manhattan. One does not declare that human behavior in either location is unnatural, even though it varies greatly and even though humans did not "always live there." We simply say that such variation is part of the definition of the human species and something we are capable of doing. When an ape's behavior is very different in New York from in the Congo, however, it is often said that the ape in New York is "screwed up" and the one in the Congo is normal. Why, then, do we not say that the behavior of people in rural Congo is more natural and normal than the behavior of people in New York?

The behavior of both ape and human is infinitely adaptable, and what is "normal" in any location is simply the strategy that a majority of group members has evolved to deal with changing environmental patterns.

Fallacy J

The argument of fallacy J is that even if one accepts all claims regarding Kanzi, they are of little consequence, because we humans acquired language without a model, and the central question of interest to Science is, how did human language emerge? Since the data from Kanzi do not speak to that question, they are said to have little relevance for Science.

As Kanzi's abilities become fully understood and realized, it will be recognized that the question of how humans alone came to invent language is based on our ignorance of the true capacities inherent in animal intelligences. Since the rise of modern Science, humans have assumed that language is a uniquely human capacity. No scientists have begun to fully study linguistic skills in any other animal. If they did, their work would not be published by a reputable scientific press.

THE MESSAGE IN KANZI'S ACCOMPLISHMENT

Kanzi provides a direct challenge to the adequacy of the belief that the communication systems of humans and other creatures differ fundamentally. Kanzi's mind permitted him to grasp our language. His mind did not evolve in the matter of a few years. Language is not unique to humans, and Kanzi would have been able to acquire it in the wild as well if other bonobos were using it there (Savage-Rumbaugh and Lewin 1994; Savage-Rumbaugh et al. 1996). What sort of language might they be using there?

Wilcox (this volume) suggests that any visible action or audible sound can become singled out and emerge as a semantically meaningfully unit. With repetition, it will become divorced from its original context of usage. Once this has occurred, the semantic unit is free to combine with others to convey new meanings. Wilcox notes that these capacities, which in his framework are all that are required for the emergence of language, fall well within the capacities of other creatures. Given this, he too concludes that language is probably not uniquely human.

Students of nonhuman primate communication have long recognized that certain sounds and gestures can occur in many different contexts and combinations, and they are repeated and even appear to form the basis of some stylized or ritualized communications between individuals. There is a great hesitancy, however, to view such signals as related to language (but see King 1994a), because it assumed that they are unmotivated—that is, they are not produced intentionally for a purpose, with the full awareness of the animals. Instead, they are assumed to be drawn from the animal unconsciously by the environment, through a process of conditioning.

Students of animal communication were not always of such persuasion. When Garner (1896) went to the field, he locked himself in a cage in the forest for the express purpose of studying the language of monkeys and apes. But that was before the withering attacks on Romanes for anecdotal evidence and the rise of Watson (1919) and behaviorism. It was before Thorndike's (1889) cat made of us aware of the subtle nature of trial-and-effort learning and before Skinner's (1969) pigeons made us aware of superstitious behavior and the conditioning of complex behavioral chains.

We now assume that because animals sometimes behave without comprehending the goals of their actions in laboratory experiments (as do we humans), animals are in fact unable to do so. When they appear to be smart—that is, when they appear to do things with intuition, insight, understanding, and purpose—we have been taught to assure ourselves that appearances are deceiving, and they really do not know what they are doing.

These myopic views have made it unnecessary for those studying primate communication to explain the true complexities of nonhuman primate vocalizations. By assuming that language is not extant in these animals and by terming the vocalizations of other primates "calls" and ours "language," we have solidified this view to the point that questions about language in natural animal communication do not arise. What kind of Scientist would try to study language by looking at calls?

Why, in the face of such extraordinarily complex vocal and gestural repertoires, have primatologists been seduced into concluding that animals cannot actually be using language, no matter how intelligent the behavior appears? Field workers continually condemn laboratory studies and their conclusions, pointing out that the true complexity of primate behavior can never manifest itself in the laboratory. Why do they not simply say, "Hey, I see some things that really look like language—it looks as if those creatures are saying something to each other, and I want to find out what it is!" How can they remain content with simplistic "call" categories when their own eyes and ears clearly tell them something different every moment they are observing a free-ranging group of nonhuman primates?

The answer lies in our ferociously anthropocentric view of language. Listening to the smooth assertions of some theorists committed to views of human uniqueness (see King, chapter 2, this volume), students of animal communication have become bound to the notion that if any creature had language, that language should, in major dimensions, look, smell, feel, taste, and act like human language. Such a view is without merit from a logical perspective, but coupled with the opinion that "all animal behavior is conditioned behavior," it has encased our minds. Add to this the fact that animals do not use their voice boxes to "speak" as we do, and the conclusion has seemed inescapable that only humans "talk."

BEYOND THE SELF-INFLICTED LIMITATIONS OF PRIMATOLOGY

A clear realization is beginning to appear that more is going on during primate signaling than just the exchange of instinctual grimaces and expression of emotion (Hauser 1996). For example, Maestripieri (this volume) alludes to conversational exchanges of the "pucker" signal. Because, for intentional communicative purposes, signals are supposed to be embedded in context rather than freed from it (Peirce 1932), it is hard to see, according to a traditional view, how they can result in "conversation." Yet what Maestripieri is wrestling with is a way to take terms such as "signal" that are permissible within the field of nonhuman primate communication and use them in a new manner, one that actually alters the traditional meaning of the term. Maestripieri also observes that submissive signals such as the hindquarter presentation are displayed not only in situations with high risk of aggression but also in the absence of such a risk, suggesting an appeasing or pre-emotive function. Clearly, if a signal such as "hindquarter present" is being used in both aggressive and nonaggressive situations, it is a behavior that, according to Wilcox's framework (this volume), has been freed to act in a semantic manner. It will surely make many linguists uncomfortable to think about a "hindquarter present" as having information value rather than existing just as a "show of feeling."

Some calls of nonhuman primates have been asserted to contain "semantic" content about specific types of predators (Seyfarth, Cheney, and Marler 1980). This work, which utilizes the "playback" of auditory calls to conspecifics, has been replicated with domestic chickens, indicating that the capacity is not specific to primate intelligence (Evans, Macedonia, and Marler 1993). Hauser (1996) suggests that in the future, playback studies with more precise controls that are coupled with measurements of neurological function will enable scientists to begin to unravel primate communication. Although the communication system of another species can be probed with such a technique, it cannot be understood. The difficulty with the call playback approach is that although playback studies demonstrate that animals can make distinctions between calls and can respond differentially (looking up for aerial predators and scanning the surround for ground predators), most complex communications in our own species do not cause listeners to look quickly in a certain direction. The playback technique, as currently developed, is useless unless the vocalization being played back is about something that requires an immediate orienting response. Generally, one would expect communications to be about many other things.

"Playback" studies, though innovative, suffer from the same binding that shackles all other forms of study of nonhuman communication. They assume that human communication is the pinnacle and that other communication systems are inherently limited by comparison. Basically, the limitation is not so much at the level of communication as at the level of cognition. Although evolutionary biologists repeatedly point out that evolution proceeds in many directions at once and that no one species is its goal or "end point," nor does evolution "strive" toward a certain form, these assertions, having been formally stated, are abandoned when discussion turns to the issues of intelligence and communication. There, humans are assumed to be the undisputed masters, and it is assumed that something of a graded scale exists in the mammalian order, moving "upward" toward human communication.

What if, instead of assuming that animals are far less communicative than ourselves, we were to assume that they tell each other things, that they have complex goals and intentions, and that they purposefully coordinate their behavior toward deliberate ends? What if, instead of asking whether they have a "theory of mind" (Premack 1988), we assume that a theory of mind and intentions are prerequisites for intraspecific vocal communication to function effectively in group-living organisms that recognize one another as distinct individuals?

Why not take as the null hypothesis the assumption that there are no major differences in intelligence between closely related species? We can then attempt to refute this perspective. Revamping the entire study of primate communication would take little more than a shift in what we take as the "null point." It will be as difficult to prove that non-human primates do not have language as it is to prove that they do have it. We can design studies and test hypotheses from either perspective. Let's choose the one most consonant with biological data and assume that it is true unless proven false. Let's assume that animals communicate intentionally, that they know what they are saying to one another, that they care whether or not the message is received, and that they can communicate about complex events, perhaps even about events removed in time and space. Then let's proceed with the collection of scientific evidence in the usual manner by devising a hypothesis about how a given animal accomplishes X, Y, or Z. How, for example, does a macaque indicate to others where it wants to go, where it wants to sleep, or when it needs a certain food?

LIMITATIONS OF AN ANTHROPOMORPHIC BIAS

While worrying that we might anthropomorphize by reading too much into the utterances of animals, we unwittingly commit a far worse error by expecting that any language, if it existed in an animal, should be speechlike—that it should have components that correspond to phonemes, vowels, and sentences. Our particular vocal apparatus results from an anatomical restructuring associated with upright posture and thus is unique in the order Primates. We also have an unusual degree of voluntary control over our breathing—something evolution generally does not leave up to a voluntary system except in aquatic mammals. Adult humans typically are able to speak at any time, without regard to mood or to what is going around them. Infants are unable to do this; they speak or babble only when in the appropriate emotional state.

Bonobos and most other animals, like human infants, move constantly between emotional states. Their states dictate whether or not voluntary vocalizations are possible, but they do not dictate the specific vocalizations that will occur. In the wild, emotional states are prompted by the surroundings and are often adaptive. For example, quiet states tend to occur on the ground, when bonobos are most vulnerable to predators. Extremely noisy states tend to occur high in the trees where bonobos can outmaneuver any predator except humans.

The ability to produce and modulate sound at will is available to humans, to the parrot, to some dolphins, and possibly to elephants. For many other animals, it remains dependent upon arousal state (Lieberman 1995). Although the ability to produce sound may be state dependent, we have no reason to assume that vocalizations serve only to indicate state or that they are involuntary once the proper state is in effect. Failure to recognize the limitations induced by the effect of state and by differences in the basic structure of the vocal apparatus has led us to conclude hastily that nonhuman primates are incapable of language. A more accurate statement would that they are incapable of a language that requires (1) control of internal state, (2) control of breathing, and (3) sound modulations similar to our own. We have every reason to believe that they are capable of a cognitively complex language that depends not upon our parameters but upon very different ones (Savage-Rumbaugh et al. 1993).

Important differences between humans and apes include our capacity to exhale air in a controlled and sustained fashion and to control inspiration in a similarly sustained manner. It is difficult, for example, for apes to acquire the ability to blow up a balloon, to blow soap bubbles, to blow a bubble with bubble gum, to hold their breath under water, to produce a sustained sound at will, to produce vocalizations regardless of emotional state, to produce loud vocalizations only on exhalation (not inhalation), to produce ascending and descending notes as we do when singing, to whistle, to produce a sustained sound from a musical instrument such as a flute or recorder, or to whisper. Kanzi has acquired many, though not all, of these skills to one degree or another, but he is unusual in this regard. His mother, who was reared in the wild, has none of them, although there are anecdotal reports of bonobos whistling in the wild. Like language, all of these physiological capacities are acquired readily by human beings, with minimal practice. The only other mammals that have equivalent control over their breathing capacities are those that either live in water or that, like elephants, regularly submerge themselves in water.

A second anthropomorphic limitation in our study of animal communication has been the assumption that we must demonstrate that animals have minds, that they know that others have minds, and that they know that the contents of these other minds are different from their own before we can began to attribute intentionality to their vocalizations, gestures, and so forth. This egocentric assumption ignores the basic issue of why animals employ gestural and vocal signals to communicate if they do not intend to convey information to conspecifics. We know that nonhuman primates can withhold communications (Hauser 1996), and so we must assume that when they do not elect to do so, it is for a reason, not because of an emotion. It is generally argued that animals do not intend such things as sexual swellings to be communicative and that many things we humans do (such as blushing) are not intentional either. The point, however, is not that we can communicate things of which we are unaware; it is to question the assumption that nearly all human communication is intentional while nearly all animal communication is not. The amount of communication we human beings engage in without awareness is probably far greater than we dare acknowledge. Similarly, the degree to which animals are aware of their "nonverbal" communications has probably been severely underestimated. Female bonobos can, for example, under some circumstances, manifest a full swelling in a matter of hours upon exposure to a male, and they appear to be quite aware of the uses of such a swelling. Male bonobos, moreover, appear to have considerable control over erections and ejaculations.

No matter how hard we try, we can never prove that animals have minds. Similarly, we can never prove that another human has a mind. It is only because they "say so" that we accept that they do. Recognizing this fundamental limitation, Gopnik and Wellman (1994) suggest that humans are literally born with some understanding of their own mental state as well as the mental states of others. In their view, thought, as well as thought about the thoughts of others, enters the child's repertoire of skills before language. Children "know" that others have minds at a very early age. Intuitively, many researchers are willing to accept this view of human children (Hauser 1996), yet we remain unwilling to credit animals with a similar capacity. Once this "thought barrier" is broken, the seeming "differences" between animal and human communication will begin to melt away and we will wonder how we could have assumed them for so long.

A third anthropomorphic limitation lies in a nearly universal misunderstanding of the true nature of "meaning" and how "meaning" is transferred between individuals (but see Taylor 1994; Savage-Rumbaugh, Shanker, and Taylor 1996, 1998). We speak of meaning as being "in" a word, as if we could open it up and find little meaning packets inside. But we all know that when we "open" a word, we find nothing but strings of letters or bits of meaningless sounds. So long as we attempt to attach a specific meaning to a specific vocal unit or units, our study of the language of animals will fail. Our own dictionaries (a rather recent invention) and our written words trick us into thinking that words have meaning and are discrete units that we package and move around just the way we move bricks around to construct a building. If, as Gopnik and Wellman (1994) assert, human infants, before language, actually understand what is in the minds of others in some way, then meaning cannot be "in" words. Words are merely things that occur while we are in the process of transferring meaning and intent. In a similar vein, smiles, head nods, flashes of the eye, and so forth are things that occur while we are in the process of transferring meaning and intent. But "content" exists "in" none of them, and to search for specific content is an elusive endeavor.

How can it be that words have meaning if meaning does not exist in words? The answer lies in the trick that language plays on our minds. It lulls us into thinking that there are units of meaning packed into words, and the conventional wisdom is that somehow we come equipped as babies to decode this complex system so that we can function as proper adults within our community. Indeed, if we do not learn to decode it and to use it appropriately, we are not permitted to function as free adults within our community. But if meaning is not in words, then where is it? It is rather frightening to think that it might be elsewhere. But meaning cannot exist in words any more than it can exist in the smile, the eye-flash of understanding, the subtle posture. Meaning can exist only in the patterning of these things, and the patterning exists not within one individual but between individuals. Moreover, the exchange of patterning between individuals is typically so rapid that the "intent" or "meaning" cannot consciously control, plan, orchestrate, and emit the flow of gestures, glances, postures, words, and so forth at the rate at which they actually occur. They occur and are patterned between individuals at a pace that is ahead of our "thought" or our conscious intent—which can plan only a few actions, words, or behaviors at a time. We behave far more rapidly than we normally understand.

This is why writing is an activity so different for us from talking, speaking, and exchanging at a meeting. This is why our behavior at conferences is so different from the behavior reflected in our written papers. Our behavior, intent, and meaning at the conference are constantly being co-constructed. When we return to our own computers, we do not have to act so rapidly, so our own intent can return more to the forefront. We can write, edit, think, rethink, plan, write, and rewrite, all before someone else says or does something in front of us to which we must respond. And we can "try" to pack as much "meaning" into our little written units as possible. But the meaning still cannot reside there. All we really can do is try to arrange our little bits of scribble in a manner that will remind some other minds of others' scribbles and hope that our scribbles have reminded some persons sufficiently that at least a bit of intended meaning has jumped from our minds to theirs.

FUZZY SETS: BLURRING THE CONSTRUCTED DICHOTOMY BETWEEN HUMANS AND ANIMALS

What if we were to assume that nonhuman primates actually do communicate—would we then become able to explain their behavior at a different level? Would we fall off the anthropomorphic deep end and find ourselves reading infinite meaning into the most insignificant actions?

Not everyone has been bound by the view that other creatures are unintelligent. Take, for example, the report that follows, quoted from the largest daily newspaper in Uganda. The report was taken from a description by local people. Any similar description, if it were of human behavior and made by the same observers, would be taken seriously and the persons involved would be punished.

> Over 30 baboons on Wednesday attacked the home of a man identified as Okecho and strangled him. The incident took place at Busitema, near the Busitema College of Agricultural Mechanization in Tororo district. The LC 1 chairman of the area, Mr Alfred Okoth, said Okecho had killed a male baboon during the day accusing it of destroying his maize and banana plantations. A troop of baboons converged at Okecho's compound in the evening and "mourned like human beings," sending Okecho to his heels. The baboons carried away the dead baboon to an unknown place. They stormed Okecho's house that night throwing the door open and strangled him. They also plucked out his heart. "We thought those were rebels but when we listened to the noise they were making and the giggling, we concluded they were baboons and confirmed with their footmarks," a frightened neighbor said. When the *New Vision* reporter visited the scene, Okecho lay in a pool of blood with a large hole on the chest where the heart was pulled out and another on the throat where the voice box was plucked out.

Is it reasonable to say that this is just an "anecdote?" Should we dismiss it as a story manufactured by untrained minds? We have evidence that chimpanzees plan and plot murder and that they deface other chimpanzee victims in a premeditated manner (Wrangham and Peterson 1997; de Waal 1986). Maybe baboons, with the right sort of leader, are capable of the same type of behavior. In Wamba, people cited an instance of bonobos lying in wait for a poacher who had killed a member of their group. They were said to have killed him by cooperatively pushing a large tree down on top of him. But I was repeatedly told not to trust any accounts by the local people—to trust only what I could see with my own eyes. I did see bonobos cooperate to push trees over, and once one intentionally knocked down a 15-pound fruit over my head. If I had not moved, I would have been knocked out and possibly injured.

It takes a great deal of intelligence to engage in premeditated murder or revenge, which involves plotting one's actions and acting at a time when the victim is vulnerable. One must keep out of sight until just the right moment, realizing that taking the victim off guard is critical. Premeditated murder, particularly that orchestrated by a group, is as complicated and intentional an act as language. Similarly, premeditated tool use is a complicated act. Chimpanzees are known to make tools and carry them long distances, revealing that they are planning to use the tool at a later time (Goodall 1986; Boesch and Boesch 1989a).

And finally, there are observations of bonobos leaving trail markers for those coming behind them, to tell them the proper direction to take (Savage-Rumbaugh et al. 1996). Indeed, any animal that follows conspecifics or tracks prey must be able to "read" tracks in a representational manner, but we reduce all of this behavior to "following a scent" and assume there is nothing to study.

TOWARD A NEW SCIENCE—WITH ANIMAL LANGUAGE/MIND AT THE CORE

So long as the reasoning fallacies of the critic remain hidden, the study of animal language cannot advance as a field. Animal language must have the right to be treated like any other field of Science and to have its data taken as data. But to do so means that we must blur the traditional human-animal dichotomy to the breaking point. This is an unacceptable proposition in today's world.

So long as people are uncomfortable with the idea of extending intention to the actions and communications of apes, we will remain unable to hear the things that apes are really trying to say to us. Apes do not need to say any more than they have said; instead, we need to learn how to listen. If we do learn to listen to apes, we may find that other animals have much to say as well.

I do not mean to imply that there are no important differences between humans and apes. Rather, the potential of animals has been so vastly underestimated because of conceptions of what ought to be that we have prevented ourselves from understanding the cognitive worlds of animals as intriguing and baffling extensions of our own.

Even more poignantly, our preconception of who we ought to be has limited us from becoming the creatures we have the potential to be—creatures far more different from apes than we have ever imagined. That Kanzi can learn a human language if no one tells him otherwise and everyone behaves as if he can is a lesson for us about the vastness of things that intelligent minds can accomplish under the proper conditions.

We have made a mistake in assuming that the way we find the behavior of animals and humans around us is the way it must be. We have asked evolutionary questions about how societies and mind evolved to be the way they are, and we have asked comparative questions about what different animal forms are capable of learning. We have assumed that the reality of social behavior and intelligence is limited to what we can see—that there are biological limits to apes and humans that are clearly reflected in their "ordinary actions." We must cast aside this assumption.

The idea that the goal of behavioral science is to explain the natural world of humans and animals neglects to recognize that behavior can be transformed by what we intend it to be. Kanzi transformed his understanding of the world by intending to learn and utilize a human language—and he did this because his caretakers intended the same for him.

Would an ethnographic approach be preferable to that espoused by the behavioral sciences? It would be ideal if an ape informant could lead researchers into a bonobo group, translate calls for them, and tell the other bonobos that the humans were not a threat. This is unlikely to happen. I have been informed by comments from Kanzi and Panbanisha, to be sure. I have also become informed by attempting to imitate their vocalizations, gestures, and glances. As I do so, I learn better ways of communicating with them, and I become increasingly able to interpret their sounds. The adequacy of my "informed" status can be evaluated to a certain extent by my ability to negotiate the bonobo world safely, without being bitten or harmed. Were my interpretations often incorrect, I would be injured. I can vocalize to them and they vocalize back to me, and I "feel" as if I know what they are saying much of the time. I can translate these things for others and assist them in learning to work with apes. But the accuracy of my translation is dependent upon my past history, my role, my status within the group as well as my own view of the ape. There can be no external judgment or validation of the immediate accuracy of any of my interpretations, other than the response of the apes themselves. That, too, must be interpreted—if not by me, then by another person whose own views, histories, and biases will inevitably affect the interpretation as well. In the final analysis, there can be no absolutely "correct" interpretation, only reasonable and less reasonable ones.

The more proficient I become at entering into the bonobos' world through their vocal system and through bringing them into a comprehension of the human vocal system, the more complex their world becomes for me. What initially appeared trivial now looms large, with ill-understood subtleties. There is little doubt that the bonobos' understanding of their vocal system is far more detailed than I will ever grasp. My knowledge will forever be limited to something less than a pidgin. I know how to get around, to ask where to use the bathroom, to express what I want to eat, whom I like, and whom I don't. But the farther I proceed in attempting to cross the species boundary, the more the ethnographic tools begin to fail. I need more than additional experience—I need to open up capacities within myself that are either nonexistent or latent. If I were again a child and my brain were open to any sort of neurological wiring, perhaps then I could travel farther with this particular tool.

No matter how far the ethnographer goes into the realm of another species, the ethnographic journey is, at heart, a personal one. Yet because the heart of the scientific process is replication and public verification, the ethnographic journey can serve us well only by proving hypotheses. From there, we must move into a different realm, the realm of what some elect to call "hard data." But no behavioral datum is ever truly "hard," for behaviors do not repeat themselves the way inanimate mechanical forces do. When behavior acts that way, it becomes "stereotypic," something we do not desire in animate creatures. Behavioral data are always "soft" in that behavior never precisely repeats itself. Can we look to "anecdotes" or "patterns of anecdotes" to fill the gap? Can the "patterned anecdotal method" transcend the problems of both the "conditioned response" explanation, on one hand, and the "unsubstantiated descriptive account," on the other? I think not, for the patterns are groupings only in the mind of the perceiver, not the mind of the perpetrator.

Where, then, does one turn? The standard ways of testing hypotheses remain open to the ethnographer who has used his or her tools to generate a reasonable, albeit complex and partially intuitive, hypothesis. One must focus on specific concepts and skills, and one must approach them from a number of different perspectives, but the important point is to begin with hypotheses that seem to fit the overall knowledge and intuition gained from the use of ethnographic and observational tools.

For example, several months after Panbanisha became pregnant, one of the caretakers in the laboratory decided to ask her where her baby was. Panbanisha responded by pointing to her abdomen, which was of course correct. But did she really know there was a baby inside her? If so, this was certainly a complex concept for an ape who had never experienced motherhood, delivery, or birth directly, only vicariously. From interviews with others associated with Panbanisha, we knew the following: (1) No person had taught her to point to her abdomen when asked this question, or even rehearsed such a question-and-answer exercise. (2) No one had pointed to her abdomen and said, "Panbanisha, your baby is in there." (3) Panbanisha had been around her mother, Matata, when Matata was pregnant and had been told that her mother's babies were coming. She had observed three births. (4) Panbanisha had seen pregnant caretakers, who had told her they had babies in their tummies. She had subsequently seen them with babies.

Still, given this history, we needed to know more. Panbanisha had answered the caretaker's question, but could she answer it (1) if someone who did not know lexigrams and did not normally work with her asked it, or (2) if it were posed by a total stranger? Moreover (3), would she answer the question differently after the baby was born? And (4) could she answer other questions such as "How do you feel about having a baby?"

We found that Panbanisha could answer this question when others asked. We also found that as the time for the birth drew near and she watched a videotape of her mother giving birth, she attempted to look inside her vaginal swelling for the baby. She then began to point to this location when asked, "Where is your baby?" We know that no one had ever pointed to this area to explain that their own baby was either located or would be located there. Therefore, she could only have deduced this from observing her mother's deliveries. When she was told, while observing a sonogram shortly before the birth, that the screen showed a picture of her baby, she went to the mirror and began to look at her abdomen in the mirror. At one point, when the sonogram showed a distinct movement by the baby, she touched the point on her abdomen that corresponded to the movement on the sonogram. Since she had never had a sonogram before and had never seen one given, and since no one told her that the movement on the screen corresponded to a feeling inside her abdomen, she must have drawn this correspondence herself. Of course, she could have touched this location by accident or in response to the movement independently of the movement on the screen. Such behavior would have been unusual, because she did not generally point to her abdomen each time the baby moved. She had, however, experienced caretakers commenting that they felt the baby move in her abdomen, and she had seen them touch the location where they felt such movement.

Following the birth, when asked "Where is your baby?" Panbanisha always pointed to the baby itself, never to her abdomen or vaginal swelling. Had she been pointing to these areas out of habit in response to the question, there should have been no change once the baby was delivered. Again, following the delivery, no one rehearsed the question or demonstrated that she should point to her baby in response to such a question. The change was a spontaneous one on her part and occurred as soon as she recognized the baby. She did not recognize her baby immediately, however. He was born with the umbilical cord wrapped tightly around his neck, and he did not move. Only after I suctioned his eyes and mouth and he began to move did Panbanisha realize that he was indeed a baby. Her behavior toward him changed immediately upon this realization.

Panbanisha did not answer additional questions such as "How do you feel about your baby?" or "Do you like your baby?" To statements such as "He is a good baby" or "You are taking very good care of him," she responded vocally in a positive manner.

Did Panbanisha really know that a baby was inside her? Additional data would be desirable, but certainly the extant data do not fit a simplistic conditioned-response explanation. A cognitive one is more appropriate at this time. With additional pregnancies, perhaps other ways of exploring the issue can be devised. The question must be considered only partially answered at this time, because no other data exist on an ape's capacity in this regard.

But one need not limit exploration to such specific questions. A more intriguing and more global question is, How is an ape such a Panbanisha created? Certainly the tools of ethnography and observation are found wanting in this case. No matter how well we learn ape vocalizations and culture or how closely we observe apes in the wild, we will not come up with a wild bonobo who appears to comprehend the question "Where is your baby?" even before the baby is born. If we are correct in assuming that Panbanisha not only comprehends this question but also knows the answer to it, how did such a state of affairs come about? How did an ape learn a human language so that she could understand and answer this question? If language is innate, as Wally would argue, then we are left with only one explanation—language must be innate in the bonobo as well, and all my colleagues and I did was provide a particular language model onto which the bonobo "universal grammar" molded itself. If language is not innate, then there must have been something powerful about the conditions that were in effect during Panbanisha's rearing, such that they promoted the acquisition of complex skills of language comprehension. Understanding these conditions may help us to learn how language gets woven into our own lives and to develop methods of repairing this weaving process when it goes awry in conditions of retardation or autism.

One cannot interact successfully with apes unless one adopts an ethnographic perspective during one's interactions. But the perspective that guides the interactions is not what must be tested and verified, regardless of how interesting it is. It is a part of the method one must employ to develop workable hypotheses about the competencies of other species, as well as hypotheses about the mechanisms by which these competencies become developed. If one does not interact, as Lorenz (1937) interacted with his geese, it is unlikely that one will see things from other than an anthropocentric point of view. To humans, it is linear hierarchies, categories, geometry, objects, and time schedules that are important. To other species, it might be an understanding of seasons, magnetic fields, wind, rain, and coincidence. To the extent that we learn to live in the worlds constructed by other species, we can develop appropriately testable hypotheses regarding their competencies.

Current methodology begins with the view that other species have no linguistic skills, and the burden of proving that language exists in another species is placed on anyone who disagrees with the "current wisdom." Indeed, the evolutionary perspective offered in this volume as an alternative to the discontinuity hypothesis contains, hidden within it, a seed of prejudice just as deceptive as that hidden in Chomsky's (1965) universal grammar. It assumes, along with Chomsky, that there are special and unique aspects of human language that separate it significantly from the communicative skills of other creatures. The evolutionary perspective differs from the discontinuous perspective only in that it searches for an evolutionary story or ladder of sorts among the living primates.

If one adopts the evolutionary position, one looks not for language in other species but only for precursors. Of course, if one adopts Chomsky's position, one does not even search for precursors, and precursors are quite fashionable now. We must be careful, however, in aligning ourselves with one side or the other in this controversy, for to do so often obscures real and difficult questions. They are questions that cannot be investigated readily, and so answers to them are often framed in theory, or rather in opposable theories, since these are the ones that seem to generate the most interest in Science today.

Having been to the Congo and observed bonobos in the wild, I find it incomprehensible that they do not have language there. Not only is their vocal repertoire immense, but they also utilize subtle gestures, drumming on trees, clicking sounds made with the mouth, whistling noises, and vegetation in communication. They coordinate their movements in time and space in a manner that would be impossible without language of some sort. I think the questions for the future will not revolve around better theories or reconstructions of the communicative competencies of past times. We cannot know what happened in the past with certainty. The theories of the future will most likely revolve around understanding the communications and the symbolic and social constructions of living primates. The issues of interest will no longer reside in deriving unverifiable evolutionary scenarios about how we came to be as we are but in deriving rearing strategies that create individuals with increasingly greater skills and capacities for social and intellectual endeavors. We will become "tinkerers" rather than post-hoc "tale spinners." Sociology and the study of behavior and culture will become sciences as we ask how to build better social worlds rather than how to build better meat-packing machines, juice cartons, or nuclear reactors. Behavioral science will be judged, like other sciences, by its creations rather than by its explanations of cognitive structure or its ability to locate visual processing areas in the brain. Such locating, while interesting, tells us little more than does knowing that digestion begins in the mouth. Knowing this does not tell us what to eat for strong bodies. Localizing skills in the brain does not build a better mind.

Knowing how to rear an ape that understands language or how to take an autistic or retarded human being and correct his language deficits does build a better mind. But these are small steps compared with the those that wait to be taken once the behavioral sciences start to "tinker" rather than to explain. Evolution itself is, of course, the greatest tinkerer of all. It has produced us and the apes. Knowing precisely how it did so will probably always remain beyond our grasp, but we do know quite a bit about the material that evolution had to work with, since apes are still alive today. Things that move modern-day apes along the same road that humans must have traveled are inevitably revealing, but never definitive. Yet each clue we uncover is all the more valuable if it not only provides a small window into our past but also opens a door into our present.

Talking with apes is a very large door. We can get into their minds in a way that breaks down "species-isms" and lets us begin to see ourselves as they see us. We should not shun this door for want of universal grammar, for fear that we will breed a race of "odd" apes, for fear that we may learn things about ourselves that we do not want to know, or for fear that the burdens and obligations may prove too great—though all of these things may come to pass. We should attempt to walk through the door and see what the path beyond species-ism looks like from the other side. We have so much to learn, and we hurt our relationships with all creatures when we shut out communication, assuming that we and we alone have evolved sentient language.

6

Language Evolution and Expansions of Multiple Neurological Processing Areas

Kathleen R. Gibson and Stephen Jessee

Ever since Aristotle stated that only humans possess a rational soul, the concept that sharp qualitative mental gaps separate humans from their animal brethren has dominated much Western philosophical, religious, and scientific thought. Twentieth-century scientific manifestations of this view have included repeated assertions of the qualitative uniqueness of varied human abilities (e.g., symbolic and syntactic capacities, tool making, self-awareness, imitation, deception, and culture) and habitual reliance on Morgan's Canon—the axiom that one must always interpret animal behavior in terms of the phylogenetically most primitive behavioral mechanism (Morgan 1894).

To be sure, these assertions have not gone unchallenged. Numerous studies now report that great apes have used gestures or visual lexigrams symbolically and combined them by means of syntactic rules, that they have used tools to make tools, that they have recognized themselves in mirrors, and that they have behaved in a deceptive fashion (see review articles in Parker and Gibson 1990; Gibson and Ingold 1993; Parker, Mitchell, and Boccia 1994). Scientific reactions to the challenges posed by apes have been varied. Many scholars, thoroughly wedded to concepts of sharp animal-human mental gaps, have redefined human cognitive uniqueness. Where it once sufficed to be able to make a tool and later to use a tool to make a tool, it eventually became necessary to use a tool to make a tool that could then be used to make another tool. Where once it was enough to use gestures symbolically, it became necessary to combine them syntactically.

Others, thoroughly indoctrinated in the techniques of modern psychology and Morgan's Canon, have focused on seemingly unending criticisms of experiments purporting to demonstrate ape abilities. The Nim experiment is a case in point. According to Terrace (1979), Nim regularly combined signs in what appeared to be a rulelike manner. The sign "give" always preceded the object that was to be given. The sign "more" always preceded the object or action that was to be repeated. Verbs always preceded objects. Terrace stated that these regularities in Nim's signing capacity could not be explained by rote learning or by imitation. He also stated, however, that they could not be interpreted as syntax so long as any other interpretation remained possible (Terrace 1979). More recent examples are criticisms leveled against mirror recognition experiments with apes. Despite published photographs of chimpanzees examining their faces in mirrors (Byrne 1995:115) and widely viewed videotapes of the gorilla Koko suddenly discovering her own blackened teeth during a bout of mirror self-inspection, some assert that there is still no clear evidence of mirror recognition in apes (Heyes 1994).

The combination of endlessly more rigorous definitions of human distinctiveness with ever more rigorous interpretations of experimental data will no doubt enable proponents of human qualitative uniqueness paradigms to continue to dismiss claims for the existence of humanlike skills in any ape, no matter how accomplished. From an evolutionary perspective, however, there are sound reasons to question such ready dismissals of the findings of ape experiments. Modern scientific data indicate a very recent phylogenetic divergence between apes and humans, as well as an overwhelming similarity between ape and human DNA and neural structures. Such findings imply behavioral and cognitive continuities and suggest that Morgan's Canon, at least when applied to the great apes, may be an anachronism more appropriate to pre-Darwinian, Aristotelian, and religious views of human uniqueness than to modern evolutionary biology.

To an evolutionary biologist, incessant criticism of the ape experiments often seems a diversion of attention from the key evolutionary questions—how human capacities evolved from those of the last common ancestor of great apes and humans and what precursors to human skills may be found in apes and other animals. Indeed, Darwin (1872) set the stage for a different view of animal capacities with his hypotheses that human intellect, emotions, and behavior evolved from those of other animals through natural selection and that the behavioral and mental differences between animals and humans are differences of degree rather than of kind.

In this chapter we approach great ape and human behavior from a strictly Darwinian perspective. We comparatively review the brains, anatomy, and behavior of humans and their closest phylogenetic kin, the great apes, from the perspective of probable evolutionary continuities rather than from a perspective of assumed human qualitative uniqueness. We suggest that quantitative differences in the size of the brain and many of its component parts distinguish humans from their closest phylogenetic kin, and these quantitative distinctions provide humans with increased mental capacities for differentiation of sensorimotor and conceptual schema and for the hierarchical construction of new schema. These capacities affect a wide variety of behavioral domains including motor, object-manipulation, social, and linguistic behaviors. They underlie most of the sensorimotor and cognitive capacities that distinguish humans from apes, and they account for many aspects of human linguistic ability. Hence, many human behavioral capacities often thought to be qualitatively unique can be interpreted as brain-size–mediated elaborations of capacities already present in apes.

These findings suggest that minimalist or other linguistic models which posit that few, if any, qualitatively unique mental capacities mediate human language are more likely to be correct than models that require the existence of numerous qualitatively unique linguistic structures. These findings also have clear implications for interpretations of the linguistic and behavioral capacities of early hominids. In particular, they suggest that quantitative expansions of multiple regions of the human brain allowed for the evolution of language, and the capacities to construct information-rich and hierarchically complex linguistic utterances may have increased in a gradual or stepwise fashion with increases in brain size.

THE VOCAL TRACT: DO DIFFERENCES IN PERIPHERAL ANATOMY ACCOUNT FOR DIFFERENCES IN SPEAKING ABILITIES?

The sounds produced by the human vocal tract reflect the size and shape of the laryngeal and oral cavities. Hence, one popular theory claims that differences in the shape of the vocal tract play a key role in human versus ape language abilities (Lieberman, Crelin, and Klatt 1972; Lieberman 1991). According to the Lieberman model, the ape larynx is situated too high in the neck to permit the proper pronunciation of certain vowels. Lieberman's presentation of this hypothesis is typological in that he implies that all apes have a similarly situated larynx—one in which the epiglottis always overlaps the soft palate. In contrast, all humans over one year of age are considered to have an epiglottis situated well below the soft palate. The result, in Lieberman's view, is that the laryngeal airway in humans is invariably longer than it is in apes.

It is interesting to contrast Lieberman's presentations of ape anatomy with drawings of ape vocal tracts based on actual dissections by Negus (1949). These drawings clearly show the tip of the epiglottis situated somewhat below the soft palate. Similarly, on the basis of his own dissections, Wind (1970) stated that in adult chimpanzees the epiglottis lies a few millimeters below the uvula. Nor is human anatomy as clearcut and invariable as Lieberman suggests. Our own investigations of adult cadavers in the University of Texas medical dissection rooms showed no constant position of the epiglottis with respect to the soft palate. In some cases the epiglottis was as little as 9 millimeters below the uvula, and in others as much as 30 millimeters (Gibson and Jessee 1994). In small children the distances would be expected to be much less. These data cast serious doubt on Lieberman's hypothesis that a specific length of the laryngeal tract or a specific distance between epiglottis and soft palate is essential for speech.

Others have noted that consonants may be more important for speech than vowels (Savage-Rumbaugh and Lewin 1994) and that human languages use an extremely variable range of sounds. Thus, an inability to pronounce a specific sound should not in and of itself prevent language or speech. What is probably more important for speech than the ability to make any specific individual sound is the ability to make many different phonetic sounds, to change them rapidly within very short time frames, and to coordinate them with breathing. Apes appear to be less capable than humans in these respects. These expanded human abilities almost certainly reflect changes in the neurological control of the vocal and respiratory musculature. They suggest that the keys to the evolution of both language and speech lie in the brain.

BRAIN SIZE IN HUMAN AND NONHUMAN PRIMATES

To date, no structures or tracts are known to exist in the human brain that cannot be found in the brains of monkeys and apes. Thus, although the possibility remains that unique structures potentially capable of mediating language may yet be found in the human brain, the preponderance of current evidence suggests that any explanation of human language founded on concepts of qualitatively unique human neural structures rests on tenuous grounds.

In contrast, definitive quantitative parameters clearly differentiate human from nonhuman primate brains and also distinguish various primate species. In absolute terms, the average human brain, as measured by weight or volume, is approximately three times the size of the average ape brain (table 6.1). Great ape brains are, on average, about twice the size of baboon brains, which are, in turn, about twice as large as the brains of any other monkeys and nearly 40 times as large as the brains of some monkeys. Many investigators have noted these relationships. Problems arise, however, in interpreting them. The large size of great ape brains in comparison with those of other primates would be in accord with much of the behavioral literature suggesting that great apes have greater tool-making, sign language, mirror recognition, imitative, and other cognitive capacities than do monkeys (Byrne 1995)—

TABLE 6.1

Absolute Brain Size in Human and Nonhuman Primates

Primate	Average Brain Weight (in grams)
Human	1,330,000
Gorilla	500,000
Chimpanzee	405,000
Hylobates	102,000
Papio	201,000
Other Old World Monkey	67,000–104,000
New World Monkey	4,500–108,000

Source: Stephan, Frahm, and Baron 1981.

if absolute brain size were considered a measure of neurologically based cognitive capacities. But some nonprimate taxa, such as elephants, dolphins, and whales, have brains larger than those of humans. Thus, the use of absolute brain size as a predictor of cognitive capacity does not place humans in the preeminent position. For this reason, many investigators have sought alternative measures of neural capacity.

Brain size correlates strongly with body size. Measures of expected brain size in relationship to body size also clearly distinguish human brains from the brains of all other vertebrates. Hence, brain size relative to body size has long been considered the best estimate of cognitive capacity. The measure of relative brain size most commonly used to predict brain size in primates is the encephalization quotient (EQ) derived by Jerison (1973) from regression equations of brain-body weight relationships in mammals. The extent to which an animal's overall brain size varies from predicted size for a typical mammal of the same body size is the EQ.

It is instructive to examine EQs in humans, monkeys, and apes (table 6.2). Humans have by far the largest EQ, over 7.0—one reason for the ready acceptance of this measure. The EQs of monkeys and

TABLE 6.2

Encephalization Quotients (EQ) for Human and Nonhuman Primates

Primate	Lowest Reported EQ	Highest Reported EQ
Human	7.39	7.79
Orangutan	1.63	1.91
Gorilla	1.53	1.76
Chimpanzee	1.48	2.17
Hylobates	1.93	2.74
Cercopithecus	1.66	2.18
Macaca	1.70	2.42
Papio	1.73	2.35
Cebus	2.54	4.79

Source: Jerison 1973.

apes vary dramatically, even among closely related taxa such as gorillas and chimpanzees. The highest nonhuman primate EQs are found in cebus monkeys, baboons, chimpanzees, and other primates that have eclectic diets and extract much of their food from matrices in which they are encased (Gibson 1986). Statistical relationships also exist between frugivory and EQ in primates (Clutton-Brock and Harvey 1980; Milton 1988). EQ, however, does not predict performance in mirror recognition tests, in tests of imitative skills or language capacity, or in common laboratory tests of primate cognition, in all of which the great apes seem to outperform monkeys, even the highly encephalized capuchins (Byrne 1995). That EQ may not be the best measure of cognitive skills is also evident from the dependence of EQ values on body size measurements. Body size varies in relationship to factors that may have little or nothing to do with intelligence, such as the size of the gut and the degree of muscularity.

Others, such as Dunbar (1992), have focused on ratios of neocor-

TABLE 6.3

Neocortical Ratios in Human and Nonhuman Primates

Primate	Neocortical Ratio
Human	4.10
Gorilla	2.65
Chimpanzee	3.22
Hylobates	2.08
Macaca	2.60
Papio	2.76
Erythrocebus	2.96

tex size to size of "lower" brain structures rather than on brain-body size relationships. The rationale for this approach is the common view that the neocortex controls intelligence while other neural areas control behaviors unrelated to intelligence. One measure that has recently gained prominence is Dunbar's neocortical ratio—the ratio of neocortex size to the size of the rest of the brain (Dunbar 1992). In primates, the neocortical ratio correlates with the size of the social group. Because Dunbar considers social group size to be a primary measure of intelligence, he concludes that the neocortical ratio is an appropriate measure of intelligence. Table 6.3, however, shows that the neocortical ratio also fails to distinguish monkeys from great apes. Hence, it fails to distinguish groups that many consider to be distinct from each other on the basis of cognitive abilities.

Other problems with the use of Dunbar's neocortical ratio are evident from an examination of the gorilla. The gorilla's cerebellum is unusually large with respect to its brain size. As a result, gorillas have a relatively small neocortical ratio, and on Dunbar's scale they appear to be intellectually impaired. In fact, the gorilla neocortex is larger in absolute terms than that of the chimpanzee or any of the monkeys.

Gorillas therefore should have neocortically mediated intellectual capacities equal to or greater than those of chimpanzees. There is no reason to believe that the enlargement of the cerebellum in any way diminishes those capacities. Indeed, much data suggest exactly the opposite—that the cerebellum may help mediate some intellectual capacities, including linguistic tasks such as generating an appropriate verb when presented with a noun (Leiner, Leiner, and Dow 1986; Peterson et al. 1988; Fiez et al. 1992).

It is also unclear whether the two premises on which the neocortical ratio is based are correct: (1) that the neocortex is the primary or sole measure of cognitive capacity and (2) that the ratio of neocortex size to the size of the rest of the brain is a better measure of cognitive capacity than is absolute size of the neocortex, other neural regions, or the entire brain. We now know, for instance, that the neocortex functions as part of complex circuitry involving both neocortical and subcortical structures. We know that subcortical structures such as the basal ganglia, cerebellum, hippocampus, and limbic system play major roles in learning and memory, and we know that the size of the motor tracts in the brain stem and spinal cord reflects the relative development of the manual and oral motor channels through which primates and humans express their cognitive and communicative capacities. These findings suggest that enlargements of entire circuits and of many interacting neural regions may be the better measures of overall capacity. In addition, all measures that involve ratios of the neocortex or cerebellum to brain stem structures commit the logical flaw of assuming that size of the motor output tracts within the brain stem is unrelated to cognition, communication, or language, even though motor structures serve as output channels for speech, gesture, art, and other communicative and cognitive behaviors.

We return, then, to absolute brain size as a potential predictor of cognitive skills in primates. As noted earlier, many researchers have discarded this measure as a predictor of species differences in intelligence, primarily because elephants, dolphins, and whales have larger brains than humans. Each of these groups, however, is now known to possess complex behavioral and communicative repertoires that may well demand great neurological capacity. Moreover, information

TABLE 6.4

Sizes of Selected Neural Structures in Baboons (Papio *spp.*), *Chimpanzees* (Pan *spp.*), *and Humans (*Homo sapiens*), in Grams*

Brain Structure	Papio	Pan	Homo
Medulla	5,297	5,817	9,622
Cerebellum	18,683	43,663	137,421
Striatum	7,182	12,246	28,689
Telencephalon	154,987	313,493	1,063,399
Piriform lobe	2,111	2,750	9,032
Septum	559	851	2,610
Diencephalon	9,280	15,392	33,319
Mesencephalon	2,711	3,739	8,087
Schizocortex	1,309	2,018	6,142
Hippocampus	3,398	3,779	10,287
Neocortex	40,142	291,592	1,006,525

Source: Stephan, Frahm, and Baron 1981.

Note: The brain structures listed are those in which all monkeys fall below all great apes and in which all great apes fall below humans. Papio and Pan were chosen to represent the upper size limit of each brain structure in monkeys and apes, respectively.

unavailable when brain size was initially discarded as a measure of behavioral capacity now suggests a prime functional importance of brain size. We now know that large-brained animals have longer lives, longer gestation periods, and longer periods of childhood learning (MacArthur and Wilson 1967; Martin 1981; Armstrong 1983; Parker 1990; Sacher and Staffeldt 1974). We also know that large brains are extremely expensive metabolically, especially during the period of growth, and can create potentially lethal problems during the birthing process. Hence, large brains would be selected against if they did not confer significant behaviorally mediated survival value.

Among the nonhuman primates, overall brain size and the size of the neocortex, cerebellum, diencephalon, telencephalon, medulla oblongata, striatum, septum, hippocampus, schizocortex, and piri-

TABLE 6.5

Correlations between Overall Brain Size and Sizes of Other Structures in Monkeys and Apes, as Measured in Grams

Structure	Correlation Coefficient
Telencephalon	.999
Neocortex	.999
Cerebellum	.986
Septum	.987
Striatum	.985
Piriform	.960
Diencephalon	.990
Hippocampus	.910
Mesencephalon	.970
Medulla	.960
Body	.940

Source: Stephan, Frahm, and Baron 1981.

form lobe clearly distinguish humans from apes and great apes from monkeys (table 6.4). These structures play diverse roles, including the mediation of both sensorimotor and higher cognitive information, emotions, and procedural and declarative learning. Statistical analysis also indicates extremely high correlations between the size of each of these neural structures and overall brain size and even body size, whether the data set includes solely monkeys and apes (table 6.5) or also insectivores, prosimians, and humans (table 6.6). Brain size also correlates with neuronal density, ratio of dendritic connections to neurons, and complexity of dendritic branching (Jerison 1979, 1980). In a series of 22 mammals, motor cortex size and size of the cortico-spinal tracts were shown to correlate with overall size of the neocortex and brain (Nudo and Masterson 1990).

These findings suggest that among primates, it is possible to predict the sizes of major neural processing areas and neuronal density

TABLE 6.6

Correlations between Overall Brain Size and Sizes of Other Structures in Insectivores, Prosimians, and Humans, as Measured in Grams

Structure	Correlation Coefficient
Telencephalon	.999
Neocortex	.999
Cerebellum	.990
Septum	.990
Striatum	.980
Piriform	.970
Diencephalon	.970
Hippocampus	.950
Mesencephalon	.950
Medulla	.890
Body	.800

Source: Stephan, Frahm, and Baron 1981.

from knowledge of brain size alone. Factor analysis confirms this suggestion and indicates that two factors account for approximately 99 percent of the variation in size of the brain and many of its component parts in primates, bats, and insectivores. One factor best defined as brain size accounts for more than 96 percent of the variation in the size of higher neural processing centers such as the neocortex, striatum, and cerebellum, and the size of the olfactory system accounts for another 3 percent of the variation (Finlay and Darlington 1995).

Taken together, these findings indicate that overall brain size in primates is a significant predictor of many neural parameters potentially related to cognition, learning, or sensorimotor skills. Although other factors may yet be found that are equally predictive of overall behavioral capacity, at the present time absolute brain size and/or the size of many neural components that strongly correlate with absolute brain size appear to have the greatest predictive value. Moreover, even if other factors are eventually found to predict behavioral capacity as well as brain size does, the major size differences between species will continue to exist. Thus, any explanation of the evolution of human language or cognitive skills must eventually come to terms with these size variations.

BRAIN SIZE: FUNCTIONAL IMPLICATIONS

Evidence that many areas of the brain have increased in size in the human lineage suggests that the evolution of language and other human capacities may have been mediated not just by expansion of one neural structure, such as the neocortex, Broca's area, or the basal ganglia, or by the acquisition of one new skill, such as syntax, but rather by coordinated changes in the sizes of many structures and tracts with diverse functions. In this section we focus on the functions of major structures that have expanded during human evolution, in order to determine what role, if any, they might have played in the evolution of language.

Neural Regions Mediating Procedural Learning

One structure that is clearly larger in humans than in great apes is the striatum, a portion of the basal ganglia. Another is the cerebellum. It has long been known that cerebellar lesions can result in slurred speech, and Lieberman (1991) reviews more recent evidence that neurological lesions in the basal ganglia may produce language deficits. Others have suggested that the basal ganglia, cerebellum, and premotor cortex play important roles in the mediation of procedural learning skills (Mishkin, Malamut, and Bachevalier 1984; Squire and Zola-Morgan 1988). Procedural learning refers to the mastery of habits, rituals, and skills that are learned slowly with much repetition and that are always used in similar contexts. Once mastered, procedural skills are seemingly never forgotten—for example, how to ride a bicycle. Almost any learned skill that is both habitual and automatic, such as automatically crossing the street on a green light, may be considered a result of procedural learning.

Procedural learning was first identified in laboratory animals such as rats and rhesus monkeys and thus is not unique to humans and great apes. That parts of the brain thought to mediate procedural learning are, however, absolutely larger in great apes than in monkeys and larger in humans than in great apes suggests a phylogenetic expansion of procedural learning skills in these taxa. Gorillas, orangutans, chimpanzees, and bonobos all use complex, learned motor routines in their nest-building endeavors, and they exhibit foraging techniques that appear more complex in terms of the organization of motor action sequences than do those of most monkeys (Byrne 1995). Possibly the expansion of the basal ganglia and cerebellum in the great apes facilitated the evolution of the ability to learn such skills. Even more advanced procedural learning skills underlie many human endeavors, including the learning of complex dance and sports routines and the use of tools such as eating and grooming utensils, vehicles, paintbrushes and other tools of the artistic trade, and musical instruments (Gibson 1996).

Many aspects of spoken, gestural, and written languages also clearly reflect procedural learning. Effective speech requires that pronunciation, routine syntactical constructions, and some vocabulary items be uttered automatically, without conscious thought about how to move the oral apparatus or about what syntactical roles to invoke. Similarly, those who are adept at gestural languages develop routine, habitual gestural movements. Most of us remember learning to write and the endless practice it entailed. Once mastered, however, writing becomes automatic. Considering the importance of procedural learning for varied aspects of linguistic communication, it seems almost certain that the evolution of language depended, in part, upon the enlargement of regions that mediate procedural learning, including the cerebellum, basal ganglia, and premotor cortex.

Neural Regions Mediating Declarative Learning and Emotions

Another region that expanded during human and great ape evolution is that encompassing the limbic system, including the hippocampus and areas of the frontal and temporal lobes that interconnect with limbic structures. This system mediates emotions, including emotional events that render learning more probable. In addition, the hippocampus plays critical roles in the learning of spatial relationships and in declarative learning—the learning of facts and information. In contrast to procedural learning, declarative learning is rapid, and the factual knowledge gained can be divorced from its original context to be used in novel contexts. Declarative learning plays a major role in the mastery of factual information pertaining to foraging (that is, what foods to eat and where they can be found), to environmental conditions, and to the composition and structure of the social group.

Declarative learning has been experimentally demonstrated in monkeys (Mishkin, Malamut, and Bachevalier 1984; Squire and Zola-Morgan 1988) and almost certainly exists in any animal whose lifestyle requires the mastery of factual knowledge of the environment. The human way of life places a great premium on declarative learning skills. Human hunter-gatherers must master large bodies of social and environmental knowledge such as the composition and structure of kin and political groups and the behaviors and spatio-temporal distributions of plant and animal foods. The enlarged human hippocampus and associated frontal and temporal lobe circuits may help facilitate this kind of learning. Declarative learning mechanisms may also play a major role in the mastery of vocabulary items. Most importantly, in the human species language serves as perhaps the primary mechanism for the social transmission and verification of factual information. Thus, irrespective of whether expansions of the limbic circuits played an integral role in the evolution of the neural substrates of language, expansions of these regions were integral for mastering the factual information transmitted by language. Indeed, without the expanded role of factual knowledge about social groups and environment in human behavior, it is doubtful whether language per se would have been selected for.

Neocortex and Sensorimotor Behaviors

The largest region of the human brain is the neocortex—a heterogeneous structure with a variety of motor, sensory, and cognitive functions. Several areas of the neocortex are considered to have expanded differentially during human evolution, including the motor and premotor cortex, the prefrontal and inferior parietal association cortices, and Broca's area.

The size of the human sensory and motor neocortical areas does not relate to the size of the body part innervated. Rather, it relates to functional capacity—specifically to the degree of fine differentiation of sensory and motor skills. For example, in humans the size of the neo-cortical motor and somatosensory representation for the hand and mouth far exceeds that for the trunk, arm, or forehead. This relates to our ability to make a greater number of highly individuated move-ments of the fingers, tongue, and lips than of the muscles of the trunk, arm, or forehead and to our ability to precisely discriminate tactile and other somatosensory stimuli applied to these areas. For example, most humans can distinguish between two points stimulated simultaneously on the tips of the tongue or fingers even if the points are only a mil-limeter apart. In contrast, to distinguish two points on the arm, the points must be two or more centimeters apart. Similar principles hold for other species. The neocortical representation for the tail of pre-hensile-tailed species such as the spider monkey is greatly enlarged (Pubols and Pubols 1972), whereas that of the hand is enlarged in rac-coons and that of the oral-facial musculature in animals with highly mobile lips and tongues (Welker and Seidenstein 1959; Welker and Carlson 1976; Welker et al. 1976).

That enlargement of neocortical sensory and motor areas should lead to greater sensory and motor differentiation is evident from a con-sideration of the possible functional roles of neurons and neuronal connections (Gibson 1988, 1990). A larger sensory or motor area potentially contains greater numbers of sensory feature detectors or motor output neurons than a smaller area would have, and it would also be expected to have a greater ratio of connections to neurons (Jerison 1979). The greater the number of feature detectors or motor command neurons, the greater the number of features or motor move-ments they can control. And the greater the interconnectivity between neurons, the greater the potential gradations between sensory and motor schemes. For example, an animal with five noninterconnected neurons controlling movement of the oral cavity would be capable of five independent oral movements at best. If these neurons were inter-connected such that the firing of any one nerve cell or any combina-tion of cells led to a different movement, then the number of possible movements would be, by simple algebra, 2^n-1, or 31. If the number of neurons was 10, then the number of possible motor movements in an interconnected system would rise to 1,023. Thus, as the number of neurons and degree of interconnectivity increase, the number of potentially independent movements increases exponentially. Increased size of a motor region is precisely what is needed to provide for unlimited numbers of movements.

All great apes appear to possess considerable oral and manual sensorimotor capacities, which they use for both communicative and manipulative endeavors. The presence of these capacities in humans and great apes suggests that the common ancestor of apes and humans also had highly developed manipulative capacities and enlarged manual and oral regions of the sensory and motor cortices. Human manual manipulative and gestural abilities, however, exceed those of the apes, and human speech places an extraordinary demand on the sensorimotor capacities of the oral cavity. For example, very tiny differences in the position of the tip or body of the tongue yield distinctive phonetic sounds, as do similarly minute differences in the position of the lips, uvula, and larynx. Hence, neurally mediated capacities to produce a large variety of tongue, lip, soft palate, and laryngeal positions are fundamental to the human phonetic capacity. An expansion of neocortical motor or premotor areas in the human lineage could well account for some of these increased capacities.

Although the ability to produce widely varied movements of the tongue, soft palate, lips, and larynx is essential for speech, by itself such mobility cannot yield speech. Speech also requires the ability to rapidly combine and recombine varied positions of the tongue with similarly varied positions of other speech organs and the ability to coordinate movements of the oral cavity with those of the respiratory system. Similarly, gestural languages require the capacity to rapidly combine and recombine varied positions of the fingers and hands.

Both the coordination of diverse oral or manual movements and meaningful, rapid, sequential changes in these movements demand parallel processing of large amounts of neural information that are held in mind simultaneously (McClelland and Rumelhart 1986; Rumelhart and McClelland 1986). Neuronal sequential processing in which one movement is elicited, feedback waited for, and then another movement elicited is too slow for speech, typing, aimed throwing, or other skilled acts. Sequences of sounds or actions must be planned in advance by multiple neural networks acting in parallel. Parallel processing of large amounts of information by multiple neural networks is also essential for the simultaneous combination of motor acts or sensory perceptions. Hinton, McClelland, and Rumelhart (1986), for example, postulate that a single neural network could perceive a chimpanzee or an onion, but the perception of a chimpanzee eating an onion requires two neural networks operating in parallel and some ability to construct relationships between the two.

The greatest increase in size of the human neocortex involves the so-called association cortices, including the prefrontal lobes, the inferior parietal association cortex, and the premotor cortex. Although these regions were long considered to be multimodal "association" regions involved primarily in higher cognitive behaviors, recent data suggest that they contain multiple sensory and motor regions (Kaas 1987). This multiplicity permits a range of sensory and motor processing functions. It may also provide for the duplication of circuits necessary for parallel processing of sensory and motor information. In other words, the expansion of neocortical association areas may have helped provide the neural processing necessary for the simultaneous and sequential combination of sensorimotor acts needed in order to construct fluent speech, gesture, writing, and other complex motor acts.

Certainly, much clinical information accords with the concept that these regions help mediate the construction of complex sensorimotor perceptions and acts. For example, on the basis of clinical deficits manifested by patients with bullet wounds to the head, the great Russian neurologist Luria (1966) hypothesized that the parietal and visual association areas function to hold several items of information in mind simultaneously and to synthesize that information to create new simultaneous wholes. He also hypothesized that the premotor area functions to organize motor acts sequentially in order to construct complex motor sequences, and that the frontal association areas function to sequentially organize more complex behaviors.

An example of the simultaneous synthesis of within-modality sensory information is the ability to simultaneously perceive and construct relationships among the separate parts of a painting or another object in order to perceive the painting or object as a whole. Patients with lesions in visual and parietal association areas often fail in such tasks (Luria 1966). For example, if presented with a drawing of a cross within a circle, patients with lesions in the visual association area may perceive the circle or the cross individually but may be unable to construct the concept that the circle encompasses the cross. Similarly, if they are blindfolded and a key is placed in their hand, patients with lesions in somatosensory association cortices may be able to discuss the shape of the object, its size, and its texture but may be unable to construct the concept "key" from the separate sensory perceptions. Examples of the sequential synthesis of motor acts include the ability, when writing or speaking, to move smoothly from one letter or syllable to another in order to construct entire written or spoken words or longer utterances. According to Luria (1966), patients with lesions in the premotor and adjacent cortices often fail in these tasks and repeat the same letter or syllable again and again. These findings suggest that the premotor cortex helps mediate the construction of separate motor acts into complex motor sequences.

Neocortical Mediation of Higher Cognitive Behaviors

Despite evidence that neocortical association areas participate in neural modulation of complex sensorimotor constructs, the major functions of these areas—at least in humans—appear to be in higher cognitive realms and to reflect cross-modal integration of sensorimotor information. Luria (1966) interpreted the cognitive deficits resulting from lesions of these areas as reflecting failure to synthesize multimodal sequential and simultaneous information into larger wholes (that is, in terms used in this chapter, to construct more complex schemes from individual units). For example, patients with lesions in parietal association areas might have difficulty dressing themselves (a skill that requires integrating kinesthetic and visual information), understanding directions and reading maps, or engaging in mathematical reasoning. Patients with lesions in the frontal association area might lack the ability to move from one complex task to another. One patient, for instance, lost the ability to prepare a meal because she

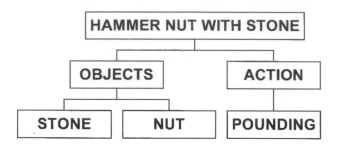

FIGURE 6.1

The hierarchy of mental constructions and relationships needed to use a hammerstone to crack a nut. Not illustrated are the varied visual and tactile elements that must be combined to construct the concepts "nut" and "stone." Great apes, some monkeys, sea otters, and some birds are capable of constructions such as this.

became fixated on single tasks such as tossing the salad and could not organize a sequence of tasks to meet the final goal of assembling the meal.

The failures of human patients with lesions in association and premotor areas to synthesize sequential and simultaneous information both within and across modalities are potentially informative about the behavioral differences among primate species that might result from relative differences in the size of these areas. Specifically, one would expect that species with larger frontal and parietal association regions and larger premotor cortices would construct more complex and information-rich sequential and simultaneous perceptions and actions. Several authors have, in fact, postulated that such behavioral differences distinguish large-brained animals from those with smaller brains (Gibson 1990), monkeys from apes (Byrne 1995), and humans from apes (Gibson 1983, 1988, 1990, 1993c, 1996; Reynolds 1983, 1993; Greenfield 1991). Gibson (1988, 1990) and Greenfield (1991) have also suggested that such constructions may often be hierarchical, in that newly constructed actions or perceptions may then be used as elements in the construction of still higher-order constructs.

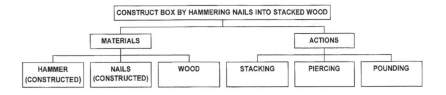

FIGURE 6.2

The hierarchy of mental constructions and relationships needed to construct a simple box from certain preconstructed elements such as hammers, nails, and wooden planks. Only humans have demonstrated this level of mental constructional skill, and only humans have demonstrated the ability to construct hammers, nails, and wooden planks.

In particular, large-brained apes seem better able than smaller-brained monkeys to organize multiple motor actions into hierarchically organized motor sequences (Byrne 1995). Humans construct even more complex relationships between actions, objects, and perceptions in order to produce hierarchically organized compound tools, athletic and dance routines, artistic designs, social organizations, theories of mind, and communicative utterances. Humans, for example, but not apes, construct tools that involve permanent junctions between diverse elements, such as a spear that is constructed from a wooden shaft, a stone point, and binding agents (Gibson 1983, 1988, 1993c, 1996; Reynolds 1983, 1993). These constructions are information rich in that they involve diverse elements, and they are hierarchical in that individual components such as stone points or wooden shafts are independently constructed and then embedded into the higher-order construct, the spear.

Figures 6.1 and 6.2 give examples of the objects and the relationships that must be created between them in order to use a hammerstone to crack a nut and to construct a box using nails and preshaped wooden blocks. The latter is more information rich, in that it requires keeping more items of information in mind simultaneously, and it is more complex hierarchically, in that there are greater numbers of embedded elements. Some monkey species and all ape species can master the first task, but only humans have exhibited constructional skills as complex as those needed to make a box. Historically, humans were first considered to be distinguished by the ability to make a tool, then by the ability to use a tool to make a tool, and then by the ability to use a tool to make a tool that could be used to make another tool. These progressively more rigid definitions focused on progressively more information-rich and hierarchically organized behaviors.

Similar information-rich, hierarchical processes are operating when humans construct the complex motor routines of sports and dance or their hierarchically complex social and political structures. Such processes are also implicit in certain interpretations of human and animal theories of mind (that is, that individuals can take the perspectives of others). For example, Dennett (1988) describes orders of theories of mind, each more information rich and hierarchically complex than the one before. In Dennett's scheme, a first-order construct would be "X believes that P." A second-order construct would be "X wants Y to believe that X is hungry." A third-order construct would be "X wants Y to believe that X believes he is all alone." In general, human performance exceeds that of the apes and ape performance exceeds that of monkeys in tests of theories of mind, as would be predicted from the hypothesis that greater brain size allows for greater information-processing capacity and more complex hierarchical constructions.

Although association cortices play integral roles in the construction of behaviors largely confined to a single sensorimotor modality or a single behavioral domain, the frontal and parietal regions have long been considered also to mediate cross-modal associations between sensorimotor modalities (Geschwind 1965). These regions emerge as the most probable coordinators of complex behaviors that cross behavioral domains. Hierarchical construction is also involved in such cross-domain and cross-modal behaviors, and many activities that are common to human societies but rare or absent in apes depend upon such constructions. For example, playing a game of cards or football requires visual, tactile, motor, and social syntheses and integrates the use of "tools" or other objects with complex social and motor routines and with the use of linguistically prescribed rules. In addition, the manufacture and use of tools in most human, but not ape, societies is profoundly social in nature (Gibson 1993c; Reynolds 1993). Such activities are far too complex to be mediated by a single neural region and no doubt require the coordinated activities of many brain regions.

Neocortical Processing and Higher Language Skills

Although some linguists argue that the brain possesses language-specific processing devices, it is clear that spoken, gestural, and written languages require information-processing, hierarchical, and cross-modal constructional capacities similar to those displayed in the other behavioral domains. Both neurological and developmental theories suggest that words are hierarchical mental constructs. For instance, the neurologist Geschwind (1965) noted that the ability to make cross-modal associations between sounds and visual images is fundamental to the generation of words. From the perspective of this chapter, such cross-modal associations make it possible to construct the concept "object name" from two separate items of information presented simultaneously—the object itself and the sound of its name. This accords with the perspective of the developmental psychologist Case (1985), who concluded from studies of young children that mental constructional abilities underlie the child's capacity to learn object names. In particular, a small child notes the object of a caretaker's attention, attends to that object, and simultaneously listens to the sounds made by the caretaker. The child then constructs a concept of the word from those diverse pieces of information. Gestural "words," of course, are also mental constructs, although the building blocks of gestural "names"—the object and its visual symbol—are both visual and thus do not require cross-modal association.

Words are not the only aspects of human languages that depend upon mental constructional skills. Words are embedded within higher-order hierarchical constructs such as phrases or clauses. These are embedded in turn within sentences, which are embedded within paragraphs and still more complex communications such as stories. As communications become more complex, they also become more information rich. For example, older children and adults string sentences together in an organized fashion in order to recount sequential events, construct stories, or describe distant objects and locations. Many of these more complex communications also exhibit a relatively simple hierarchical structure in the sense that single words or phrases are subordinate to an overall hierarchical structure. Thus, human language demonstrates hierarchical information-processing capacities similar to those seen in other human behaviors.

A critical question is whether or not human language requires cognitive abilities in addition to these general mental constructional skills. Some linguists (e.g., Pinker 1994) maintain that language has many unique properties such as syntax and passive voice that are unrelated to other cognitive domains and that require specific, neurologically determined syntactical capacities. Other linguists believe that human language can be accounted for on the basis of very few processes, most of which may be shared with other cognitive domains (see Wilcox, this volume, for a review of these two contrasting positions). Resolving disputes among members of the linguistic community is not within the purview of this chapter. What can be said is that some linguistic perspectives are extremely compatible with the model of brain-size–mediated, hierarchical construction, and they suggest that much, if not necessarily all, syntax reflects these processes.

For example, Berwick (1997), a follower of Chomsky's minimalist school, concludes that human syntax requires just three components: words, word features (such as sounds and meaning), and the ability to "merge" words and word groups into higher-order hierarchical constructs. We have already argued that words and word sounds are mental constructs produced by joining diverse units of information together (that is, merging). In his detailed analysis, Berwick further argues that the use of one complex mental process, which he terms "merge," can account for such linguistic "universals" as the joining of word parts into larger words, the joining of words and phrases into sentences and clauses, the affixing of grammatical suffixes to words, recursive generative capacity, the construction of routine or "core" relationships between sentence parts such as subject and object, and the ability to move words or phrases from one sentence position to another—as when changing between active and passive voice, when changing from a declarative sentence to a question, or when simply reordering a sentence such as "The guy ate the ice cream" to "The ice cream, the guy ate." Thus, in Berwick's view, "merge" is a neurological process that can explain most, if not all, aspects of human syntax.

Although Berwick does not extend his concept of the neurological capacity "merge" from the linguistic to other cognitive domains, from our perspective it is clear that "merge" could well be the fundamental process that permits the construction of relationships between diverse items of information processed in parallel and held in mind simultaneously. Thus it could underlie the hierarchical mental constructions that clearly exist in a variety of human and ape cognitive domains.

Wilcox's perspective (this volume) is also compatible with the mental constructionist perspective. He proposes 13 abilities that he considers essential for language. None of these is specific to language, however; they all enter into other human abilities such as object manipulation, art, music, and mathematics. Many, if not all, seem to be present in apes, if not in other animals, and none has been demonstrated to be absent in apes. Many mammals, for example, can make associations, detect differences between two more structures, and engage in selective attention. Two key cognitive skills delineated by Wilcox appear to be identical to processes described in this chapter and postulated to have expanded in the human lineage. Wilcox's "entrenchment" appears to be identical to what we have described as procedural learning, and his "composition," to what we have described as hierarchical construction.

Considering that some linguists have proposed models that posit few, if any, cognitively unique human mental structures and that are fully compatible with the mental constructionist approach, it seems incumbent upon those who continue to postulate language-specific cognitive skills to heed Wilcox's words (this volume): "The cognitive linguistic approach does not permit the linguist to posit a new, language-specific cognitive ability until it can be demonstrated that basic cognitive abilities are insufficient to account for some facet of linguistic behavior; no such need has yet arisen in accounting for any facet of language." If some unique linguistic structures and processes are eventually demonstrated, it will merely mean that the processes we describe account for many, but not all, aspects of human language. The finding of

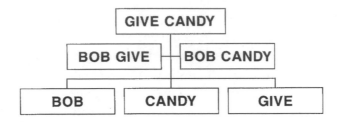

FIGURE 6.3

The hierarchical mental construction needed for a simple two-word utterance. The first symbolic constructions of very small children are two-word utterances like this one. Great apes have demonstrated the ability to regularly construct similar combinations of two gestural or visual signs and to do so with apparent combinatorial "rules" (Greenfield and Savage-Rumbaugh 1990).

such structures will not negate our basic thesis—that brain-size–mediated, hierarchical mental construction is a critical linguistic and cognitive process.

It is instructive to examine the claims of the ape-language experiments from the perspectives of hierarchical mental construction and overall information-processing abilities. It is clear from this work that apes do have some rudiments of "merge" and of hierarchical mental construction, because they can learn to recognize English words and English names of objects and to produce their own gestural or visual words and object names. They can also regularly combine two visual gestures or symbols according to apparent syntactic rules (Greenfield and Savage-Rumbaugh 1990), and they can understand English sentences of moderate syntactic complexity, such as "Make the doggie bite the snake" or "Go get the apple that is in the refrigerator" (Savage-Rumbaugh et al. 1993).

Even if the ape experiments are accepted at face value, however, without resorting to Morgan's Canon or other strict experimentalist criticisms, the linguistic productions of even the most linguistically adept apes, such as Kanzi, a bonobo trained to use visual signs in a languagelike manner (Savage-Rumbaugh and Lewin 1994), do not approach human linguistic production in terms of hierarchical com-

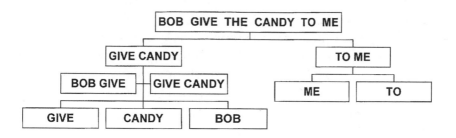

FIGURE 6.4

The hierarchical construction of a simple sentence. By three years of age, human children routinely construct sentences similar to this one. Although apes often combine three or more signs, they have never demonstrated that they can do so in accordance with any system of rules. The hierarchical constructional capacity required to construct a sentence of this type is far beyond that which has ever been demonstrated by an ape.

plexity or information content. At best, productive ape language remains information poor in comparison with that of even two-and-one-half- to three-year-old human children in terms of vocabulary size and size of mean length of utterance. Similarly, the most complex sentences produced by apes fall short of those routinely produced by two-and-one-half- to three-year-old children in terms of hierarchical constructional complexity. Figures 6.3 and 6.4, for example, compare two utterances exhibiting two differing levels of information processing and hierarchicalization. The first corresponds to a level of hierarchicalization common to human children who are just beginning to use two- and three-word utterances. The second corresponds to a level of hierarchicalization generally reached by human children by two and one-half to three years of age. The spontaneous utterances of language-trained apes often approach the first level but rarely, if ever, reach the second. In other words, in terms of the hierarchical constructional abilities that underlie language, even the most linguistically adept apes fall far short of the capacities of small children and do not remotely approach the hierarchicalization capacities of human adults.

One reason apes fall short of humans in mental constructional capacity may relate to overall information and parallel processing ability as might be exhibited in the form of working memory—that is, the ability to keep many concepts in mind simultaneously. It is now clear that in humans, working memory capacity underlies the ability to perform optimally on intelligence tests of varied kinds (Wickelgren 1997). Savage-Rumbaugh and colleagues (1993) have hypothesized that Kanzi may have less working memory than humans. Kanzi, for example, clearly performed less well than a two-year-old comparison child in tasks that required keeping two objects in mind simultaneously, such as "Take the apple and the carrots outside." The ability to keep more than one concept in mind simultaneously is an essential component of hierarchical constructional capacity. The other essential component is the ability to construct relationships between objects held in mind—that is, to "merge." Whether or not Kanzi and other apes also fall short on this ability is less clear from existing data.

Summary of Brain-Size Data

The functional implications of the increased size of the human brain and its critical neural processing areas suggest that human linguistic, technical, athletic, and social abilities reflect (1) the increased sensory and motor capacities essential for the precise pronunciation of phonetic sounds and the precise use of manual gestures and tools, (2) increased procedural learning skills, (3) increased information-processing and hierarchical constructional capacities, and (4) increased interactions among these diverse behavioral capacities. Thus, the evolution of language clearly reflects the coordinated evolution of many neural regions. Even if linguists or others eventually succeed in isolating a gene for syntax or some other critical linguistic parameter, such a gene could not, by itself, produce meaningful language in the absence of expansions of other neural regions.

MODELING EARLY HUMAN MINDS

The neural hypotheses we have presented hold clear implications for interpretations of the fossil and archaeological records. They suggest quantitative continuities between early hominids and the common ancestor of apes and humans in a variety of behavioral domains essential to the linguistic enterprise. Thus, they imply that models suggesting a sudden, all-or-none emergence of fully formed language at some point in the human fossil record are likely in error. Rather, language evolution was probably gradual or stepwise in nature (Gibson 1988, 1996). Fossil populations with brain sizes intermediate between those of apes and modern humans would also have possessed intermediate levels of information-processing and hierarchical constructional skills, which would have resulted in intermediate levels of linguistic, technical, and other cognitive capacities.

Although human hierarchical mental constructional skills underlie our advanced cognitive capacities and are essential to such behaviors as language, tool-making, and social perspective-taking, it is also important to recognize that the essence of human, as opposed to ape, cultural achievements does not reside merely in the possession of any one ability. Rather, the interaction of various human skills propels achievements in each behavioral domain to higher levels than could be achieved by expansion of any one behavioral domain alone (Gibson 1993b, 1996). Thus, human procedural skills such as dance, gesture, speech, art, and the manufacture of tools serve as means of acquiring and transmitting declarative knowledge. Similarly, accumulated factual knowledge permits the manufacture of ever more complex tools and other items of material culture, which lead to further linguistic and social changes. Thus, the cultural differences between humans and apes (or between various human societies) are far greater than can be explained simply on the basis of differences in any one behavioral domain (Gibson 1996). The interacting and reverberating effects of differing cognitive-behavioral domains in producing material culture render it quite possible that modern cognitive skills existed prior to anything resembling "modern"—that is, Upper Paleolithic—technologies. The interactive nature of human behavioral domains also indicates that modern cultural capacities required the evolution of fully modern abilities and accomplishments across an entire span of learning, sensorimotor, linguistic, social, and technical domains. A time lag in the evolution of any of these capacities could have prevented the emergence of fully modern human cultural capacities (Gibson 1996). Hence, the emergence of the Upper Paleolithic signifies the emergence of a complex, interacting, sensorimotor-cognitive-learning suite, not just the emergence of language.

An examination of the fossil and archaeological evidence enables one to determine in rough outline the emergence of increased cranial capacity (see Davidson, this volume). One can also infer the emergence of the sensorimotor, imitative, and planning skills essential for the manufacture of tools, along with the emergence of more complex forms of foraging. By about 2 million years ago, at the latest, African hominid populations of the genus Homo exhibited absolute brain sizes that clearly were larger than those of the apes. These hominid brains also possessed humanlike expansions of Broca's area and of the parietal lobes (Falk 1983; Tobias 1987). By this time, early hominids were also making stone flake tools with sharp cutting edges that were used for butchering game and preparing plant materials for use as tools such as digging sticks (Harris and Capaldo 1993). Although these tools differ only minimally from those produced by Kanzi (Savage-Rumbaugh and Lewin 1994), their regular use to exploit a new life-style represents some behavioral divergence from anything seen so far in wild apes.

Using this information, what can we infer about language in these early hominids? Certainly, the hand-ax makers possessed at least as much mental constructional skill as do extant apes, and perhaps more. Their linguistic capacity—the ability to make gestural signs and to combine small numbers of gestures according to rudimentary syntactic rules—would have at least equaled that of the enculturated apes. Such capacities, if realized, would have sufficed for the communication of desires, wants, and intended travel sites, just as the symbolic capacities of language-trained apes and very small children suffice for similar purposes. The critical issue is whether such capacities were actually used in this manner by early hominids.

Resolving the issue of when early hominids actually began to use, in a languagelike way, the rudimentary linguistic capacities inherited from the common ape-human ancestor requires some understanding of early hominid life-styles and the types of communicative behaviors they might have encouraged. Several authors have suggested that natural selection for rudimentary manual or oral gestural communication skills would have begun once early hominid young became dependent on adults for the provisioning of difficult-to-process foods, including foods that could be processed only by skilled tool-users (Parker and Gibson 1979; Borchert and Zihlman 1990; King 1994a). Under these conditions, young who could signal needs for food or desires for help in obtaining food might well have had survival advantages over those who could not. Such conditions might also have selected for the ability to imitate novel motor routines and for adults who took sufficient interest in their young to demonstrate tool-use and other complex motor routines. Indeed, the one clear report of attempted teaching by a wild chimpanzee in the Taï forest in Ivory Coast occurred under just these conditions (Boesch 1993; Gibson 1993b; King 1994a; Parker 1996). An adult chimpanzee attempted to demonstrate the proper method of holding a wooden hammer to one of her offspring, who was attempting to extract nut meat from a hard shell. By at least 2 million years ago, early hominids were regularly using tools for complex scavenging and extractive foraging tasks in environments in which the fresh fruits and leafy vegetation that serve as back-up foods for the young of most tool-using chimpanzees were scarce. These are just the conditions that would have encouraged foraging dependency by post-weaning young.

Others have noted the potential use of vocalizations to coordinate group travel (Maestripieri, this volume) and have suggested that a possible early selective pressure for rudimentary syntactical communications was the need to communicate group rendezvous sites among hominids who regularly coalesced and dispersed (Peters 1974). That such a function could have been among the earliest functions of language is evident from the behavior of both wild chimpanzees and wild bonobos. In each species, adults often disperse from and hours later aggregate at the same place (Goodall 1986; W. McGrew, personal communication, 1990; Savage-Rumbaugh 1996). Although the archaeological evidence remains tenuous on this point, it is plausible that the assumption of the scavenging mode of life represented such aggregation-dispersal circumstances. Hominids might have dispersed in search of carcasses and then informed each other of any that were located.

Thus, while there is no reason to assume the existence of complex language by 2 million years ago, these hominids most likely possessed the mental capacity for using simple manual or vocal symbols and very minimal syntactic rules. Their lifestyle may have provided them with the motivation to use such symbols to communicate desires for food, requests for help in obtaining food, or possible locations of rendezvous sites.

Somewhere between 2 million and 1.5 million years ago, an even more modern, larger-brained form of hominid, *Homo erectus,* appeared on the African scene. This form survived in Africa and parts of Europe and Asia until approximately 200,000 to 300,000 years ago. About 1.5 million years ago, *Homo erectus* began making hand axes—bilaterally symmetrical tools with sharp tips. Many early hand axes were crude in shape and may have been by-products of flake production (Davidson and Noble 1993a). Many later ones, however, were finely made, exhibiting regular geometrical proportions (Gowlett 1996). Some of them, such as those from the English Boxgrove site, were clearly used in butchering meat (Mitchell 1996). Indeed, in an interesting recent experiment, a modern butcher found hand axes to be ideal tools for skinning and butchering game animals (Mitchell 1996). Their construction was such that they could also have served admirably as throwing tools for the felling of prey (Calvin 1993). These considerations suggest that even if some hand axes were accidental by-products of flake production, others were clearly made to a predetermined form (Gowlett 1996), and that form had several outstanding functional qualities.

Examinations of hand axes make it clear that those fashioned to a predetermined shape required cognitive skills greater than any exhibited by apes, including the ability to make bilaterally symmetrical objects with strict geometric proportions and to do so according to a prearranged mental template. Wynn (1979) has gone so far as to state that hand axes required a level of intelligence equivalent to that of a child in Piaget's concrete operations stage, or about 7 to 11 years of age. Regardless of the actual level of Piagetian intelligence achieved by *Homo erectus,* its greatly enlarged brain size suggests that *Homo erectus* had more mental constructional and other cognitively relevant neurological capacities than do any of the extant apes.

How much of *Homo erectus*'s increased neurological capacity was applied to linguistic endeavors remains open to interpretation. One difficulty is imagining what can be communicated with linguistic capabilities intermediate between those of modern toddlers and modern older children and adults, and how such intermediate levels of communication might have been selected for in hominid evolution. Little research has been directed toward the pragmatic use of language in children—especially among children communicating with other children as opposed to linguistically sophisticated adults. Prior to about seven years of age, modern children lack the ability to communicate, by means of language alone, descriptions of absent objects or of previous events with enough precision to be understood by a listener who has not seen the objects or experienced the events (Piaget 1955; Karmiloff-Smith 1979). Apparently such communications require advanced syntactic skills such as the use of deictic modifiers, which some children fail to master completely until the school-age years (Karmiloff-Smith 1979).

What young preschoolers do appear to be able to communicate, according to Piaget (1955), is information about events, actions, and objects present in the immediate environment or known to both speaker and listener. Even then, much gestural demonstration is involved. Piaget notes that preschool children, when playing with each other, often engage in a kind of monologue in which a child states what he or she is doing—"I am coloring the car blue"—or wants the other to do—"You go there and do that." Considering the enlarged size of the *Homo erectus* brain, the complexity of the hand ax, and the simplicity of the grammar needed for such constructions, we have to assume that *Homo erectus* was capable of such communications, at least in the gestural mode. The question is, what types of environmental circumstances would have facilitated such communications? It has previously been suggested that a lifestyle demanding cooperation in endeavors that required individuals or small groups to assume divergent tasks might have fostered the need for linguistically simple communications of this type (Gibson 1988). Such tasks could have included cooperative hunting in which individuals assumed divergent roles, food sharing in which individuals agreed in advance to focus on differing food collection tasks, or cooperative shelter building. To determine whether or not *Homo erectus* actually engaged in such behaviors requires further archaeological analysis. It does appear, however, that *Homo erectus* had moved into a lifestyle with heavy reliance on animal prey and could well have been engaged in complex cooperative hunting.

Homo erectus and its descendants in Africa and Europe continued to manufacture hand axes for approximately 1 million years, until the emergence of Middle Paleolithic Mousterian tool traditions about 200,000 years ago. Mousterian tools, which were produced by both Neandertals and early anatomically modern humans from about 100,000 to 40,000 years ago, reflected two major technological advances: prepared stone cores from which multiple stone flakes could be readily produced and the hafting of stone points to wooden spears (Shea 1989, 1993; Churchill 1993). If Reynolds (1993) is correct that the creation of junctions between tools and between linguistic expressions evolved simultaneously, then hafting in particular serves as a clear sign that these hominids had far surpassed any ape in hierarchical mental constructional skills and had possibly attained modern human cognitive abilities. Since both Neandertals and early anatomically modern humans possessed brain sizes equal to or greater than those of modern humans, as well as an external brain form that was essentially modern (Holloway 1985), it is reasonable to assume that both had modern human cognitive capacities (see Davidson, this volume).

One common objection to this interpretation focuses on the anatomy of the Neandertal cranial base. As noted earlier, Lieberman (1991) hypothesizes that differences in the position of the larynx partially account for human speaking capacities as compared with those of apes. Our examination of the range of variation in ape and human laryngeal positions indicates that this assumption is dubious.

Even if the assumption of distinct, nonoverlapping positions of the larynx in apes and humans could be proved correct by means of solid scientific studies, this would not demonstrate a lack of speaking abilities in Neandertals. Lieberman's allegation that Neandertals could not pronounce several vowel sounds is based on analyses of the shape of one Neandertal fossil—that of La Chapelle aux Saints (Laitman,

Heimbach, and Crelin 1979). In Lieberman's view, the position of the larynx can be determined by the degree of flexure of the cranial base (Lieberman, Crelin, and Klatt 1972; Lieberman 1991). We tried to replicate these findings in cadavers in the University of Texas Medical School anatomy facilities (Gibson and Jessee 1993, 1994). We could find no correlation between degree of flexure of the cranial base and position of the larynx. Others have also questioned Lieberman's hypothesis on anatomical grounds (Falk 1975; Burr 1976; Heim 1989; Arensberg et al. 1990; Duchin 1990).

The primary anatomical support for Lieberman's hypothesis derives from the work of Laitman, Heimbach, and Crelin (1979). Laitman and his colleagues examined the exocranial flexure of the cranial base in an age-graded series of modern human skulls. According to Laitman, the anatomy of the exocranial base in human infants resembles that of the apes in that it is very flat. In his view, the flexure of the cranial base changes rapidly about the time the infant begins to babble and talk. Laitman also measured exocranial flexure in Neandertal and "Cro-Magnon" fossils. He concluded that the flexure of the cranial base in the "Cro-Magnon" fossils was identical to that of modern human adults, and the cranial bases of most Neandertals were within the range of variation of modern human children with full speaking capacity. The La Chapelle fossil, however, had an exocranial base anatomy outside the range of modern human variation. Even if taken at face value, Laitman's work provides no support for the hypothesis that the shape of the cranial base prevented Neandertals from pronouncing vowels, because most Neandertal skulls fell within the range of variation of modern humans with full speaking capacity. The La Chapelle fossil was fragmented when found and lacked critical points of the exocranial base, which had to be estimated by Laitman. Since Laitman's work, the skull has been reconstructed with a more highly flexed exocranial base (Heim 1989).

In addition, we replicated Laitman's study on a different age-graded series of modern human skulls, those in the anatomy laboratory at the University of Texas Dental Branch in Houston. The infant skulls in our series had a human, rather than an apelike, anatomy. Moreover, even Laitman's estimate of the degree of exocranial flexure of the unreconstructed La Chapelle fossil fell within the range of variation of skulls of modern human older children in our skeletal collection. Consequently, we conclude that the shape of the cranial base cannot be used to argue that Neandertals lacked full speaking capacity.

The other frequently invoked argument against Neandertal speaking abilities involves the Neandertals' alleged lack of art and complex technology, which are presumed to be indicators of spoken communication. Certainly there was an explosion in nonperishable art forms and finely worked stone, bone, antler, and ivory tools in Europe about 40,000 years ago, coincident with the arrival of modern humans (Mellars 1992, 1995). The technologies of anatomically modern humans and Neandertals, however, were highly similar throughout the 60,000 years or more of their coexistence, and traces of Neandertal art do exist (Marshack 1989). There also have been many nonindustrial cultures in historic and modern times that neither produced cave, stone, or other nonperishable forms of art nor used bone, ivory, or other complex tools. And of course millions of people in technologically modern societies can speak but cannot produce cave art or stone carvings. Indeed, children develop rudimentary symbolic linguistic facilities long before they can draw objects to a predetermined shape using modern pencils, crayons, paper, and blackboards. If the presence of nonperishable art forms or complex tools were used as a yardstick of language facility, we would have to conclude that many modern humans lack language.

That Neandertals had a modern brain size and external brain form, shared a common ancestor with modern humans for several million years after the ape-human phylogenetic divergence, hafted tools, lived in harsh environments, and occasionally produced jewelry and nonperishable art suggests that they possessed fully modern cognitive and linguistic capacities (Gibson 1996). The same can be said for anatomically modern humans during the period of 60,000 to 70,000 years that they existed in the Levant prior to the beginning of the Upper Paleolithic. The critical questions are, what in the lifestyle of these early big-brained forms might have selected for cognitive and linguistic capacities greater than those of *Homo erectus,* and what happened about 40,000 years ago that led to an explosion in technology and nonperishable art forms?

Work by Piaget (1955) and Karmiloff-Smith (1979) suggests that at about seven to nine years of age, children develop a more sophisticated use of deictic devices, and the use of such forms allows them to demarcate distant objects, events, and actions more precisely. Piaget writes about an explosion in the ability to use language to share and verify factual knowledge. This may partially account for the fact that cultures throughout the world entrust children of about seven with greater responsibilities and sometimes enter them into formal schooling. According to Piaget, children at about seven also begin to argue on the basis of facts. No longer do arguments such as "My Daddy is bigger than yours" hinge on mere assertion. Children begin to understand that factual knowledge can be investigated and verified.

Collaborations in the acquisition of factual knowledge are the hallmark of almost any modern human society. The sharing and verification of facts, perhaps more than any other features, differentiate modern human hunting, gathering, agricultural, and industrial lifestyles from those of the apes. Modern hunter-gatherers procure food over very large home ranges, often in dangerous environments. They require knowledge of weather conditions and of animal and plant natural histories far too comprehensive to be gleaned by a single individual. An examination of ethnographies clearly indicates that hunter-gatherers discuss such things as where salt licks are located and whether a tuber that an entire group has been watching for months is now ripe or has been eaten by a member of the group. They also discuss water and weather conditions and the behavior, location, and well-being of distant kin and tribes (Marshall 1976; Lee 1979; Silberbauer 1981; Smith 1981; Winterhalder 1981; Mithen 1990). Such discussions demand full capacity for language and declarative knowledge. False information about the presence or absence of edible items or about the locations of friendly and hostile tribes can be a life-or-death matter.

The question is whether the foraging skills of Neandertals, early anatomically modern humans, or the common ancestor of the two groups required such collective knowledge. Much evidence suggests that the skills of the Neandertals did. At a time when anatomically modern humans were still confined to moderate climates, Neandertals flourished in cold European climates and did so for at least 100,000 years. In-depth archaeological analyses indicate that European Neandertals intensely exploited relatively impoverished areas and readily adapted their foraging styles to changing environmental conditions (Stiner 1994; Kuhn 1995). They were also highly mobile people who opportunistically moved short distances in search of changing foraging opportunities. Thus the entire Neandertal lifestyle suggests intensive factual knowledge of the environment and hence highly developed declarative memory and linguistic communication skills. Early anatomically modern humans also practiced complex foraging styles demarcated by seasonal migrations to food resources (Lieberman 1993; Lieberman and Shea 1994). This lifestyle would have demanded intensive factual knowledge of environmental conditions and so would have placed a premium on the linguistic communication of factual knowledge.

If this analysis is correct, then both Neandertals and anatomically modern humans possessed advanced linguistic communication skills long before the Upper Paleolithic. A hundred thousand years from now, archaeologists may well view the emergence of the Upper Paleolithic in the same way we view the origins of agriculture or the industrial revolution. That is, neither of these technological revolutions required increased cognitive capacities or the emergence of a new species. Rather, technology and increased population density spurred their onset. It has been suggested elsewhere that the behavioral pattern we call the Upper Paleolithic can be viewed in the same light—as a technological and social revolution among groups that had long possessed modern linguistic and cognitive capacities (Whallon 1989; Hayden 1993; Gibson 1996). In particular, many of the technological and social inventions of the Upper Paleolithic may reflect new patterns of seasonal mobility and intensive seasonal exploitation of specific prey species.

SUMMARY

Comparative data indicate that human evolution was demarcated by the quantitative expansion of neural areas that function to provide advanced sensorimotor skills, increased procedural and declarative learning abilities, and complex hierarchical mental constructional abilities. Each of these capacities is essential for language. Thus, language evolution is likely to have involved the coordinated evolution of numerous neurally based capacities. That the brain had reached modern size and external form in Neandertals and early modern humans suggests that modern cognition and language had evolved by 100,000 years ago and that the Upper Paleolithic demarcates one of many technological revolutions in our species rather than the first emergence of language.

7

The Game of the Name

Continuity and Discontinuity in Language Origins

Iain Davidson

King (1994a) has shown that some adult nonhuman primates donate to infants significant amounts of information essential for their survival, without this donation's being identifiable as teaching. In reaching this conclusion, King recognized that there are so many similarities between nonhuman primates and humans in the process of information acquisition that it is preferable to consider the continuities between the two groups rather than the discontinuities. Despite King's observation, language appears to be a distinctively human behavior that represents a discontinuity within the continuum of primate communication. We might, therefore, ask for what purposes it is preferable to emphasize continuity over discontinuity. This chapter is about the evolutionary emergence of language and how evidence from nonhuman primates can be used in constructing arguments about that emergence. I argue that the very use of language by humans ensures that the emergence of language is seen as a discontinuity in an evolutionary process that can, otherwise, be understood as continuous.

I begin by emphasizing that language is communication using

symbols and that the arbitrary but conventional nature of symbols ensures that however shaded the meanings of words, their very nature makes for discontinuities in the descriptions of the entities they define. Language use itself, therefore, encourages analysis in terms of discontinuity in the evolutionary emergence of language.

Evolutionary arguments are historical arguments. On one hand, they concern the relationships of descent from ancestors that provide continuity between past and present. On the other, they concern the modifications arising during the process of descent that created discontinuities between past and present. I suggest that most historical arguments involve identification of discontinuities through the definition of words to describe the elements of historical processes.

Indisputably, there are differences between nonhuman primates and humans; otherwise, the category "nonhuman primate" would be meaningless. In consequence, assessing the evidence from nonhuman primates involves discussing appropriate ways to use the evidence of similarity and difference in understanding evolutionary processes. I canvass four types of evidence use: (1) the use of arguments from analogy; (2) the use of inferences about ecological function and evolutionary convergence; (3) the use of arguments derived from cladistics to define the features of the common ancestor from which modern African apes and humans both derived; and (4) the use of common features of primate behavior to provide the control circumstances against which claimed human uniqueness can be assessed. Consideration of how these arguments can be used in accounting for aspects of behavior suggests that each addresses causation at a different scale.

Next I examine some arguments about continuity. In particular, Dunbar (1996) elaborated an argument about the sizes of human groups and about the role of language in maintaining such groups. In doing so, he considered the common features of group sizes and mechanisms for group maintenance across a wide range of nonhuman primate species. There appear to be problems in identifying the size limits of groups to which nonhuman primates and humans each belong, but the important point is that these problems are not the same in both cases. This highlights a more general issue about the comparability of evidence between humans and nonhuman primates, owing to the ability of humans—and the inability of nonhuman primates—to describe in language what they are doing.

Discontinuity between humans and nonhuman primates is obvious, or no distinction could be made between the two categories. The issue is how these differences emerged—differences that are, at least in part, due to the evolutionary emergence of language among humans. The major source of evidence about that process of emergence is the archaeological record. I discuss in detail one of the sets of evidence— the pattern of changes in brain size since the time of the common ancestor we share with chimpanzees and gorillas—which shows that the process was simultaneously continuous and discontinuous.

In all of this I emphasize that the story we humans tell is strongly influenced by our practice of using language to assign names to elements of processes and to parts of continua. I close with a brief discussion of this practice as a defining feature of humans, who play the convention-bound game of naming. Through the arbitrariness of the relations between names and things, we can also change the rules of the game.

NAMING AND THE NATURE OF HISTORICAL ARGUMENTS

Once of the conclusions reached by Noble and me in our *Human Evolution, Language and Mind* was this: "The concept which is key to our argument has been distinguished by Terrace (1985) as the capacity to understand that entities can be referred to by use of their jointly known names" (Noble and Davidson 1996:224). What are the implications of "naming" for our understanding of the evolution of language?

King (1994a) classified our approach to language origins as a "discontinuity approach" (but see King, chapter 2, this volume). I have always thought that the arguments Noble and I developed were firmly grounded in evolutionary theory, which is essentially a continuity argument. Yet our emphasis on the symbolic nature of language requires a discontinuity because of the practice of naming, without which there can be no discussion of the archaeological evidence for language origins. Thus, ours is deliberately both a continuity and a discontinuity approach. Moreover, following the argument of Abler (1989), one of the essential features of language is its particulate nature (involving discontinuity between the elements of utterance—the names); it is this which permits the "infinite use of finite media." Discontinuity *within* language, then, is one of the features that establishes a discontinuity *between* language and other communication systems. Our task in studying the evolution of language is to see how this discontinuity arose "by gradation," in Darwin's phrase, from other aspects of nonhuman primate behavior. How is the discontinuity of language part of a continuous process?

Origins

It is possible to discuss the origins of language and mind from the evidence of archaeological research. As a crude characterization, it might be said that most historical arguments can be expressed as statements about origins. Clearly this oversimplification undervalues the study of processes of change, but many historical questions can be well characterized as a search for origins. Among prehistoric processes, this generalization would apply to the emergence of bipedalism, stone tool making and use, the habitual carrying of infants, handedness, hominid colonization of Asia and Europe, the control of fire, the use of shelter, secondary altriciality (the human pattern of prolonged infant dependency outside the womb), aimed throwing, pointing, the colonization of Australia or the Americas, symbol use, body modifications, art, the fisher-gatherer-hunter way of life, agriculture, pottery, wine- and beer-making, writing, urban dwelling, and metallurgy. Among historic processes, the generalization would apply to the emergence of printing, perspective painting, the theory of evolution, the industrial revolution, the railroad, the internal combustion engine, the telephone and radio, the transistor, and the microchip.

All of these features of the prehistory and history of humans represent discontinuities within a continuous historical process. Darwin's theory of evolution was the culmination of a long series of speculations by others about how variation in organisms might have arisen, as well as the culmination of a long gestation in Darwin's own thinking. But publication of *The Origin of Species* was an identifiable moment of appearance for the theory. Similarly, each of the prehistoric or historic features I listed marks a discontinuity between nonhuman primates and humans (even though wild chimpanzees use stone tools), yet they result from historical processes—processes of biological descent from nonhuman primate ancestors—that can be seen as continuous. The processes of emergence of each of these named features can be studied either as continuous processes of change or as stories of the origins of the named feature from a preceding state that could not be identified by that name.

What are origins? They are a product of naming, one of the distinctive features of language. Language as a means of defining arbitrary yet conventional categories splits the world up into manageable portions. In a historical sequence of human or hominid behavior,[1] an origin is where behavior that fits into one category changes enough to fit into another category. Usually, the behavior for which we seek an origin already has a name; often, the precursor behavior does not. One of the things we discover in approaching the origins of particular categories is that we know little explicitly about those categories, particularly about the behaviors that preceded the origin in question. Questions about the precursor behavior reveal how much of our intuitive understandings of certain categories are really the results of reifications of oversimplifications created by naming, as we can show by considering the origins of language.

In looking for the origins of language, we need to ask what language is. Importantly, "language" does not exist (and Taylor [1996] suggests that it had no origin). The word is a name used to describe the general category of communication among present-day people represented by the existence of separate languages, themselves reifications of ways of talking about the ordinary means by which humans communicate with each other in communities. It is, at least in part, a result of this reification of means of communication that leads to the question of whether or not this "thing"—"language"—is innate. Unmask the reification of the name, and the question (of what language is) is more difficult to ask but easier to answer. Language is not any "thing," but we use the word as a name for a particular set of communicative practices, namely, communication using symbols. Immediately, questions arise. What was communication like before symbols—what was the precursor behavior? What is primate communication like without symbols, and can it be considered similar to hominid communication before language? Is it appropriate to think of any communication outside human communities as language? Would any behavior without language be human? Are there any humans who do not use, and so do not "have," language?

Once we recognize that the study of origins in hominid or human behavior is really about how those hominids or humans changed their behavior from one named category to another, we recognize that the study of origins is about the practice of naming and about the conventional limits on the arbitrary boundaries of names. This is not to say that the study of origins is a futile exercise in semantics; in fact it is a valuable study of conventions—of the behavior of people who name. Somehow our discourse about origins has to get over the problem of naming—that is, naming creates discontinuities, however continuous the process.

In studying the evolution of language, Noble and I (1996) defended a definition of language as communication using symbols and a definition of symbols as entities that stand, arbitrarily but by convention, for something other than themselves.[2] Because language and symbols are tightly defined in this way, we are content that there can be no halfway houses. Something either is or is not a symbol. We eschew the range of apologetic quasi-categories such as protolanguage (something that isn't language but also isn't not-language), full-blown language (implying a precursor that resembles a partly inflated balloon), language as we know it (implying some sort of undefined language as we do not know it), and so on. This is part of the problem that Burling (1993; Davidson and Noble 1993b) identified in arguments about continuity between nonhuman primate call systems and language. Regardless of recent claims about referential communication in nonhuman primates (see King, chapter 2, this volume; Snowdon, this volume), there is no present-day continuity between nonhuman primate communication systems and human language. Over the course of evolution since the common ancestor of humans and other primates, however, there has been continuity (fig. 7.1). If we could be satisfied with names given to postulated precursor states, we could label the

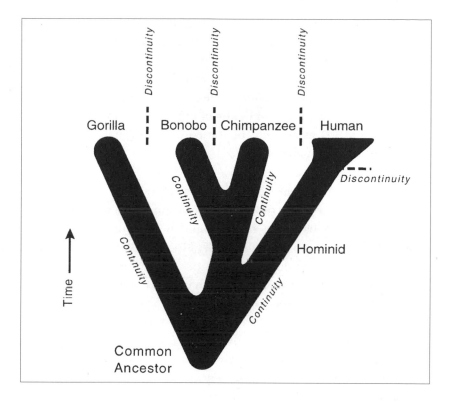

FIGURE 7.1

Continuity and discontinuity between human and nonhuman primate communication.

sequence of connections linking present-day nonhuman primate communication back to its precursor in a common ancestor at some remote date and then back up through the precursor communication states of ancestral humans to the communication of present-day humans that we know as language. Difficulty arises from naming language as an entity that has an origin and at the same time not naming a precursor state. Further difficulty stems from the absence of direct evidence for precursor states (before the appearance of writing). The nature and timing of passage through these states must necessarily be speculative, unless archaeological evidence can be pressed into service. The task for serious research is to reduce the degree of speculation.

Given that there is no continuity between modern nonhuman primates and humans, then the evidence from nonhuman primates can be used to discuss issues about human behavior only through some form of argument or inference. I identify four forms of argument here: (1) analogy; (2) the specification of ecological function; (3) identification of features of the common ancestor of humans and some nonhuman primates; and (4) assessment of the common primate baseline for some features of human behavior.

Analogical Argument from Nonhuman Primates

Others have considered the appropriate forms of argument in comparing the behavior of humans and nonhuman primates (see Hinde 1986; Tooby and DeVore 1987; Moore 1996; Zihlman 1996). The explosion of data on nonhuman primates over the last 20 years (e.g., Smuts et al. 1986; McGrew, Marchant, and Nishida 1996) means that anthropomorphism (Kennedy 1992) and mere metaphor (Fedigan 1982) can now be avoided.[3] In the case of comparison between humans and nonhuman primates, it is still necessary to ask what it is we are trying to infer and whether it is the humans or the nonhuman primates that are incompletely known. As Hinde (1986) points out, with so many species of nonhuman primates and with such diversity of behavior among humans, it is not difficult to find superficial similarities "to prove whatever one wishes."

I take analogy to be primarily a form of inference in which comparison between an incomplete set of evidence about situation A and a complete set of evidence about situation B can enable a plausible argument for the presence in A of some characteristic that is not directly observable, on the grounds that it is present in B (Davidson 1988). Analogy is one of the ways in which evidence from living nonhuman primates can be used to discuss evolutionary issues, particularly about the behavior of extinct nonhuman primates.

Analogies use chimpanzee (or baboon, or vervet) models to say, "If hominids were like chimpanzees (or baboons, or vervets), then..." The problems and pitfalls of such analogies are well discussed by Fedigan (1982), King (1994a), and Moore (1996). One problem concerns the functions of arguments that use primates as models for some aspect of hominid behavior. Tooby and DeVore (1987) distinguished between referential models and conceptual models. Referential models appeal to analogy. They take a single species, assume that some hominid ancestor was more or less like that model, and then explore the implications. Tooby and DeVore point out that these models tend to force an undue emphasis on early periods of hominid evolution, when differences between hominids and the model species might have been relatively small. Thus Tanner (1981), by exploring a chimpanzee model, raised new questions about the roles of female hominids early in hominid evolution. But because this is an analogy (and not a homology), such a model is primarily heuristic and is best controlled very carefully, preferably by reference to evidence from the archaeological or paleoanthropological record.

Arguments from Ecological Function

An alternative to referential models is the use of conceptual models (Tooby and DeVore 1987), which is akin to Hinde's (1986) preference for principles drawn from a range of species. One way to understand the difference between referential and conceptual models is to recognize that conceptual models, by explaining processes that apply to both the known reference species and the less-known object of comparison, offer theoretical reasons why referential models have some success. Referential models that are closer to the unknown referent in ecological circumstances and phylogenetic relationship are more likely to be conceptually appropriate if there is a theoretical argument about ecological determination of behavior (such as optimal foraging theory) or about phylogenetic inertia. In the best of circumstances, common evolutionary background makes referential models meaningful. At a much simpler level, the question of convergence may be crucial, particularly when making comparisons between species that are relatively or completely unrelated but occupy similar ecological niches (Altmann 1974).

As an example of the problem of convergence, we might consider vocalization. Some chicken vocalizations (Evans, Evans, and Marler 1993) are made under conditions very similar to those of vervet monkey vocalizations, a phenomenon we can hardly attribute to common phylogeny. These similarities may be due to common features of the ecologies of the two taxa: open country, small body size, and predators in the sky, in the bush, and on the ground. The distinction between convergence of ecological function and commonality due to phylogenetic descent is relatively simple when contrasting vervet monkeys and chickens. It is rather more difficult when reference species are more closely related. Thus we are more inclined to give credence to arguments for continuity of behavior between nonhuman primates and humans—because of common phylogenetic history—than we are to arguments about chickens and humans. But an instructive insight comes from interpretation of the ontogenetic development of communication among New World primates, which have been separated from Old World primates for about 40 million years.

In the ontogenetic development of human communication, there is a stage of production of vocal utterances known as babbling that usually precedes the production of utterances meaningful to adults. A wide range of parallels for infant babbling can be found among primates. In particular, Pola and Snowdon (1975; and see Snowdon, this volume) demonstrated seven major features of babbling in human infants that have parallels in the vocalizations of infants among the New World monkeys called pygmy marmosets. In marmosets as in humans, this babbling is closely related to emergence of the utterances of adulthood, and the process of emergence is strongly influenced by the richness of the learning environment of conspecifics. In this regard, Snowdon (1993a) suggested that patterns of ontogenetic development of vocalizations have as much to do with ecological function as with common phylogeny.

We might, therefore, seek to define in an increasingly specific way the ecological conditions in which communicative acts are performed, in order to identify the precise determinants of utterances. But this path is doomed. First, at base it is too deterministic, and there clearly are some aspects of volitional control in nonhuman primate communicative acts (however difficult the animals find these to achieve). Second, it is unlikely that ecological description can ever proceed beyond approximations. And third, the huge environmental range of humans (and the comparatively wide range of their ancestors during the last 1 million years or more) makes it difficult to introduce ecological functionalism into an argument about the emergence of a distinctively human communication system. We must take ecological function into account when arguing about primate and nonprimate communication, but we cannot easily base inferences about the evolutionary process of change in hominid communication on ecological function alone.

"Cladism" and the Evolution of Language

The approach Noble and I adopted in *Human Evolution, Language and Mind* (1996:chapter 2) was to use evidence from the behavior of nonhuman primates to construct an argument about the last common ancestor of apes and humans. We did this through an approach similar to the cladistic approach to identifying closeness of relationship among organisms (Groves 1989), a technique used by others with similar aims (Wrangham 1987; McGrew 1989; Cameron 1993; Byrne 1995). By this process we were able to argue that the common ancestor lived and nested in trees on the edges of the tropical forests of Africa, was rarely bipedal, and had a small brain and body size (equivalent to that of an olive baboon) but an encephalization quotient (a measure of brain size relative to body size) similar to that of chimpanzees. The diet was primarily fruit and leaves with some insects but no meat. Social organization involved association between females without alliances and often solitary males who had little involvement in rearing infants. Communication was primarily nonvocal with some limited vocal utterances, and both forms of communication were honed by observational learning and conditioning. Symbols were not part of these communication systems. The evidence on which these conclusions were based is summarized in table 7.1.

There are two problems with this approach. The first is that of distinguishing between common ancestry and convergence. The second is that of identifying the processes by which the differences between the common ancestor and the modern species emerged.

The first problem is illustrated by the example of vocalization. Rich interpretation of vervet calls could imply that semantic communication is very old, at least as old as the common ancestor of humans and vervets. This sort of argument would produce an expectation that apes

TABLE 7.1

Summary of Features of the Common Ancestor of Humans and Other Apes

Variable	Gibbon	Orangutan	Gorilla
Habitat	Asian tropical forests	Sumatra and Borneo tropical forests	Central African highland and lowland rain forests
Sexual Dimorphism	Little: F 5–7 kg; M 11 kg	F 37 kg; M 70 kg	F 70–100 kg; M 140–160 kg
Locomotion	Brachiation	Aboreal quadrupedal	Knuckle-walking and quadrupedal climbing
Brain Size	100 ml		470 ml
Diet	Leaves and fruit	Leaves and fruit	Leaves and fruit
Meat	No	Very rare	No
Tools	Very few	Very few	No
Nests	?	Yes	Yes
Vocalization Types	11	21	17
Nonvocal Communication Types	31	20	8+
Symbols	No	No	No
Social Organization	Monogamous	Solitary	Harems

Note: For discussion, see Noble and Davidson 1996:chapter 2.

Chimpanzee	Bonobo	Common Ancestor
Central African rain forests to savannas	Congo rain forests	Edge of African tropical forests
F 30–34 kg; M 39–40 kg	F 30 kg; M 40 kg	Probably avg. 19 kg
Versatile knuckle-walking and quadrupedal climbing	Versatile knuckle-walking and bipedalism, quadrupedal climbing	Occasional bipedalism
380 ml		210 ml
Fruit, leaves, and insects/meat	Fruit and leaves	Fruit, leaves, and insects
Hunting?	No	No
Frequent	Frequent	No
Yes	Yes	Yes
34	14	Restricted
37	47	Yes
Not really	?	No
Alliances among males	Alliances among females (weaker among males)	Closed society; little male parental investment

have a similarly "semantic" call system, but Mitani (1996) has argued that ape communications are not very semantic. One option here is that all of the nonhuman apes have diverged from the common pattern, but this seems implausible. The alternative is convergence on a gesture-call system of apparently discrete utterances for specific contexts, doubtless affected by natural selection in much the same way as the chicken call system.

The second problem is solved by appropriate inspection of the copious evidence in the archaeological record. Continuity is all too easy to claim when the only known parts of a process are its beginning (whether inferred by using an ape as a referential model or by working out the characteristics of a common ancestor) and its end (represented by some named category of modern human). There are few methodological options in this situation beyond drawing a straight line between the two points. Archaeology has the potential, albeit difficult to realize, to show in detail the stages in the evolutionary emergence of aspects of human behavior. We can improve on the simplistic drawing of a straight line (upward) from starting point to end point and offer more credible hypotheses about the gradations between. In particular, we can offer some evidence about whether these gradations occur in steps or along slopes. Snowdon (1993a) may protest that "conclusions about...language are highly speculative inferences that can probably never be confirmed or refuted," but the possibility of reducing the extent of speculation is something we can aspire to—and the archaeological record is a much better place to look than anywhere else (Davidson and Noble 1998). Conclusions from archaeological evidence, properly interpreted, should be no more hazardous than inferences about cognition in nonhuman primates. To suggest otherwise is to risk ignoring the best evidence there is, in favor of far riskier arguments.

Humans as Primates

Perhaps one of the most respectable uses of nonhuman primate evidence in the study of humans is in setting the primate baseline for what might be expected to occur in humans. This, I believe, is the important contribution of syntheses by, for example, McGrew (1992) and Byrne (1995): despite massive efforts, ingenious experiments, and meticulous fieldwork, the uniqueness of humans is intact. Defining a baseline in this way enables archaeologists to identify what signatures to seek in the archaeological record in order to reduce speculation about processes in the past.

Byrne's conclusion was that the difference between common ancestor and human is a "bridgeable one," but the bridge nevertheless spans a "gulf" between human and animal. Gibson (1993a) may well be able to defend a view that "few, if any, behavioral discontinuities appear to separate ape and human," but it is a view that needs defending.

No one now would defend a definition of humans as the unique tool makers, because Goodall (1964) demonstrated that chimpanzees also use and make tools—a finding confirmed by many others, to the extent that McGrew (1987, 1992, 1993) could synthesize the variety of ways in which the behavior of chimpanzees in making and using tools is similar to human behavior. It is now well established that chimpanzees eat the meat of other vertebrates (Teleki 1973; McGrew et al. 1978; Harding and Teleki 1981; Hasegawa et al. 1983; Boesch and Boesch 1989b; Boesch 1994; Stanford et al. 1994; Wrangham and Peterson 1997), although the appropriate naming of the ways in which they get the meat is more controversial. Similarly, there is a wide measure of agreement that humans can use symbols to communicate with chimpanzees in certain laboratory settings (Premack and Premack 1983; Gardner and Gardner 1985; Savage-Rumbaugh 1986; Savage-Rumbaugh and Lewin 1994), although the extent of success in these experiments is disputed by some (Seidenberg and Pettito 1979; Terrace 1979; Wallman 1992).

Whatever the interpretation of these data, the important point is that we are left with a catalogue of the features of nonhuman primate behavior that should be expected in the behavioral repertoire of humans. We might, therefore, expect humans to make tools as well as chimpanzees (McGrew 1992); to eat meat as frequently as chimpanzees (Stanford et al. 1994) but more often than gorillas; to have a communication system of vocal utterances (a "gesture-call" system, in Burling's [1993] telling phrase) as complex as that of vervet monkeys (Cheney and Seyfarth 1990) and more complex than that of chimpanzees (Mitani 1996); and to have social relationships maintained by some equivalent of grooming in the manner of all sorts of nonhuman primates (Dunbar 1991). But all of this tells us nothing about how or when distinctively human differences from this nonhuman primate pattern emerged. In particular, it tells us nothing about evolutionary processes in the emergence of language as a form of communication distinct from that of other primates. Evidence from the behavior of modern nonhuman primates may sharpen the focus of our understanding of features of difference observed in the archaeological record, but it is silent about process and timing.

Continuity, Discontinuity, and Types of Causality in Language Evolution

To draw together the threads of my argument about uses of evidence from nonhuman primates for discussing the evolution of language, I return to some old principles of questioning about animal behavior. Tinbergen (1951) specified that in studying the causes of animal behavior, it is possible to ask about four different aspects: (1) the behavior's proximate cause, (2) its ontogenetic development, (3) its evolution, and (4) its ultimate cause. It is these questions we might address in looking at the evolution of language.

Clearly, any language event can be described in terms of its immediate communicative intent (whether or not that intent is adequately described by the meaning of the content of the utterance). And describing the immediate communicative intent might describe the proximate cause of the event. Studies of nonhuman primates cannot get at the "meaning" of communications, but they may be able to specify the contexts of communicative acts precisely enough to show the sorts of proximate causes for some forms of communication. We should expect communication in such contexts to have been available as an option for early humans and their nonhuman hominid ancestors. They should have had a repertoire of gesture-calls in situations of danger, as well as other calls equivalent to the grunts and wrrs of interindividual intercourse among vervet monkeys (Cheney and Seyfarth 1990).

Much effort is expended in describing and analyzing the processes by which humans acquire language during their lives—the ontogenetic development of language (e.g., Lock 1980). That there is still a controversy about the innateness of "language" is testament to the difficulty of interpreting these data. Certainly, Chomsky's argument (e.g., 1971:122, 125) depended critically upon his assertion of the "poverty of the stimulus," the assertion that neither the positive models children hear nor the scarce negative corrections they receive are sufficient to account for the forms of language children learn. (This claim leads me to question whether Chomsky has ever brought up children!) And while this may be an underresearched criticism of the nativist position, the few instances in which the stimulus has been truly poor, as in the case of Genie, a severely abused child kept almost completely isolated from language from the age of 20 months to 13 years (Rymer 1993), suggest that language acquisition is not inevitable in humans. Moreover, by contrast, some languagelike communication has been demonstrated in interactions between humans and some captive apes. Importantly, the developmental circumstances of the enhanced communicative abilities of the bonobos Kanzi and Panbanisha suggest that appropriate developmental context may be crucial in the acquisition of language (Savage-Rumbaugh et al. 1993; Savage-Rumbaugh and Lewin 1994; Savage-Rumbaugh, this volume), and absence of appropriate context can result in an ape's failure to learn the novel behavior. Evidence of this type from nonhuman primates can provide control data showing that language is not innate, particularly where the relevant experiment on human subjects is beyond the limits of ethical behavior.

The position that language is innate fails fundamentally because it offers no well-formed argument about how language evolved (see, e.g., Dennett 1995). It seems to Noble and me that arguments about the evolutionary emergence of language might be crucial to understanding its emergent role in consciousness (Davidson and Noble 1989, 1993a; Noble and Davidson 1991, 1993, 1996). The difficulty for any argument about language origins is that all language users (including Kanzi and Panbanisha) acquired this special form of communication from other (human) language users. The first language users, being first, could not have acquired it this way. However simplistic this may seem, it still needs to be pointed out that the origin must, therefore, have involved at least two individuals who together discovered the symbolic potential of their communicative utterances. They must, in short, have been communicating beforehand. I regard this as a compelling reason why language must have emerged from a preexisting communication system. Noble and I have argued that this continuity was not necessarily with the gesture-call system (Burling 1993) but was perhaps with communication through iconic gestures (Davidson and Noble 1993b). The evidence from nonhuman primates is shadowy here, but there are rare instances of iconic communication among nonhuman primates with greater or lesser degrees of opportunity to have derived this practice from humans (Savage-Rumbaugh, Wilkerson, and Bakeman 1977; Tanner and Byrne 1996).

It is the behaviors of nonhuman primates which are rare that provide the clue to the relevance of nonhuman primates for understanding the evolutionary emergence of differences between humans and other primates. The reasons for this are straightforward: in an evolutionary argument, we take it for granted that for any character under natural selection, selection tends to operate at both ends of the character's range of variation, so that values in the middle of the range are more frequently expressed. Natural selection militates against rare characters. When selective pressure is reduced at either end of the range, characters that once were rarely expressed might be found in more cases. Thus, rare instances of what looks like teaching among the wild chimpanzees of the Taï forest in the Ivory Coast (Boesch 1991, 1993) are not themselves indications of the importance of this behavior for the particular animals, but they are precisely the stuff of evolution (Noble and Davidson 1996:42)—they are part of the variation of behavior on which natural selection might operate. Under changed circumstances (changed selective pressures), teaching could become an important part of the behavior of the descendants of these modern animals. By analogy, it is such rare behaviors of the ancestors of modern humans that led to the behaviors that distinguish us from nonhuman primates.

Finally, we move to the question of ultimate causes of language. This question is usually posed in terms of adaptive value, often involving interpretations of ecological function. This is problematic, given the domination of adaptive arguments by plausible, or "just so," stories for which there is little possibility of evidence. It is in this category that

I would place Dunbar's arguments about grooming, group size, and language origins (Aiello and Dunbar 1993; Dunbar 1991, 1992, 1993, 1996). Dunbar argues that considering appropriate subsets of nonhuman primates, there is a strong correlation between group size and percentage of time spent grooming and between group size and relative size of neocortical regions of the brain. Thus for humans, for whom neocortex size is known, it is possible to predict the proportion of time spent grooming and the appropriate sizes of groups. Because the predicted time is as high as 40 percent, Dunbar argues that language replaced the function of physical grooming as a means of ensuring group cohesion by reducing the cost of grooming.

The point is not whether Dunbar is right or wrong but that he demonstrates a method for using nonhuman primates in arguments about hominid and human evolution. Humans are considered in the context of the whole range (actually a selection) of primates and as necessarily involved in solving a range of problems of survival similar to that of other primates. The particular solutions are unique (language), but they fall within a range of solutions comprehensible in the context of nonhuman primates. Thus humans (and our language use in particular) again show both discontinuity and continuity with nonhuman primates.

The conclusion is that different forms of argument about the uses of evidence from nonhuman primates in discussions about the evolution of language seem to address different questions about the causes of animal behavior. At the risk of oversimplifying, it might be said that analogy equates roughly with proximate explanations, ecological function arguments tie in with ontogenetic development, cladistic use of primate evidence relates to evolutionary explanations of behavior, and assessment of humans in the context of the whole spectrum of primate behavior concerns ultimate causation.

THE NATURE OF CONTINUITY

I characterized studies such as Dunbar's as emphasizing continuity between human behavior and that of a range of other primates. Closer examination of this theory of continuity reveals some of the strengths and weaknesses of continuity arguments.

In his investigation of the relationship between neocortex ratio and group size, Dunbar was forced into the discovery of an important intermediate size grouping of modern humans of about 150 people. There is little acknowledgment that because these are already modern people, the existence of groupings of this size might depend on language. Johnson (1982) argued that in modern human groups using language, stress due to the scale of necessary communication increases with the size of the society in question. Various hierarchical organizational institutions have emerged to deal with the levels of disputation that may arise, presumably permitting larger group sizes. Fletcher (1981) showed something rather similar: that for fisher-gatherer-hunter communities there is a maximum population size of about 150, which is, in addition, limited by residential density. Moreover, in societies with fixed residential bases—mostly agricultural, trading, or industrial societies—the possible residential density decreases as population size increases, partly due to the spatial exigencies of communication: as population increased, for example, paths became inadequate to deal with the volume of traffic and became streets. Thus, I suggest, hominid and human evolution can be described in terms of the varying relative importance of unvarying vocal or gestural signals (like those of vervets), coded vocal signals or gestural signs (language), unfading coded signs (paintings or writing), transport of unfading coded signs (borne "in a cleft stick" by a messenger on foot, horse, or vehicle), and transfer of communication without a messenger (e.g., electronically). Whereas Fletcher (1981) emphasized the spatial importance of such different modes of communication, Noble and I have pointed to the psychological or perceptual importance of at least two of these communicative contexts: language itself (Davidson and Noble 1989; Noble and Davidson 1991, 1993, 1996) and literacy (Olson 1986). Presumably the perceptual abilities of primates with nothing more than vocal or gestural signals are different again from those of humans.

Dunbar argues that humans adopted language as a means of solving the problems of living in large groups with conspecifics. This does not constitute an argument about the mechanism of the emergence of the distinctive behavior called language. Group size maintenance through grooming may provide a selective context for the success of language. It seems plausible that language, when it emerged in a creature with an appropriate neocortex ratio, ultimately permitted a range of hierarchical organizational institutions and a range of innovations in communication: coded vocal signals or gestural signs, unfading coded signs, transport of unfading coded signs, and transfer of communication without a messenger. The process of emergence of these innovations was slow and variable (Davidson 1997a) but seems plausibly implicated in the extinction of nonhuman hominids.

All of which brings into play the problem of the identification of groups, since it seems to be a product of language use that the collectivities of about 150 people identified by Dunbar can be recognized as groups at all. Language makes possible the symbolic identification of membership in such a group without actual physical proximity. Without this sort of symbolic identification, it is doubtful whether such groups of humans could be said to exist. Indeed, I would argue in the context of this chapter that it is only the naming of the human collectivities as "groups" that makes it possible to compare them with groups of nonhuman primates. Whether or when such groups or such symbolic identification can be found during prehistory is open to much the same sort of speculation that Snowdon (1993a) deplored. Consideration of the archaeology of the earliest "art" from two continents shows that symbolic identification does not seem at all likely before the advent of language (Davidson 1997a).

Social Groups

One of the requirements for the evolution of separate populations that may turn into separate species is some form of reproductive isolation. This may happen through geographical separation when founder groups colonize islands or cross rivers or mountain ranges. It may also arise through behavioral separation of groups. Crucial here is the means of identifying groups. For most purposes that are of any interest to us (from our connection with biology and evolution), groups are usually identifiable by their members' coresidence and common use of space. Grave problems arise if we lose sight of this.

Boesch (1996) recently assessed the evidence for different party sizes among chimpanzees in his research region of the Taï forest. Parties are groups of animals that travel together, and their sizes in

Boesch's study varied from 1 to 41 members, with a mean of 8 and a heavy preponderance of parties of fewer than 15. But these parties were fluid, and the mean duration for which the members of a party stayed together was 17 minutes. Nevertheless, Boesch was able to ascertain that the parties he had studied belonged to a community of 76 individuals, the largest of 7 communities across the whole range of well-studied wild chimpanzees or bonobos. Although Boesch and others (Wrangham et al. 1996) can investigate meaningfully the determinants of party size, it is more open to question whether community size can be determined in similarly meaningful ways, given that it depends on the criteria by which human researchers recognize the limits of the community and on the modern ecological pressures that define the limits of distribution of primate species.

Interactions between individuals occur at several different levels, such that identification of groups may be contentious. Dunbar cites Hinde (1976) as arguing that it is "the observer, and not the animals, who creates the groups by abstracting an overall picture of the network of relationships that are the main concern of the individual animals" (Dunbar 1988:12). Although this is a process well understood among humans as they interact with other humans, where all participants in a group can name the group, it is less clear how group identity is understood or recognized for the nonhuman primate "groups" so named by ethologists. How do nonhuman primates achieve this abstraction, and how can ethologists determine that that is what the primates have done? In one attempt to demonstrate patterns of grouping, Goodall (1986) published data on patterns of association among the Gombe chimpanzees, from which she identified six different levels of association defined, for any individual, in terms of percentage of time spent in the company of another individual. Although these data might be susceptible to many different levels of analysis, the important question is how different patterns of association can be compared across species, and in particular how the comparison can be made with named groupings of humans. For how many humans are there comparable studies of the amount of time spent in each other's company? If Goodall's methodology were applied to humans, then for many people workmates would be seen to be in a closer relationship than sexual mates who cared for many children! But humans avoid potential confusion in this regard by naming relationships (for example, with kinship terms), which allows the maintenance of relationships without close physical proximity.

For humans, identification of group membership can occur through a number of markers that may have the effect of allowing group identification when individuals move beyond coresidence. In this circumstance, the group exists only symbolically. This sort of group identification is familiar to all humans in our habit of referring, while we are traveling, to family or friends "at home." The issue of what constitutes "home" is probably more complex than it seems, but the important point is that such an entity is really defined symbolically through language, and this symbolic definition is achieved through the naming of a place as "home." By the same token, it is difficult to see how studies of nonhuman primates can identify the sorts of distinctions between workmates and sexual mates (generally in the absence of observations of sexual activity) that are commonplace in symbolic representations of the daily lives of humans.

Canvassing All Options

Dunbar's approach to the continuity between the human experience and that of nonhuman primates canvassed all options of group size and grooming time seen among nonhuman primates. He considered humans as necessarily involved in solving a range of problems of survival similar to that of other primates. As such, his is what others would call a "conceptual model" based on understandings of ecological frameworks shared by humans and nonhuman primates. Foley and Lee (1989) used the same technique to consider the "core social systems" of all extant hominoids defined in terms of the usual social distribution of males and females (that is, with nonkin, solitary, with kin, or with kin and lineage). In this way Foley and Lee canvassed all options for social combinations. While this method shows that humans are embedded in the same matrix of relationships as nonhuman primates—continuity—it also shows discontinuity between humans and nonhuman primates. For Foley and Lee, humans are creatures who uniquely have a social system involving relatively stable relationships based either on males living with kin and lineage and a solitary female or on both males and females living with kin and lineage.

This appears to be a straightforward identification of a discontinuity between humans and nonhuman primates, but in reality it depends again on some subtler arguments. First is the language-determined ability of Foley and Lee to classify (to name) the male and female distribution states (and note the caution by Dunbar [1988:9–10] about the subjectivity of identifying these distribution states). Second, and perhaps more important, is their ability to identify humans as "distributed with" particular categories of other humans. This is what I refer to as the "ethologist's bind." We are continually confronted with two problems in comparing humans and nonhuman primates: we cannot ask the nonhuman primates to account for their lives (in this case to define their perceptions of their relationships), and we cannot (or will not) act as nonparticipant observers in human communities (with rare and controversial exceptions such as Denham 1975). These problems create a fundamental disparity in the quality of observations about humans and nonhuman primates—an insoluble bind.

The result of the ethologist's bind is crucial to understanding the types of continuity between humans and nonhuman primates. In particular, we must exercise caution when the understanding that is sought involves the aspect of human behavior that makes us distinctive— namely, language. Very few of the observations that can be compared between humans and nonhuman primates are of equivalent quality. There tend to be observations of nonhuman primates by humans who are separate from the behavior of the nonhuman primates—what some would call etic observations—and observations of humans by humans who are, more or less unconsciously but inevitably, enmeshed with the behavior of the observed humans—emic observations. Paradoxically, continuity arguments may depend on an invalid assumption that there is continuity in the quality of observations. The discontinuity of observations derives from the fundamental way in which language use transforms perceptions by naming distinctions between categories.

THE NATURE OF DISCONTINUITY

The paradox that emerges from this consideration of attempts to show continuity by canvassing all options is that it clarifies the particulate nature of the observations and the extent to which an appearance of discontinuity is also created by the use of language to describe phenomena in discrete categories. I earlier proposed that the archaeological record provides access to the steps and slopes of the evolution of human behavior by gradation. I next discuss this in the context of one set of data generally held to be relevant to the origins of language: the increase in cranial capacity (and hence brain size) during the emergence of humans from a nonhuman hominid past. The paradox here is that a set of data that show discontinuity is itself continuously distributed.

Patterns of Change in Brain Size

Issues about interpretation of prehistoric evidence might be clarified by some concrete examples related to the question of the evolution of language. The pattern of changes in brain size during the course of hominid and human evolution (see Noble and Davidson 1996:figs. 28–29, 33–35) is often discussed but rarely evaluated. The pioneer in this field is Holloway (e.g., 1983). Data are summarized in Aiello and Dunbar (1993), and there is a recent discussion by Ruff, Trinkaus, and Holliday (1997).

In figure 7.2 I show the general envelope of values of cranial capacity by enclosing all the known measurements in a dark shaded region. Between 3 million and 2 million years ago, the range of cranial capacities of hominids was small (about 400–450 ml) and showed little or no change over the period. Between 2 million and 1.5 million years ago, cranial capacity increased in both size and range of variation (about 450–950 ml) when all hominids are considered together. (The naming of hominid species is especially problematic because skeletal morphology is an imprecise guide to breeding potential; see Noble and Davidson 1996:142–45.) At about 1.5 million years ago, the smaller end of the range of variation disappeared, and if modern scientists name the small-brained hominids as a separate species (which they do), they say that that species became extinct. The new lowest values were about 650 milliliters. Between 1.5 million and about 400,000 years ago, there was very little change in cranial capacity, although both lower and upper limits increased slightly (by about 100 ml). At 400,000 years ago,

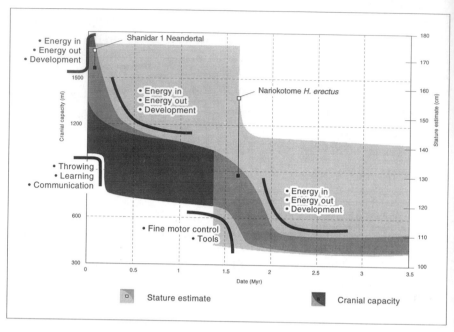

FIGURE 7.2

Major elements of change in cranial capacity during hominid and human evolution.

the upper limits of hominid cranial capacity increased, reaching a maximum about 50,000 years ago with the now-extinct Neandertals. About 200,000 years ago, the smaller end of the range of variation again disappeared (or, if named as a separate species, that species became extinct).

Also shown in figure 7.2, in paler shading, is the evidence for changes in the stature of hominids. I choose stature as a measure of body size because it seems to be relatively uncomplicated (calculated by regression equations of one sort or another, mostly associating postcranial bones with stature), whereas estimates of body mass usually involve a wider set of assumptions (such as about state of nutrition) in addition to regressions. With the exception of the Nariokotome *Homo erectus,* there are no remains earlier than Neandertals (represented here by the Shanidar 1 specimen) for which an estimate of cranial capacity can be associated directly with the estimate for stature. Moreover, because naming of specimens as belonging to one species or another depends crucially on classification of features of the skull, whereas estimates of stature depend on postcranial remains, it is also very difficult to split up the stature estimates by species. I believe that this comparison, stripped of the species names invented and assigned by physical anthropologists, gives a much clearer picture of the pattern of evolution among our ancestors in the relationship between cranial capacity and body size. Ruff, Trinkaus, and Holliday (1997) sought to overcome the problem I have outlined here by dividing the set of skeletal remains into separate samples defined not solely by species attributions.

The pattern of changes in stature is slightly different from that of changes in cranial capacity. On the evidence, the range of variation in stature remained fairly constant (at 1.05–1.40 m) from before 3 million years ago until after the increase in cranial capacity had begun. About 1.6 million years ago, the range of statures increased dramatically (to 1.75 m). Since 1.4 million years ago, individuals of small stature (below 1.40 m) have rarely been found. From 1.4 million years ago to the present, stature has remained relatively constant in range and size (1.40–1.75 m). Thus, the way in which change took place is similar to that for cranial capacity: an initial expansion of range followed by extinction of the lower end of the expanded range of variation. The significant difference, however, is that there was only one major change in stature during the course of hominid evolution.

The implication is clear: the early change in cranial capacity is closely related to changes in body size. The sequence of causation appears to be that large body size followed large brain size. But the second increase in cranial capacity was not accompanied by (and does not appear, give or take a few basketballers, to have been followed by) another increase in body size. This was an unequivocal increase in relative brain size, completed about 250,000 years ago.

The final point about the pattern of changes in cranial capacity and stature is that some Neandertal cranial capacities were greater than those of modern humans but Neandertal stature was less. Why should this be, given all our assumptions about the fundamental good of large brain size for hominids? The answer to this question seems to me to be crucial, but it needs to be considered in the context of all of the other changes and in the form of thinking about evolutionary questions that I posed previously.

Explaining Brain Size Increase about Two Million Years Ago

Many factors have been linked to patterns of brain size among primates and other mammals. Foley (1990) collected references to arguments about gestation length, life span, neonate weight, weaning age, age at first reproduction, interbirth interval, home range area, dietary quality, maternal metabolic rate, group size, social complexity, grooming rate, and communicative ability. The key point is that the range of variation in any character is constrained by selection. Thus, the initial stage of stable cranial capacity needs to be considered in terms of the selective pressure against large brains as well as that against small brains.

The first phase of brain expansion, about 2 million years ago, was cited by Tobias (1987) as evidence for an early origin of language (see also Davidson and Noble 1998; Noble and Davidson 1996). Although this is a possibility that some will wish to consider, I prefer to consider the pattern of changes in terms of the relaxation of selective pressures against large brains (Davidson and Noble n.d.). These pressures result from the energy balance of the brain—the costs of providing energy and of preventing overheating that might arise from the consumption of energy. These two costs were addressed partly by changes in the diet of early hominids, with the incorporation of more meat and other scavenged tissue (such as brains and marrow), and partly by changes in blood flow around the skull consequent upon bipedalism, which provided some measure of thermoregulation (Falk 1986). In addition, any expansion of cranial size must have been weighed against the size of the birth canal, which was in turn related to effective bipedalism. By 2 million years ago, all of these changes were in place. The constraints were removed, but was there a significant selective advantage for individuals with increased brain size? Some insight may be provided by considering why the small-brained hominids (named Australopithecines by physical anthropologists) became extinct.

The major behavioral change at around 2 million years ago was the regular manufacture of stone tools. As might be expected, stone tools have been found in earlier contexts (Chavaillon 1976; Semaw et al. 1997), but regular use seems to be little older than 2 million years. Stone tools were used for cutting many things, but significantly for this argument, for cutting meat (Bunn 1981; Keeley and Toth 1981; Potts and Shipman 1981). The main requirement for consistent production of stone flakes from cobble cores was not brute force but precision of application of force in appropriate places on the core. Such an activity would have selected for fine motor control, and thus extinction of the Australopithecines might have been due to their inability to compete with larger-brained hominids capable of fine motor control. By implication, there might have been an expansion of the regions of the brain associated with fine motor control—those closest to Broca's area in modern humans. The presence of changes in this region of the brain has been claimed by Falk (1983) for fossils dated at 1.8 million years ago.

In addition, bipedalism had emerged by this time, together with a strong probability of hairlessness (Wheeler 1985). In all likelihood this created the necessity for mobile, bipedal hominids to carry infants in front of them more frequently than is the case among knuckle-walking apes (Noble and Davidson 1996). The opportunities afforded in this context for adults and infants to attend visually to the same object or event (joint attention) created a selective context for teaching. Boesch (1991; Boesch and Boesch 1993) suggested that the "teaching" of nut-cracking was relatively unsuccessful among infant chimpanzees because of their lack of strength. Considering all of these arguments about stone tools and learning together, it may be that stone tool making provided the context for learning to teach younger infants by example (Noble and Davidson 1996:42–43, 199–200).

Explaining Brain Size Increase between 400,000 and 200,000 Years Ago

The second episode of cranial capacity increase must be considered in terms of a similar set of selective pressures: acquisition of energy and dissipation of heat, as well as selective pressure during ontogenetic development. Thermoregulation may have been less a problem for later hominids in this sample because the majority of the prehistoric specimens later than 250,000 years ago are from the cooler latitudes, between $30°$ and $60°$ from the equator, whereas those earlier than 400,000 years ago are almost all from latitudes between $0°$ and $30°$. In addition, Falk (1986) showed that the pattern of emissary veins that she claims to be a heat-dispersing radiator changed among later hominids to be more effective in this role.

The question of dietary input of energy is more complex. Brace (1995) argued (on little evidence) that there was an increase in the amount of cooking during the relevant time period. Others have suggested that pointed wooden sticks discovered from the period of the second brain expansion reflect improved possibilities for obtaining food (Oakley et al. 1977; Thieme and Veil 1985; Thieme 1997). But there remains strong evidence that scavenging continued to be a major source of meat (and brains and marrow) until after 50,000 years ago (Stiner and Kuhn 1992; Stiner 1994). The systematic killing of prime-age animals that is characteristic of hunting came rather later in the story (Davidson 1989; Stiner and Kuhn 1992). Nevertheless, one of the most intriguing recent discussions concerns the apparent trade-off during the course of hominid evolution between the relative sizes of two energetically expensive tissues: the brain and the gut.

The increase in size of the brain in humans relative to nonhuman primates has been accompanied by a concomitant reduction in the size of the gut (Aiello and Wheeler 1995). Because gut tissue does not fossilize or leave an endocast, it is difficult to specify the timing of this change. However, there are differences between apes and humans in the shape of the rib cage that are probably related to gut size. The changes seem not to have occurred by 3 million years ago in *Australopithecus afarensis*—"Lucy" (or "Luke," if, as seems likely, it turns out to be male and not female [Husler and Schmid 1995])—but they had occurred by 1.5 million years ago in the *Homo erectus* from Nariokotome (Ruff and Walker 1993). It seems likely, therefore, that dietary changes had occurred by the time of the second increase in brain size—which was an increase relative to body size—in order for the relatively small gut to provide enough energy to feed a very large brain.

The other distinctive feature of the human brain relative to that of nonhuman primates is the extent of its growth outside the womb (Foley and Lee 1991). This is known as secondary altriciality. The timing of the emergence of this feature is highly uncertain. Consideration of the life history parameters of the *Homo erectus* from Nariokotome (Smith 1993) suggests that the pattern of maturation had some features more in common with apes than with humans, suggesting that secondary altriciality might not have emerged by 1.5 million years ago. Its emergence may therefore be associated with the second increase in brain size. This would have reduced the selective pressure against large brains still further.

The combination of carrying infants, joint attention, and increased time for brain growth outside the womb doubtless had a dramatic effect on the extent of learning in hominid infants. It is not difficult to argue that this would have put larger-brained hominids at a selective advantage over smaller-brained ones (which perhaps did not have secondary altriciality). Noble and I would add that it was at this stage of hominid evolution that throwing (perhaps of pointed sticks) became important. The Nariokotome individual had a smaller spinal cord than modern humans in the region of the thorax (MacLarnon 1993), and it has been suggested that this individual had a reduced ability for the muscle control necessary for throwing and for the fine breath control needed for the sorts of vocal utterances we associate with speech (Walker 1993).[4] According to Calvin's (1993) argument (adapted in Noble and Davidson 1996:chapter 8), throwing had important consequences for the expansion of the motor strip adjacent to Broca's area and for selection for sequenced actions, which are essential for many aspects of spoken and manual gestural communication, as well as for throwing. It would be consistent with our argument if hominids of smaller brain size succumbed to selective pressure in competition with hominids that had expanded brains, enhanced learning, and complex sequenced actions.

Explaining the Reduction of Brain Size after Neandertals

Finally, I want to consider why modern humans have brains smaller than those of some Neandertals.[5] The explanation must be consistent with those I have just offered for the selective disadvantages of large and small brains, first for Australopithecines and second for *Homo erectus*. Large brains are costly to feed and difficult to keep cool, and pose problems for development. All of these problems presumably were solved in the Neandertals. Nevertheless, if the same functions could be performed with smaller brains, there would presumably have been a selective advantage for the smaller-brained hominids (humans) because of the lesser energy cost.

The functions of larger brains that I have suggested produced selective advantages over smaller brains were increased joint attention and enhanced learning, fine motor control, sequenced vocal and manual control, and perhaps teaching. It is difficult to see how bigger brains could somehow be disadvantageous for any of these functions. The issue of the large brains of Neandertals requires an argument that goes beyond the scope of the usual explanations of large brain size.

Noble and I have consistently argued for a fundamental distinction between Neandertals and modern humans in the production of symbols (Davidson 1991; Noble and Davidson 1993). We argue that because symbols stand for things other than the symbol itself, they produce displacement. Behavior interpreted as involving displacement is rare in apes and other nonhuman primates but is the norm among humans. The timing of its emergence (by any interpretation) during the course of hominid and human evolution can be suggested only from archaeological evidence.

Gibson (1993c) comments that none of the reported utterances of "language-trained" apes extends beyond the shared experience of the participants in the exchange. Language in humans is replete with such utterances. Neandertals were not apes, of course, at least in any conventional sense of the name "ape," but their archaeological record is also unlike that of any humans except their exact contemporaries in the eastern Mediterranean region (Lieberman and Shea 1994). Gibson also draws attention to the lack of long-term planning among apes, and Noble and I have argued that the earliest evidence for the sort of displacement and planning at issue is the fact of colonization of Australia (Davidson and Noble 1992). Gibson attributes some of the abilities implied in these differences between humans and other apes to humans' capacity for breaking up "perceptions, motor actions and concepts into smaller component parts" (Gibson 1993c:252; see also Gibson and Jessee, this volume), together with construction and hierarchization of these components. But Gibson's model of increasing information-processing capacity as a direct product of increasing brain size founders on two features of the archaeological record. First is the lack of fit between the archaeological evidence of behavior and changes in cranial capacity (Noble and Davidson 1996:chapters 6–7), and second is the greater brain size of Neandertals. If Gibson's model were correct, we would expect modern humans to exhibit the greatest brain sizes. I suspect there is something different about the ways in which Neandertals and modern humans used their brains.

It is difficult to be precise about how brains function as animals perform various behaviors. This is true for all primates, including modern humans. Making any statement from the archaeological evidence is even more hazardous, for most of the behavior must be inferred without any evidence of the bodies that produced it, and when there are skeletal remains, even if they include the skull, no brain remains to function. What follows, therefore, is speculative, but it is consistent with the archaeological record.

Noble and I (1996) have argued that when two individuals spoke the first language, it was indistinguishable from the communication last uttered by the same individuals (this is the ultimate continuity argument). The origin of language was a discovery of the symbolic potential of the referential utterances of hominids that did not use language. An appropriate comparison would be with the effectiveness of the vervet gesture-call system, but, we speculate, with a hugely increased range of referents (supposing that is what vervets have). Our scenario for this (Davidson and Noble 1989; Noble and Davidson 1996) sees two hominids communicating with each other using a bodily gesture (-call) that indicates the observable presence of prey or predator through iconic movements of hand and arm (see Burling, this volume; Wilcox, this volume). If that gesture were accidentally or incidentally traced into a more permanent medium (such as the side of a stream channel), then the trace itself might become an object of attention in the absence of the prey or predator. In this way, the communicative act could be seen to refer in the absence of the referent. Some such trick is needed to achieve the distinctive discontinuity between nonhuman primate and human communication represented by the uniquely human, and languagelike, ability to pay attention to the communicative act itself, rather than to the object of communication.

I continue the speculation wholly on the basis of a familiar computer model.[6] To retain a large number of such gesture-calls requires a large memory, and I speculate that in hominids memory was enhanced with increased brain size. Once humans discovered the symbolic potential of their utterances, the way was open for utterances to have meanings outside the context of their uttering, together with hierarchization of utterances. To continue the computer analogy, this would allow a reduced instruction set, so that less reliance would be placed on keeping whole utterances in memory: they could be constructed anew each time as necessary. With reduced need for memory, hominids with smaller brains were at no disadvantage. Here the speculation ends.

Given the greater power of language (this symbol-based, meaningful, particulate, hierarchized communication system) over a vervetlike communication system, those humans who possessed it would have had enormous competitive advantages over hominids that did not. Moreover, in the competition where brains are costly, those who could achieve the same (or better) results with smaller brains would have required less energy input and less fine-tuning of their thermoregulatory systems and would have given birth more easily. I think I understand why Neandertals became extinct—always supposing that there really were creatures that correspond to the category we name and understand as "Neandertals."

Extinction

Evolutionary argument requires there to have been continuity. Even if monsters were to emerge as a result of massive genetic mutations, such "hopeful monsters" had parents. But it is an inevitable consequence of evolution that there has been extinction. Among hominids, Australopithecines (small-brained hominids) have become extinct, and so have Neandertals (large-brained hominids). Most importantly, so have the creatures that link modern gorillas, chimpanzees, and bonobos to the last common ancestor they all shared with humans (see fig. 7.1). When we compare modern humans with chimpanzees we see discontinuity, but there is an unbroken chain that goes back from us to the common ancestor and from the common ancestor forward to modern chimpanzees.

I have expressed this argument about discontinuity in terms of a continuous sequence of changes of cranial capacity. The argument forces us to consider what is involved in extinctions. The extinction of Australopithecines can be expressed as a shift in the range of cranial capacities. Yet some would say that the argument should be expressed in terms of the named genera *Homo* and *Australopithecus*. This argument would state that there was a discontinuity at about 2 million years ago with the appearance of the genus *Homo*. Note that identification of specimens as one genus or the other is not necessarily straightforward in the initial stage: two fossil skulls (ER 1805 and ER 1813) are particularly controversial (Falk 1983; Wood 1992). My point in this chapter is that the only candidates for ancestry of the genus *Homo* are a mother and a father from the genus *Australopithecus*. If we choose to see the two genera as separate we can see a discontinuity; if we choose to emphasize the continuity we can still confront the problem of extinction, but in a different way. It depends on how we play the game of the name.

Similarly, some would argue that there are no real distinctions between *Homo erectus* and *Homo sapiens*, and given that there has been continuity of ancestry, there is an inescapable argument for this. But how would we refer to the smaller-brained hominids that became extinct about 250,000 years ago if a naming practice were adopted that called all *Homo erectus* and *Homo sapiens* together *Homo sapiens*? And finally, there is dispute (sometimes vicious) over the role (or lack thereof) of Neandertals in human ancestry (Stringer 1992; Aiello 1993; Frayer et al. 1993; Stringer and Gamble 1993; Trinkaus and Shipman 1993; Mellars 1996; Tattersall 1996; Stringer and McKie 1997). Clearly there was a biological reality that could be said to be the resolution of the dispute, but scholars are uncertain what it was (Corruccini 1994).

The conclusion, therefore, is that a continuous process links humans with nonhuman primates through our fossil ancestors. Discontinuity occurs through the extinction of some parts of the range of variation of organisms. On the evidence of changes in brain size, this seems to happen after the range of cranial capacities has expanded to larger values and small-brained creatures have become extinct. Our naming practices are heavily implicated in the way in which we see these processes.

WHAT IS A HUMAN?

The fear of species solipsism should not keep us awake at night. We all know that humans are different from all other animals, even while acknowledging the difficulty of believing in Cartesian dualism. We do not invite Kanzi to our symposia or expect to find the Karisoke gorillas organizing one of their own to ask what they can learn about the nature of being a gorilla from the study of humans. No vervets ask how humans see the world; no nonhuman primates construct mirrors or televisions or wonder whether humans see themselves there as others see them. There are no ape or monkey humanologists, archaeologists, psychologists, or linguists. Only humans play word games; only humans pun. Discontinuity is absolute, but it has not always been. While I am happy with the thought that to be an archaeologist is to be human, the discontinuity deserves further exploration.

In reviewing the evidence for the mental abilities of apes, Byrne (1995:233) concluded that chimpanzees could be said to "demonstrate impressive cognitive skill: intentional teaching, intentional deception, grammatical comprehension, distinguishing between malice and accident...extensive tool-making and mechanical comprehension....Why these animals, which give evidence of the insight that we humans consider so crucial to behavioral intelligence, show so few signs of its use in everyday life, remains a mystery."

We may wish to criticize one or another of these claims in detail (Kennedy 1992; Heyes 1994), however much they have become the orthodoxy of primatology, but that is not the issue. Rather, the significant point is that Byrne juxtaposed this generous characterization with the recognition that the "other great qualitative change in cognition during [hominid and] human evolution was that of language." He pointed out that there may be no sign of language in the communication of other species, but if we overlook the critiques by Heyes and Kennedy, there may be precursors in chimpanzee cognition.

Let us consider the question of the origins of language. We run up against the consideration of hominid behavior before language and against the rich field of what is possible in animal behavior without language (Snowdon 1990). We also run up against all the linked biological and behavioral features of language. Noble and I (1996) argued for the

importance of the evidence of bipedalism and cranial thermoregulation in understanding the process of increasing absolute and relative
brain size. Brain size increased most markedly long after hominids
began to walk bipedally and to have skeletal proportions much like
those of modern humans. The major stage of brain size increase took
place within the last 400,000 years, without major modification to the
pelvis. This seems to have been possible only through an evolution of
the relation between brain growth and gestation length such that
humans, of all primates, have the longest period of brain growth outside the mother. In consequence, human infants are dependent for a
high proportion of their infancy, with much brain growth taking place
during that critical period. Hairlessness, unidentifiable archaeologi-
cally but inferred as part of the thermoregulatory package, also leads to
the need for human mothers to carry their children face to face more
than hairy apes do, since ape infants can cling either to the back, where
they are out of sight, or to the belly. Noble and I suggest that this leads
to an increased incidence of joint attention between mother and infant
and more opportunities for learning.

None of these yielded language, but all are essential to creating
the circumstances by which modern human infants acquire it. Thus, at
one level we are no closer to understanding the precise moment when
the first two people recognized the symbolic nature of their utterances,
but we are aware of how that moment was translated into the modern
process of language ontogeny.

And the importance of this is that it gives a credible basis for arguing about the nature of language as symbolic communication and
about its relation to the abilities of humans. Emphasizing the symbolic
basis of language allows an argument based on the archaeological evidence, not for the origin as a moment in time but for the process of
emergence over a longer time period. This was a process not just about
vocal or nonvocal utterances, communication, or symbols themselves
but about the evolutionary emergence by gradation of human anatomical form, function, and ontogeny from ancestors different in all of
these. All of these elements were involved in the final step that sharply
distinguished communication using symbols from its precursor, nonsymbolic communication. This is more constructive than a belief that

language is so complex that there are no naturalistic explanations for its origins (Chomsky 1972).

The first appearance of symbols represented a true threshold: something either does or does not stand for something else. One test of this raises the further issue of displacement: can the reference occur when the referent is absent? There is no sign that vervets ever chat about eagles once the eagle has landed (indeed, they have been observed to make the leopard call to eagles on the ground). The archaeological record is full of evidence of the sudden appearance of symbols, both as material objects that can be construed only as standing for something other than themselves and through evidence of displaced reference, most eloquently in the construction of a watercraft that brought people to Australia. The archaeological evidence following this threshold represents the working out of all the implications of the new symbolic capacities of humans (Davidson 1997a, 1997b). Nonhuman primates may be able to learn to use symbol systems in company with humans, but none has discovered a symbol system by itself, with the possible exception of bonobos (Savage-Rumbaugh et al. 1996), and none has worked out the potentials of the system.

I conclude, therefore, by emphasizing the nature of humans as creatures that play the game of names. The game is not only one in which categories can be named and entities real and imaginary can be assigned to those named categories but also one in which the boundaries of the categories can be changed, arbitrarily and by convention. Depending on where we draw these boundaries, we can see continuity and discontinuity in the same evidence. The game of changing the rules of the game is truly human.

Notes

I would like to name the players who have helped me with this game. As usual, discussions with Bill Noble influenced my writing on these themes, and Helen Arthurson contributed in more ways than she knows. I also thank Peter Jarman and Fred d'Agostino for helpful advice. Rob Burling and Robin Dunbar made very constructive comments that enabled me to improve the chapter. Barbara King and Stuart Shanker provided the stimulus for further sharpening the argument. I thank them all with the usual disclaimers. The School of

American Research advanced seminar was a very stimulating occasion, and I particularly want to thank Sue Savage-Rumbaugh, Charles Snowdon, and Talbot Taylor for their interactions. Figure 7.1 was drawn by Doug Hobbs, and figure 7.2 by Heather Burke and Doug Hobbs. I thank them both.

1. A further illustration of the power of naming lies in the use of the word "hominid." Generally speaking, it refers to members of the category of animals named by zoologists as the family Hominidae, where both giving the name "family" to a grouping of genera and species and giving that "family" the name "Hominidae" are inventions of those zoologists. Hominidae originally included humans and their ancestors, since we shared a common ancestor with other apes. In this classification, the Hominidae stand in contrast to the Pongidae, a grouping of all the nonhuman apes. It is now recognized that humans have a close ancestral relationship with chimpanzees (and gorillas) and that such a grouping should be contrasted with the Asian apes (which include the orangutan of the genus Pongo). A more appropriate classification (see also Groves 1989) would put the African apes together as Hominidae with subfamilies named Homininae (including humans, Australopithecines, and human ancestors of the genus Homo) and Gorillinae (including gorillas, chimpanzees, and bonobos) (Jones, Martin, and Pilbeam 1992). Hence, the convenient shorthand for the taxonomic grouping to which humans and their ancestors belong would be hominin. But the name hominin has no currency (yet) outside a small specialist field, and so I have avoided it here. Moreover, I use the name hominid to refer only to those extinct creatures that have no signs of being human by the definition used here—the use of language. This can cause confusion for those who are committed to strict application of the rules of zoological nomenclature, but by explicitly defining the term this way, I avoid other confusions.

2. There are, so far as I know, two exceptions. The words "word" and "symbol" are symbols that stand for themselves!

3. Anthropomorphism is a form of analogy in which humans are used as the source of an analogy for interpreting the incompletely known behavior of nonhuman animals. The form of argument is illustrated by a trivial example: an animal exhibits a form of behavior (e.g., baring the teeth) that looks like a form of behavior in humans (smiling). Therefore, the animal is happy because humans smile when they are happy. It is circular to use anthropomorphic interpretations of nonhuman primate behavior (derived in this way) in arguments that seek to infer something about human behavior.

4. I recognize the danger of arguing from selected instances and samples where n = 1. MacLarnon (personal communication) has now shown a similar pattern in Australopithecines, so it seems unlikely that the small thoracic spinal cord was a pathology that caused the death of the Nariokotome individual.

5. There are serious problems in this assertion arising from sampling and attribution of specimens to species. Nevertheless, the popular wisdom is that Neandertals had big brains, and there is no evidence that they were systematically smaller. Ruff, Trinkaus, and Holliday (1997) have argued that the size of Neandertal brains relative to body mass was smaller than that of early anatomically modern humans.

6. There are many reasons why computer models are inappropriate for understanding how brains work, not least that connections within the brain are transmitted both electrically and chemically (Greenfield 1997). In addition, much attention is paid to analogies with memory (as here) or central processing units but little to the vexed question of operating system.

8

Children's Transition to Language

A Human Model for Development of the
Vocal Repertoire in Extant and Ancestral
Primate Species?

Lorraine McCune

The evolution of language is shrouded in mystery. We infer and theorize about communicative and linguistic skills that might have characterized our hominid ancestors. Perhaps the developmental trajectory observed in current humans can provide direct evidence of pre-human abilities, as "ontogeny recapitulates phylogeny." Such a global hypothesis would prove difficult to test. I would like to propose a more powerful, if indirect, developmental approach. Given that the linguistic skills of hominid ancestors—whatever those skills might have been—developed during the period from birth to maturity in each individual of the species, *attention to the comparative development of the communicative repertoire in extant species, including human infants, can provide clues to pre-human developmental trajectories* (Parker and Gibson 1979). Where humans and other extant primates share developmental processes, these processes are implicated for common ancestors. The transition of interest in this chapter is a specific aspect of language communication, the beginning of linguistic reference in humans. How can this developmental transition be described? Can similar processes be identified by taking a broadened view of the communicative development of extant primate species (King 1994b)?

Vocal communication involves respiratory, phonatory, and articulatory components. In addition, a motivational component is needed. The motivational component varies greatly across species and situations. For example, an "expression" that follows with some inevitability from an experience such as pain and a proposition instigated by the "intention to mean" (Searle 1969) derive from distinct physiological and psychological motivations. By definition, communication includes an emitting and a receiving organism. Communication may occur by virtue of an organism's meaningful expression in the absence of a clear intention to convey a message to another organism. Indeed, some communicative signals in both evolution and development may derive from functional activities of organisms (Darwin 1965 [1872]; Tinbergen 1952).

This chapter first describes human infants' transition to referential language as a framework for considering comparative developmental data later in the chapter. Vocalizations occurring autonomically in response to metabolic demand are accorded a prominent role in this transition. These vocalizations, termed "grunts," can prompt the recognition of sound-meaning correspondence because of their occurrence in consistent metabolic circumstances. Since grunts are used communicatively by adults across primate species, their autonomic occurrence in infancy is broadly implicated in the transition to the communicative repertoire in both extant species and in evolutionary forebears, thus implicating this vocalization in the evolution of language.

The capacity for communicative signaling is one prerequisite for attributing language to an individual or species. For communication to succeed, the signal must produce a response in the recipient related to both the internal experience and the external behavior (the signal) of the signaler. The communicating (signaling) individual experiences an internal "state of meaning" (perhaps the sense of attending to an object or event) and must produce some signal indicating that meaning. When communication is successful, the receiving individual experiences an internal state of meaning closely related to that expressed by the sender. Searle (1983, 1992) terms such internal states of meaning "Intentional states" or "I-states." (Following Searle [1983], I capitalize

"Intentional" as distinct from the common definition of "intentional" meaning "purposeful.") While an I-state describes internal experience without necessarily including external purposeful goals or actions, I-states may include such purposeful goals or accompany such purposeful actions.

Intentional states characterize all conscious experiences of organisms that are in some sense paying attention to their surroundings (Searle 1992). Analysis of Intentional states is used here to describe and compare characteristics of the hypothesized internal states of organisms that can be inferred from external behavior and circumstances. An I-state is defined as a mental state directed at objects or states of affairs in the world. The following characteristics of I-states are useful for comparative study: (1) the sense of the self in relation to the environment, (2) a focus that selects some stimulus and leaves the rest as (3) periphery, and (4) an affective tone (Searle 1983, 1992; Bloom 1993). Other aspects of the environment are considered as background, of which the organism maintains awareness. An I-state analysis permits consideration of both referential (focus) and motivational (affective tone) aspects of a given signal event (see Marler, Evans, and Hauser 1992), allowing consideration of human and other animal signals within an equivalent framework.

For example, a person might experience an I-state upon noticing a fire in a crowded theater. This state would include visual and other sensory experiences of the fire as focus, a sense of the self as surrounded and threatened, the aspects of the theater itself and the other patrons as periphery, and an affective tone of fear. That I-state might be expressed by an involuntary scream or by a shout of "Fire!" without the explicit purpose of warning the other patrons. Alternative or additional I-states are possible in this situation. The person might suppress any vocalization and quickly and silently head for the exit, experiencing an I-state including the purposeful goal of escape as focus, with the other theater patrons and their potential as obstacles to escape as periphery. That is, the person's fear now encompasses being trampled by an exiting mob. Alternatively, the person might experience an I-state including the purposeful goal of warning the other theatergoers and yell "Fire!" with this goal in mind. The other patrons, receivers of the communication "Fire!"—whether it is expressed with communicative purpose by the speaker or not—will experience an I-state at least partially matching that of the sender. They might scan the environment, discover the flames, and experience an exact match of focus—the fire itself—while sense of self, periphery, and affective tone might vary from that of the first individual. Other patrons might repeat the call "Fire!" while taking protective action.

Recent findings regarding infant use of the "grunt," a simple laryngeal vocalization accompanying consistent I-states, provides the impetus for examining the transition to the adult vocal repertoire across primate species (McCune et al. 1996). Vocalizations termed "grunts" with the physiological character of human grunts function communicatively in a large number of nonhuman primate species including chimpanzees, *Pan troglodytes* (Marler 1976; Goodall 1986; Hauser et al. 1993), vervet monkeys, *Cercopithecus aethiops* (Seyfarth and Cheney 1986), gorillas, *Gorilla gorilla* (Fossey 1972; Harcourt, Stewart, and Hauser 1993; Seyfarth et al. 1994), and baboons, *Papio hamadryas* (Andrew 1976).

Within one month of beginning communicative grunt production, children in a study by my colleagues and me (McCune et al. 1996) first exhibited linguistic referential ability. Reference entails recognition that a given lexical item could be used to designate a range of categorically related entities or events. Those children with appropriate phonetic resources began referential language production and showed a sharp increase in lexical frequency; those with limited phonetic resources demonstrated referential understanding by the use of gestures. When we examined the context of all grunt vocalizations occurring between 9 and 16 months of age in the sample of five subjects, we observed a developmental sequence in contexts of grunt use. The earliest grunts ("effort grunts") occurred under conditions of physiological effort, such as attempts to reach a toy or change position (see Stark 1993; Stark, Bernstein, and Demorest 1993). We next observed grunts occurring under conditions of attention ("attention grunts") while the child examined a toy or shifted from one activity to another, with no evidence of physiological effort or communicative intent. Attention grunts occurred as early as nine months but increased in frequency thereafter. Finally, grunts accompanied communicative gestures and looks to the mother ("communicative grunts") and often entailed repetition until a response was forthcoming. This use heralded the transition to reference. Human adults also grunt in conversational contexts (Schegloff 1972).

My colleagues and I (McCune et al. 1996) found evidence that grunt vocalization can occur as an epiphenomenon of physiological stress. The larynx interacts with the lungs in maintaining appropriate oxygenation of the blood under conditions of increased metabolic demand. This process involves reflexive relationships between the intercostal and laryngeal muscles mediated by the vagus, the tenth cranial nerve (Remmers 1973; De Troyer et al. 1985). Under conditions of metabolic demand, activation of the intercostal muscles to maintain lung inflation during expiration sets in motion reflex contraction of laryngeal muscles, thus creating a system under pressure that lengthens the expiration phase of the breath and enhances oxygenation of the blood. Expiration against the constricted glottis produces pulses of sound, audible as grunts in humans and some larger mammals and ultrasonic in small rodents (Blumberg and Alberts 1990). Rat pups' ultrasonic grunt vocalizations ("isolation calls") induce retrieval to the nest (Allin and Banks 1972; Hofer and Shair 1978, 1993). The vocalized autonomic grunt can thus be seen as an epiphenomenon of complex physiological processes of response to metabolic demand (fig. 8.1). Porges, Doussard-Roosevelt, and Maiti (1994) define this laryngeal mechanism as part of a larger system regulating processes of motion, emotion, and communication.

Following Darwin's (1965 [1872]) propositions regarding the derivation of purely expressive acts from those originally serving some basic function for the animal, we proposed (McCune et al. 1996) that children's experience of their own grunts leads to representational sound-meaning correspondence. Both physiological effort and visual attention suggest a consistent I-state: directedness to environmental stimuli. Given the capacity to form symbol-referent relationships, the child might form such a relationship between the I-state of specific environmental focus and the accompanying autonomic grunt vocalization and then might employ the vocalization in communication with

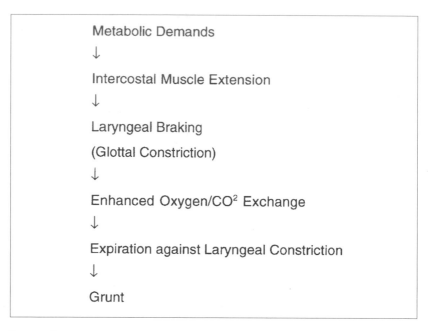

FIGURE 8.1

Physiological processes underlying autonomic grunt production.

the caregiver. The communicative grunt is thus a personal symbol with unstable meaning, varying with what the infant has in mind. This experience may facilitate children's recognition of the variety of sound-meaning correspondences available in the adult repertoire. Infants of other primate species might similarly benefit from the experience of autonomic grunts in recognizing the meaning potential of their species' vocal repertoire.

Comprehensive study of the acquisition of species-specific call repertoires in other primates is only beginning. Whereas it was previously assumed that calls were fixed emotional responses triggered by innate releasing mechanisms, the influence of learning must now be acknowledged (Newman and Symmes 1982; Hauser 1988, 1989, 1996). Field studies of vervet monkeys (Seyfarth and Cheney 1986) and chimpanzees (Plooij 1984), as well as conditioning studies using various species (Pierce 1985) and language studies with chimpanzees (e.g., Gardner and Gardner 1975, 1989; Savage-Rumbaugh et al. 1989), have contributed to the view that communication is a developmental accomplishment.

In the following sections I present a view of children's transition to referential language, providing, where possible, comparative information. I then consider this human model in relation to available developmental data regarding chimpanzees and vervet monkeys in the wild and cross-fostered chimpanzees and bonobos experiencing human-derived symbol systems. To what extent do other species exhibit the skills known to contribute to human infants' transition to speech? Is it possible that autonomic grunt vocalizations influence other species' apprehension of the significance of vocal signals?

PARAMETERS OF LANGUAGE ACQUISITION IN CHILDREN

Previously (McCune 1992) I proposed that a number of critical capacities developing in the first two years of life could together predict the onset of referential language in human infants. Rather than acting independently and in a fixed order, these parameters interact in a dynamic system, influencing one another developmentally and predicting the referential transition when all variables are in place (see Thelen 1991, 1993). The relationship with a caring adult provides the critical context for these human infant developments. The abilities identified are the following: (1) mental representation (the capacity for internal representation of meanings), often observed in *representational play*, (2) recognition of sound-meaning correspondence as expressed in communicative use of a consistent vocal form to solicit adult attention to the infant's attentional focus (*communicative grunt*), and (3) phonetic skill sufficient to produce consistent and differentiated vocalizations (*vocal motor schemes*). Recent reports provide empirical support for this proposal (Vihman and McCune 1994; McCune 1995; McCune et al. 1996; Roug-Hellichius 1998; McCune and Vihman n.d.). The developmental sequence culminating in referential language is summarized in figure 8.2.

Parent-Infant Communication

Initial communicative exchanges between infants and parents involve infant "expressions" of internal states, without the specific

FIGURE 8.2
Steps toward language in human infants.

Birth	3 Months	7–9 Months	9–11 Months	11–15 Months	13–28 Months
Cry	Effort grunt	**Attention grunt**	Communicative gestures (context-limited words)	**Communicative grunt**	Early talkers: 13–16+ months
Grunt	Coo	Babble		Representational meanings in pretend play	Vocal motor schemes for 2 consonants
				Language comprehension	Later talkers: 18–28 months
					Vocal motor control in words/sentences
					Referential words

intention to convey a meaning to the parent and, by that means, alter the parent's I-state. Rather, parents learn to recognize their infants' signals and respond in ways that both meet needs and convey understanding to the infant. Davidson (this volume) recognizes that the evolutionary origin of language required "at least two individuals who together discovered the symbolic potential of their communicative utterances." This same fact characterizes infants' initiation into language: infant signals develop symbolic potential for parents, who then act as mediators in the infant's transition from motivated to symbolic signaling.

The earliest phase of infant-mother interaction is characterized by mutual attunement (Stern 1985), such that the infant experiences multisensory familiarity and responsivity from the caregiver. The acoustic form of parental expression is keyed to the infant, including the prevalence and effects of "Infant-Directed Speech" ("motherese"), which is uniquely suited to the acoustic abilities of human infants in the early months of life (e.g., Fernald 1989, 1992). This process is matched by the infant's instinctual capacity for both eliciting and responding to specific forms of adult activity. Mutual understanding between parent and infant is experienced in bodily action. By virtue of attunement as expressed and experienced during the first year of life, the parent is in a unique position to comprehend the infant's earliest preword and wordlike utterances. Such comprehension by at least one conspecific is essential for the evolution of symbolic signals in a species (Burling, this volume.)

Maestripieri and Call (1996) describe similar processes of mutual tuning of behavior in other primates. Infant distress calls (isolation calls) are a nearly universal feature across primate species, with form, conditions of expression, and maternal response varying by species and developmental status. Howler monkey mothers retrieve whimpering infants who have fallen, and the mothers whimper in return, but they do not retrieve squeaking or barking infants from rough play. In both macaques and vervet monkeys, patterns of distress call frequency and maternal responsiveness suggest developmental patterns of mutual regulation similar to those characterizing attachment relationships in humans.

Plooij (1979) provides detailed descriptions of mutual regulation of chimpanzee mother-infant interaction in the wild. Infants solicit maternal interest by vocalizing and biting their mother's body and hands in the first few weeks of life. By four months the infants solicit face-to-face play. Mother-infant play is most frequent at six months, when mothers seem expert at keeping babies engaged at a comfortable level, which the baby signals by staccato grunts. If interaction becomes too intense, the infant's vocalizations shift into screams, and interaction ceases. Plooij attributes the social difficulties of infants reared without mothers to the lack of opportunity to learn mutual regulation through mother-infant interaction.

In humans, development of an attachment relationship affects every area of psychological functioning (Ainsworth et al. 1978). Throughout the first year of life, maintaining physical proximity and a sense of psychological unity is a primary motivator of infant behavior. Availability of an attachment figure reduces distress reactions and enhances exploration and play in humans and other primates (Ainsworth and Bell 1970; Miller et al. 1986, 1990; Slade 1987a, 1987b).

Apes clearly develop attachments to human caregivers as well as to conspecifics. Hayes (1951) reported contact demands typically addressed to a chimpanzee mother from her fostered chimpanzee, Viki. Gardner, Gardner, and Drumm (1989) found that their chimpanzees showed negative reactions to all caregiver departures, even though one friendly caregiver always remained, whereas the comings and goings of technical support staff went unremarked. Maki, Fritz, and England (1993) found that five- to seven-year-old chimpanzees reared without an available attachment figure in the first two years of life engaged in more self-clinging, self-sucking, and object attachment than those reared by chimpanzee mothers or human caregivers. Russon and Galdikas (1995) reported that orangutans selectively imitated important human caregivers and older siblings.

In comparison with humans, other primate infants have major responsibility for acquiring information as they develop. By contrast, donation of information from adults to immatures is rare. For example, despite the constant contact between chimpanzee adults and immatures in the first five years of life, adult influence on infant food choice is minimal (King 1994a).

Mental Representation as a Social-Cognitive Development

Werner and Kaplan (1963) proposed that children's development of language and reference was the culmination of a symbolic or representational ability derived from (1) their need to maintain psychological contact with their caregivers and (2) their attention to objects in the environment. A state of psychological unity characterizes the human infant's initial experience of self and mother (see Mahler, Pine, and Bergman 1975). From this sense of unity, a sense of self-other individuation emerges, partly due to experiences of physical separation occasioned by motor developments (creeping and walking) and occasions of maternal absence, and partly due to a cognitive construing of the physical and affective experience of separation. Joint attention and later reference to the external world of objects become the major vehicles for maintaining a state of mutuality.

Werner and Kaplan (1963:20) asserted that "[t]he nonrepresentational construing of objects as expressive is basic, and genetically prior to, the use of expressive properties in representation. Dynamic-vectorial characteristics, physiognomic qualities, rhythms, etc., inhere in the objects and events of our experience. . . . Such expressiveness also inheres in the actions of organisms, for example, in their bodily movements, vocalizations, and so on." This function, termed "mimesis," is implicated in a recent theory of the evolution of language (Donald 1991, 1993). Human infants demonstrate a developmental trajectory of mimesis culminating in representational play, and studies of other primates reviewed later in this chapter suggest that imitation and representational play are not exclusively human. Werner and Kaplan (1963) considered this mimetic process to be the source for the development of mental representation. They proposed that the earliest expressions of object knowledge are imitative, such as the onomatopoetic sound made by one child in response to the sound of a coffee grinder or the rhythmic rocking back and forth of another in response to a ticking clock. Both signals later became detached from the original situation and developed designatory function.

Early acts of designation are expressed in both vocal and gestural channels. The relationship of infant and adult in mutual contemplation of objects provides the framework for the development of a representational referential ability that is independent of present objects and events. From this basis the development of communicative symbols, including words and gestures, proceeds. Vocal and gestural channels have equipotentiality for symbolic development (see Burling, this volume; Wilcox, this volume), which involves both an internal relationship between symbol and referent and a process of mutual structuring such that both participants in the communicative exchange come to a joint understanding of representational meanings (Vauclair 1990). Parent-infant communication thus often includes "private" words and expressions understood only by the dyad.

Reference is thus derived from social rather than individual experience (see Davidson, this volume; Snowdon, this volume). Extension of the index finger to touch a near object of interest or to point toward a distant object is a common accompaniment of infant attention beginning around the end of the first year of life. Finger extension is used in service of cognitive understanding to focus attention and examine objects (Ruff 1984) and for communication. Franco and Butterworth (1996) found pointing, frequently accompanied by visual checking with the social partner, well established by 12 months of age as a communicative gesture by infants seeking to establish joint attention. For the age of 10 months, they found a lower mean frequency of pointings, and infants often pointed alternately between the object of interest and the social partner rather than maintaining an object-directed point while shifting gaze to the social partner. This transitional behavior suggests the infant's gradual differentiation of self, social partner, and object that Werner and Kaplan claim to be the genesis of reference. Object attention is reported less frequently for primates in the wild; however, Plooij (1984) found a brief period of object play in chimpanzees between two and five months of age, and cross-fostered chimpanzees are known to explore objects and share them with caregivers in ways similar to human infants. Cebus and macaque monkeys show visual, tactile, and oral exploration of objects similar in kind if not in frequency to that observed in children (Natale 1989a).

Lennon (1984) found that pointing for self and communicative pointing were first observed close in time between 9 and 11 months of age in a longitudinal sample. When infants isolate the index finger to focus their own attention on an object, they also begin to use this same gesture to actively solicit joint attention. The grunt vocalization under conditions of focal attention, also occurring between 9 and 11 months, may be a vocal expression of the infant's experience of directedness to the world of objects.

Vihman (1996) summarized human infants' development of gestural communication: gestures such as pointing to direct the social partner's attention, open-handed arm extension to request objects, and offering and giving objects develop between 10 and 15 months, usually before word use is well established. Semantic gestures such as spread hands indicating "all gone" or a head shake expressing denial are more likely to occur during the period of early vocabulary development. Children also may express symbolic gestures such as sniffing to indicate flowers or lifting a finger to the lips to indicate a sleeping doll or baby.

Chevalier-Skolnikoff (1979) reported gestural development in both chimpanzee and gorilla infants in the wild, including hand extension for begging and a "let's go" gesture—hand extension in the desired direction—on the part of one gorilla infant. Bard (1990) reported development of begging gestures between two and three years of age in orangutans, noting that chimpanzees in the wild may develop pointing within a time frame similar to that for human infants. Leavens, Hopkins, and Bard (1996) reported the spontaneous development of communicative pointing in two captive chimpanzees without relevant training.

Representational Play: A Predictor of Language Developments

The most appropriate indicator of the capacity for mental representation in the second year of life is the development of representational play. Object permanence, also a useful indicator, reaches its ceiling at the point when language begins, so it is less valuable as a predictor of developmental milestones (McCune-Nicolich 1981a). Careful study of the child's changing relations with objects and social partners in play demonstrates developmental steps that follow from Werner and Kaplan's theoretical framework regarding the development of symbolization.

The earliest level (level 1) merely imitates the expressive acts characteristic of use of particular objects. These are brief, isolated actions, without evidence that the child is aware of the relationship between the played acts and the routines of life they mimic. With differentiation come new forms of integration as the child uses sound effects and elaborations to link the played act (symbol) with the referenced real experience (level 2). The child then includes a broader range of participants in play (level 3), begins to construct sequences of acts (level 4), and eventually demonstrates a hierarchical structure in planning and executing representational acts in play (level 5). Specific milestones in the transition to language are predictable from representational play development (Piaget 1962; Nicolich 1977; McCune-Nicolich 1981b; McCune 1995).

First words, associated with specific events, may develop contemporaneously with *single representational play* acts (level 2). Earlier (McCune 1992) I found referential words as well as first word combinations occurring only after *combinatorial pretend play* (level 4) had been observed. The play sequences (e.g., feed mother, feed doll; place doll in car, roll car) may involve repetitions and do not necessarily follow the appropriate order of the portrayed events. First rule-based or syntactic combinations in language occur at level 5, *hierarchical pretend*. In hierarchical pretend, a single act (which may be part of a sequence) exhibits hierarchical structure in one of the following ways: planning of the act is indicated by search or announcement; one object is substituted for another; a doll is treated as if it could act independently (e.g., place a cup in its hand rather than to its lips) (see McCune 1995 for a review of these findings).

This sequence of developments demonstrates the growth of an internal representational ability that can, in conjunction with additional capacities and an appropriate social and linguistic environment, serve the development of reference and syntactic ability. In producing referential words, the child demonstrates internal representation of both meaning and representational form (word or gestural sign)— hence the co-occurrence with combinatorial representational play. Syntactic language exhibits a hierarchical structure first observable in children's simple ordered utterances and hierarchical representational play.

Representation in Nonhuman Primates

Formal study of mental representation in monkeys and apes has emphasized the development of object permanence and tool use in captive animals. These skills are taken in the literature on humans to mark the transition from sensorimotor to representational intelligence, culminating at sensorimotor stage 6 (Piaget 1954, 1962), which marks the onset of mental representation. Self-pretend behavior is indicative of stage 6 representation expressed in play, although all of these skills may not develop in synchrony in humans and may not characterize different species to the same extent. Sensorimotor stages 5 and 6 correspond roughly with symbolic play levels 1 and 2, respectively; play levels 3, 4, and 5 designate increasingly advanced mental representation.

Three studies provide information on representational play in apes. Mignault (1985) assessed representational play in four chimpanzees over a period of three and a half years, beginning when the animals were between ten months and two years of age. They had been raised by humans in an environment containing objects typically encountered by young children and in which they could observe the activities of their caregivers. During the period of the study, all of the animals exhibited increasing frequencies of presymbolic acts (level 1) and exhibited a few instances of self-pretend (level 2) or imitative pretend (level 3) after these acts were modeled. In follow-up studies several months later, the two oldest subjects (age five and a half) both exhibited pretend grooming behavior—brushing a doll—and one exhibited a pretend combination (level 4) by scraping an empty plate with a spoon handle and "eating."

Russon and Galdikas (1995) observed the spontaneous imitation of formerly captive adult orangutans that were being rehabilitated to free living. The animals tended to imitate favored human caregivers and high-ranking conspecifics, selecting actions within their competence. These included complex "real" activities imitated some time after they were observed, such as hanging a hammock and then swinging, and untying a canoe and then taking a ride. However, "some cases were empty functional routines, often performed after delay (e.g., making motions of brushing teeth or siphoning fuel from an empty drum)"

(Russon and Galdikas 1995:13), suggesting representational play.

Hayes (1951) provided optimum conditions for representational development as defined by Werner and Kaplan. The infant chimpanzee Viki was continually with her foster parents, living in a manner differing from that of a human child only in those areas demanded by species differences (e.g., her crib was roofed to prevent wandering by a motorically sophisticated infant). Hayes reported imitative caregiving and household routines beginning at about 16 months of age (comparable to humans), as well as putting on makeup and primping at the mirror (play combination). Hayes's observations suggested that at 18 months Viki developed a play routine involving an imaginary pull toy. If this indicated a general skill rather than a unique activity, then Viki could be credited with level 5 representational play, hierarchical pretend.

Apes' performance on sensorimotor tasks, in contrast with monkeys' performance, indicates representational ability on the part of apes, suggesting that pretend play might be within their competence. Natale (1989b) confirmed stage 5 object permanence in small samples of crab-eating macaques and cebus monkeys and in a single gorilla and Japanese macaque. By controlling for learning of operant strategies that might improve success over trials, Natale and Antinucci (1989) found that only the gorilla exhibited stage 6 object permanence, suggesting the initial phase of mental representation. Filion, Washburn, and Gulledge (1996) reported representation of the trajectory of an invisible moving target in rhesus macaques. In human infants as well, motion events enhance cognitive performance; this skill is observed as early as four months in human infants (Kellman 1993).

Confirming stage 6 representational tool use with Piagetian tasks requires the difficult judgment that the same problem is solved by "insight" rather than by trial and error. Chevalier-Skolnikoff (1989) examined spontaneous tool use, categorizing the observations by stage, and found that cebus monkeys and chimpanzees, but not spider monkeys, showed tool use that could be characterized as stage 6. This is in keeping with recent findings by Visalberghi, Fragaszy, and Savage-Rumbaugh (1995), who found cebus and three species of apes (chimpanzees, bonobos, and orangutans) capable of modifying sticks presented to them and successfully solving a tube-retrieval task. The apes, however, in contrast with the monkeys, showed a decline in errors across blocks of trials. This result suggests that the apes but not the monkeys used representation or remembered experience rather than continued trial and error in solving the task on subsequent trials. Limongelli, Boysen, and Visalberghi (1995) modified the tool-retrieval task by introducing a trap into which the lure would fall if pushed from the "incorrect" end of the tube. Two of five chimpanzees solved this task and demonstrated in a follow-up experiment that their success was based on prediction of the trajectory of the lure. The single cebus monkey that solved this trap problem demonstrated rote responding on the control task (Visalberghi and Limongelli 1994). Despite the need to overcome extensive technical difficulties, researchers have demonstrated representational abilities in apes, suggesting that they may exceed the abilities of monkeys in this domain.

Evidence also indicates that representational skills are used in the wild. Boesch and Boesch (1984) observed that chimpanzees were able to recall the locations of up to five stones appropriate for nut-cracking and to retrieve the stone nearest to the goal tree. This would require keeping the goal (e.g., nut-cracking) in mind while retrieving the tool, an act similar in representational structure to level 5 play. Byrne (1995:137–40) summarized observations of possible instances of representational play in captive and wild apes.

Phonetic Development

Children's earliest vocalization is crying as an expression of their state of discomfort. Noncry vocalizations termed "coos" begin to occur shortly, often in pleasant social situations. Both cries and coos exhibit primarily laryngeal modulation of the air stream. Babbling, beginning in the later half of the first year, involves at least rhythmic jaw opening and closing, coordinated with breathing, and may also include fine motor control of the tongue in relation to other oral structures.

Human infant babbling is characterized by rhythmic repetition of consonant-vowel syllables in sequence and by a developmental increase in both the proportion of vocalizations including a consonant and the size of the consonant repertoire (Stoel-Gammon and Otomo 1986; Roug, Landberg, and Lundberg 1989; Oller et al. 1992). The phonetic parameters of babbling also characterize infant speech (Vihman et al. 1985; Vihman and Miller 1988). In contrast with earlier studies, Snowdon (this volume) presents evidence of "babbling" in certain marmoset species. These vocalizations involve production of portions of the species' call in repetitive bouts out of context. Because monkey vocalizations are laryngeally based, the babbled vocalizations no doubt share this property.

Vihman and I (McCune and Vihman 1987, n.d.) described children's development of "vocal motor schemes" that served to organize their babble and predicted the individualized phonetic forms of their early words. The rhythmic structure and repetitive character of babbling is similar to other rhythmicities, such as kicking and manual banging, that emerge around the same time (Thelen 1981). Vocal motor skill, seen as a particularly complex subtype of motor skills (Thelen 1991), may be expected to develop toward more organized vocal patterns in much the same way that changes are exhibited in manual activities such as rhythmic banging, which gives way to more discrete manual activities such as picking up a small pellet with thumb and index finger.

Early talkers (those who showed the transition to referential word use by 16 months) exhibited vocal motor schemes suggesting systematic organization and motor control in their babble, whereas later talkers omitted babble or failed to show systematic organization in babble (McCune and Vihman 1987, n.d.). Later talkers' vocal motor control was exhibited in words and sentences developing between 18 and 28 months without a prior organized babbling period. By three years of age, the early and later talkers showed indistinguishable language abilities. Vihman, Velleman, and I (1994) identified individual patterns of development in the phonological expression of early language learners' lexicons, some traceable to the child's preverbal vocal motor schemes (see also Vihman and Velleman 1989; Vihman 1996).

Initial Semantic Development
The nature of children's early words has been the subject of controversy. Are children's words referential from the beginning? If not, how might reference emerge? Werner and Kaplan described an initial

period in which wordlike forms were limited to familiar event contexts and were imbedded in those contexts. Fully referential words symbolic of specific semantic content emerged later. Vihman and I (1994) reported that situationally limited words—those limited in occurrence to specific events and objects—developed prior to referential words in some children. These situationally limited words included social expressions (e.g., "please," "hi," "yay") and words accompanying baby games (e.g., "peek-a-boo" in a hiding game or "baa" in response to "What does the sheep say?"). These expressions are notable as parts of "interindividual routines" (Bruner 1975; Savage-Rumbaugh et al. 1993; King 1994a), some of which also characterize adult social interaction and others of which are designed by adults for the purpose of interacting with children.

Unlike referential words, these and other situationally dependent expressions are elicited by consistent and recurrent events and may be learned from adults as routine aspects of such events; in the latter case, the child relies on more general processes of learning and memory rather than on the referential construing of generalizable symbol-referent relationships (Bloom 1993; Rovee-Collier 1995). These words convey information about the child's I-state (involvement in the ongoing event) and may express the child's desire to experience I-states matching those of other participants from whom the words have been learned.

Werner and Kaplan (1963:20) claimed that "an *intentional act of denotative reference* is required" for referential language in which one entity (e.g., an acoustic pattern) is construed as a symbol designating another (e.g., an internal meaning exemplified in various external objects). Similarly, Donald (1991, 1993) claimed "lexical invention" to be the outgrowth of the mimetic skill that is the foundation for language systems. He described a mutually influential creative tension between phonetic form and meaning. Unlike theorists who discuss the mapping of meanings onto forms or vice versa, Donald, like Werner and Kaplan, believes that an analogical and metaphorical process underlies symbol-referent relationships in language and that these relationships always involve linguistic creativity. According to Donald, the capacity for lexical invention was a precursor to, or a concurrent development with, phonetic skill. He doubts that humans, without phonetic skill, would have been able to "sustain the expansion of the lexical capacity" (Donald 1993:743).

Two forms of early referential expression occur in the single-word period: nominal expressions referring to entities and persons and relational expressions referring to the dynamic aspects of ongoing events (Bloom 1973; McCune-Nicolich 1981b; Vihman and McCune 1994; McCune and Vihman 1999). Nominal expressions refer to entities exhibiting physical characteristics in common (e.g., "ball" applied to round objects). Relational expressions, which have been studied infrequently, refer to dynamic aspects of events unfolding in space and time (Talmy 1975; Langacker 1991a). The meanings of these words reflect the child's earliest perceptual experience of objects in motion (Kellman 1993). Familiar examples are "up," indicating positive vertical movement or position, "allgone," when an object disappears from view, and "stuck," when objects are attached. While both nominal and relational expressions refer, by their relational quality the latter prefigure predicative language.

In summary, entry into language for young humans involves parallel and interlocking developmental changes across several domains within the child, in the context of species-typical experiences of social relationships and a culturally maintained linguistic system. The development of referential speech requires (1) representational ability, (2) phonetic skill sufficient for vocal expression, and (3) recognition of sound-meaning correspondence. The child gradually experiences the self in relation to social beings external to the self. Phonetic skill develops through babbling and experiencing acoustic and proprioceptive aspects of the infant's own and others' sounds. A capacity for representation comes to support the construction of meaningful symbol-referent relations.

The communicative grunt, derived from physiological experience, may be the child's initial personal symbol. Experience of laryngeal vocalizations (grunts) accompanying consistent psychological experiences of meaning leads to "invention" of a relation between such meaningful states and the grunt vocalization. The integration of these experiences yields the capacity for the intentional acts of denotative reference by which the child comes to acquire referential words accepted as part of the linguistic system of the community.

COMMUNICATIVE DEVELOPMENT: A COMPARATIVE APPROACH

Given the proposed model for the transition to language in human infants, one can examine the extent to which the same underlying abilities characterize the transition of other infant primates into the species-specific vocal repertoire, and for cross-fostered chimpanzees, their transition into human-devised symbol systems. Genetic and neurological similarities between humans and other primates suggest continuities in communicative development, despite the radical dissimilarities in behavior obvious from birth. Gibson and Jessee (this volume) suggest that uniquely human neural structures underlying language are unlikely; rather, a number of critical structures shared with other species have undergone expansion and reorganization in the course of evolution. Deacon (1992, 1997) presents evidence of the integration of those brain structures that underlie vocalization in other primates with neocortical structures in humans, and of a facilitating role for neocortical structures in the vocalizations of other primates. Bastian (1965) observed that laryngeal and sublaryngeal mechanisms shared by humans and other primates account for differences in pitch, timing, and intensity that are important for both linguistic and nonlinguistic communication.

Indeed, descriptions in the literature show cross-species similarity in the form of communication of interest here, the communicative grunt. According to Goodall's observations of chimpanzees, "[v]ocalized communication among friendly individuals comprises, for the most part, a variety of soft grunt-like sounds" (1986:128). In vervet monkeys, Cheney and Seyfarth (1982) have demonstrated the use of acoustically distinct grunts that discriminate individuals by rank and familiarity. An additional distinct grunt form is used when the animal giving the call or others in view are moving into an open area. Gorillas' grunts seem predictive of group movement (Stewart and Harcourt 1994). Thus, despite differences between human language and primate vocal communication, laryngeally based vocalizations mediating social relationships are characteristic of both.

Communicative Exchanges of Vervet Monkeys

Vervet monkeys use acoustically distinct alarm calls in response to eagles, leopards, snakes, and minor mammalian predators (Struhsaker 1967; Seyfarth, Cheney, and Marler 1980). Animals hearing a call first scan the area to sight the predator, then take suitable protective action. Adults may repeat alarm calls in chorus, including infant calls, when given in the correct context. Examination of the probable I-states of signaler and receiver suggests explanatory mechanisms for this sequence of events. The I-state of the calling animal probably includes focus on the specific predator with continuing peripheral awareness of the presence of other vervets, an affective tone relevant to the imminent danger, and an intention to take protective action. The behavior of the animals within hearing seems similar to that of human occupants of a crowded theater upon hearing the shout "Fire!" Upon hearing the call, the animals probably experience an I-state related to that experienced when they themselves make the same call in the presence of the specific predator. Like the occupants of the theater, they may scan the environment in search of the predator. Upon noting it, they experience the full I-state elicited by this experience, with expression of the call and escape behaviors following from this I-state.

This vocal exchange and its behavioral consequences suggest that the initial caller and animals within hearing are acting on the basis of equivalent or matching I-states, with the hearer taking action functionally the same as that of the speaker. Communication by matching I-states may be achieved adventitiously, without the speaker's intending to communicate by means of the vocal expression, just as the frightened theatergoer may shout "Fire!" without a communicative goal. Hearing the word "fire" with an excited intonation induces an I-state in the hearer like that experienced in the presence of an observed fire. Hearing an alarm call may serve as a "reminder" for the vervets, beginning a reactivation of the I-state experience of previous encounters in which the hearer had produced this call in the presence of the predator (Rovee-Collier et al. 1980; Rovee-Collier 1995). Seeking the predator visually suggests the effects of the reactivation process. By visually searching, the hearer either completes the reactivation of the full I-state, calls, and takes protective action, or else fails to find the predator and thus does not experience the I-state matching that of the animal giving the original alarm. In this case, the monkey neither repeats the alarm nor takes protective action.

Vervet grunts provide an additional example in which call exchanges can be described by matching I-states. Cheney and Seyfarth (1990) reported that examples recorded and analyzed up until the time of their writing indicated that interindividual grunt exchanges involved repetition of the same grunt. For example, a dominant animal who received a "grunt to a dominant" from a subordinate animal "replied" with the same form, a "grunt to a dominant," rather than a "grunt to a subordinate," even though he was addressing a subordinate animal. The authors suggested the possibility that "the function of these calls was to communicate 'message received'" (1990:127). Consideration of I-states provides a mechanism in support of this interpretation, as follows. Hearing a grunt to a dominant induces in the individual some aspects of the I-state he or she experiences when producing the same grunt form to a dominant animal. Based on this I-state, the hearer, although interacting with an animal subordinate in rank, produces a grunt to a dominant, thus allowing a match or symmetry of I-states between animals differing in rank. This exchange thus neutralizes the otherwise more volatile affective experience of both animals, allowing them to remain in proximity.

Since vervet grunts are discrete elements of a general form with continuous acoustic properties, Cheney and Seyfarth (1990) questioned why vervets have not developed additional vocalizations useful for survival, such as a grunt that a mother might use to convey to an infant in danger the message "Follow me" (1990:119). In the cases of alarm calls and grunts discussed so far, the communicating animal produces an expression of its own ongoing I-state, which leads to a matching I-state in the receiving animal. The message "Follow me" requires instatement of an I-state in the receiving animal somewhat different from that experienced by the communicating animal. For both, the focus would be the extant danger—for example, an observed predator—and the affective tone would be one of fear. However, the communicating animal experiences, in addition, the desire to influence the behavior of the receiver and must encode a message to that effect. For communication to succeed, the receiving animal must experience and act upon the additional intention to move toward the communicating animal. Descriptions of vervet communication in the literature give no evidence of the capacity to convey an I-state beyond that matching the caller's ongoing experience.

Unlike human infants, vervets and other nonhuman primates may produce vocalizations highly similar to the adult repertoire from birth. However, these may not be produced in the correct adult context initially, nor do juveniles exhibit comprehension of adult calls from birth (Seyfarth and Cheney 1986). It seems that primates other than humans must also learn something about sound-meaning correspondence as it functions within the species. I propose that for other primate infants, as for humans, the reflexive accompaniment of movement and effort with grunted vocalization forms the bridge to productive comprehension and use of the species-specific repertoire found in adults. Preliminary evidence in support of this hypothesis includes the observation that earliest grunts occur only with movement or effort and are followed by grunts in the absence of effort that take the specific adult form and are limited to appropriate contexts. Consistent comprehension of alarm calls and their production limited to appropriate circumstances should follow appropriate comprehension and use of one or more of the species' grunt vocalizations.

Development of the Vervet Vocal Repertoire

Cheney and Seyfarth (1990) reported that vervet infants grunted with high frequency from birth. Seyfarth and Cheney (1986) found that the acoustic features of infant and juvenile grunts, including call length and unit length, differed significantly from those of adult grunts, a finding that could not be accounted for by anatomical growth. Infant grunts only gradually approached the adult forms. The earliest grunts reported (at one to eight weeks of age), regardless of which adult form they resembled, tended to occur in the context of movement or struggle, a context similar to that of human infants' effort grunts.

Between 9 and 16 weeks, the infants used the grunt form produced by adults when they themselves or others moved into an open area (a "MIO grunt") both in the appropriate context and when following another animal. Some of these grunts apparently accompanied the infants' own movement and might be analogous to the "effort grunts" of human infants, whereas other grunts took notice of other animals and might be analogous to human infants' "attention grunts." This distribution continued throughout the second and third years, only gradually becoming restricted to the adult context of announcing, noticing, or predicting movement into an open area. Infant grunts resembling the grunt to a subordinate and the grunt to another group also accompanied movement between 9 and 16 weeks. During this same period, the seven grunts recorded that resembled the grunt to a dominant occurred while the infant was in observation of other animals, with no movement reported. If vervets develop attention grunts, these may begin during the three- to four-month age range, with other animals as the focus of attention.

The next age category reported spanned 17 weeks to 2 years. Except for a few examples in each category where the infant grunted as it followed its mother, movement was associated only with the species-specific, movement-related adult grunt. Among observed young between two and three years of age, all four categories of grunts used in vervet communication displayed adult acoustic features and use. These seem analogous to the communicative grunts observed in human infants at the transition to language, but the specificity to particular situations seems analogous, as Cheney and Seyfarth note, to words.

It seems plausible that the association of movement and effort with reflexive grunts assists vervets in apprehending the "meaning" of adult vocalizations. That vervets have a grunt appropriate for observed and predicted movement may further assist the animal in making the initial transition to appropriate species-specific vocalization. In fact, the grunt associated with movement is the first one used appropriately by the infants.

Unlike grunts, alarm calls were infrequent in infancy and were not observed prior to one month of age. The few calls recorded prior to six months of age were acoustically indistinguishable from those of adults. Infants' early use of alarm calls is not random. For example, the eagle alarm is from the beginning restricted to birds and other items "in the air." This use may be learned initially as part of an interindividual routine in which the infant observes conspecifics to vocalize and look up. However, appropriate responses to alarms and the limiting of production to those predators eliciting alarms from adults develop only gradually during the early years.

Infants may learn from adults' tendency to repeat alarm calls after confirming the presence of the predator, although such repetition is no more likely following an infant's than an adult's initial alarm. Caro and Hauser (1992) reported that appropriate alarm calls in subsequent predator encounters were more likely for infants whose correct alarm calls had been repeated by adults. They further observed four cases of "punishment" in which vervet mothers who initially fled in response to an incorrect infant alarm call subsequently returned to bite or slap the infant. Vervet monkeys make use of alarm calls given by starlings to species that prey on both starlings and vervets. Hauser (1988) demonstrated that infants' development of the ability to respond appropriately to the alarm calls of starlings varied with extent of exposure, demonstrating the effects of learning. It may be the case that vervet infants' apprehension of the relevance of vocal signals to I-states is derived from or facilitated by the early experience of their own reflexive grunts. This understanding would render them sensitive to developing comprehension and production of vocal signals that correspond to relevant I-states within the capacity of the species. The proposed sequence of development is summarized in figure 8.3.

Alarm calls are referential, in the sense that they select out a type of predator in contrast to other predators. They also function to communicate. Evidence is clear that calls are voluntary and more likely in the presence of other animals, but as Cheney and Seyfarth report, strategies to ensure successful communication or to repair failed communication have not been observed, leaving open the question of whether the vervets intend their calls to communicate with others.

Communicative Exchanges of Chimpanzees in Natural Environments

The vocal repertoire of chimpanzees, although highly varied both in the range of circumstances for which calls are used and in the qual-

Birth	1–3 Months	3–4 Months	6–7 Months	1–2 Years
Scream (adultlike)				
Wrr (adultlike)				
Grunt: Some features adultlike but others significantly different				
	Effort (?) grunts: Often accompany movement	**Attention (?) grunts:** 60% predict or notice movement (adult use)		**Communicative (?) grunts:** Develop all adult acoustic properties and appropriate use
	Alarm calls begin. They are acoustically like the adults' but applied to broader categories of species	Same response to all alarm types	Consistent adultlike response to each alarm type	Alarm calls develop appropriate use

FIGURE 8.3

Steps toward adult communication in vervet infants.

ity of vocalization by individuals, involves variation on four themes: hoots, barks, screams, and grunts and pants (Van Lawick, Marler, and Van Lawick-Goodall 1971; Marler 1976; Goodall 1986). Boehm (1989) highlighted the potential of grunts, noting that they are occasionally employed in conversational bouts and are prevalent in open country, although their functions are poorly understood. Grunts "relating to nesting and travel...must be considered to be one possible additional source of preadaptation useful to evolutionary development of vocal communication in the human direction" (Goodall 1986:377). The "rough grunt" is known to be specific to situations involving food (Marler and Tenaza 1977). Goodall reported grunts serving to "regulate group movement"; these were likely to occur when animals foraging together but out of sight of one another paused before moving on (Goodall 1986). Rough grunt production varies with the quantity of food found (Hauser and Wrangham 1987; Hauser et al. 1993), and chimpanzees patrolling the edges of their range refrain from vocalizing (Goodall 1986), thus demonstrating voluntary aspects of their vocalization.

Boehm (1992) indicated that gestural communication is as important as vocal communication in chimpanzees, with overlapping messages sometimes conveyed in the two modalities. Some vocalizations such as food grunts and grunts associated with travel probably function to induce matching I-states between the communicating animals. These vocalizations express the I-state of the feeding or traveling individual directly. As discussed earlier, hearing such vocalizations would tend to induce in hearers some aspects of their own typical experience when they produce such vocalizations, thus achieving matching I-states with the calling animal.

As de Waal (1984) describes it, the greeting ritual accorded to dominant males seems to exemplify communication leading to reciprocal I-states between the participants. The subordinate animal approaches the dominant with ever deeper bows accompanied by a series of short panting grunts, while looking up at the individual he is greeting. The chimpanzee receiving a greeting to a dominant, unlike a vervet in similar circumstances, does not repeat the vocalization heard. Rather, he rises to his greatest height and, making his hair stand on end, presents a visual representation of his dominant position. As the subordinate animal expresses the weakness of its position, the dominant animal, rather than experiencing a matching sense of weakness, expresses a reciprocal (in this case opposite) sense of strength and potential aggression.

Boehm described an interchange between a mother and daughter (Wunda and Winkle) at Gombe in which the mother repeatedly attempted to induce her daughter to follow, while the daughter attempted to induce the mother to stay. The mother eventually succeeded in calling her daughter to her by producing a whimper after a long series of slight movements away and pauses to look at the young chimpanzee. Examples such as these suggest that chimpanzees in the wild are capable of communicating I-states distinct from but related to their own current behavior and thus of coordinating reciprocal roles in a communicative event. Similarly, in laboratory experiments chimpanzees (but not monkeys) trained in only one of two cooperative roles in a problem-solving task successfully perform the reciprocal role without further training (Povinelli, Nelson, and Boysen 1992; Povinelli, Parks, and Novak 1992; Byrne 1995). The superior mental representation of apes described earlier contributes to these abilities.

Chimpanzee Communicative Development

Chimpanzee infants, like human babies, are completely dependent on maternal care from birth. They are supported by the mother against her body for the first two months, gradually increasing the frequency of independent ventral clinging (Plooij 1979). Between three and five months of age they become capable of quadrupedal locomotion and begin to cling to their mothers' backs while traveling. Infants are carried by their mothers for three or four years and commonly nurse for four to five years (Teleki 1989). Plooij (1984) studied six mother-infant pairs of the Gombe Stream group described by Goodall (1986). The observational study used a quasi-longitudinal multiple case study design covering the age span of birth to 30 months. Vocalization data were reported in detail on two infants for the first six months. Detailed case reports included evaluation of three classes of vocalizations: effort grunts, "uh-grunts" singly and in series, and whimpers. These data can serve in a pilot examination of my thesis regarding the role of autonomically produced grunts in the development of vocal communication in chimpanzees.

Plooij described the effort grunt as an explosive expulsion of air "resulting when breath, after being held while making some physical effort, is released." It might be "vocalized," was produced "with mouth and lips slightly open," and was used "whenever a baby was moving or struggling over its mother in search of the nipple" (Plooij 1984:47). Of effort grunts observed, 87 percent accompanied movement. Observations in which effort grunts occurred without movement (n = 72) involved the infant lying prone over its mother's thigh, head outward. The author speculated that "the baby was keeping balance, which involves muscular effort not visible in gross movement" (1984:46). Plooij added: "Although much rarer, effort-grunts were observed in other age classes and in both sexes, and again in combination with an increased effort." Plooij noted effort grunts, for example, from a juvenile who was standing on his head and from an adult male who was trying unsuccessfully to break open a wasps' nest using a large branch as a lever (1984:46-47).

There was an increase in frequency of effort grunts associated with struggling over the mother toward the end of the first month and with reaching for things toward the end of the second month. Between months two and five, the frequency declined to near zero. A vocalization termed the "uh-grunt," produced with lips pushed forward and closed, occurring singly or in series, was also observed frequently from birth. In the early months it seemed to be a startle response to various sudden stimuli. From three months on it was limited to situations in which other chimpanzees were in view or their vocalizations were noticed. In the early months, uh-grunt series occurred frequently with whimpering, and the two could grade into each other on the same exhalation. Between three and five months, the infants discriminated uh-grunts from whimpers and restricted uh-grunt series to adult males and females at close range. Unfortunately for my purposes, the Plooij report includes no further data on the development of the species-typical adult vocal repertoire. The uh-grunt "series and staccato," as it was described, may be the infantile precursor of the "soft grunts," "pant-grunts," and "laughter" described by Goodall.

The data available can be interpreted as demonstrating a shift in function for grunts in chimpanzees analogous to that proposed for human babies. Effort grunts, identified as such by Plooij, and an additional (probably reflexive) grunt—the uh-grunt in response to startle—occur from birth. Effort grunts decline with increasing motor ability, and uh-grunts come to mark notice of other chimpanzees, perhaps analogous to human infants' attention grunts. Finally, uh-grunts are directed to adult animals, a use overlapping with the adult communicative repertoire. This sequence is described in figure 8.4 in the context of additional developmental variables.

Along with chimpanzee infants' total dependence on maternal care come opportunities like those experienced by human infant-parent dyads for developing intense affective connections. The changing use of whimpers demonstrates this bond as well as the developmental effects of cognitive and motor progress (Plooij 1984). Initially, whimpers occur whenever the infant is out of ventral contact with the mother. With development, the infant can tolerate loss of ventral contact so long as the mother is in view. A two-month-old infant in close proximity to the mother who is out of the line of vision whimpers until visual contact is restored. During this time period the infant has a brief phase of interest in the mother's face and begins to grasp objects. These activities are reminiscent of behaviors characterizing human infants at a slightly older age. Such activities are precursors to the development of individuation and of joint attention to objects, which form the foundation for I-states related to referential understanding in human infant-parent dyads. By seven to nine months the chimpanzee infant, like the human baby, is taking brief excursions away from the mother and whimpers only when out of arm's reach. The infant also begins to follow others and to use gestures such as begging for food with arm outstretched to mother's mouth. At around 12 months of age, gestures inviting activities are observed, and the infant "plays" at nest-building, an activity that seems to echo the dawn of representational play in human infants. This developmental sequence suggests the preparatory phases noted in figure 8.2 for human infants as they approach language.

Birth	2 Months	3–5 Months	7–9 Months	12 Months
			Vocal data limited	Vocal data unavailable
Effort grunts accompany movement	**Attention (?) grunt:** Uh-grunt at sight or sound of other chimps	Mutual regulation in mother-infant play		
Uh-grunts and series are reactions to starting stimuli		**Communicative grunt:** Uh-grunt and series to adult chimps		
Whimper: loss of ventral contact	Whimper: out of contact + out of sight		Whimper: out of arm's reach	
Scream: distress	Clings ventrally without support	Clings on back	Follows familiar others	
Clings: mother supports	Interest in mother's face	Walks in quadruped position	Communicative gestures such as begging	Gestures inviting activities, e.g., tickle
	Grasps objects			Plays at nest-building

FIGURE 8.4

Steps toward adult communication in chimpanzee infants.

Chimpanzees in Human Homes and Laboratories

In the context of spontaneous interactions beginning early in development, chimpanzees can learn to name, request, comment, and combine symbols using elements of a human language (American Sign Language; Gardner and Gardner 1975, 1989). Loulis, a chimpanzee who experienced signs only from other chimpanzees, developed a repertoire of 50 signs during a 5-year period (Fouts, Hirsch, and Fouts 1982; Gardner and Gardner 1992). When offered opportunities to expand the range of meanings they can express along with the means to express them, chimpanzees incorporate these into their daily existence.

Chimpanzees are capable of I-states overlapping with those of humans, in addition to those expressed in the species-typical repertoire. Specifically, the I-state of joint attention to objects and contemplation of their names and relationships seems to be induced by socialization in human culture. Such modifiability of I-state, a powerful mechanism for change in response to environmental contingencies, is also a capacity of the human species. Initially chimpanzee language projects incorporated such operant methods as structured reinforcement and shaping. Monitoring of the animals' progress under differing learning conditions has demonstrated that they acquire symbols most effectively in the kinds of routine and caregiving interactions that characterize the verbal environment of human infants (Gardner and Gardner 1975; Bruner 1983; Nelson 1985; Savage-Rumbaugh et al. 1993).

Savage-Rumbaugh (1986) demonstrated the importance of the animal's developing an I-state appropriate to the communicative goals identified by experimenters. Although chimpanzees have something like a "name" for food (the rough grunt and its series), the I-state underlying the vocalization includes imminent availability of the food for consumption. In the chimpanzee-typical I-state, food exemplifies what Werner and Kaplan (1963) term a "thing of action," where functional aspects may predominate. "It is our view that those objects which enter into symbolic activity must be things-of-contemplation, that is, objects that one 'regards out there,' rather than things upon which one merely acts in the service of immediate biological need satisfaction" (Werner and Kaplan 1963:67).

Initially, Sherman and Austin (chimpanzees aged two and a half and one and a half, respectively) made no progress in learning to "name" foods that were not available to be eaten. Only through a lengthy and arduous process of "fading" (providing smaller and smaller bits of the food to be named, along with a consistent but different food reward) did the animals learn to distinguish the "referential" value of their symbols from the signal value indicating a food to be eaten. In order to name foods, the chimpanzees needed to treat foods as "things of contemplation."

Once foods were named, this ability was not extended immediately to tools. Tool names could easily be elicited in contexts where the tool was about to be used, but not in the context simply of contemplation in the absence of imminent use. Chimpanzees use and modify tools in the wild (McGrew 1992), so they experience I-states in which such objects and their functions are the focus. The I-state of "naming" and contemplating nonfoods required further extensive training. It is of interest that the animals did not learn these skills gradually over many trials. Rather, they experienced large numbers of trials over several days with nearly random responses and then suddenly began performing almost 100 percent correctly. This pattern suggests the induction of an I-state underlying these new performances, of which the animals were previously incapable (perhaps another phase of the shift in meaning from objects of action to objects of contemplation), and it recalls the sharp upswing in lexical expression following human infants' transition to reference (Bates, Dale, and Thal 1995; McCune and Vihman n.d.). The solidity of the knowledge eventually attained by the animals was demonstrated in their ability to name foods and tools and categorize both the real items and their symbols based on category membership as humans experience it.

Foods are a privileged category for chimpanzees in the sense that identifying and acquiring them is critical to survival. Chimpanzees must devote a large proportion of their time to food acquisition and consumption (McGrew 1992). Savage-Rumbaugh (1979) reported unsuccessful attempts to teach object reference using other objects before discovering the successful strategy of training for names of foods and of tools used to extract food. Food is equally important to humans, but adult culture provides for feeding of the young until maturity. Thus human infants and children spend a small proportion of time seeking and consuming food but a larger proportion interacting with objects. Such interaction with objects is critical to the cognitive development appropriate for human society. The young of both species are socialized from the early weeks in the species-appropriate direction through participation in adult activities and/or provision of specific opportunities for learning.

The combination of conspecific socialization with socialization into a human symbol-using community from early infancy provides an ideal opportunity for young animals to develop appropriate psychosocial bonds while experiencing the broader range of meanings offered in human culture. The bonobos *(Pan paniscus)* Mulika and Kanzi acquired nearly 50 lexigrams through a combination of observing the "lessons" of older bonobos and participating in caregiving and game routines in which lexigram symbols and spoken English were incorporated (Savage-Rumbaugh et al. 1986). Brakke and Savage-Rumbaugh (1993) reported the results of rearing a chimpanzee (Panpanzee) and a bonobo (Panbanisha) together while providing access to older animals and the same opportunities for acquiring lexigram symbols that Kanzi and Mulika had experienced, with similar results.

Kanzi first learned symbol use without specific teaching by observing training sessions with his foster mother, Matata. Consequently, his skills were not tested until he was two and a half years of age, when they were discovered upon his separation from Matata. Mulika experienced both observational learning and the use of lexigrams by humans in interactive contexts from the early months of life. She began to use a single lexigram, "milk," at 12 months with a generalized meaning that seems similar to the use of communicative grunting in human babies, including the specification of the referent of her communicative expression by an accompanying point. Panbanisha began symbol use at 11 months, also with the lexigram for "milk," which was initially overgeneralized. Savage-Rumbaugh and colleagues (1986) noted the similarity of Mulika's use of "milk" to conventionalized vocal gestures, including grunting as reported by Bates and colleagues (1979) for human children. The authors attributed the use of "milk" to the insight that the keyboard was a communication tool, much as we interpret communicative grunts as indicating that a vocal form can represent an I-state, a forerunner of the development of specific "names" for "things." It is probably not accidental that the infants used a name associated with their most salient food as their first acquired human symbol.

The Hayeses (Hayes 1951) adopted the chimpanzee infant Viki at birth and treated her as much as possible like a human baby, allowing her to sleep in their room and to have free run of the house in play. Viki exhibited species-typical behavior toward her adopted mother as described in table 8.3, including the demand for close physical contact. The Hayeses had anticipated that Viki might develop a communicative vocal repertoire under these circumstances, much as a human baby might. Noting that Viki vocalized very little after a brief period of vocal play at one to four months, the Hayeses began training her to vocalize to gain attention and have her needs met. Of interest here is the form of her initial vocalization, produced under these circumstances: a spontaneous grunt ("ah"). Viki's first word ("mama") was formed by manually closing her lips as she produced this vocalization. The exact status of her words as such (three were reported: "mama," "papa," and "cup") remains in question, but she continued to use variants of the "ah" sound for communicative purposes. Although this study is often remarked for its failure to train Viki to use vocal language, it seems just as remarkable for the evidence it provides of the relationship established between a human adult and an infant chimpanzee and for demonstrating that the chimpanzee could gain voluntary control and communicative use of a laryngeal vocalization.

In summary, there is evidence that the development of grunt communication in nonhuman primate infants parallels that in human infants. Both vervet monkeys and chimpanzees exhibit effort grunts in infancy, prior to use of a related, laryngeally based grunt form for communication. In vervets, appropriate use and comprehension of alarm calls, with their referential quality, appears to occur later than competence with grunt communication, showing similarity to the sequential development of communicative grunts and referential language in human infants. Communication appears to be limited, however, to expression of the animals' ongoing experience. In chimpanzees, longitudinal study of a few infants has demonstrated effort grunts and uh-grunts as startle responses prior to grunts in communicative contexts, but data are unavailable on the transition from infant vocalizations to the full vocal repertoire in chimpanzees. Observation of apes both in captivity and in the wild, in contrast with monkeys, finds manual gestures and representational activities. Studies of chimpanzees exposed to human symbol systems have demonstrated the animals' capacity for symbolic communication. Chimpanzees are capable of purely referential communication, which develops spontaneously in the context of human interactions that include exposure to a symbol system. When operant learning procedures were used, extensive structured experience was needed before the animals could treat symbols for food as purely referential. Rather than being a representational constraint, chimpanzees' limitation in expressing referential meaning appears to be phonetic, related to limited fine motor control of the articulatory organs, and conceptual, related to the limitation on meanings and relationships that they are capable of entertaining.

CONCLUSION

I have proposed a human model for the development of reference. In the context of close affective bonds with primary caregivers, infants develop the capacity for symbolic representation, refine the vocal motor skill needed for producing words of their language, recognize the function of sound-meaning correspondence, and proceed to referential language production and comprehension. Numerous studies have revealed attachment relationships and development of representational abilities in nonhuman primates, the latter usually distinguishing apes from monkeys.

Human infants demonstrate development from metabolic to communicative function for a simple laryngeal vocalization, suggesting a developing ability to control what is initially an involuntary vocalization. Both vervets and chimpanzees have shown such control (Cheney and Seyfarth 1990; Hauser et al. 1993). In human infants who develop physiological and neurological structures suited to speech, communicative grunts herald the onset of referential language. In other species, too, the grunt may provide a foundation for other controlled signals. Might a consistent developmental process affect the transition to controlled vocal signaling across primate species? If so, calls in which referential qualities accompany or dominate reflexive or motivational aspects (Marler, Evans, and Hauser 1992) would be expected to develop after grunt vocalizations shift from autonomic accompaniments of effort to communicative use. This seems to be the case for vervet monkeys, whereas developmental data remain incomplete for chimpanzees. Among cross-fostered chimpanzees, Viki's learned communicative vocalization to her caregivers took the grunt form. Grunts are produced by Kanzi and other apes studied by Savage-Rumbaugh and associates, but grunt development has not been systematically studied. It is of interest that the animals' initial keyboard use involved broad communicative use of a single symbol, prior to referential use of a range of different lexigram words. This seems analogous to the human infant's use of grunts indicating recognition of the representational and communicative value of vocalization, prior to referential word use.

Consistency across extant species implicates a similar process in hominid ancestors. Perhaps parent-infant dyads provided the cradle of meaning for primates, with adult-adult communication building on the initial parent-infant repertoire (Parker and Gibson 1979). According to the model proposed here, the meaning potential of vocal communication is discovered by young primate individuals, including humans, because an autonomically produced vocalization accompanies a related class of physiological and psychological states (e.g., effort, attention). This accompaniment is an essential aspect of the metabolic functioning of the animal, thus ensuring that this adventitious discovery will be replicated across phylogenetic time. Differences in other aspects of biological endowment and environmental circumstances (e.g., cognitive or representational capacity; vocal repertoire of the natal social group) could explain differential paths from this common beginning.

9

Motivation, Conventionalization, and Arbitrariness in the Origin of Language

Robbins Burling

In this chapter I explore the role of what I call "motivated" signs in the origin of language. By motivated signs I mean signs that are not arbitrary and that are, therefore, very different from the typical arbitrary signs of language. At least since the time of Ferdinand de Saussure, early in the twentieth century (Saussure 1959 [1916]:69), linguists have generally insisted upon the arbitrary relationship between the form and the meaning of linguistic signs. The substance that English speakers call *bread* is called *pain* by the French and *roti* by speakers of Hindi, and any other name would do as well. All that is required is that everyone in the speech community agrees on some consistent convention. To be sure, a few onomatopoetic words echo the bleats of animals or the twitterings of birds, but these words have generally been looked upon as exceptions to the more general pattern of language.

Nevertheless, I argue that motivated signs are likely to have been important in the earlier stages of language.[1] I start by proposing a typology of the various forms of human and primate communication and by exploring the role of motivated signs within the context of other forms of communication. Next I survey the various kinds of motivated signs that are found in contemporary human languages. I then move on to diachronic change and consider several examples in which signs that began as motivated were gradually conventionalized until, having lost their motivation, they became totally arbitrary. The background having been given, I turn in the final sections of the chapter to phylogeny. There I consider the part that motivated signs could have played in the early stages of human language I conclude with some suggestions, admittedly speculative, about the stages through which the early antecedents of language could have passed.

ARBITRARY AND MOTIVATED SIGNS

To sort out the varieties of signs that human beings use, we can do no better than return to the American philosopher Charles Sanders Peirce and his famous three-way division of signs among "icons," "indices," and "symbols" (Peirce 1955). Figure 9.1 shows Peirce's classification of signs, except that I have added the level including "motivated" and "arbitrary," which Peirce did not make explicit.

Peirce used the term "symbol" for signs like the word "bread" whose form and meaning are related only by convention—that is, arbitrarily. Neither Peirce's indices nor his icons are arbitrary. An index is associated with the object or idea to which it refers—its referent—by proximity or causality. The pointing gesture by which I indicate a cat is an index. A footprint that tells me someone has passed and the smoke that indicates a fire are indices related to their referents by causality.

Peirce recognized three kinds of icons: images, metaphors, and diagrams. Images have a physical resemblance to their referents. Both pictures and onomatopoetic words resemble their referents, so they are obvious images. By moving my hand I can represent the direction or the manner in which an object moves, and these gestures, too, are images. Metaphors are more abstract. They need not literally resemble the physical form of their referent but relate to it in a more abstract way. When talking about a plan of action, I might hold my hands with the palms facing each other, in the same way that I might show the size of a fish. I would not suggest that a plan has an absolute size, but I do reveal a feeling that it is similar to a bounded object, something that

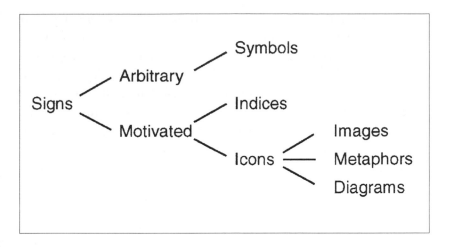

FIGURE 9.1

Varieties of Peircian signs.

has a beginning and an end. My hands do not form a picture of a plan, so they do not shape an image, but they relate to the idea of a plan (or at least to this particular plan) in a metaphorical way. Diagrams show the relationships among the parts of the object, but they need not resemble either the whole object or its parts. A wiring diagram shows how the parts of a circuit are connected, but neither the overall shape of the diagram nor the representations of the individual parts need to resemble the physical circuit. In the following pages, I often refer simply to "icons," but it will occasionally be helpful to distinguish among Peirce's three types of icons.

In their enthusiasm for arbitrariness, linguists have tended to minimize the role of iconicity and indexicality in language, but as soon as we widen our perspective to include the full range of human communication, motivated signs can no longer be so easily dismissed. Our gesticulations—the waving of our arms and the molding of our hands with which we accompany speech—are pervasively iconic. The sign languages of the deaf have more obvious iconicity than do the spoken languages of the hearing. All the earliest writing systems of which we have knowledge, such as Sumerian, early Egyptian, and ancient Chinese, were iconic in their extensive use of pictographs. Even spoken language shows more iconicity than Saussure and many later linguists have led us to expect. Not only do languages have the phonological iconicity of onomatopoeia and sound symbolism, but they have considerable syntactic iconicity as well.

I return to all of these varieties of iconicity later in the chapter, and I argue that the ability to produce and to interpret motivated signs, both icons and indices, could have been an important part of the cognitive foundation upon which the early language of our evolving human ancestors was built.

THE VARIETIES OF HUMAN COMMUNICATION

Human beings have several different forms of communication, and if we are to understand the evolutionary role of motivated signs, it is important to keep them distinct. Our two most distinctive forms of communication are language itself and what I have called our system of "gesture-calls" (Burling 1993). Our gesture-calls include our laughs and sobs, our smiles and frowns, our looks of puzzlement, annoyance, anger, and joy. Some of these are audible and some are visible, and several, such as laughs and sobs, are both. Some of our gesture-calls, including many facial expressions, are silent, but most of our calls are associated with characteristic gestures, so I find it artificial to separate the visible and audible components of our gesture-call system. What can be seen and what can be heard work so closely together that they have to be considered as constituting a single, unified communication system, and this is the reason for my hyphenated term. Our gesture-call system constitutes a large part, though by no means all, of what we often call our "nonverbal communication."

Our gesture-calls differ radically from language, not only in their form but also in the messages they characteristically convey. With our gesture-calls, including our facial expressions, bodily postures, and laughs and cries, we subtly convey the details of our emotions, and for the most part these signals are easily understood even when used by people of widely differing cultures.[2] Languages are more variable and require more learning.

It would be much too simple, however, to suppose that gesture-calls are determined entirely by our genetic inheritance while language has to be learned. We have to learn some particular language, but it is our biological inheritance that endows our minds with the potential for learning a language. The same thing is true of our gesture-calls. Much about them is set by our inherited human nature, but they are by no means immune to experience. Thus, like everything else that we are and do, both language and our gesture-calls are formed by the way our experiences act upon our inherited biological potential. Nevertheless, the learning that is required for language is certainly greater than the learning required for gesture-calls. With no training at all, we can understand a large part of the gesture-call system of the most culturally remote people on earth. We need years to achieve an equivalent control over a language not our own.

A more fundamental difference between our gesture-calls and language may be that gesture-calls form an analog system, with graded signals, while language is fundamentally digital. Graded signals, such as those that lie along the continuum from a giggle through a laugh and on to a guffaw, can no more be counted than the positions of a slide rule or of a continuously variable meter. Language, on the other hand, is constructed from units such as phonemes, words, and sentences that stand in contrast with one another. We cannot compromise between two different words, or between their meanings, in the way we can compromise between gesture-calls or slide rule positions. The units of language can be counted because they fall into contrastive sets.

Our gesture-call system is excellent for conveying our emotional state and for indicating our intentions. With our gesture-calls we can show that we are friendly and cooperative or, conversely, that we are angry or bored. We modulate all of our social relationships with our gesture-calls, offering polite smiles of deference and reassurance or suggesting subtly that it is time to break off a meeting. Most of us can probably convey the subtleties of our emotions, intentions, and degree of cooperative inclinations more successfully with our gesture-calls than with language.

Our gesture-calls, on the other hand, give us less help when we want to convey factual information about the world, and it is there that language comes into its own. Only with language can we describe things distant in time and space. We can feign with our gesture-calls but we cannot really lie. A proper lie requires language. We can do our best to laugh at a joke that we do not find funny, but most of us are not very skillful at conveying a misleading impression without words. When someone conveys one message with words but a different message with his facial expression, it is his face, not his words, that we believe. We have a strong sense of voluntary control over language. Voluntary control over our laughs, cries, and facial expressions is much more difficult to achieve.

.   The words of a language are organized by means of a complex syntax that makes it easy to form sentences that no one has ever said before. Lacking in syntax, gesture-calls never allow us to say anything really new. Quite apart from the productivity allowed by syntax, we can also add entirely new words to our language. New gesture-calls are impossible. Speakers of all languages control tens of thousands of distinct words. In order to keep all these words distinct from one another we need a phonological system that gives language its characteristic dual level of patterning. Lacking a huge contrastive vocabulary, our gesture-call system has no need of a separate phonological level. Even the neurology of the gesture-call system is different from that of language. Language is under cortical control; gesture-calls are under the control of the limbic system. In sum, language and gesture-calls use different machinery and convey different kinds of messages.

It should hardly have to be emphasized that the human gesture-call system closely resembles the gesture-call systems of other primates and even more distantly related mammals. Indeed, by using the label "gesture-calls," I have anticipated the conclusion that this part of human communication has a quite typical primate, and even mammalian, character. Of course the particular calls and gestures we use are not the same as those of any other species, although ours are quite similar to those of chimpanzees and are so close to those of bonobos that both they and we find it easy to understand each other's facial expressions and body language. Savage-Rumbaugh and Lewin (1994:106–7) give stunning examples of the ease with which humans and bonobos are able to communicate by means of what I am calling their gesture-call systems, a confirmation of the close relationship of our two species. As would be expected, our gesture-calls are less like those of more distantly related primates, but because every species has its own character-istic signals, our special signals give no grounds for surprise.

I emphasize the distinction between our gesture-calls and our language because I want to be clear about the questions I raise. Language is a relatively recent evolutionary development, and I want to ask how an animal without language could have evolved into an animal with language. I also want to ask what earlier behavior and aptitudes might have formed the background out of which language grew. Of course gesture-calls also evolved, but their evolutionary roots go back very much farther than language, and only confusion results from a failure to distinguish them.

The dichotomy between gesture-calls and language is basic to an understanding of human communication, but of course the story is more complex. To see the part that motivated signs play in communication, more detail is needed. Figure 9.2 adds several types of communication to those that I have already considered.

The double horizontal line in figure 9.2 divides the analog part of our communication at the top from the digital part at the bottom. The vertical line divides visible communication from audible. Only the cell for gesture-calls at the very top lacks the vertical division, for there it would be artificial to divide the visible from the audible. Elsewhere the diagram is arranged in a way that suggests the close parallelism between our audible and our visible communication. Wilcox (this volume) makes a strong case for the primacy of visible signals in language evolution. I remain agnostic on this issue, although, as I point out later, it is certainly easier to construct a hypothetical continuum that yields visible signals than to construct a corresponding continuum for audible signals. I do think it is worth emphasizing that every kind of communication we find in one modality has a close parallel in the other, and selection for skills in one modality is likely to have carried with it increased skills in the other.

At the bottom right of figure 9.2 is spoken language, balanced on its left by sign language. Since signing can exploit the three dimensions of visible space as well as the dimension of time, its organization can differ in significant ways from spoken language, but except for being visible rather than audible, it shares most of the characteristics of spoken

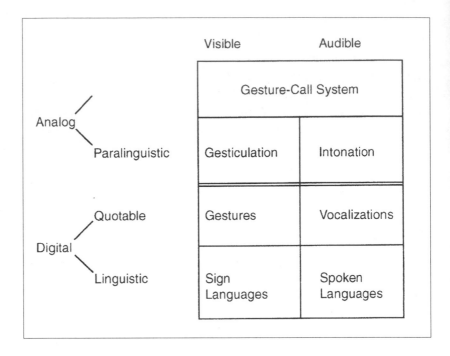

	Visible	Audible
Gesture-Call System		
Paralinguistic	Gesticulation	Intonation
Quotable	Gestures	Vocalizations
Linguistic	Sign Languages	Spoken Languages

Analog — Paralinguistic

Digital — Quotable — Linguistic

FIGURE 9.2

Types of human communication.

language. It is utterly different from a gesture-call system.

Just above the row for language are spaces for what Kendon (1988, 1992) has aptly called "quotable gestures" and for what might in symmetry be called "quotable vocalizations." Quotable gestures include such things as nods, head shakes, the V-for-victory sign, and the head screw that suggests someone is crazy. These are learned, conventional, and variable from culture to culture. They also contrast with one another, and it is this that makes them quotable. They share most of the characteristics of language, but because they are visible rather than audible, they cannot be incorporated into the phonology or syntax of a spoken language.

Nor are quotable vocalizations incorporated into phonology or syntax, and it is this that keeps them on a separate row from language in figure 9.2. Not conforming to standard phonology, the quotable vocalizations are difficult to spell, but they include the expressions we some-times write as *oh-oh* ("oops"), *tsk-tsk* ("shame!"), *m-hm* ("yes"), and *uh-uh* ("no"). Like the proper words of a language and like quotable gestures, these vocalizations need to be learned and are culturally variable. They also contrast, both with each other and with proper words. In all these respects they are much like quotable gestures.

In the remainder of this chapter I will have little to say about quotable gestures or quotable vocalizations. I mention them in order to make clear that quotable vocalizations are not the same as calls, and quotable gestures are very different from both the gestural component of our gesture-call system and from the gesticulation that accompanies language. The word "gesture" is dangerously ambiguous. Quotable ges-tures are much more languagelike than are our other facial or manual movements, and they are properly placed on the digital side of our communication system along with language.

Only one row of figure 9.2 remains to be considered. It includes gesticulation in the visible column and intonation in the audible. The purpose of this typology has been to isolate these two types of commu-nicative signals, and they will be the topics of the next three sections.

First, however, it is important to recognize that human beings make gestures of one other kind that is not included in figure 9.2. These can be called "instrumental gestures," and they are omitted from figure 9.2 because their basic function is not communication at all. They are the movements that all animals, including humans, need to make in the ordinary business of life. We move ourselves from place to place, we manipulate objects, we eat, we kick, we scratch. Wilcox (this volume) emphasizes the importance of instrumental gestures as grounding for human cognitive abilities and language capacity, and they may have played an important part in the evolution of communi-cation. Although instrumental gestures are designed to deal with the environment rather than to communicate, animals easily interpret many of the instrumental gestures made by conspecifics and even by members of other species. We understand what others are up to by the way they behave, so their instrumental gestures do communicate even if that is not their primary purpose. Because they must be adapted to the environment, instrumental gestures are inherently motivated. The shape of our hand iconically reflects the shape of the object we are about to grasp. The direction of our gaze indexes the object at which we look. Instrumental gestures, moreover, are capable of being conventionalized for communicative purposes, and in this way they serve as the foundation upon which a good deal of communicative gesturing can be built. I return to instrumental gesturing in later sections of this chapter and suggest its importance for the launching of language.

PARALINGUISTIC SIGNS

Like gesture-calls, gesticulation and intonation are analog signals, but they are both used more intimately with language than are gesture-calls. All of us sometimes mold our hands and move our arms as we speak, and these gesticulations so closely reflect the meaning of our talk that they form a sort of counterpoint to it (McNeill 1992). "Gesticulation" refers most specifically to hand and arm gestures, but we often bob our heads and even hunch our shoulders at the same time, and the bobbing and hunching belong with gesticulation in a broader sense. Intonation refers to the melody of language, to the rises and falls of pitch that accompany our words and sentences. Intonation works closely with rhythm, pauses, and intensity (loudness), and together these form the prosodic system of a language. I limit my observations primarily to intonation and consider the other aspects of prosody only tangentially.

Intonation must not be confused with the contrastive system of tones in languages such as Chinese. Syllables in all languages are characterized by particular consonants and particular vowels. Chinese syllables are also characterized by particular tones, and these tones are as much a part of the contrastive system as are the consonants and vowels. Tones do not prevent Chinese from having intonational patterns like other languages. Tones and intonation readily coexist, but tones, like consonants and vowels, are used to distinguish words from one another, whereas the primary function of intonation is to express our emotions and our attitudes toward the things we are talking about.

Word stress, in languages such as English, works in ways that resemble tone. Roughly speaking, one syllable of each English word can be said to have stress. "Dífficult" is stressed on its first syllable, and "understánd" is stressed on its third. Although there are complications and a few exceptions, the location of stress is generally fixed, and this location, along with the sequence of vowels and consonants, is a part of the contrastive system of the language. When a word is spoken in isolation, the stressed syllable is almost always given an accent. This means that it is pronounced a bit longer or louder than surrounding syllables or with a higher, or occasionally lower, pitch. In one way or another, it is set off from the neighboring syllables. In the flow of speech, when a word is accented, it is the stressed syllable that receives the accent, but not every stressed syllable receives an accent every time the word is used. Some stressed syllables are said no higher, longer, or louder than the surrounding syllables, although we know the location of stress so well that it may be hard for us to realize that a stress has not received an accent. It is the ability of a stressed syllable not to receive an accent that forces us to make a distinction between stress (a fixed location in a word) and accent (the setting off of a stressed syllable by pitch, intensity, or length). Because stress, like tone, is an inherent part of the word, its location is a part of the contrastive system of the language. The accent given to a stressed syllable can vary continuously from nothing at all to a scream. The degree of accent reflects the emotions and attitudes of speakers toward what they are talking about. In spite of its close association with language, accent is used in ways that recall the gesture-call system.

Traditionally, linguists have regarded intonation, but not gesticulation, as belonging to language. The only reason to treat them differently is that intonation is produced by the voice, so its association with the spoken language that most linguists study seems more intimate. If we can ignore their differing visible and audible modalities, however, it is clear that gesticulation and intonation have such similar relationships with (the rest of) language that it is difficult to find any solid basis for considering one but not the other to be a part of language. I prefer to define language in a way that excludes both. If we were to define language broadly enough to embrace gesticulation and intonation, we would still have to acknowledge their differences from the rest of language. It seems easiest to recognize the distinction from the beginning by defining language more narrowly. We can even look upon both intonation and gesticulation as a sort of invasion of language by the kind of signaling system that forms our gesture-calls. We hear the degree of excitement or fatigue in other people's voices, and we see the same emotions in their gesticulations.

The movements and noises that we use in gesticulation and into-nation sometimes escape their usual association with language. We use our voices iconically without language whenever we imitate a noise. Occasionally we even hum an intonation in the absence of words. In the right context it is possible to answer a question simply by humming the tune of "I don't know." Even without vowels and consonants, the intonational contour sounds enough like the sentence to convey its meaning (Bolinger 1986:211). We can also use our hands without lan-guage to form iconic movements and shapes. We lean our bodies or thrust our shoulders indexically in the direction we are concerned with. Watching something being pushed, we move our hands or our bodies in sympathy. Our gesticulations often reflect the manipulation of real objects in the world, so they reflect our instrumental gestures. For present purposes, the important thing about paralinguistic signals is that they are the most consistently motivated component of human communication.

I have now located motivated signs within the broad range of human communication. The next step is to survey the several types of motivated signs that human beings use.

GESTICULATION

In this and in the following two sections, I survey the main varieties of motivated signs that are used in human communication. Motivation is probably easiest to recognize in gesticulation, in no small part due to the careful work of McNeill, reported in his book *Hand and Mind* (1992). McNeill uses the word "gesture" for what I, following Kendon and others, have called "gesticulation." Although I follow McNeill's analysis, I substitute "gesticulation" for his "gesture" because I want to be careful to distinguish it both from quotable gestures and from the hand and facial movements of the gesture-call system.

McNeill recognizes several kinds of gesticulation. First, what Peirce would have called images, McNeill calls *iconics*. These imitate the shape or movement of something that is being talked about. We may move our hand upward when talking about someone who is climbing. We may wiggle our fingers to represent moving legs. When offering to get someone a cup we may form our hand into the shape that would hold a cup. We hold our hands wide when talking about something big. We may pinch our faces together for something small or trivial. We outline the shape of almost anything with our hands.

McNeill's *metaphorics* correspond to Peirce's metaphors. They are similar to iconics but represent more abstract ideas. We may direct our palm first one way and then the other to show that there are two sides to some issue. We move our hand back and forth several times when talking about something repetitious. Metaphorics are not pictures of physical objects, but they are representations of ideas.

McNeill's *deictics* are pointing gestures, and they would be included among Peirce's indices. We may point to physical objects, including people, when we talk about them. We may also point more abstractly, as when we point first in one direction and then in another to refer to two absent people, to two different events, or even to two opposing viewpoints.

McNeill's final two types of gesticulation are not so easily assigned to one of Peirce's types of signs, but in their own ways they also point, so both have an indexical component. We may mark the places in our sentences that we find important with *beats*. These can be slight movements of the finger or hand, or they can be bobs of the head. Of all gesticulations, beats are generally the least conspicuous, but they are also the most tightly tied to language. Try saying "I ábsolútely will nót dó it" very forcefully, by placing a firm accent on *áb-, lút, nót,* and *dó,* but lift your head slightly on each beat instead of bobbing it downward. Then try bobbing your head downward on unaccented syllables instead of on accented ones. You will quickly discover how tightly you are constrained in the way you form and place your beats. Beats generally coincide with intonational accents and point to the important parts of our discourse.

Finally, *cohesives* are made by repeating any of the other four types of gesticulations. A point in one direction may be followed by a point in another direction. The repetition itself carries a meaning, for it ties different parts of the discourse together and announces that the two places that are marked by the same gesticulation have something in common. Cohesives can be regarded as pointing to each other. In Peircian terms they diagrammatically reflect the relationships among the things we are talking about. All these gesticulations are well motivated. Some are iconic and some are indexical, but none is arbitrary. Like gesture-calls, gesticulations are analog signals, but they are much less stereotyped.

We have little systematic cross-cultural knowledge of gesticulation. A good deal of cross-cultural variation in the amount of gesticulation is sometimes presumed to exist, and possibly there is variation in the types. Southern Europeans are supposed to wave their arms more freely than northerners, although the apparent variation may be due more to differing uses of quotable gestures than to differing patterns of gesticulation. In any case, all people do, sometimes, gesticulate, and so far as we now know, everyone uses the same basic types of gesticulation that McNeill has identified among American speakers of English.

INTONATION

Because intonation is produced with the voice rather than with the hands, it is more difficult to extract from the rush of spoken language than is gesticulation, but the pitch of intonation is iconic in at least two different ways.

First, high pitch is associated with high tension, arousal, excitement, eagerness, and activity, and low pitch with low tension, relaxation, completion. These relate to the pervasive metaphor of "up and down" and to inconclusiveness and conclusiveness. As Bolinger put it (1985:99): "In the course of an action we are up and moving; at the end, we sit or lie down to rest. In a discourse this translates to higher pitches while [an] utterance is in progress and a fall at the end." Mothers soothe their infants with low-pitched, reassuring sounds. High-pitched enthusiasm is stimulating. We raise our voices in fear, anger, excitement, or intense interest. Our voices drop with boredom and fatigue. We hold the floor with a rising intonation. We yield to another speaker with a fall.

Rises and falls of pitch modulate the meaning of the words with which they are used. The end of a statement most often has a fall in pitch, sometimes gradual, sometimes quite abrupt. In English, as in most other languages, questions that can be answered "yes" or "no" usually end with a terminal rise. It is wrong, however, to consider this rise to be a "question intonation," for questions do not always rise, and rises are found in places other than questions. Subordinate clauses, for example, typically rise: "If I had some fish, I'd eat it." Rises are more accurately described as indicating incompletion. Like a subordinate clause, a question shows that something else is expected, although it invites someone else to supply the rest. Statements that end with a terminal rise often suggest uncertainty on the part of the speaker. "I think I have enough," with a rise at the end, leaves room for doubt. A falling pitch would show more certainty.

Any sentence type can be used with any intonation. We say that we "soften" a command by putting it in the form of a question. Instead of saying "Hand me the chisel," it is more polite to say "Can you hand me the chisel?" Even in its question form, however, the sentence is likely to end with a fall rather than a rise, and this shows that it is not really a question at all but a request. No verbal reply is expected. Conversely, if I say "That's a turnip" with a terminal rise, I show my own uncertainty. I leave something unfinished. I have asked a question without using question syntax.

The close association of intonation and gesticulation is shown by the fact that raised eyebrows, like a raised voice, can signal uncertainty, lack of completion, or a question. A more persistent association between gesticulation and intonation is the synchronization of spoken accents with gesticulated beats of the hands or head. In English, we most often accent the points of a discourse that interest and excite us with a rise in pitch. The more interesting and exciting the point, the greater the rise. These accents generally coincide with the beats of gesticulation, and it is this kind of close coordination of intonation and gesticulation that makes it awkward to consider intonation to be a part of language while excluding gesticulation. Because accents mark important points of the discourse, often the points where new information is introduced, they reflect the pragmatic flow of information rather than the syntax, and so do the beats of gesticulation.

If a syllable is accented, the strength of its accent can be continuously graded, and the strength is proportional to the strength of the emotion. "His name is John" can be said with a barely perceptible peak in pitch on "John" and then a fall. With progressively stronger accents, the assertion becomes progressively more forceful (Bolinger 1978:474) until it finally becomes a scream.

The second iconic association of pitch is with size. A high or rising pitch suggests small size, weakness, helplessness, submission, courtesy, and a lack of confidence. A low or falling pitch suggests large size, assertiveness, authority, aggression, confidence, self-sufficiency, and threat (Ohala 1944). The iconicity here is obvious. We expect high pitches from small musical instruments and small people—women and children. Large musical instruments and large people—men—are pitched lower. Even among animals, high pitch is associated with submission. A dog's submissive whine is pitched higher than its threatening growl, just as an infant's pleading whine is high while a sergeant's forceful command is low.

We try to project an image by the way we speak. Hoping to sound more authoritative than we feel, we may try to mask our nervousness by lowering our voice. In many languages, a rise in pitch is used for polite speech (Brown and Levinson 1987:267–68). Women's speech is said to be more often characterized by hesitant and deferential rising intonation than is the speech of men (Lakoff 1975:17). Both raising and lowering pitch can be useful for getting one's way, but a careful assessment of one's relative social position is needed before deciding which is more likely to be successful. We easily recognize the meaning of these pitch differences. We react to the degree of deference or authority shown by a person's speech.

Intonation is linked to the structure of sentences in one important way. The rises, falls, and discontinuities of the melodic line mark the syntactic divisions of sentences. Each phrase is likely to have one particularly important point marked with an accent. That accent helps to set the phrase off from its neighbors. The melody helps the hearer to untangle the structure of sentences. In most respects, however, intonation expresses the attitude and emotions of the speaker.

SYNTACTIC ICONICITY

In addition to the iconicity of onomatopoeia, sound symbolism, and intonation, spoken languages exhibit considerable iconicity in syntax, and since Jakobson (1965, 1966) first opened the subject, syntactic iconicity has drawn the attention of a growing minority of linguists (Haiman, ed., 1985; Givón 1989).

Syntactic iconicity shows up most clearly in the order of words and morphemes. Word and morpheme order cannot be used for imagistic or even metaphoric iconicity, but it can stand in a relationship of diagrammatic iconicity to the meaning (Matthews 1991:12). The most obvious example is the tendency for the words of a sentence to follow the order of the events they describe. We understand the famous *veni, vidi, vici* to mean that Caesar's first action was to come. Then he saw, and only after that did he conquer. Languages do give us ways to say things out of chronological order, but this comes at the cost of more complex syntax: "Before conquering I saw and before seeing I came." A logician might argue that "I went inside and ate" reveals nothing about where I did my eating, but nonlogicians will normally understand the sentence to mean that the eating took place after going in, so it must have taken place inside. Someone who says "I ate and went inside" will be understood to have eaten outside.

A less obvious form of syntactic iconicity is revealed by the order of words in an English noun phrase. Consider *the old red iron steam engine,* as shown in figure 9.3. The order of the words in this phrase is almost fixed. It is not quite impossible to say "the red old iron steam engine" or even "the old red steam iron engine," but neither of these is quite natural. Why do we prefer "the old red iron steam engine" over any alternative order? Do we simply learn this order as an arbitrary characteristic of the English language?

The order turns out to be far from arbitrary, for it diagrams the relationship among the concepts. The modifiers that stand closest to the noun are also closest to its meaning. "Steam" is used with only a handful of nouns, such as "steam boiler," "steamroller," "steamship," and "steam shovel." These are so few and distinctive that dictionaries list them as lexical items. "Iron" can modify far more words than "steam," among them "nail," "hinge," and "key," but only rarely and

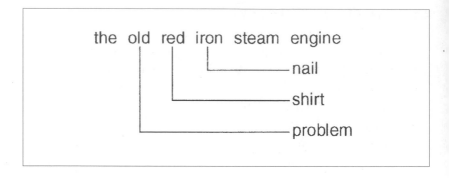

FIGURE 9.3
Word order iconicity.

metaphorically would "iron" ever be used to modify a word that refers to something soft. "Red," on the other hand, can be used as easily with soft things like shirts and cheeks as with hard things like nails or engines. The meaning of "old" is even more general, for unlike steam, iron, or red, it can easily be used with words for abstractions, such as "problem," "question," or "argument." Finally, "the" is the most general modifier of all, for it can be used with any common noun (that is, not a "proper" noun) in the language. The pattern is consistent: the modifiers whose meanings are most specific to the meaning of the noun are placed closest to the noun. The most general modifiers are the farthest away.

If this word order conforms diagrammatically to the relationships among the concepts, we should expect to find the same order in other languages. I know of no systematic cross-linguistic study of noun phrases that tests this expectation, and any test would be complicated by languages in which some or all modifiers are placed after the noun rather than before it. The languages whose data I have looked at give me the strong impression that when modifiers precede the noun, they appear in the same order as in English.

Other examples have been investigated more carefully, the best known being Bybee's study of verbal affixes (1985). Verbs in many languages can have prefixes or suffixes that mark aspect, tense, mood, and person. *Person* refers to the difference between first, second, and third person and between singular and plural. *Mood* distinguishes assertions (indicative), nonassertions (subjunctive), and commands (imperative). *Tense,* of course, locates the action in time. *Aspect* is not prominently marked by affixation in English, but languages with morphological aspect use it to indicate such things as the beginning, continuation, or completion of an action. English often has separate verbs to make distinctions that could be made by aspect markers in some other languages. For example, we use distinct verbs to show the difference between moving into a state and being in it: fall asleep/sleep, sit down/sit, learn/know, grow/be big, grab/hold, lift/carry. In some languages, this distinction is made by aspect affixes. A distinction that is made by using two different words instead of by means of an affix is said to be *lexicalized,* so we can say that aspect is often *lexicalized* in English.

When the verbs of a language carry affixes that distinguish more than one of these four distinctions, the affix for aspect is almost always placed closest to the verb—just before the verb if it is prefixed, just after the verb if suffixed. Affixes for tense, mood, and person are placed at increasing distances from the verb. As with the noun modifiers, the order of these affixes is diagrammatically related to the degree of involvement of the concepts with the verbs. Lexicalization shows the closest involvement of all. This means that even though English does not have grammatical aspect, the intimate involvement of aspect with the verb is shown by its lexicalization. Tense affects the meaning of the verb less closely than aspect, and mood even less so. Person refers to the participants in the action rather than to the action itself, so it is reasonable to find person markers farthest from the verb.

Syntax can be motivated in still another way. Generally, the categories that linguists refer to as "marked" are expressed by longer forms than unmarked categories. The obvious example is plurality. When a language distinguishes plural from singular nouns, it is almost always the plural that is "marked" by the longer form. English, of course, conforms to this rule by forming the plural with a suffix that is added to the singular form of the noun. Logically, it should be possible to leave the plural "unmarked" and to form the singular by adding a "singular marker" to the plural form. Languages almost never do this, presumably because the singular is cognitively central. Marking something as plural adds an idea, as well as a suffix, to the core word.

If morpheme and word order were consistently motivated, we might expect morphemes and words to occur in the same order in all languages. Of course they do not, and we must ask why. In some cases different orders seem to have little difference in motivation. Whether an adjective comes before or after its noun, for example, seems to matter less than its distance from the noun. In other cases, historical processes of various sorts probably drag languages away from perfect motivation. We might expect that if languages lost too much motivation, pressures would build that would push them back to greater motivation. It is clear, for example, that children learn motivated constructions more easily than those that violate motivation (Slobin 1985). Children make more mistakes with nonmotivated constructions. If they made enough mistakes they could gradually force the language back to a form that was more clearly motivated.

English has one strikingly nonmotivated suffix: the third person singular -s, as in *I drive/she drives*. Languages more often mark first- and second-person verbs or plural verbs and leave the third person singular unmarked. The history of this English anomaly is well known, and it resulted from entirely ordinary processes of linguistic change. English once had a rich system of person markers, but most were progressively lost until the third person singular -s is all that remains, the final relic of verb agreement. If this suffix is as nonmotivated as it appears to be, we might expect it to be unstable. Its loss would remove an anomaly. In fact, the third person singular suffix has already disappeared from a few dialects of English, including those spoken by some African Americans, who can say "She drive tomorrow" as easily as "I drive tomorrow." Perhaps in the course of the next century or two the loss of the third person singular -s will spread. Some day it may be remembered only as a historical oddity.

The iconicity and indexicality found in gesticulation, intonation, and syntax are more extensive than linguists have sometimes acknowledged, but linguists have still been justified in emphasizing the arbitrary nature of many other aspects of language. In the concluding section of this chapter, I suggest that motivated signs could have had a much greater importance during the early evolutionary stages of language than they do today. First, however, I must consider the competing advantages of conventionalization. Conventionalization leads to a decline in motivation and a corresponding increase in arbitrariness.

CONVENTIONALIZATION IN HISTORY

Having surveyed the use of motivated signs in contemporary languages, I turn in this and the following section to several examples in which signs that began as motivated icons or indexes gradually became standardized and conventionalized. When conventionalization goes far enough, motivation can finally be undermined and the signs can be drawn into a contrastive system of communication.

To one who has no knowledge of American Sign Language (ASL), its signs are by no means transparent, but many have an underlying motivation (Frishberg 1975; Klima and Bellugi 1979). Without an explanation, the sign in which the thumbs and index fingers of both hands are formed into a horizontal "o" shape and moved alternately up and down will appear completely obscure. Once told that the sign represents a balance scale whose pans swing up and down, the motivation for its meaning, 'judge', becomes obvious. A large number of ASL signs are as clearly iconic as judge but still arbitrary enough to require learning. These signs have become partially conventionalized but have not yet lost all motivation.

When signers lack a name for something, they find it easy to invent one, and their newly invented signs are often clearly iconic. Klima and Bellugi (1979:11) described a sign for 'cinnamon roll' that was invented by a three-year-old child. The girl held one hand in a cupped position, and just above it she circled the index finger of her other hand. She sketched the roll's swirls, its most salient feature. Klima and Bellugi also described deaf researchers who needed a sign for 'videotape recorder'. The machine they needed to talk about had two spools that spun together as the tape moved from one to the other. In the sign invented by the researchers, the two index fingers outlined circles in imitation of the turning reels. Gestures like those for cinnamon roll and videotape recorder are not very different from the gesticulations that a hearing person might make while mentioning these objects, except that from the start they need to carry the full burden of communication. This forces them to be correspondingly explicit, and unlike gesticulations, the invented signs of the deaf tend quickly to become conventionalized. At first the sign for videotape recorder had both fingers circling in the same direction, just like the spools. Soon, however, the signers began to circle their fingers in opposite, complementary, directions. At the cost of reduced iconicity, this made the sign easier to form and also brought it closer to the style of established ASL signs. Many ASL signs have had a similar history. They started as clear iconic representations of the objects or actions to be talked about but were then adapted to the established patterns of the language.

With enough time, the original iconicity of a sign can be completely lost. ASL grew from a form of signing that was brought to the United States from France in the early nineteenth century, so its history in America is relatively short and many of the changes it has undergone are well known. An example is the sign 'home'. Since home is the place where you eat and sleep, its sign began as a compound, formed from the sign for 'eat' followed by the sign for 'sleep'. 'Eat' is made by a gesture that suggests bringing food to the mouth, and 'sleep' is made by placing the palm of the hand beside the head, as if sleeping. Both signs are transparently iconic, and their meanings could unite in the sign for home. With time, however, the two parts of the compound merged. Today home is made with two taps of the extended fingers on the cheek. The hand shape of EAT has been retained but is now made in approximately the position for SLEEP. The revised sign is quicker to form than the original, but it has lost all trace of the earlier iconicity of its parts. It has become as arbitrary as the English word "home."

Early writing was gradually conventionalized in much the same way as ASL. Sumerian, ancient Egyptian, and early Chinese all made extensive use of pictographs. A picture looking a bit like a mountain might represent the word for mountain. A picture of a hand could represent 'hand'. Pictographs offered an obvious, though only partial, solution to the problem of representing the huge number of words in a spoken language on clay or papyrus. Even in the earliest surviving examples of writing, however, the pictures are often quite stylized. For example, the earliest form of the Sumerian word for water consisted of two wavy but generally horizontal lines, easily understood as representing waves. This was a pictograph, but already highly stylized. Later, for unknown reasons, this sign, along with all the rest of Sumerian writing, was rotated 90 degrees so that the wavy lines were written vertically instead of horizontally, a considerably less iconic representation. Then, with the development of a stylus that made triangular impressions in clay, the sign was further stylized into one long vertical stroke that replaced one wavy line, and two shorter strokes, one above the other, that replaced the second wavy line. By then the sign had lost any hint of iconicity (Kramer 1963). The same kind of conventionalization came to all other Sumerian signs and to the signs of other writing systems as well. The earliest surviving Chinese characters are much more iconic than modern ones. A trace of iconicity can still be seen in a handful of modern Chinese characters, but most have become completely arbitrary symbols that represent the syllables of the spoken language.

It is more difficult to point to convincing cases in which intonation has become conventionalized. Bolinger (1989:27) speculates that intonation could have contributed to the development of tones in some languages, and this would amount to a conventionalization of intonation. If one looks hard enough, it is possible to find examples of tone-like distinctions even in English. "That's fùnny," pronounced with a low pitch on *fùn-*, is likely to be understood as meaning "that's strange." "That's fúnny," with a high pitch on *fún-*, is more likely to be understood as meaning "that's laughable." English has not become a tone language, however, and there are other well-known ways for tones to arise than by conventionalization of intonation. I know of no certain cases in which intonation has been conventionalized into contrastive tone.

Clearer examples of the conventionalization of pitch differences are found in sound symbolism. In many languages, words meaning 'little' have high front vowels, whereas words meaning 'large' more often have vowels that are lower and farther back. "Itsy bitsy" and "teeny weeny" are obvious examples. Part of the appeal of "humungus" lies in the sound symbolism of its vowels. High front vowels have high second formants and are perceived as high pitched and thus as appropriate for words meaning 'little'. Back vowels have low second formants and are perceived as having low pitch and so as more appropriate for words meaning 'large'. It is true that "big" and "small" are counterexamples of the generalization, but so many examples from so many languages fit the generalization that the relationship is convincing in spite of the exceptions.

CONVENTIONALIZATION IN THE INDIVIDUAL

Centuries were needed for writing to be conventionalized; a few generations have brought considerable conventionalization to American Sign Language. We can watch conventionalization happening even more quickly as every child learns to talk. A compelling example is found in Goldin-Meadow's study of deaf children of hearing parents (1993). The children with whom Goldin-Meadow worked had no contact with an established sign language, but their deafness cut them off from the spoken language of their homes. In spite of the absence of linguistic input, these deaf children devised elaborate gestural systems by which to communicate with other members of their families. The signs they used were all iconic or indexical in origin, and at first they were not so different from the gesticulations of hearing people. The children pointed to things as a way of naming them, and they formed shapes with their hands just as everyone sometimes does while speaking. The gestures of these children had to stand alone, however, and like the signs of ASL they became conventionalized into something more like words than like gesticulations. The children created what amounted to simple languages.

> All of the children used their gestures as "tools" for communication—to convey information about current, past, and future events, and to manipulate the world around them. Like children learning conventional languages, the deaf children requested objects and actions from others and did so using their gestures; e.g., a pointing gesture at a book, a "give" gesture, and a pointing gesture at the child's own chest, to request mother to give the child a book; or a "hit" gesture followed by a pointing gesture at mother, to request mother to hit a tower of blocks. Moreover, like children learning conventional languages, the deaf children commented on the actions of objects, people, and themselves, both in the past (e.g., a "high" gesture followed by a

"fall" gesture to indicate that the block tower was high and then fell to the ground) and in the future (e.g., a pointing gesture at Lisa with a head-shake, an "eat" gesture, a pointing gesture at the child himself, and an "eat" gesture with a nod, to indicate that Lisa would not eat lunch but that the child would). Gestures were also used to recount events which happened some time ago; e.g., one child produced an "away" gesture, a "drive" gesture, a "beard" gesture, a "moustache" gesture, and a "sleep" gesture to comment on the fact that the family had driven away to the airport to bring his uncle (who wears a beard and a moustache) home so that he could sleep over. (Goldin-Meadow 1993:65–66)

Goldin-Meadow recognized three different kinds of gestures. "Pointing gestures" indicated a person or an object, but unlike the points of hearing people, which indicate the location of an object but do not name it, the pointing gestures of the deaf children came to function like the nouns and pronouns of an established language. They served as names for objects and people. Mostly the children pointed to things present in their immediate environment, but as they grew older they invented a more abstract kind of pointing. One child, for example, made a round gesture to indicate a Christmas tree ball and then indicated its hook by pointing to the place in the gesture where the hook would belong.

Goldin-Meadow gave the name "characterizing gestures" to iconic gestures that denoted actions and attributes. Chewing movements made while a fist was held near the mouth meant 'eat'. A hand moving forward in the air when describing the movement of a toy meant 'go'. Each child devised his or her own idiosyncratic signs, of course, but each settled on stable forms that, while iconic or indexical in origin, became conventionalized by repetition. At least one child constructed some signs by combining one set of fixed hand shapes with another set of fixed motions.

The term "marker" was used for a third type of gesture. Markers included nods and head shakes to indicate affirmation and negation, and a finger held in the air to mean 'wait'. These, of course, are conventional gestures for hearing speakers of American English, and they were learned from family members, but they were incorporated securely into the children's linguistic system.

The signs invented by the deaf children came to differ from the gesticulations of hearing people in two ways. First, they were segmented into a linear sequence, and second, they became sufficiently standardized to contrast with one another. The signs of the deaf children had a more consistent form than the gestures of the hearing members of their families, for whom the gestures stayed closer to ordinary gesticulation, but even the children's signs never became so conventionalized as to be arbitrary. They always retained their motivated character. An isolated deaf child who is trying to make his or her needs known to people who do not control the system as well is limited to signs that are clearly motivated. Goldin-Meadow suggests (1993:78) that at least two language users may be needed before arbitrariness can be introduced into a communication system. Two users can more easily agree on arbitrary conventions.

Hearing children sometimes conventionalize gestures in such subtle ways that we hardly notice. Consider the "arms-up" gesture by which toddlers ask to be picked up. This begins as an instrumental gesture, a part of the baby's adaptation to the impinging world, in this case a part of his interaction with bigger people. After being lifted often enough by adult hands that have been placed under his armpits, a baby learns to spread and then raise his arms in anticipation. The gesture then becomes conventionalized and turns into a stylized request. This arms-up gesture is so common that we might almost imagine it to be an inborn gesture-call, but it is more dependent upon learning than true gesture-calls. Unlike the words of a language or quotable gestures such as the "bye-bye" wave, however, it is learned through practice in interaction, not by either imitation or direct instruction. If adults make an arms-up gesture to a baby, they are more likely to be imitating the baby than offering instruction. The arms-up gesture is not as clearly culturally patterned as words or quotable gestures, and it is not used symmetrically. Adults do not seriously ask babies to pick them up. The begging gesture—hand extended, palm upward with the fingers together—is learned in much the same way. The communicative grunts of human and primate infants that are described by McCune (this volume) are a parallel vocal example of a signal that is conventionalized from an instrumental act. These and many other common gestures are conventionalized from the background of our instrumental activities, and they remain more clearly iconic than many quotable gestures. I return later to chimpanzee infants, who conventionalize gestures just as human infants do.

The spoken language of hearing children also progresses from motivated to increasingly conventionalized and arbitrary forms. This can be seen in the word order that often appears in early child language. Small children often use word order that is "incorrect" by the standards of the adult language but that is also more motivated. Slobin (1985) gives exhaustive documentation from many languages in which children's "incorrect" order is more iconic than the "correct" order. Logically, for example, most negatives negate their entire sentence. It would be diagrammatically reasonable to negate "The train will come on time" as "Not—the train will come on time." By placing the sign for negation outside the rest of the sentence, we could show that the meaning of the entire sentence, rather than the meaning of just of one of its parts, has been reversed. In ordinary speech we tuck the negation inside the sentence and say "The train will not come on time," but this loses diagrammatic iconicity. As they begin to learn English, small children often place the negative outside the rest of the sentence: "No sit there," "No the sun shining," "No fall," "No play that." (Both the examples and the suggested analysis are from Klima and Bellugi 1966). The order violates adult rules of grammar, but it diagrams the meaning of the sentences better than adult grammar does.

Children sometimes make their first questions simply by using a rising intonation, but a bit later they may attach question words to the beginning of the sentence: "What he can ride in?" or "What you eat?" To make the first of these examples conform to adult standards, the subject and auxiliary verb need to change places ("What can he ride in?"), and the second example requires an added "do." These changes appear to be unmotivated, and children generally learn them later than the use of the question word itself.

Even more obviously motivated than word order are the stereotypic children's words that are, to some degree, onomatopoetic: "choo-choo," "bow-wow," "honk-honk," and so forth. Children learn these words from older people, of course, but adults recognize children's affinity for motivation and expect such motivated forms to appeal to children.

In special circumstances, even adults can conventionalize signals in the course of a single conversation. With sufficiently imaginative gesturing, two adults who share no common language can communicate a good deal. They can use the gestures and calls that all humans share: smiles to show good will, laughs to show solidarity, frowns to show puzzlement, and all the rest. They may also share quotable gestures such as nods and head shakes even if they share no spoken language. In addition, they are likely to make heavy use of pantomime, the most motivated of all gestures. They will point and make shapes with their hands, hold up fingers to represent numbers, and even move their entire bodies to show their meaning. They may draw pictures on paper or in the dirt. With enough patience it is possible to explain to someone that he should "go three blocks that way, turn right, walk two block more, and find the tall building." It does not take long, in encounters like these, for conventions to arise. Whatever is understood can be seized upon as useful for the future, even if it is soon abbreviated. It may take a good deal of initial effort to get across the idea of 'blocks' in "three blocks," but once that has been accomplished, it will be much easier to explain that after turning right the person should go two more 'blocks'. A start is made in agreeing on a conventional way to name 'blocks'.

Groping to give directions to someone with whom one shares no language represents a stage of communication that amounts to a sort of pre-pidgin—communication with no spoken language at all. When people with good ears but no common language are thrown together for any length of time, they soon find spoken words to support, and then to replace, the frantic gesturing with which they must begin. Efficiency of communication quickly encourages the development of conventionalized sequences of sounds with consistent meanings.

CONVENTIONALIZATION AND ARBITRARINESS

I have described a process that has taken place repeatedly. The early stages of several types of communication relied heavily on motivated signs, but as each communication system became established, the signs became more and more conventional. Finally they lost all the motivation with which they began and reached the point of arbitrariness. The transparency of motivated signs would seem to give them a clear advantage over those that are arbitrary, but conventionalization and arbitrariness have so regularly won out that they must have important advantages that compensate for the loss of motivation.[3] What are they?

Conventionalization represents, in part, the victory of the producer (signer, writer, speaker) over the receiver (reader, listener). Even more, it is the victory of skilled and experienced users over learners. Motivated signs are much easier to learn than arbitrary ones, so learners should have a clear preference for extensive motivation. Unfortunately for learners, their power over the form of a communication system is limited, and for the most part they must take signs as they find them. Experienced producers have more control, and they find it advantageous to cut corners—to make a diagram instead of a picture, a stylized hand movement instead of a pantomime, a conventionalized sequence of sounds instead of a realistic imitation of a noise. Receivers may understand more easily when the signals are clear and well motivated, but skilled receivers are also producers, and once they have learned the code they can generally understand the same conventionalized and arbitrary signs that they can produce. The learner, with no more power over the communication system than our own schoolchildren have over the irrationalities of English spelling, must adapt to the abbreviations and conventionalizations that producers find convenient and that skilled receivers have learned to cope with.

Conventionalization speeds up communication and makes the job of the producer easier, but these are not its only advantages. As signs become standardized they also become less ambiguous, and clarity can be enhanced if the signs are made to contrast with each other. In a highly iconic system, we might expect the signs for 'cat', 'tiger', and 'leopard' to be quite similar. The signs for 'dog', 'fox', and 'wolf' ought to differ somewhat from those for the cats, but they would differ less from the signs for the cats than from those for body parts or clothing. For practical communication, it is more important to keep similar objects distinct. It is much more dangerous to risk confusing 'cat' with 'leopard' than with 'hat'. The context will generally suggest whether "cat" or "hat" is the intended word. It is less likely to help us decide between "cat" and "leopard." Too much iconicity invites ambiguity.

With an increasingly complex syntax, conventionalization and arbitrariness would have had still other advantages. People who are clever enough to agree to keep their words in a consistent order should be able to communicate more successfully than those who jumble their words at random. If modifiers are always kept on the same side of the word they modify, listeners will understand them more easily, simply because they will know which word is the modifier and which is modified. Even this modest degree of conventionalization implies the beginning of syntax and rudimentary parts of speech.

Conventionalization and arbitrariness have one final implication. Conventionalization implies that different people and different groups can create quite different conventions to represent the same meaning. Different groups can agree on different shapes for individual words and different orders in which to string these words together. Conventionalization, then, opens the way for different dialects and languages. I return to conventionalization in the final section of this chapter, where I suggest some reasons for the decline in the iconicity with which language may have begun.

MOTIVATED SIGNS IN GORILLAS, CHIMPANZEES, AND BONOBOS

Human beings easily produce and understand motivated signs of many sorts, but such signs appear to be rare among other species. It is true that ordinary gesture-calls have sometimes been said to be iconic. Since gesture-calls ordinarily develop by the ritualization of some other behavior, they start with the inherent iconicity of instrumental acts. When a dog snarls in order to threaten, his lip is drawn back as if to bite, so a snarl can be interpreted as an icon of a bite.

Nevertheless, even if animal signals are regarded as iconic, they are also highly stereotyped, and the kind of productive iconicity that lets human beings so easily discover similarities between objects, pictures, gestures, and sounds is hard to find among animals. Bonobos, chimpanzees, and gorillas, however, have demonstrated a degree of productive iconicity that brings them closer than other animals to humans. Even the ability to recognize their own reflection in a mirror suggests that these animals are closer than any others to the recognition of icons, and their ability to recognize objects, people, and animals in pictures unambiguously demonstrates an iconic capacity that most animals never show. A number of captive chimpanzees have also been reported to have gestured spontaneously in iconic or indexical ways in order to indicate their wants. Viki, the chimpanzee who was raised by Keith and Catherine Hayes (Hayes and Nissen 1971) and who is remembered most often for her failure to learn to talk, was skillful at other kinds of communication.

> At times her gestures became very explicit. Watching bread being kneaded, she begged for a sample of dough by going through the motions for a while, and then holding out her hand, palm up, moving her fingers in the gesture which means "give me" to both her species and ours. A similar incident occurred during the weekly ironing as she grew impatient for her turn to do the napkins. She stood on a nearby table, moving one clenched fist slowly back and forth above the ironing board while her other hand tried to take the iron away from "mamma." (Hayes and Nissen 1971:107)

Gardner and Gardner (1969:670) reported that when the chimpanzee Washoe wanted to go through a door, she would hold up both hands and pound on it with her palms or knuckles. The Gardners encouraged Washoe to develop this gesture into a sign, but even without the conventionalization that we expect in a sign, it was certainly motivated. Many of Washoe's other gestures seem also to have been motivated, although this is obscured in the Gardners' description by their eagerness to interpret them as signs and by their efforts to persuade Washoe to make them in a way that would conform more closely to the conventional signs of ASL.

More recently, iconic gesturing has been observed in an adult male gorilla named Kubie who lives among other gorillas in reasonably

ROBBINS BURLING

naturalistic conditions in the San Francisco Zoo (Tanner and Byrne 1996). Kubie interacted frequently with a female named Zura, and he used iconic gestures to show her what he wanted her to do. By moving his hand downward, either while touching Zura's body or simply while moving it where she could see it, he indicated that he wanted Zura to move downward like his hand. Kubie also patted his own chest in a gesture that seemed to call attention to himself. He, and to a lesser extent Zura, used many other gestures in what appears to have been a rather subtle form of communication. These gestures were spontaneous, not taught by humans.

Savage-Rumbaugh gives a striking example of the ability of a chipanzee named Booee to read a novel iconic gesture made by a human being.

> One time [Booee] hung by his hands from the top of the cage and did a 360° turn while we were playing. I laughed and, wanting to see that again, held up my hand and spun my index finger around in a 360° arc and pointed to the top of the cage. Booee at once grasped my intent and proceeded to repeat his flip for my benefit. This gesture was not one of Booee's signs. In fact no one had ever made that sort of gesture or request to him before.... Yet he was immediately able to comprehend the meaning of my gesture—repeat that flip you did up there. (Savage-Rumbaugh and Lewin 1994:36)

When he was a year and a half old, Kanzi, the famous bonobo studied by Savage-Rumbaugh and her colleagues, began to extend his arm, though not his index finger, to indicate the direction in which he wanted to travel. When riding on Savage-Rumbaugh's shoulders he would sometimes lean his whole body in the desired direction or even forcefully turn her head to show the direction he wanted to go. He used hitting motions to show that he wanted nuts cracked and a twisting motion to show that he wanted a jar opened (Savage-Rumbaugh and Lewin 1994:134). Even more striking, perhaps, because no human participants are involved, bonobos use iconic hand and arm gestures to indicate the positions they desire others to assume for copulation

338

(Savage-Rumbaugh and Lewin 1994:112). Finally, Savage-Rumbaugh (this volume) reports that Kanzi's half-sister, Panbanisha, referred to a visitor as "mushroom" because she recognized the similarity of the visitor's hairdo to a mushroom.

These examples of motivated signs among apes are all drawn from captive animals, and almost nothing seems to be known about the use of motivated signs in the wild. It is difficult to imagine that the iconic gestures used by Kubie when communicating with Zura, or those used by bonobos during copulation, would be possible unless they were based upon behavior that is used in the wild as well. It must be very difficult to observe motivated signs among wild apes, but so far as I am aware no one has looked very hard for them. As far as we know now, the ability to communicate by means of motivated signs sets apes apart from other animals, even monkeys, but it is an ability that apes share with human beings.

In addition, chimpanzees appear to come closer than other animals to the human ability to conventionalize instrumental gestures. Human children conventionalize the originally instrumental arms-up gesture and use it to make a request. Tomasello and his colleagues (1985, 1994; Tomasello, Gust, and Frost 1989) have studied a wide variety of gestures that were conventionalized by young chimpanzees living in a seminatural group at the Yerkes Regional Primate Research Center field station. Some of these young chimpanzees learned to touch their mother's side in a characteristic way in order to get her attention when they wanted to nurse. They learned to hold their hand in a begging position below the adult's mouth while looking at the adult's face when hoping to be given some food. They engaged in a whole series of stereotyped acts in order to invite other young chimps to play.

Although many of these chimpanzee gestures are used by more than a single individual, they are not universal in the species. They have to be learned in the same way that a human child learns the arms-up gesture, but there is no indication that they are learned by imitation. This means that they lack any kind of traditional continuity within a community, and this makes them quite different from the signs and words of human languages. Individual chimpanzees differ in the gestures they use and in the forms of their individual gestures. In particular, the gestures used by a young chimpanzee with its mother can be quite idiosyncratic, since the mother and her child use them only with each other, never with other individuals. Like human children who conventionalize a request to be carried, each young chimpanzee is capable of conventionalizing his own gestures and putting them to communicative use.

COMPREHENSION AND PRODUCTION

I need to digress long enough to deal with an old puzzle that hovers over the first stage of language and that concerns the relation between comprehension and production. What could the first speaker have hoped to accomplish with her first words if no one else could understand them? An answer to this puzzle can begin with recalling the way in which other communicative signals have become established in other species; the most important observation is that it is not production but comprehension that makes a sign. In every case that we understand, the noises or movements that became communicative signals were first made for reasons other than communication (Tinbergen 1952). Only later did they become communicative. A dog's snarl is the classic example.

Snarls began as part of the preparation for a bite. They helped to get the dog's teeth into the proper position, but at first they had neither communicative intent nor result. Only when victims began to notice that retracted lips tended to be followed by a bite did the movement become communicative. Potential victims might even be able to use the information provided by retracted lips to try to avoid the bite. Then, with victims understanding, the aggressor had a new opportunity. By developing a ritualized lip movement, perhaps more stereotyped and even exaggerated than before, the dog might reduce the ambiguity of the sign and even be able to frighten off its enemy while avoiding the riskier activity of biting. The lip movement, originally instrumental, had evolved into a communicative snarl, sending information that was useful both to the aggressor and to its potential victim. The snarl was ritualized by being built into the genetic endowment of the species, so it did not need to be conventionalized by each individual, but the essential point is that it was comprehension that started this process. The movement of the lip could start to be ritualized only after it was understood. Other animal signals seem to have begun in parallel ways, with comprehension as the first and crucial step. Could the communication that we recognize as language also have begun at the point where it was understood rather than the point at which it was produced?

It helps to recognize that at every stage of language as we use it today, individuals are better at comprehension than at production. Linguists have not always acknowledged the precocity of comprehension, in part because it is much more difficult to study than production, but also in part because of a rather behaviorist bias that makes the "behavior" of speaking seem more important than "passive" compre hension. In spite of pious assertions that their theories are neutral with respect to speaker and hearer, linguists have generally focused on production. Studies of comprehension are better established in primatology, particularly by the playback experiments of observers such as Cheney and Seyfarth (1990). Savage-Rumbaugh has stressed the importance of studying comprehension if we are to understand ape capabilities (Savage-Rumbaugh et al. 1993).

At every stage of their development, children understand more than they can say. It is difficult to prove this to the satisfaction of a hardnosed experimental psychologist, but parents are rarely in doubt. The implication is that much that is essential about language is learned silently as children learn to understand. Speaking may be only the final stage, the point at which language that is already under passive control is finally made active. Even as adults, we can understand more than we can say. We all understand dialects that we cannot produce, and we all understand words that we would not use. In some parts of the world, people learn to understand most of what is said in a second or third language without ever saying much of anything in it. In New Guinea people sometimes say, "I can hear that language but I cannot speak it" (Aram Yengoyan, personal communication).

As soon as we recognize that human beings can understand more than they produce, we ought to wonder how much spoken human language primates can learn to understand. Even if they are incapable of uttering a single spoken word, an ability to understand would demonstrate some genuine knowledge of a language. Numerous anecdotal reports have described captive chimps who, in spite of their inability to say anything at all, appeared to understand quite a bit of spoken human language. These reports have been met with some skepticism, partly for the bad reason that our biases push us to emphasize production, but partly for the much better reason that it really is very difficult to demonstrate comprehension skills. Apes, like people, can infer a great deal from the context in which language is used, so it is always difficult to know how much a listener depends upon context and how much upon the language itself. Hayes and Nissen suggest that Viki learned to understand a considerable amount of spoken English, but they were so eager to teach her to articulate words that they did not systematically study her comprehension.

The ability of apes to learn to comprehend a significant amount of spoken language has now been dramatically confirmed by Savage-Rumbaugh and her colleagues (Savage-Rumbaugh et al. 1993) who have worked with Kanzi. At the age of eight, Kanzi was able to respond correctly to a large number of different words and to a considerable variety of spoken sentences. His ability was compared with, and found remarkably similar to, that of a two-year-old human girl. Kanzi's skills impress me as a far better demonstration of linguistic ability than has ever been shown by any other nonhuman primate who has been trained to produce language or languagelike signals, whether by articulating spoken words, by signing, by manipulating plastic chips, or by pressing buttons. Indeed, Kanzi's ability to comprehend a human language seems extensive enough to force us to grant him a degree of linguistic competence that linguists, at least, have generally presumed to be exclusively human. Neither Kanzi nor any other bonobo is ever likely to give serious competition to human children, who learn a language with such apparent ease, but I do not doubt that Kanzi has learned a good deal of English. This does not really change the evolutionary question. We must still ask how a language-using animal like ourselves could have evolved from an earlier animal that lacked language, but we must either suppose that there has been some remarkable parallel evolution of the human and bonobo lines or else push back the beginning of linguistic ability to a point before the split between humans and bonobos.

The priority of comprehension over production suggests that when a few individuals began to produce increasingly wordlike signs, others would have been able to understand them. This would remove any mystery about the communicative usefulness of the first words or wordlike signs, except that it is no more likely that those first signs were produced with communicative intent than was a dog's first snarl. The question that remains is, Why would anyone produce languagelike signs in the absence of communicative intent?

PHYLOGENY

Up to this point I have tried to remain sober enough to stick to arguments that I am willing to defend, but the time has come to stop being cautious. In this last section I offer some speculations about how language might have been launched. The speculations grow out of arguments already offered, and I believe the speculations are not implausible. I claim no more.

At least since the time when Hockett was writing (Hockett 1960; Hockett and Ascher 1964), it has seemed obvious to many workers that if we are to understand language evolution we must explain how primate calls could have evolved into human spoken language. The tradition continues in the enthusiasm with which skilled fieldworkers such as Cheney and Seyfarth (1990) focus on calls rather than gestures and search for parallels between calls and language rather than between nonhuman primate and human calls. In searching for similarities between ape calls and language, I believe some primatologists miss the more important continuities between apes and humans. Earlier in this chapter I reviewed the profound differences that separate human gesture-calls from language. Human gesture-calls are manifestly homologous to those of apes (Hooff 1972, 1976), but radical changes would be needed to transform a call into anything resembling a word or a sentence. The more promising continuities, I believe, are to be found in the workings of human and ape minds.

I find it much more difficult to distinguish language from the other capabilities of the human mind than to distinguish it from our gesture-call system. The evolution of language has transformed the human mind but has disturbed our gesture-call system only marginally.

If we want to understand how language has changed our species, it is our mind rather than our gesture-call system that requires our attention. Indeed, I believe that the most productive way to understand evolving language is to see it as emerging as one component of an evolving mind.

Even the fact that deaf people so readily develop sign languages that are as rich and versatile as spoken languages argues strongly that what changed most crucially in the course of human evolution was the human mind rather than a preexisting call system. People who can hear find it convenient to use their voices for language. People who cannot hear simply use an alternative medium—awkward in the dark or when using tools but fully equal in most respects to the tasks that we give to any language.

Motivated signs depend on a cognitive ability that human beings have in abundance but that neither humans nor animals need for their gesture-calls—the ability to recognize similarities between a sign and the thing it stands for. This ability is one part of a more general human ability that allows us to make and understand not only icons and indices but also analogies and metaphors. Any animal that can produce motivated signs must be able to perceive connections between disparate phenomena: between an object and the gestured shape of the object; between a bird and an imitation of its call; between a pointing hand and the thing it points to. Motivated signs like these become possible only with a growing ability to puzzle out the interrelations among the phenomena of the world. They depend on a recognition of co-occurrence and an increasingly nuanced understanding of cause and effect. Most animals show little ability to use motivated signs, but apes do, and apes have clearly moved part way along the same path that has brought to human beings such an extensive ability for motivated signs.

It now possible to summarize the themes of this chapter by proposing several stages by which a species without language might have evolved into a species with language.

1. Let us start with an ancestor living some time back before the split between humans and apes, a species with a versatile mammalian gesture-call system but nothing we would want to call

language. Like most other mammals, individuals of this species would have used their gestures and calls to convey a limited amount of referential information and a great deal of information about their own emotions and intentions. They would also have used their bodies in all sorts of instrumental ways, and although their instrumental gestures were not intended for communication, conspecifics and even members of other species would have profited from being able to interpret them. Wilcox (this volume) also points to the importance of "actions with instrumental functions" during the early stages of language.

2. Of necessity, these instrumental gestures had to be adapted to the physical world, and so they would have been inherently iconic. In a species that, we assume, was becoming increasingly adaptable and increasingly dependent on learning and on living by its wits, those individuals who were most skillful at interpreting each other's instrumental gestures should have been advantaged. Chimpanzees are so famously skilled at interpreting the behavior of conspecifics that they find it profitable to act so as to deceive one another, but they must also find it profitable to comprehend well enough to detect attempted deception by others (Byrne and Whiten 1988). Improving comprehension would have allowed and encouraged the conventionalization that makes gestures easier to produce and that reduces their ambiguity. Chimpanzees, as Tomasello and his colleagues have shown, have reached this stage.

3. The growing ability to understand instrumental gestures, with their inherent iconicity, would have fostered, in turn, the ability to produce iconic signs for specific communicative purposes. Since chimpanzees and bonobos can understand and produce iconic signs, they appear to have reached this stage, although their abilities have been demonstrated more clearly in captivity than in the wild.

4. Individuals who were skillful at learning to understand conventional and iconic signs would have had an advantage over those less well endowed. Those who could use imitative learning as a

shortcut to the acquisition of these signs would have been particularly advantaged. Individuals who could learn by imitation would no longer need to invent all of their conventionalizations. It has been difficult to find convincing examples of wild primates that learn communicative signals by imitation. Indeed, a good deal of skepticism has recently been expressed about the ability of primates, even of apes, to imitate much of anything (Visalberghi and Fragaszy 1990; Tomasello 1996), but imitation is essential for our kind of language. Only with imitation did traditional transmission become possible.

5. It is easier to outline a hypothetical sequence for the evolution of visible signs than for audible signs, but since the basic adaptations are cognitive, we should expect the increasing flexibility of visual communication to entail a corresponding flexibility in audible communication. The close parallels between visible and audible communication that I outlined earlier suggest that they evolved together. At some point, our ancestors needed to develop better voluntary control over what has become the vocal tract than our even more remote ancestors once had, but this should be seen as an adaptation to improved communicative ability rather than as a prerequisite for it.

6. As learning by imitation became increasingly important, the retention of iconicity would have mattered less, and the stage was set for conventionalization to move on to the point of arbitrariness. The development of arbitrariness, however, could have been a very long process. The degree of arbitrariness that took a few generations for American Sign Language and a few centuries for writing may have required tens of thousands of generations for spoken language. We know by the results that conventionalization and arbitrariness won in spoken language, just as they later won in writing and as they continue to win in sign language, but we do not know the steps by which this happened during the early stages of language. With arbitrariness came the likelihood that different groups of people would settle on differing conventions. Differing dialects and languages would have become possible.

7. Clarity of communication would have been improved if the increasingly arbitrary signs could be kept safely distinct from one another. Contrast would be especially important for signs whose meanings could be easily confused, so contrast would have encouraged arbitrariness. Early contrast, however, did not require duality of patterning.

8. The capacity for storing and retrieving what I will now call "words" must have grown relentlessly. Modern humans are able to learn tens of thousands of distinct words, and this ability could have developed only through a long evolutionary process. Successive generations of our ancestors must have passed through many stages of growing vocabulary size. The time when humans and apes first started to diverge may be as recent as 5 million years ago, hardly a long period in which to have evolved our astonishing capacity to learn and store words. If bonobos can store as many words as is suggested by Kanzi's receptive ability, however, the expansion of storage capacity would seem to have begun well before the point of divergence.

9. An expanding vocabulary entails, among other things, a phonology. A few score words, conceivably even a few hundred, could have been kept distinct in the same way that we still keep our quotable gestures and quotable vocalizations distinct. Each word would have had its own form and its own meaning, but even these early words could have been in contrast with each other, just as our quotable vocalizations and gestures still contrast with each other, without any need to build up the words from smaller distinctive phonological units. As the capacity for learning words expanded, however, a point would have come when their numbers required a more orderly way to keep them all distinct. This implies the need for a phonological system built with such units as the distinctive features of spoken language or the contrastive hand shapes, orientations, and movements of sign language. Perhaps there are other ways in which thousands of words could be kept distinct, but the method with which evolution has endowed us is the capacity to use a contrastive phonological system.

347

10. There would be no reason for vocabulary to keep expanding unless it helped people to think and communicate about ever more complex matters. At some point, thought and communication would have been made richer by the ability to use words in orderly combinations, and syntax would have been born. It is hard to imagine any basis by which people could start to join words except in motivated ways. (Armstrong, Stokoe, and Wilcox [1995] suggest ways in which motivated gestures could have fostered the growth of syntax; see especially their chapter 7, "The Origin of Syntax.") Words used in temporal sequence could have reflected the temporal sequence of the speaker's experiences, just as they still do. Objects closely related in the world could be named by words placed close to each other in speech.

By the time a species had passed through this sequence, most of the general features that we associate with human language would have been in place, although an enormous number of details remain to be accounted for. The sequence is a hypothetical one, of course, but the individual steps seem plausible. The sequence avoids entirely the mysterious process that would be required to turn a gesture-call system into language, but it ties every stage of developing language to expanding cognitive abilities. Motivated signs may have played an important role at the launch, but we find good reasons for their partial replacement under the pressures of conventionalization and arbitrariness.

The ability to use motivated signs was probably one important prerequisite for language, but I do not mean to suggest that it was the only one. The brain is a complex organ. Its evolution must have responded simultaneously to many selective pressures, and I see no reason to single out just one as central. Calvin, for example (1983, 1987), has suggested that precision throwing required the nervous system to evolve in ways that could also have supported linguistic ability. Wallace (1989, 1994) has pointed to the importance of cognitive mapping as a component of developing cognitive skills. Dunbar (1993) has argued that early language replaced grooming as a means of social bonding. Donald (1991) has argued for the importance of mimesis as a prerequisite for language. Sorting requires the same kind of sharp discriminations that are needed to assign names to objects, and Hayes and Nissen (1971) have described the enthusiasm with which the chimpanzee Viki sorted small objects. All of these evolving cognitive skills, and many others, could have contributed to a growing ability to use language. I see no inconsistency in supposing that they all worked together.

We would like to know much more than this about the sequence of stages through which evolving language passed, but this should be enough to suggest that although modern spoken language seems to be characterized more by arbitrariness than by motivated signs, a stage during which communication depended upon motivated signs could have helped to push our ancestors onto the path that led, after a long evolution, to the ability to learn a language of the type we have today.

I hope that primatologists will look more closely at motivated signaling, not only among captive animals but among those in the wild. The ability to understand and use motivated signs seems to distinguish primates, or at least gorillas, chimpanzees, and bonobos, from other mammals. The use of motivated signs is a plausible step along the path toward language. By learning more about the cognitive foundation of the anthropoid ability to produce iconic and indexical signs, we should improve our model of the cognitive abilities of our own ancestors.

Notes

1. Armstrong, Stokoe, and Wilcox (1995, especially 191–94, 226–29) have also emphasized the importance of motivation in the evolution of language, and in particular they have stressed the role of iconic manual signs. See also Noble and Davidson 1996:220ff.

2. Ekman and his coworkers (1972) convinced most readers of the fundamental universality of the basic facial expressions. Recently, Russell (1994, 1995) and Fridlund (1994) have sharply criticized Ekman's and related work. Ekman (1994) has defended himself, as has Izard (1994), in my opinion effectively. I find it difficult to take seriously Russell's apparent belief that any slight degree of cultural variation rules out the possibility of any universal component of behavior. I also feel that Russell greatly overestimates the likelihood that superficial Western influence could cause older and different patterns of facial expressions to disappear. It is hard for me to believe that any anthropologist who has lived

among a geographically and culturally remote people and who has struggled to understand and to be understood has failed to exploit the commonalities of human facial expressions. Until an anthropologist acquires some rudimentary language skills, facial expressions are likely to be the most effective means of communication.

3. Snowdon (this volume) credits some animal calls with arbitrariness. By the definition of arbitrariness that he gives ("signals are not iconic or ono-matopoetic; the denotation is independent of any physical or geometric resemblance to the signal"), this is surely correct. Nevertheless, when linguists use "arbitrary" they generally have something more in mind. I began this paper by calling the word *bread* "arbitrary" because the same meaning could be expressed by any sequence of sounds on which a speech community agreed. It is a matter of convention. A choice has been made. The denotation of an animal call may have no physical resemblance to the signal, but unless it can be shown to have been set by convention and to vary among groups of the same species as do words, linguists will find it odd to call it "arbitrary." It is fixed not by arbitrary convention but by the genetic endowment of the animal.

10

The Invention and Ritualization of Language

Sherman Wilcox

The use of language to convey and acquire ideas is an
extension and refinement of the principle that things gain
meaning by being used in a shared experience or joint action.
— John Dewey, *Democracy and Education*

In her study of information donation as a framework for understanding the evolution of language, King (1994a) took a perspective
that can be called an explicit continuity approach (but see King, chapter
2, this volume). The continuity approach, she wrote (1994a:131), "does
not deny the unique properties of human language, but it rejects the
view that such properties set human language sharply apart from other
forms of information donation." The best continuity approaches, she
observed, go beyond comparing and contrasting nonhuman primate
communication with human language; they also attempt to suggest
how and why evolutionary changes might have occurred. "Human language is acknowledged to be different from other communication systems, but the focus remains on understanding what other primates
actually do and how behavior changes over time. Instead of undertak-
ing a top-down analysis, the continuity approach works from the bottom up, asking what monkeys and apes do, not just whether or not they
can do what humans do" (King 1994a:138).

I, too, take a continuity approach in discussing how human
language might have emerged in an evolutionarily plausible way. I pro-

pose that language grew out of existing cognitive abilities, social processes, and visible gestures. I attempt to develop my proposal within four constraints that I view as crucial to a scientifically valid continuity approach to language evolution: (1) the key elements required for the emergence of language must already have been present in hominids' abilities, behaviors, and social life; (2) language-external factors were acting to select these elements; (3) none of the key elements is language specific; and (4) these elements are sufficient to account for present-day human language (although I do not rule out further evolutionary development of particular abilities).

I also make a few assumptions about what is not required in a continuity approach. For example, I do not assume that a continuity approach implies that evolution has to plod along at an infinitesimally slow rate (consider the research on Darwin's finches by Peter and Rosemary Grant, as reported by Weiner [1995], which shows selection at work within very short time periods). I also assume that a continuity approach does not rule out the possibility that discontinuities can arise in evolving complex systems. An example from the physical world is state change in complex systems: when we continuously change temperature, for example, water undergoes a sharp state change to ice (for an example of how self-organization in complex systems is relevant to language, see Steels 1997).

Finally, I assume that invention—the creative power to see some aspect of the world in a new way—is not inconsistent with a continuity approach so long as the invention relies on existing abilities and processes. The emergence of language does not, I assume, rest entirely on forces beyond our ancestors' control (such as a beneficial genetic mutation; see Bickerton 1990)—forces that became grist for the mill of natural selection and alone account for language. "The human brain," writes Dawkins (1987:195), "is an inveterate analogizer." I assume that even our more distant primate ancestors possessed cognitive abilities to analogize: to form structured conceptualizations; to establish correspondences between components of these conceptualizations; and to classify new experiences as similar to old experiences on the basis of these correspondences. Clearly, these abilities are within the grasp of modern nonhuman primates (Savage-Rumbaugh et al. 1993; Byrne 1995; Savage-Rumbaugh, this volume).

Even if the best continuity approaches go beyond comparing and contrasting nonhuman primate communication to human languages, this remains a good starting point. What do humans do when we do language?

VIEWING LANGUAGE UP CLOSE

It is certainly true, as Bickerton suggests (1995:35; see King, chapter 2, this volume), that if we are to account for the evolution of language, we must have a clear understanding of what language is in all its detail, complexity, and knotty peculiarities. Linguistic theories that attempt to account for a full range of data—grammatical, historical, psychological, and neurological—provide such an up-close view of language. Yet, as King notes, this does not mean that all linguistic theories see language the same way or come to the same conclusions about how to account for the data. It follows that how a particular linguistic theory views language will significantly affect how that theory explains the emergence of language.

There are many linguistic theories. Two that I discuss in this section are the Cartesian approach (Chomsky 1966; Bickerton 1990; Pinker 1994) and the cognitive approach (Lakoff 1987; Langacker 1987, 1988, 1991a). I focus on these two because they provide strikingly different views of language and its relation to other perceptual and cognitive abilities. A third approach to language, the functional approach (Haiman 1985, 1994, 1998; Givón 1989, 1995; Bybee, Perkins, and Pagliuca 1994), is also relevant to my discussion of language evolution. I explore in detail some of Haiman's proposals (1994, 1998) for the role of ritualization in the evolution of language.

The Cartesian approach is the one most familiar to nonlinguists, and it is the approach that many primatologists and anthropologists investigating the evolution of language respond to. Many attempts to find precursors or analogues to language abilities in modern nonhuman primates or to speculate about possible language precursors in hominid abilities and social life begin with a search for the language abilities posited by Cartesian linguists. The problem is, the Cartesian approach makes inherently discontinuous assumptions about how language might have emerged. For example, addressing the possibility that language emerged from previous communicative abilities, Chomsky (1972:70) wrote:

> When we ask what human language is, we find no striking similarity to animal communication systems. There is nothing useful to be said about behavior or thought at the level of abstraction at which animal and human communication fall together. The examples of animal communication that have been examined to date do share many of the properties of human gestural systems, and it might be reasonable to explore the possibility of direct connection in this case. But human language, it appears, is based on entirely different principles. This, I think, is an important point, often overlooked by those who approach human language as a natural, biological phenomenon; in particular, it seems rather pointless, for these reasons, to speculate about the evolution of human language from simpler systems.

Beyond the dissociation between animal communication and human language, Cartesian linguists also insist on a dissociation between general cognitive abilities and the unique, autonomous, modular language ability. This dissociation can be traced back to Descartes' position on the relation between two modes of conceptualization: understanding, or reasoning, and imagination (Descartes 1980 [1641]:90): "I believe that this power of imagining that is in me, insofar as it differs from the power of understanding, is not a necessary element of my essence, that is, of the essence of my mind; for although I might lack this power, nonetheless I would undoubtedly remain the same person I am now. Thus it seems that the power of imagining depends upon something different from me."

In the Cartesian approach, language is built upon reason—the mind—not imagination (which has its basis in the body). This position on language has tremendous ramifications for how the language ability is situated in regard to general cognitive abilities. The Cartesian linguistic approach holds that language and general cognition are autonomous (Chomsky 1966:4–5): "In short, man has a species-specific capacity, a unique type of intellectual organization which cannot be attributed to peripheral organs or related to general intelligence and which manifests itself in what we may refer to as the 'creative aspect' of ordinary language—its property of being both unbounded in scope and stimulus-free."

This claim, in turn, can be linked to the Cartesian position that our mental processes, our cognitive abilities, are not grounded in our bodily based perceptual or manipulative abilities (Descartes 1980 [1641]:93):

> Although perhaps...I have a body that is very closely joined to me, nevertheless, because on the one hand I have a clear and distinct idea of myself—insofar as I am a thing that thinks and not an extended thing—and because on the other hand I have a distinct idea of a body—insofar as it is merely an extended thing, and not a thing that thinks—it is therefore certain that I am truly distinct from my body, and that I can exist without it.

Cartesian linguistics considers the essence of language to be grammar, and grammar to be a self-contained system describable without reference to other cognitive abilities—a separate mental module. The Cartesian approach treats grammar as an autonomous system distinct from both lexicon and semantics. Under this approach, the best model for understanding this self-contained linguistic system is that of a formal, algorithmic device for generating well-formed sentences. Redundancy is avoided in describing such a system because redundancy implies a loss of generalization, a lack of parsimony; economy is a prime goal in developing a Cartesian theory of language.

Cognitive linguistics makes quite different assumptions about the nature of language and is, I believe, much more compatible with selectionist approaches to language evolution. In contrast to Cartesian linguists, cognitive linguists insist that language relies on basic cognitive abilities. The goal of cognitive linguistics is to determine what these abilities are and how they operate in the use of meaning-making that we call language. This leads to a different understanding of how to develop theoretical models. For example, the cognitive linguistic approach takes a very different view of the role of theoretical economy from that of Cartesian linguistics. The cognitive linguistic approach does not permit the linguist to posit a new, language-specific cognitive ability until it can be demonstrated that basic cognitive abilities are insufficient to account for some fact of linguistic behavior; no such need has yet arisen in accounting for any facet of language ability.

Under the cognitive linguistic view, biology is seen as a better model for understanding how language works than is formal logic or mechanistic metaphors. Language, like biology, is considered to be inherently uneconomical and redundant. Language, in the cognitive linguistic approach, is not generated by an algorithmic grammar module; it is constructed by humans using general cognitive abilities. All grammar does is supply speakers with an "inventory of symbolic resources" (Langacker 1988:5).

The presuppositions and perspectives of these two approaches to language have profound implications for what must be accounted for in order for language to emerge. For the Cartesian linguist, grammar is structure that exists independently of use and general cognitive abilities. In order to account for the emergence of language, the Cartesian linguist must directly account for how grammar-as-structure emerged. It is little wonder that such a model leads to proposals that language emerged all of one piece (Bickerton 1990:190): "[S]yntax must have emerged in one piece, at one time—the most likely cause being some kind of mutation that affected the organization of the brain."

Although cognitive and functional linguists differ in some fundamental ways in their approach to the study of language, they share the view that grammar as structure is an emergent phenomenon. For the cognitive or the functional linguist, grammar emerges from use in social situations and from individual cognitive abilities. In order to account for the emergence of language, cognitive and functional linguists need not account for how grammar emerged; rather, they must account for the presence of certain cognitive abilities, study their use in nonhuman primates, and hypothesize about their selection in our hominid ancestors.

ABILITIES, PROCESSES, AND RAW MATERIALS

The essence of my proposal is that three critical elements were implicated in the evolution of language: cognitive abilities, the process of ritualization, and visible gesture. It is tempting to regard cognitive abilities as essentially focused on the individual and the process of ritualization as a social process. This dichotomy, however, is ultimately misleading. Cognitive abilities surely develop in the context of social life, and the process of ritualization depends on cognitive abilities. Nevertheless, the cognitive abilities that I describe are abilities individuals bring to bear on their perceptual and motoric interactions with the world.

Ritualization is a process driven by repetition. A ritualized activity need not ever occur in a social environment. I may, for example, develop a certain ritual for the way I shave in the morning; no one else affects or is affected by my ritual. Clearly, when we regard ritualization in this way, it is not independent of cognitive abilities such as automaticization. Nevertheless, ritualization can also have a significant social aspect. Conventionalization, an important aspect of language (Burling, this volume), is clearly a related phenomenon, a type of socially agreed-upon ritual (see also Tomasello 1990, 1994, for a discussion of ontogenetic ritualization in the development of chimpanzee gestural signals).

Visible gesture, I argue, is a critical raw material on which cognitive abilities and the process of ritualization may act. It plays a mediating role in the emergence of language, providing, at different levels and stages of development, various semiotic potentials upon which natural selection may act. My definition of visible gesture is based on an understanding of gesture as action. According to this model, gestures range from the articulations made during the production of language (phonetic gestures, which are not, for the most part, visible) to non-symbolic actions that serve only instrumental and not communicative functions.

Cognitive Abilities: Grounding Language in the Body

In cognitive linguistics, language is analyzed as a structured inventory of conventional linguistic units (Langacker 1987). Cognitive linguistics imposes a content requirement on linguistic units: "[T]he only units permitted in the grammar of a language are (i) semantic, phonological, and symbolic structures that occur overtly in linguistic expressions; (ii) structures that are schematic for those in (i); and (iii) categorizing relationships involving the structures (i) and (ii)" (Langacker 1991a:18–19). Thus the content requirement directly addresses one of the assumptions of the Cartesian approach, the grounding of language. "It rules out all arbitrary descriptive devices, i.e., those with no direct grounding in phonetic or semantic reality...[devices] introduced solely to drive the formal machinery of autonomous syntax" (Langacker 1991a:19).

Cognitive linguistics claims that grammar (that is, syntax) is intrinsically symbolic. By using the term symbolic, cognitive linguists do not mean that grammar is describable in terms of symbols that are manipulated by a set of rules that make no reference to the meaning of the symbols.[1] Rather, the term "symbol" is used to refer to a unit that has both phonological and semantic substance. Although symbolic units may exist at various levels of abstraction, they are restricted to structures that possess both form and meaning. Symbolic units are the building blocks of grammar in the cognitive linguistic approach; grammar is nothing but highly schematized symbolic units. It is for this reason that cognitive linguists claim that lexicon, morphology, and syntax form a continuum of symbolic structures (Langacker 1988).

A basic claim of cognitive linguistics is that grammatical constructions embody conventional imagery, where imagery is taken to mean the ability to mentally construe a situation in alternative ways. The cognitive linguistic approach depends on a number of basic cognitive abilities to account for grammatical functioning. Among these abilities are the following:[2]

1. The ability to form structured conceptualizations.
2. The ability to establish correspondences between components of different conceptualizations.
3. Entrenchment (also called routinization, automaticization, and habituation). This is the process in which, through repetition, a complex structure comes to be manipulable as a prepackaged assembly. It is through entrenchment that a complex structure becomes manipulable as a unit; the unit becomes reified.

4. Abstraction, or the emergence of structure through reinforcement of the commonality inherent in multiple experiences.

5. Schematization. This is a special case of abstraction in which a coarse-grained commonality emerges when distinct structures are viewed with less precision and specificity (from a distant vantage point). A schema is the commonality that emerges from distinct structures when one abstracts away from their points of difference by portraying them with lesser precision and specificity.

6. Comparison, or the ability to detect differences between two (or more) structures. Comparison involves an inherent asymmetry whereby one structure serves as a standard against which a target is evaluated.

7. Categorization. This is a type of comparison in which the standard is an established unit and the target is originally novel. When there is no discrepancy, the target elaborates (provides more detail about) the standard; when there is, the target extends (goes beyond) the standard.

8. Composition, or the ability to combine simpler structures into more complex ones. Composition involves the ability to integrate two or more component structures to form a composite structure.

9. Association, or the process in which one kind of experience evokes another.

10. Symbolization, which is a particular kind of association in which conceptualizations are associated with (mental representations of) observable entities such as sounds, gestures, or written marks.

11. The ability to impose figure-ground organization on a scene. That is, scenes do not come with "objective" figure-ground organization; instead, this organization is a matter of construal. Describing a situation as "the couch is under the picture" or "the picture is above the couch" imposes figure-ground organization upon an objective scene.

12. Focusing (profiling). This is the ability to select or focus attention on one aspect of a complex scene (for example, the

ability to select a standard and a target).
13. The ability to track an entity through time. This cognitive
ability depends on perceptual continuity.

The way in which cognitive linguistics uses cognitive abilities such
as these to account for grammatical phenomena is beyond the scope of
this chapter—a price to be paid for viewing language up close. For an
example of how the cognitive linguistic approach works, the interested
reader is referred to Langacker (1990), who presents an account of the
grammatical functioning of the English future *go,* epistemic modals (as
in "You must be tired"), and perfective *have* that relies on perspective
(analogously to the way a perceiver views a scene).

There are, however, a few generalizations I should note about
these cognitive abilities. First, they have a deep association with spatial
abilities; indeed, Langacker first dubbed his particular branch of cognitive linguistics (now called cognitive grammar) "space grammar"
because of this link between the abilities that underlie grammar and
spatial cognition. The connections between language ability and spatial
cognition are also explored by another branch of cognitive linguistics
called "mental spaces" (Fauconnier 1994; Fauconnier and Turner
1996). Deane (1992) describes a unified theory of syntax consistent
with the tenets of cognitive linguistics. He provides compelling linguistic evidence and neurological data from aphasia to support his claim
that there is a "close connection between bodily experience, spatial
thought and grammar" (Deane 1992:4). The evolutionary role of spatial cognition in the emergence of language is clearly an important concern (see Snowdon, this volume).

Second, these cognitive abilities have a close connection with
vision and visual cognition. This is clear not only in those abilities that
are explicitly tied to vision, such as imagery, focus, and figure-ground
organization, but also in such basic cognitive abilities as schematization
(viewing structures at lower resolution, such as from a distant vantage
point, so that details are lost) and categorization, which relies on comparison grounded in visual features (see Biederman 1990).

This link between vision and language has been noted by others as
well. For example, the cognitive scientist Sereno (1991a, 1991b) claims

that language may well have emerged from a fairly simple modification of visual cognition. He notes analogies between "scene perception" and language:

> [T]he integration of successive glances in the comprehension of a visual scene requires a kind of serial assembly operation similar in some respects to the integration of word meanings in discourse comprehension….[T]he underspecified, context-free information in an isolated glance is sharpened and focused by context (cf. polysemy); information from temporally distant glances must be tied together (cf. anaphora). (Sereno 1991b:82)

The main difference between scene perception and language, according to Sereno, is that comprehending a scene is closely tied to the current scene, whereas language "might best be thought of as a kind of fictive visual scene comprehension, in the case of spoken language comprehension, by sequences of phoneme[s]" (Sereno 1991b:82).

The difference is less stark, however, when we broaden our view to include language or communicative behavior that is not spoken. Here we see the first example of how visible gestures play a mediating role. If we imagine a case in which a story is presented primarily by means of visible gestures, we see immediately that visible gestures are both a part of the current visual scene and about some fictive (remembered or hypothetical) scene.

Givón (1995:393–448) presented a proposal for language evolution that is compatible in many respects with the one I am proposing. Givón suggested that language arose "through co-evolution of the neuro-cognitive mechanisms, socio-cultural organization and communicative skills of pre-human hominids" (1995:444). A central thesis of Givón's proposal is that "the supportive neurology specific to the processing of human language is an evolutionary outgrowth of the *visual information processing system*" (1995:394). Givón noted that the visual processing system splits into two streams: a ventral visual processing stream that analyzes visually perceived objects as belonging to particular types, and a dorsal visual processing stream that is responsible for analyzing spatial relations and spatial motions among specific objects (that is, visual states and events). He found correspondences between these two visual processing systems and linguistic processing: (1) Recognizing an object as a member of a generic type is the visual equivalent of lexical-semantic identification, which involves recognizing a specific token of a word as an exemplar of a generic type; and (2) recognizing spatial relations among objects, or between an object figure and its spatial ground, is the visual equivalent of recognizing propositional information about states or events, because propositions include an element of relationship (Givón 1995:408–9).

A third generalization about cognitive abilities that I should mention is that there is a strong manipulative component to many of them. The connection between manual activity such as tool-making or tool use and cognitive abilities has been explored by a number of researchers, including Calvin (1982), Davidson and Noble (1993a), Gibson (1993c; Gibson and Jessee, this volume), Toth and Schick (1993), and Wynn (1993). It is no mere etymological accident, I think, that we resort to using words that originate in manipulative actions to describe certain cognitive abilities. Consider how Tattersall (1995:241) relies on manual (and visual) imagery in discussing hominid evolution:

> If general lifeways changed so little prior to the advent of *Homo sapiens,* why do we see so much physical change—and particularly brain enlargement—in the course of human evolution? One possibility is that even relatively small technological advances—changes simply in the way in which the manipulability of the world was viewed by hominids—may have handed an evolutionary advantage to those individuals capable of grasping and exploiting them.

I might sum up these observations by noting that the cognitive abilities I listed, which form the foundation for the human language capacity, are grounded in the visual perception and manipulation of objects and events in the world. While this conclusion is compatible with the cognitive linguistic view of human language, it is exactly contrary to a pivotal claim of Cartesian linguistics—that language is not grounded in peripheral (perceptual, motoric) systems.

The Process of Ritualization

Haiman (1994, 1998) has presented a compelling case for the role of ritualization in the evolution of language. He argues that the driving force behind ritualization is the repetition of a behavior or activity. He identifies three major processes associated with ritualization: emancipation, or the freeing of instrumental actions from their primary motivation; habituation, or a decline in the strength of response or even the tendency to respond to a repeated stimulus; and automaticization. Berger and Luckmann (1967:53) defined automaticization by noting that "any action that is repeated frequently becomes cast into a pattern, which can then be reproduced with an economy of effort."

All three processes are at work across human and nonhuman behaviors and across linguistic and nonlinguistic behaviors. The first, emancipation, plays a key role in semanticization, or the transformation of an instrumental act into a sign. Automaticization is responsible for the emergence of double articulation (or duality of patterning), which many regard as a criterial feature of human language. Habituation brings about the erosion of icons into arbitrary symbols, signs that are not motivated by their external links and that therefore are susceptible to systemic or internal constraints. I discuss all three processes later in the chapter.

Visible Gestures: Meaningful Actions

My colleagues and I have recently proposed a gestural model of language evolution (Armstrong, Stokoe, and Wilcox 1994, 1995) that claims that all language, whether spoken or signed, is articulatory gesturing (Neisser 1967). We define gesture as a functional unit, an equivalence class of coordinated movements that achieve some end. Of course we recognize that in defining gesture in this way, we are juxtaposing two senses of the word: the more commonsense use in which gesture refers to bodily actions that are expressive or meaningful, and a more technical sense that is used in the speech and phonetic sciences of articulatory gesture as a dynamic, coordinative structure without symbolic meaning (Fowler 1986; Kelso, Saltzman, and Tuller 1986; Browman and Goldstein 1989).

Clearly these two senses are related; at the very least, gestures of the first type are composed of gestures of the second type. This is true across "commonsense" gestures and speech gestures. A "thumbs up" gesture is composed of a coordinated assembly of nonsymbolic gestures (closing the fingers, extending the thumb, raising the arm, etc.). Words are likewise assemblies of nonsymbolic gestures into larger, symbolic gestural complexes. Thus, our gestural view considers the word "Great!" and the "thumbs up" gesture to be remarkably similar. Each is a coordinated assembly of nonsymbolic gestures into a larger symbolic unit: "[W]ords [or symbolic gestures] are not simply strings of individual gestures, produced one after the other; rather, each is a particular pattern of gestures, orchestrated appropriately in time and space" (Kelso, Saltzman, and Tuller 1986:31). Our claim is that this perspective on gesture is necessary for understanding the evolution of neural mechanisms that form the basis for perceptual categorization, memory, and language (Edelman 1987; Studdert-Kennedy 1987; Kimura 1993).

I have found it useful (Wilcox 1996) to examine according to various criteria the types of gestures that can be produced and received by animals. For example, we might consider which parts of the animal's body are engaged in the production of gestures and thus unavailable for other activities, or conversely, which activities preclude the production of gestures. It is difficult to produce a manual gesture while engaged in an activity requiring the use of both hands.[3]

We might also consider how the receiving animal perceives the sender's gesture—or, more correctly, how it perceives the proximal signal (acoustic or optic for our discussion) produced by the distal gesture—and the properties of the environmental signal. Optical gestures require a visual system and a source of light for perception—visible gestures are less efficient in the dark and in environments that block vision (e.g., in arboreal environments; see Maestripieri, this volume). They also require that the receiver's eyes be looking at the signal source. We cannot optimally receive visual gestures unless we are looking at them. Equally important, we cannot receive other visual signals at the same time, because we are not attending to them. Other sources of visual information that might be available in the environment become less accessible or even inaccessible to an animal that is required to visually attend to a visible gesture.

We get a different set of characteristics for acoustic signals. The ear does not have to be directed at the signaling source in order to receive an acoustic signal; acoustic signals work as well in the dark as in the light and are better suited to arboreal environments than are optical signals. Ears are not engaged in any other activities except receiving acoustic information. Though auditory attention can certainly be directed, it is also true that we can perceive auditory information to which we are not attuned (consider the common experience of being engaged in a conversation yet overhearing your name spoken). Acoustic information is complementary to optical information.

Visible gesture plays a pivotal role in the framework I am developing. I suggest that visible gesture provided the raw material on which cognitive abilities and the process of ritualization acted. Visible gesture was no ordinary raw material, however; it was, I suggest, a highly volatile element, poised to serve as a catalyst in the crucible of evolving cognitive abilities and social processes.

Visible gesture was a critical element in the early emergence of language for several reasons. First, visible gestures are implicated in the grounding of cognitive abilities. As we have seen, the basic cognitive abilities upon which language can be built are themselves grounded in our bodily interactions with the world, interactions that rely on visual perception and manual manipulation. Visible gestures also mediate the individual and the social. Visible gestures, including manual and facial gestures, are an important means by which social order is regulated and social interaction is conducted (Zeller 1996; Maestripieri, this volume).

Gesture is a fundamental unit of organization in an organism's motoric interactions with the world (Edelman 1987:221-31). Our motoric actions, though, are bound up with perception. As Churchland (1986:473) notes, "evolution being what it is, pattern recognition is there to subserve motor coordination.... [I]f we ignore motor control as the context within which we try to understand pattern recognition, we run the risk of generating biologically irrelevant solutions." Visible gesture also mediates action and perception.

Finally, and perhaps most importantly for the early stages of language evolution, visible gestures mediate action and communication. Visible gestures are at once actions in the world, actions with instrumental function (grasping a prey), and, at least potentially, communicative actions, acts that convey information and intent ("grasp that prey!"). It is not merely that visible gestures are iconic for objects and events in the world—they are that and more. Visible gestures are objects and events in the world.

It is this potential for gesture to serve a communicative function, like the potential of a ball poised to roll down a hill, that I suggest is a key feature of visible gesture. Cognitive abilities and ritualization nudged the ball and got language rolling.

RITUALIZATION: SEMANTICIZATION AND GRAMMATICIZATION

Ritualization plays two roles in the overall framework that I am developing. First, it is implicated in the initial emergence of communication, a process that can be equated with the sociobiological notion of semanticization: "In the course of evolution, both locomotory movements and acts (concerned with comfort, with heat regulation, and with the capture of prey) have been selected and modified to produce signals" (Blest 1963:102). Givón (1995) describes the process of semanticization as a transformation of instrumental behavior into communicative signals. The process, he claims, may be broken down into several conceptually distinct components (Givón 1995:429):

1. A complex thick band of co-occurring features of behavior co-occurs reliably with a unique referent
2. Attention is gradually narrowed from the entire thick band to a few or one of its salient features
3. The single salient feature is then reinterpreted as a communicative clue
4. All other features of the behavior are disregarded

Second, ritualization is involved in the transformation of these primitive signals into grammaticalized signs—signs with features that we regard as criteria of human language, such as double articulation (duality of patterning), arbitrariness, and digitization. Thus, ritualization is implicated both in the emergence of communicative signaling and in the transformation of nonlinguistic signals into linguistic signs.

From Action to Meaning

Semanticization is driven by the first of the three types of ritualization mentioned earlier, emancipation. Emancipation refers to the transformation of objects and events in the world into signs, objects, or events that stand for or mean something other than what they are.

As behaviors and activities become emancipated from their instrumental function, they can become selected and modified to produce signals. Acts that formerly served an instrumental function become free to take on meaning. Haiman cites a paradigmatic example from Kessel's (1955) research on the mating activity of balloon, or dancing, flies. The male balloon fly signals the female that he is available for mating by giving her a "wedding present"—a balloonlike object made of bodily produced silk. He does this, apparently, to distract the female, who would rather eat the male than mate with him. While she is busy opening the present, he mounts and mates with her. According to Haiman (1994:4), the explanation for the male's ritualized gesture is this:

> Originally, the male dancing fly distracted the predaceous female with a distracting gift of a dead insect: at this point, the gift was purely instrumental. Later, the gift was interpreted as a signal to the female, a signal whose message was something like "this fly is available for mating." Originally, also, the male partially wrapped his tiny prey up in silk exuded from his anal glands, probably in order to subdue it: the silk, like the dead insect, had an instrumental function, and its similarity to "wrapping" was incidental. Finally, however, the mate achieved his original "purpose" by giving the female the elaborated wrapping alone, and it is the wrapping which serves as the mating signal.

Thus, in the nonlinguistic realm, instrumental actions—movements or gestures—are ritualized through repetition and become meaningful acts—signals. These basic, paradigmatic cases of semanticization invariably involve the transformation of instrumental, visible gestures into meaningful signals.

Haiman also suggests that emancipation transforms connotation into denotation—that denotation is emancipated connotation. The process, according to Haiman (1998:153), looks like this:

> A symptomatic gesture or fidget (let us say, a cry of pain like [aaaa]) accompanies a psychological state. That is, originally the gesture co-occurs with the state. It becomes a signal which connotes that state once it is recognized and responded to by some other animal. Finally, it becomes a sign (say, the English word "ouch") which denotes the state only when it becomes emancipated both from the stimulus which produced it originally and from the motivated state of which it served as a signal.

It is at this early stage of semanticization, which Haiman regards as marking the true origin of language, that I suggest visible gestures played a key role. Visible gestures were readily recruited into service as meaningful signs because of their unique quality of being both actions in the world and actions about the world. Visible gestures are iconic with what they mean (a type of iconicity that Peirce [1955] called "image" iconicity: the sign in some way resembles its referent). Because of this quality, they can serve for the motivated naming of objects and actions in the world (for a fuller discussion of motivated signs and their significance in the evolution of language, see Burling, this volume).

But we require more in order to get to language. It is one thing to account for the emergence of meaningful signs—signs that can iconically represent objects and events. It is another to account for linguistic signs, which do more than name; they also enter into relations with other signs. Visible gestures have the capacity to go beyond representing actions and events in the world. They also carry the seed of syntax: visible gestures are both name and relation (Armstrong, Stokoe, and Wilcox 1995:chapter 7). As such, they exhibit a second type of iconicity, "diagrammatic" iconicity: the relations among parts of the sign correspond to or reflect relations among parts of the referent (Peirce 1955).

The diagrammatic iconicity of visible gestures is both externally and internally directed. Visible, particularly manual, gestures not only iconically represent event structures in the world but also stand in an iconic relationship to the internal structure of linguistic signs. Events in the world can be construed as involving objects and interactions. Objects are prototypically time-stable entities capable of moving about and interacting with other objects. Objects are conceptually autonomous with regard to interactions. These characteristics and valences map onto linguistic signs, which not only represent event structures in the world but also consist of prototypical objects (nouns) and interactions (verbs) with their own autonomy-dependency relationships.

The same characteristics apply to visible gestures: they are diagrammatically iconic for syntactic relations. They are objects that move about and interact with other objects. Hands are prototypical nouns, and their actions are prototypical verbs. Hands, as objects, are conceptually autonomous with respect to the interactions they can enter into (grabbing, pulling, tearing, hitting, etc.).[4] The production and perception of visible, manual gestures ground grammar in action and perception. Archetypal semantic roles such as agent and patient, and archetypal events such as transitive actions, are grounded in our visual perception of manual gestures and our experience as "mobile and sentient creatures and as manipulators of physical objects" by means of manual action (Langacker 1991b:285).[5]

In summary, it is this nexus of functions and correspondences that I suggest made visible gestures a key element in the emergence of language. Visible gesture, like the Roman god Janus, faces in two directions simultaneously: toward the perceived world of objects and events and toward the conceived world of grammar. Visible gestures are (1) instrumental actions in the world; (2) potentially communicative actions about the world; (3) diagrammatically iconic with objects and events in the world; and (4) diagrammatically iconic with syntactic dependencies and relations.

Semanticization provides a mechanism by which we can get from instrumental gestures to meaningful gestures—primitive linguistic signs. But two problems remain. First, if visible gesture was so critical to the emergence of language, then why is language not now based on visible gesture? Kendon (1991:215) also posed this question: "All forms of

SHERMAN WILCOX

language that we encounter today (with the exception of the relatively rare occurrence of primary, i.e., deaf sign languages and the even rarer development of alternative sign languages in speaking communities) are, of course, spoken. If language began as gesture, why did it not stay that way?" In an earlier work (Wilcox 1996), I called this the "Great Switch" from visible gesture to speech. How can my framework account for this switch?

The second problem concerns what happened after the switch. If, in the switch to speech, we find a sudden appearance of those critical features of language such as arbitrariness, double articulation, and digitization, then we have in fact explained very little. How do we account for the appearance of grammaticalized speech?

From Visible to Audible Gesture

I propose that the same cognitive abilities, ritualization processes, and characteristics of visible gesture that were used in accounting for the emergence of the first linguistic gestures can also account for the switch to speech and the appearance of the features that are criteria of modern spoken language.

First, I claim that there was in fact no Great Switch from gesture to speech. One answer to Kendon's question is that speech is still gestural. The difference between visible gestures and speech is not that one is gesture and the other is not; they are both gestural. The operative difference is that one is visible-optical and the other is audible-acoustic (see Fónagy 1988; Farnell 1995; Fowler and Levy 1995).

The unique semiotic qualities of visible gestures as both actions-in-the-world and communicative actions were critical in moving from action to meaning—in semanticizing visible actions.[6] But these visible gestures did not occur alone; our ancestors were not mute. Visible gestures and audible gestures—vocalizations—were surely both present in a rich, holistic, action-communication system. Once visible gestures became emancipated from their instrumental functions and became primitive signs within this complex visible-audible gestural system, the same process of emancipation came to bear on this system. Only now, audible gestures came to be symptomatic for the visible-audible gestural complex. Here is how this process maps onto the steps involved in emancipation that Givón (1995:429) described:

1. "A complex thick band of co-occurring features of behavior co-occurs reliably with a unique referent": visible gesture and audible gesture co-occur as a complex, multimodal signal.
2. "Attention is gradually narrowed from the entire thick band to a few or one of its salient features": attention is redirected from the multimodal signal to the acoustic portion of it.
3. "The single salient feature is then reinterpreted as a communicative clue": audible gesture is construed as representing the entire signal.
4. "All other features of the behavior are disregarded": the visible gestural portion of the complex signal decreases in communicative salience and is able to serve other functions.

In other words, I am claiming that a sudden switch from gesture to speech never occurred. In this scenario, there was never a time when visible gestures were unaccompanied by vocalizations. Rather, I am suggesting that there was a gradual realignment of information transmission from a wide-band signal in which the optical portion (visible gesture) initially played a critical role to a wide-band signal in which the acoustic portion (vocal tract audible gesture) became predominant.

It is worth noting that this claim provides for a unified account of the relation between language and gesture. Several researchers (for example, Blake et al. 1992; McNeill 1992; Blake and Dolgoy 1993; Kimura 1993) have noted the deep neurological and psychological connections between language and gesture. We might ask how these connections came about. As we saw earlier, the Cartesian position claims that animal communication and human gestural systems share many properties and might be directly connected: "The examples of animal communication that have been examined to date do share many of the properties of human gestural systems, and it might be reasonable to explore the possibility of direct connection in this case" (Chomsky (1972:70). But the Cartesian position goes on to claim that there is no direct connection between human language and animal communication—that they are based on entirely different principles.

The neurological and psychological convergence of human language and gesture must then be some evolutionary fluke.

Under the scenario I am presenting, the links between gesture and language can be traced far back into our evolutionary history. This suggests that there was no convergence of the cognitive abilities involved in, or of the neurological structures responsible for, gesture and language. They have been essentially the same structures and abilities from the start.

What might have caused such a realignment to take place? What were the adaptive pressures that might have caused the acoustic signal to become the salient, representative clue for this wide-band communication signal? Previously (Wilcox 1996), I described one example of how selection pressures might have come into play based on King's (1994a) notion of social information donation. King proposed a model explaining how and why increased information donation was selected for. "The clearest pattern for information donation," she wrote, "is found in the foraging context and correlates with food sharing and extractive foraging with tools" (1994a:117). King claims that "a likely selection pressure for greater donation of information is a shift to dependence on foods that require a significant investment by immatures in acquiring foraging skills and the information on which those skills depend" (1994a:119).

Acquisition of foraging and tool-making skills relies critically on at least two processes. First, adult and immature must jointly attend to the task. This means cognitively sharing a focus on, say, digging up a tuber in a certain way or producing a tool with a certain technique, as well as visually attending to the task. As tasks become increasingly difficult, the demand for information donation to take place through explicit instruction will also become greater. This is precisely where visible gestures are at a disadvantage. They require the hands, which are already engaged in another activity, and the eyes, which must divide their attention between attending to the task and attending to the gesturer. This would put pressure on the acoustic channel to carry the communicative load, simultaneously freeing the optical channel to receive important visual information. The same case can be made for other situations in which competing sources of optical information are present, such as in the acquisition of predator avoidance skills. It would be more efficient, not to mention more effective, to be able to attend simultaneously to a vocalizing, information-donating adult and to an approaching predator than to divide visual attention between the two.

Of course, other selectional pressures were possible. My point is that the same process of ritualization that accounted for the transformation of visible actions into meaningful gestures can also account for the realignment of a visible-audible gestural complex in which visible gestures initially were most informative into a system in which audible gestures came to carry the burden of communicative information.

Linguistic Ritualization: From Vocalizations to Phonemes

Burling (1993) suggests that of the many features of human language, the most important is the principle of contrast. "Language," he writes, "is characterized by pervasive contrast" (1993:28). The principle of contrast is closely related to another feature of language, digitization: "The phonological system of a language, by imposing absolute distinctions on the phonetic continuum, is almost pure contrast, but we can also speak of words and even sentences as being in contrast....The result is a digital system of communication constructed from contrasting signals" (Burling 1993:28). Burling is not alone in noting that an overriding distinction between language and communication is that the former is digital while the latter is analog. Chomsky (1972:69) also claims that the distinction between animal communication and human language is that "the animal system admits in principle of continuous variation along the linguistic dimension [Chomsky refers here to variables such as pitch alternation]...whereas human language is discrete." Although animal communication has an indefinitely large range of potential signals, "the mechanism and principle...are entirely different from those employed by human language" (Chomsky 1972:69).

Other features have also been noted as separating language from other forms of communication. Among the most commonly offered are duality of patterning and arbitrariness (Hockett 1960). One concern for those attempting to account for the evolution of language is to locate these features of language in nonlinguistic animal communication (Snowdon, this volume) or else to explain how they could have emerged from earlier communication systems that were not arbitrary, were not pervasively contrastive or digital (that is, were continuous), and did not display duality of patterning. Haiman (1994, 1998) provides what I regard as a satisfying answer: linguistic contrast, digitization, duality of patterning, and arbitrariness are emergent properties, the artifacts of ritualization.

First, let us consider the principle of contrast and digitization. As we saw earlier, emancipation is implicated in the transformation of instrumental actions into signals. Emancipation also is implicated in the further transformation of these signals—it is involved in codification, or the creation of signs. Codification operates on actions in two ways. First, the activity, through ritualization, becomes routinized: its form remains relatively stable, independent of the stimulus. Second, the ritualized activity becomes decontextualized. Because it does not occur in response to the same stimulus, it can now occur in a variety of contexts. One result of codification in an emerging linguistic system is that what were originally random fluctuations become both distinctive and uniform, precisely because they are emancipated from their conditioning environments (see Haiman 1994).

It is this process by which signals become distinctive and uniform that is related to digitization. Another way to look at this process is as an example of what ethologists have called "typical intensity," or the tendency for a ritualized gesture to remain constant irrespective of the presence or strength of the stimulus that produced it. The close connection between typical intensity in ritualized animal behavior and the property of digitization and contrast in human language is revealed in the following observation from Blest (1963:104): "Whereas stimuli of varying strength for the release of the unritualized precursors of display movements elicit responses of varying intensity and form, following ritualization, the derived responses acquire an almost constant form and intensity to a wide range of stimulus strengths."

Thus, when applied to the emergence of linguistic behavior, ritualization has two results. First, it can explain how previously variable or analog signals can become digital, so that linguistic units—phonemes, for example—impose absolute distinctions. Second, these emerging linguistic units begin to form a system and thus enter into intrasystemic relations; that is, they become contrastive. "As signs become emancipated from, and autonomous relative to, their extralinguistic real-world referents, they may be free to become more sensitive to their linguistic context, that is, the other signs with which they co-occur" (Haiman 1998:149). As we will see, ritualization is also implicated in the rise of the principle of contrastiveness in emerging linguistic systems.

What about duality of patterning (Haiman calls this "double articulation")? Duality of patterning is the property of language by which it is structurally organized at two levels: in terms of combinations of meaningful units (such as morphemes or words) and in terms of sequences of units that lack any meaning in themselves (phonemes) (Crystal 1980). But meaningless units do not have to start that way. The process that drove duality of patterning was erosion of meaningful units into meaningless units. This process is also identified with grammaticization, the erosion of meaning or substance through repeated use (Bybee, Perkins, and Pagliuca 1994).

As a driving force in the emergence of duality of patterning, grammaticization is important because it leads to the erosion of large units into increasingly smaller units. Thus, as Haiman suggests, "rather than accepting double articulation as an irreducible given, we might get a handle on its origins by thinking of degrees of significance, with signs arranged in a hierarchy" (Haiman 1994:11). His scheme is shown in figure 10.1.

There is clear cross-linguistic evidence that this grammaticization process is pervasive and unidirectional. The suggestion I make here is that the process is essentially one of ritualization, and it can be continued backward to include the ritualization of instrumental, nonlinguistic gestures—that is, it can account for the evolution of language out of nonlanguage.

What about arbitrariness? Certainly, the roots of arbitrariness are also revealed in many of the facets of ritualization just described. First, we saw that one result of ritualization is the emancipation of a signal from its motivation—the form becomes unmotivated. Second, the beginnings of arbitrariness are also implied in the emergence of typical intensity. Manning (1967:138) elaborates: "Postures or movements which have a typical intensity are more easily recognized but corre-

Biggest (most "wordlike")	1. Words, lexical morphemes
	2. Affixes, grammatical morphemes
Intermediate signs	3. Submorphemic sounds with associations
Smallest (most "soundlike")	4. Phonemes

FIGURE 10.1

Hierarchy of double articulation (after Haiman 1994).

spondingly convey less information about the signaller's motivational state." As we have less and less information about the motivation for a particular form, that form becomes more arbitrary.

Finally, arbitrariness has its beginnings in another result of ritualization, the tendency for the form of the ritualized activity to become stylized. Stylized gestures or signals are hypertrophied to the point that they are instrumentally dysfunctional. Once emancipated from their functional motivation, they are free to take on a life of their own. We see two results that, at first glance, appear contradictory.

First, we see the rise of style for style's sake: increased sensitivity to system-internal constraints as opposed to system-external (motivated or iconic) constraints. Freed from practical, functional demands, stylization runs riot. Cartmill (1993) provides a particularly telling example. Among the fourteenth-century English aristocracy, hunting was no longer a necessary activity. Freed from necessity, hunting became ritualized, stylized, and thus associated with upper-class status and gentility. Being familiar with the obligations of style became so important that the aristocracy spent a great deal of time and effort in learning proper hunting behavior (Cartmill 1993:61–62): "The growth of ritual in the upper-class medieval hunt is documented in the how-to books produced for the education and training of aristocratic hunters....[These books] became progressively more concerned with the forms of hunting etiquette and ceremony than with the practical task of bagging game." The well-heeled medieval hunter had to learn a vast terminology for the various kinds of animal droppings, for the common configurations of antlers, for the hoofprints of deer, for the places where deer left signs of having lain or stood or walked or galloped, and for the different kinds of hunting dogs and their anatomy, behavior, and so forth. He had to learn the appropriate signals to be given to fellow hunters, and much, much more (Cartmill 1993:64).

Second, stylization leads to the development of standardization. Freed from external and idiosyncratic motivations or stimuli, activities, gestures, and signals become uniform. When stylization is applied to material culture, such as the production of tools and art objects, it places increased demands on explicit instruction and thus on information donation (King 1994a:102–9). In language, these two properties are manifested in two ways essential to our understanding of modern human language. First, standardization implies internal structure or "standards of well-formedness"—that is, grammar. Second, since these standards have only internal coherence and little, if any, external motivation (that is, they are "grammar for grammar's sake"), the only way they can persist is through convention.

The ritualization account has one significant benefit that seems to be lacking from other accounts of what distinguishes language from nonlanguage: it suggests an explanation for how these features might have emerged. For example, Burling (1993, this volume) builds the case that the human language (and languagelike) system is sharply distinguished from the human gesture-call system (and from animal gesture-call systems). He does not, however, offer an explanation for how the features of language that he claims separate it from nonlanguage came to be, other than that they reflect how animals used their minds more than how they communicated. Saying that "language emerged as a product of our evolving mind" (1993:36) does not explain why language has the features of contrast and digitization, arbitrariness, and duality of patterning. Are these essential properties of the mind?

Burling's belief that cognition was significant in the origins of language is one that I obviously share. He is undoubtedly correct that cognitive abilities were critical in the emergence of language. But this is only part of the story. When Burling (1993:37) says, for example, "I suspect that we will learn more about the origins of language by studying how apes and other primates use their minds than by studying how they communicate," I want to respond in two ways. First, although I agree that it is important to study how animals use their minds (indeed, merely acknowledging that animals have minds is a great step forward), we must also recognize that minds have a social basis (Vygotsky 1978; John-Steiner 1985; Wertsch 1985, 1991; Sinha 1988, 1989). Because of this we cannot extricate the mind from communication. Minds did not emerge in individual animals living in isolation; they emerged in individuals who were a part of a social unit and among whom communication was taking place. Nonhuman primate minds as well as human minds are surely shaped by how they communicate.

Second, ritualization is implicated in all facets of language evolution. I suspect that we can learn a great deal by studying the multifaceted transformations that behaviors such as visible gestures or audible signaling undergo when they are repeatedly used by ever larger and ever changing groups of individuals.

THE EMERGENCE OF GRAMMAR: AN ONGOING PROCESS

I return now to the issue of how ritualization can lead to standardization. One implication of my previous discussion is that there was no single event that occurred at a particular point in time (such as a genetic mutation or the sudden "discovery" of symbols or symbol traces) that we can identify as the origin of language. Evolution is not a process that happened only once in the past; it goes on continuously. Likewise, the evolution of language and grammar is occurring continually. Grammar is always emerging. In this respect, I agree with Taylor (1996) that the origin of language never happened—it is, I would claim, always happening.

This is the view of functional linguists such as Hopper (1987), who argue that grammar is an emergent property of language. But this view of language also suggests something more fundamental. Not only do the grammars of existing languages continue to emerge, but we might see the emergence of language itself if only we look in the right place.

A particularly instructive example is given in a recent study of the evolution of language on a microgenetic time scale. Singleton, Morford, and Goldin-Meadow (1993) present evidence that when individuals invent symbols to communicate de novo, they can generate a system of symbols that is characterized by what the authors call "internal standards of well-formedness." Their data come from two sources: gestures invented by a deaf child, David, over a period of years, and gestures invented by nonsigning hearing individuals on the spot.

This important study provides a glimpse at the emergence of language in action. Standards of well-formedness are "the organization of information in contrastive and productive categories" (Singleton, Morford, and Goldin-Meadow 1993:705). The authors note that David's gestures displayed two features: they conveyed information about the referent of the gesture (that is, they were iconically motivated), and they fit into a contrastive system of form-meaning categories. The difference between gestures that conform to standards of well-formedness and those that do not is captured in the difference between gestures invented by novice gesturers for the first time and David's system of home-grown signs (Singleton, Morford, and Goldin-Meadow 1993:703–4):

> When the novice gesturers generated a gesture, their goal was to produce a handshape that adequately represented the object, and their choice of handshapes appeared to be constrained only by their imaginations and the physical limitations imposed by the hands themselves. In contrast, when David generated a gesture, his choice of handshapes was (we suggest) guided not only by how well a handshape captured the features of an object, but also by how well that handshape fit into the set of handshapes allowed in his system.

The novice gesturers' creations were motivated. David's gestures, although perhaps still partially sensitive to external motivation, "conformed to an internally consistent and contrastive system; that is, they appeared to have standards of form."

My only quibble is with the ontological status of these standards of well-formedness, because clearly their manifestation in David's gestures amounts to the appearance of grammar. Throughout the study, the authors seem to assume a Cartesian view of language. They state, "In this paper, we explore the forces propelling a communication system toward standards of well-formedness" (Singleton, Morford, and Goldin-Meadow 1993:684). The authors imply that these standards are preexisting and that they direct the course of the emerging language system. For example, they state that "David appeared to rely on standards of form that guided the way in which he constructed his gestures" (Singleton, Morford, and Goldin-Meadow 1993:698). The authors seem to be saying that David relied on an innate, mental representation of standards of well-formedness. In this sense, then, David did not really create language, and certainly not grammar; under this view, a preexisting grammatical system directed the way in which he constructed gestures. This implies that grammar did not emerge in this situation but only became manifest.

This is precisely what Hopper (1987), in proposing that grammar is emergent, argues against. Such a view of language "provides for a logically prior—perhaps eventually even biologically prior—linguistic system which is simultaneously present for all speakers and hearers, and which is a pre-requisite for the actual use of language. It is, in other words, the scenario that when we speak we refer to an abstract, mentally represented rule system, and that we in some sense 'use' already available abstract structures and schemata" (Hopper 1987:140–41).

How would the alternative view explain the appearance of standards of well-formedness in David's gestures? As we have seen, once a behavior or gesture becomes emancipated from its external stimulus—becomes ritualized—as a matter of course it becomes less externally motivated and more sensitive to internal constraints. I suggest that standards of well-formedness in David's gestures are emergent properties of a system undergoing ritualization. Because these standards of well-formedness are the products of ritualization, we would expect that repetition, the prime mover of ritualization, would be required in order for the standards to appear. As the title of their article—"Once Is Not Enough"—suggests, this is precisely what the authors conclude: "These findings suggest that it is possible for an individual to introduce standards of form within a communication system, although it appears to require a period of time, perhaps years, for such standards to evolve" (Singleton, Morford, and Goldin-Meadow 1993:710).

This section has been primarily an ontogenetic story. My claim is that this ontogenetic, developmental scenario has implications for phylogenesis, the evolution of language. What it suggests, I believe, is that language or grammar is not an innate predisposition of the brain; structure is not innately specified. Rather, innate predispositions of the brain are more like developmental engines (Gómez 1997). What is selected for is not some innate grammatical system present in adults but developmental trajectories, "certain starting points for development (brain genotypes) which in interaction with the environment give way to successful or unsuccessful ontogenies (brain phenotypes). . . . [I]n the case of language evolution, we are not looking for 'innate grammars,' but for mechanisms capable of developing grammars" (Gómez 1997:134–35). I suggest that the process of ritualization, which relies critically both on interaction with the social and physical environment and on general cognitive abilities, is such a mechanism.

CONCLUSION: NOT UNIQUELY HUMAN

I have attempted in this chapter to expand on previous work (Armstrong, Stokoe, and Wilcox 1994, 1995; Wilcox 1996) and to develop a unified account of language evolution that is compatible with evolutionary theory. By unified, I mean that the account places the evolution of language within the domain of other behaviors, abilities, and processes that are observed across animal species. I see this as a necessary position to take if we are to explain the evolution of language. As Cartmill (1993:226) has noted, "to explain something is to show that it is an instance of some general rule, familiar to us from other instances." If, as Chomsky claims, language relies on a "species-specific capacity, a unique type of intellectual organization," then it is beyond our scientific powers to explain. Again, Cartmill (1993:226): "If there really are human peculiarities that find no parallels in other creatures, then they are inexplicable. As long as we insist on hearing stories that 'explain' human uniqueness, we will have to forgo genuine explanations and content ourselves with narrative fables, in which all the causal links are supplied by the imagination."

I do not think we have to resort to fables in examining the evolution of language. This means we must search for parallels, for instances of the general rule familiar to us from other instances. If, as King (1994a) notes, the phenomena we are attempting to explain are by definition unique, then we are forever destined to tell miracle stories.

The framework I have proposed allows for a scientific explanation of how language emerged. It does this by relying on the four constraints I described at the beginning of the chapter. The key elements of the framework were in place and available for selection prior to the emergence of language. None of the elements is posited solely to account for language, and none is uniquely human. Finally, though I have offered no linguistic argumentation or examples, the elements of the framework have been demonstrated by a number of linguists to be sufficient to account for modern human language.

The framework also unifies several aspects of language and language-related behaviors. For example, it provides a unified explanation for (1) the intimate relationship between language and gesture (McNeill 1992); (2) the common neurological substrates controlling manual and speech gestures (Kimura 1993); (3) the connections between language and vision (Sereno 1991b); and (4) the connections between sign and speech (Poizner, Klima, and Bellugi 1987; Kimura 1993; Farnell 1995).

Clearly, this framework depends on a particular way of looking at language. Although the cognitive-functional linguistic framework is widely accepted and, to my mind, the most satisfying of current linguistic approaches, it is still a minority view within the field. The claim that grammar is grounded in perceptual and cognitive abilities or that historical processes such as ritualization play a role in shaping grammar, although uncontroversial among cognitive or functional linguists, would certainly be challenged by others.

Finally, the framework raises further questions about human and nonhuman primate communication. Do nonhuman primates use gesture in ways compatible with the claims presented in this chapter? To what extent do nonhuman primates possess the cognitive abilities upon which this framework relies? Is the evolution of these cognitive abilities in nonhuman primates and hominids compatible with this framework?

What can we learn about the evolution of language by studying the joint development of activity, gesture, and language in human ontogeny? What role do motivated signs play in nonhuman primate communication? What do we know about the ritualization of behavior, particularly in information-sharing settings, in nonhuman primate communities? Many of these questions have already been posed and explored by other contributors to this volume. As we begin to discover more complete answers to such questions, the mystery of how language could have evolved in a continuous manner will surely begin to fade. The mist will rise, and our vision of language as a cognitive ability embedded within social processes will become clear.

Notes

This paper could not have been imagined, much less written, without the benefit of discussions, guidance, and encouragement from my friends, colleagues, and mentors: Barbara King, Bill Stokoe, David Armstrong, Joanne Scheibman, Larry Gorbet, Joan Bybee, and Phyllis Wilcox. The inadequacies are, of course, my own.

1. In fact, cognitive linguistics has no "rules" per se; the closest analogue would be a highly general and fully productive constructional schema. Most such "rules," however, are seen as "special and actually rather atypical cases in the overall spectrum of linguistic patterns, most of which exhibit some lesser degree of generality and/or productivity" (Langacker 1995:17).

2. The list of cognitive abilities is extracted from various sources including Langacker 1987, 1991a, and 1995 and unpublished materials by Langacker.

3. When I began my involvement in the American Sign Language (ASL)–using community, I was always struck by the complementarity of eating and talking/signing. Speakers talk while preparing their food; once the food reaches the mouth, conversation ceases or is restricted. For signers, preparing food precludes conversation; once the food is in the mouth, conversation continues. I recognize that this complementarity depends on cultural taboos against talking with food in one's mouth; my observation is meant only to demonstrate that these means of action and communication are susceptible to such restrictions.

4. It would be instructive, but again beyond the scope of this chapter, to explore these relationships in modern, fully grammatical, visible-gestural languages such as ASL. Despite claims to the contrary, I believe it is possible to

demonstrate that the same iconic mappings not only still appear but also emerge in newly evolving signed languages (Goldin-Meadow et al. 1994). For example, entity qualities are mapped onto features of hand shape; verbal qualities (such as temporal aspect) are mapped onto movement features; relationships (whether spatial, temporal, or logical) among entities (whether real or construed) are mapped onto spatial relations among the hands and body; and so forth.

5. Readers might wonder whether I am not confusing syntax and semantics in saying that grammatical relations such as subject and object are grounded in semantic archetypes such as agent and patient (see Beakin 1996:66 for such a charge). Within the cognitive linguistics framework, grammatical-syntactic relations are derived from semantic archetypes such as those mentioned here (see Langacker 1991b:282–329).

6. McCune (this volume; McCune et al. 1996) describes the development of human infant vocalizations along a course in which vocalizations start under conditions of effortful activity, then accompany acts of focal (visual) attention without communicative intent, and finally are used as communicative tokens. This developmental course not only reflects the role of gesture in the ontogenesis of human language but also mirrors the transition of instrumental actions into meaningful actions through emancipation.

References

Abler, W. L. 1989. On the particulate principle of self-diversifying systems. *J. Social & Biol. Structures*, **12**, 1–13.

Aiello, L. C. 1993. The fossil evidence for modern human origins in Africa: a revised view. *Am. Anthropol.*, **95**, 73–96.

Aiello, L. C., & Dunbar, R. I. M. 1993. Neocortex size, group size, and the evolution of language. *Curr. Anthropol.*, **34**, 184-93.

Aiello, L. C., & Wheeler, P. 1995. The expensive-tissue hypothesis: the brain and the digestive system in human and primate evolution. *Curr. Anthropol.*, **36**, 199–221.

Ainsworth, M. D. S., & Bell, S. M. 1970. Attachment, exploration and separation: illustrated by the behavior of one-year-olds in a strange situation. *Child Devel.*, **41**, 49–67.

Ainsworth, M. D. S., Blehar, M. C., Waters, E., & Wall, S. 1978. *Patterns of Attachment*. Hillsdale, New Jersey: Lawrence Erlbaum.

Alcock, J. E. 1996. The propensity to believe. In: *The Flight from Science and Reason* (Ed. by P. R. Gross, N. Levitt & M. Lewis), pp. 64–78. Annals N.Y. Acad. Sci., **775**.

Alexander, R. D. 1974. The evolution of social behavior. *Ann. Rev. Ecol. Syst.*, **5**, 325–83.

REFERENCES

Allin, J. T., & Banks, E. M. 1972. Functional aspects of ultrasound production by infant albino rats (*Rattus norvegicus*). *Anim. Behav.*, **20**, 175–78.

Altmann, S. A. 1974. Baboons, space, time, and energy. *Am. Zool.*, **14**, 221–48.

Andrew, R. J. 1964. The displays of the primates. In: *Evolutionary and Genetic Biology of Primates* (Ed. by J. Buettner-Janusch), pp. 227–309. New York: Academic Press.

Andrew, R. J. 1976. Use of formants in the grunts of baboons and other nonhuman primates. In: *Origins and Evolution of Language and Speech* (Ed. by S. R. Harnad, H. D. Steklis, & J. Lancaster), pp. 673–93. New York: New York Academy of Sciences.

Arensberg, B., Schepartz, L. A., Tiller, A. M., Vandermeersch, B., & Yak, Y. 1990. A reappraisal of the anatomical basis for speech in Middle Paleolithic hominids. *Am. J. Phys. Anthropol.*, **83**, 137–46.

Armstrong, D. F., Stokoe, W. C., & Wilcox, S. E. 1994. Signs of the origin of syntax. *Curr. Anthropol.*, **35**, 349–68.

Armstrong, D. F., Stokoe, W. C., & Wilcox, S. E. 1995. *Gesture and the Nature of Language*. Cambridge: Cambridge University Press.

Armstrong, E. 1983. Relative brain size in mammals. *Science*, **220**, 1302–4.

Baars, B. J., & Bernard, J. 1996. Understanding subjectivity: global workspace theory and the resurrection of the observing self. *J. Consciousness Studies*, **3**, 211–16.

Baptista, L. F., & Gaunt, S. L. L. 1997. Social interaction and vocal development in birds. In: Social Influences on Vocal Development (Ed. by C. T. Snowdon & M. Hausberger), pp. 23–40. Cambridge: Cambridge University Press.

Bard, K. A. 1990. "Social tool use" by free-ranging orangutans: a Piagetian and developmental perspective on the manipulation of an animate object. In: *Language and Intelligence in Monkeys and Apes* (Ed. by S. T. Parker & K. R. Gibson), pp. 356–78. Cambridge: Cambridge University Press.

Bard, K. A. 1992. Intentional behavior and intentional communication in young free-ranging orangutans. *Child Dev.*, **63**, 1186–97.

Bastian, J. 1965. Primate signaling systems and human language. In: *Primate Behavior: Field Studies of Monkeys and Apes* (Ed. by I. DeVore), pp. 585–606. New York: Holt, Rinehart and Winston.

Bates, E., Benigni, L., Bretherton, I., Camaioni, L., & Volterra, V. 1979. *The Emergence of Symbols: Cognition and Communication in Infancy*. New York: Wiley.

Bates, E., Dale, P., & Thal, D. 1995. Individual differences and their implications for early language development. In: Handbook of Child Language (Ed. by

P. Fletcher and B. MacWhinney), pp. 96–151. Cambridge, Massachusetts: Blackwell.

Bates, E., Elman, J., Johnson, M., Karmiloff-Smith, A., Parisi, D., & Plunkett, K. 1996. *On Innateness.* Technical Report no. 9602. La Jolla, California: Center for Language Research.

Bates, E., & Marchman, V. A. 1988. What is and is not universal in language acquisition. In: *Language, Communication and the Brain* (Ed. by F. Plum), pp. 19–38. New York: Raven Press.

Bauers, K. A., & Snowdon, C. T. 1990. Discrimination of chirp variants in the cotton-top tamarin. *Am. J. Primatol.,* **21,** 53–60.

Beakin, M. 1996. *The Making of Language.* Edinburgh: Edinburgh University Press.

Beckoff, M., & Jamieson, D. 1996. *Readings in Animal Cognition.* Cambridge, Massachusetts: MIT Press.

Berdecio, S., & Nash, L. T. 1981. *Chimpanzee Visual Communication.* Anthropology Research Papers, vol. 26. Tempe: Arizona State University.

Berger, P., & Luckmann, T. 1967. *The Social Construction of Reality.* Garden City, New York: Doubleday.

Bernstein, I. S. 1970. Some behavioral elements of the Cercopithecoidea. In: *Old World Monkeys: Evolution, Systematics, and Behavior* (Ed. by J. H. Napier & P. H. Napier), pp. 263–95. New York: Academic Press.

Bernstein, I. S. 1980. Activity patterns in a stumptail macaque group. *Folia Primatol.,* **33,** 20–45.

Bernstein, I. S., & Ehardt, C. L. 1985a. Agonistic aiding: kinship, rank, age, and sex influences. *Am. J. Primatol.,* **8,** 37–52.

Bernstein, I. S., & Ehardt, C. L. 1985b. Intragroup agonistic behavior in rhesus monkeys, *Macaca mulatta. Int. J. Primatol.,* **6,** 209–26.

Bernstein, I. S., Williams, L., & Ramsay, M. 1983. The expression of aggression in Old World monkeys. *Int. J. Primatol.,* **4,** 113–25.

Bertrand, M. 1969. *The Behavioural Repertoire of the Stumptail Macaque.* Basel: Karger.

Berwick, R. C. 1997. Syntax facit saltum: computation and the genotype and phenotype of language. *J. Neuroling.,* **10,** 231–49.

Bickerton, D. 1990. *Language and Species.* Chicago: University of Chicago Press.

Bickerton, D. 1995. *Language and Human Behavior.* Seattle: University of Washington Press.

Biederman, I. 1990. Higher-level vision. In: *Visual Cognition and Action* (Ed. by

D. N. Osherson, S. M. Kosslyn, & J. M. Hollerbach), pp. 41–72. Cambridge, Massachusetts: MIT Press.

Blake, J., & Dolgoy, S. 1993. Gestural development and its relation to cognition during the transition to language. *J. Nonverbal Behav.*, **17**, 87–102.

Blake, J., McConnell, S., Horton, G., & Benson, N. 1992. The gestural repertoire and its evolution over the second year. *Early Devel. and Parenting*, **1**, 127–36.

Blest, A. 1963. The concept of "ritualization." In: *Current Problems in Animal Behavior* (Ed. by W. Thorpe & O. Zangwill), pp. 102–25. Cambridge: Cambridge University Press.

Bloom, L. 1973. *One Word at a Time.* The Hague: Mouton.

Bloom, L. 1993. *The Transition from Infancy to Language.* New York: Cambridge University Press.

Blum, D. 1994. *Monkey Wars.* New York: Oxford University Press.

Blumberg, M. S., & Alberts, J. R. 1990. Ultrasonic vocalizations of rat pups in the cold: an acoustic by-product of laryngeal braking? *Behav. Neurosci.*, **104**, 808–17.

Boccia, M. L. 1989. Comparison of the physical characteristics of grooming in two species of macaques (*Macaca nemestrina* and *M. radiata*). *J. Comp. Psychol.*, **103**, 177–83.

Boehm, C. H. 1989. Methods of isolating chimpanzee vocal communication. In: *Understanding Chimpanzees* (Ed. by P. Heltne & L. Marquardt), pp. 38–59. Cambridge, Massachusetts: Harvard University Press.

Boehm, C. H. 1992. Vocal communication of *Pan troglodytes*: "triangulating" to the origin of spoken language. In: *Language Origin: A Multidisciplinary Approach* (Ed. by J. Wind, B. Chiarelli, B. Bichakjian, A. Nocentini, & A. Jonker), pp. 323–50. Boston: Kluwer Academic.

Boehm, C. H. 1993. Egalitarian behavior and reverse dominance hierarchies. *Curr. Anthropol.*, **34**, 227–54.

Boesch, C. 1991. Teaching in wild chimpanzees. *Anim. Behav.*, **41**, 530–32.

Boesch, C. 1993. Aspects of transmission of tool-use in wild chimpanzees. In: *Tools, Language and Cognition in Human Evolution* (Ed. by K. R. Gibson & T. Ingold), pp. 171–83. Cambridge: Cambridge University Press.

Boesch, C. 1994. Chimpanzee–red colobus monkeys: a predator-prey system. *Anim. Behav.*, **47**, 1135–48.

Boesch, C. 1996. Social groupings in Taï chimpanzees. In: *Great Ape Societies* (Ed. by W. C. McGrew, L. F. Marchant, & T. Nishida), pp. 101–13. Cambridge: Cambridge University Press.

Boesch, C., & Boesch, H. 1984. Mental maps in wild chimpanzees: an analysis of hammer transports for nutcracking. *Primates,* **25,** 160–70.

Boesch, C., & Boesch, H. 1989a. Tool use and tool making in wild chimpanzees. *Folia Primatol.,* **54,** 86–99.

Boesch, C., & Boesch, H. 1989b. Hunting behavior of wild chimpanzees in the Taï National Park. *Am. J. Phys. Anthropol.,* **78,** 547–73.

Boinski, S. 1993. Vocal coordination of troop movement among white-faced capuchin monkeys, *Cebus capucinus. Am. J. Primatol.,* **30,** 85–100.

Bolinger, D. 1978. Intonation across languages. In: *Universals of Human Language, II: Phonology* (Ed. by J. H. Greenberg et al.), pp. 471–524. Stanford, California: Stanford University Press.

Bolinger, D. 1985. The inherent iconism of intonation. In: *Iconicity in Syntax: Proceedings of a Symposium on Iconicity in Syntax, Stanford, June 24–26, 1983* (Ed. by J. Haiman), pp. 97–108. Amsterdam: John Benjamins.

Bolinger, D. 1986. *Intonation and Its Parts: Melody in Spoken English.* Stanford, California: Stanford University Press.

Bolinger, D. 1989. *Intonation and Its Uses: Melody in Grammar and Discourse.* Stanford, California: Stanford University Press.

Borchert, C. M., & Zihlman, A. L. 1990. The ontogeny and phylogeny of symbolizing. In: *The Life of Symbols* (Ed. by M. LeC. Foster & L. J. Botscharow), pp. 15–44. Boulder, Colorado: Westview.

Boughman, J. W. 1997. Greater spear-nosed bats give group distinctive calls. *Behav. Ecol. Sociobiol.,* **40,** 61–70.

Boughman, J. W. 1998. Vocal learning by greater spear-nosed bats. *Proc. Royal Soc. Lond.,* **265,** 227–33.

Brace, C. L. 1995. Biocultural interaction and the mechanism of mosaic evolution in the emergence of "modern" morphology. *Am. Anthropol.,* **97,** 711–21.

Brakke, K. E., & Savage-Rumbaugh, E. S. 1993. Patterns of productive vocabulary growth in bonobo and chimpanzee. Poster presentation, biennial meeting of the Society for Research in Child Development, New Orleans, Louisiana.

Brockelman, W. Y., & Schilling, D. 1984. Inheritance of stereotyped gibbon calls. *Nature,* **312,** 634–36.

Browman, C. P., & Goldstein, L. 1989. Articulatory gestures as phonological units. *Phonology,* **6,** 201–51.

Brown, P., & Levinson, S. C. 1987. *Politeness: Some Universals in Language Usage.* Cambridge: Cambridge University Press.

Bruner, J. S. 1975. The ontogenesis of speech acts. *J. Child Lang.*, **1,** 1–19.

Bruner, J. S. 1983. *Child's Language: Learning to Use Language.* New York: Norton.

Bunge, M. 1996. In praise of intolerance to charlatanism in academia. In: *The Flight from Science and Reason* (Ed. by P. R. Gross, N. Levitt, & M. Lewis), pp. 96–116. Annals N.Y. Acad. Sci., **775.**

Bunn, H. 1981. Archaeological evidence for meat-eating by Plio-Pleistocene hominids from Koobi Fora and Olduvai Gorge. *Nature,* **291,** 574–77.

Burling, R. 1986. The selective advantage of complex language. *Ethol. Sociobiol.,* **7,** 1–16.

Burling, R. 1993. Primate calls, human language, and nonverbal communication. *Curr. Anthropol.,* **34,** 25–53.

Burr, D. 1976. Neandertal vocal tract reconstructions: a critical appraisal. *J. Hum. Evol.,* **5,** 285–90.

Butovskaya, M. L. 1993a. Kinship and different dominance styles in groups of three species of the genus *Macaca* (*M. arctoides, M. mulatta, M. fascicularis*). *Folia Primatol.,* **60,** 210–24.

Butovskaya, M. L. 1993b. Intrusion into agonistic encounters in three species of genus *Macaca* (*Macaca arctoides, M. mulatta, M. fascicularis*) with reference to different dominant styles. *Primate Rep.,* **37,** 41–50.

Bybee, J. 1985. Diagrammatic iconicity in stem-inflectional relations. In: *Iconicity in Syntax: Proceedings of a Symposium on Iconicity in Syntax, Stanford, June 24–26, 1983* (Ed. by J. Haiman), pp. 11–47. Amsterdam: John Benjamins.

Bybee, J., Perkins, R., & Pagliuca, W. 1994. *The Evolution of Grammar: Tense, Aspect, and Modality in the Languages of the World.* Chicago: University of Chicago Press.

Byrne, R. W. 1995. *The Thinking Ape: Evolutionary Origins of Intelligence.* Oxford: Oxford University Press.

Byrne, R. W., & Whiten, A., eds. 1988. *Machiavellian Intelligence.* Oxford: Clarendon Press.

Caldecott, J. O. 1987. *An Ecological and Behavioural Study of the Pig-tailed Macaque.* Basel: Karger.

Calvin, W. H. 1982. Did throwing stones shape hominid brain evolution? *Ethol. Sociobiol.,* **3,** 115–24.

Calvin, W. H. 1983. A stone's throw and its launch window: timing precision and its implications for language and hominid brains. *J. Theoretical Biol.,* **104,** 121–35.

Calvin, W. H. 1987. The brain as a Darwin machine. *Nature,* **330,** 33–34.

Calvin, W. H. 1993. The unitary hypothesis: a common neural circuitry for novel manipulations, language, plan-ahead, and throwing? In: *Tools, Language and Cognition in Human Evolution* (Ed. by K. R. Gibson & T. Ingold), pp. 230–50. Cambridge: Cambridge University Press.

Cameron, D. W. 1993. The Pliocene hominid and protochimpanzee behavioral morphotypes. *J. Anthropol. Archaeol.,* **12,** 386–414.

Candland, D. K. 1993. *Feral Children and Clever Animals.* New York: Oxford University Press.

Carlson, A. A., Ziegler, T. E., & Snowdon, C. T. 1997. Ovarian function of pygmy marmoset daughters (*Cebuella pygmaea*) in intact and motherless families. *Am. J. Primatol.,* **43,** 347–55.

Caro, T. M., & Hauser, M. D. 1992. Is there teaching in non-human animals? *Q. Rev. Biol.,* **67,** 152–74.

Cartmill, M. 1990. Human uniqueness and theoretical content in paleoanthropology. *Int. J. Primatol.,* **11,** 173–92.

Cartmill, M. 1993. *A View to a Death in the Morning: Hunting and Nature through History.* Cambridge, Massachusetts: Harvard University Press.

Cartmill, M. 1994. Reinventing anthropology. *Yearbk. Phys. Anthropol.,* **37,** 1–9.

Case, R. 1985. *Intellectual Development: Birth to Adulthood.* New York: Academic Press.

Chapman, C. A., White, F. J., & Wrangham, R. W. 1994. Party size in chimpanzees and bonobos. In: *Chimpanzee Cultures* (Ed. by R. W. Wrangham, W. C. McGrew, F. B. M. de Waal, & P. G. Heltne), pp. 41–57. Cambridge: Harvard University Press.

Chavaillon, J. 1976. Evidence for the technical practices of early Pleistocene hominids, Shungura Formation, lower Omo valley, Ethiopia. In: *Earliest Man and Environments in the Lake Rudolf Basin* (Ed. by Y. Coppens, F. C. Howell, G. L. Isaac, & R. E. F. Leakey), pp. 565–73. Chicago: University of Chicago Press.

Cheney, D. L., & Seyfarth, R. M. 1982. How vervet monkeys perceive their grunts: field playback experiments. *Anim. Behav.,* **30,** 739–51.

Cheney, D. L., & Seyfarth, R. M. 1990. *How Monkeys See the World: Inside the Mind of Another Species.* Chicago: University of Chicago Press.

Chevalier-Skolnikoff, S. 1979. The gestural abilities of apes. *Behav. Brain Sci.,* **2,** 382–83.

Chevalier-Skolnikoff, S. 1989. Spontaneous tool use and sensorimotor intelligence in *Cebus* compared with other monkeys and apes. *Behav. Brain Sci.,* **12,** 561–627.

Chomsky, N. 1965. *Aspects of the Theory of Syntax.* Cambridge, Massachusetts: MIT Press.

Chomsky, N. 1966. *Cartesian Linguistics.* New York: Harper and Row.

Chomsky, N. 1971. Recent contributions to the theory of innate ideas. In: *The Philosophy of Language* (Ed. by J. Searle), pp. 121–29. Oxford: Oxford University Press.

Chomsky, N. 1972. *Language and Mind.* New York: Harcourt Brace Jovanovich.

Christopher, S. B., & Gelini, H. R. 1977. Sex differences in use of a species-typical facial gesture by pigtail monkeys (*Macaca nemestrina*). *Primates,* **18,** 565–77.

Churchill, S. E. 1993. Weapon technology, prey size selection, and hunting methods in modern hunter–gatherers: implications for hunting in the Paleolithic and Mesolithic. In: *Hunting and Animal Exploitation in the Later Paleolithic and Mesolithic of Eurasia* (Ed. by G. L. Peterkin, H. M. Bricker, & P. Mellars), pp. 11–24. Washington, D.C.: Archaeological Papers of the American Anthropological Association.

Churchland, P. 1986. *Neurophilosophy.* Cambridge, Massachusetts: MIT Press.

Cleveland, J., & Snowdon, C. T. 1982. The complex vocal repertoire of the adult cotton-top tamarin *(Saguinus oedipus). Z. Tierpsychol.,* **58,** 231–70.

Clutton-Brock, T. H., & Harvey, P. 1980. Primates, brains, and ecology. *J. Zool. Lond.,* **190,** 309–32.

Colmenares, F. 1990. Greeting behaviour in male baboons, I: communication, reciprocity and symmetry. *Behaviour,* **113,** 81–116.

Corballis, M. C. 1992. On the evolution of language and generativity. *Cognition,* **44,** 197–226.

Corruccini, R. S. 1994. Reaganomics and the fate of the progressive Neandertals. In: *Integrative Paths to the Past: Paleoanthropological Advances in Honor of F. Clark Howell* (Ed. by R. S. Corruccini & R. L. Ciochon), pp. 697–708. Englewood Cliffs, New Jersey: Prentice Hall.

Crystal, D. 1980. *A First Dictionary of Linguistics and Phonetics.* London: Andre Deutsch.

Darwin, C. 1872. *The Expression of Emotions in Man and Animals.* London: Murray. Reprint. Chicago: University of Chicago Press, 1965.

Davidson, I. 1988. The naming of parts: ethnography and the interpretation of Australian prehistory. In: *Archaeology with Ethnography: An Australian Perspective* (Ed. by B. Meehan & R. Jones), pp. 17–32. Canberra: Department of Prehistory, Australian National University.

Davidson, I. 1989. *La economía del final del Paleolítico en la España oriental.* Valencia: Diputación Provincial.

Davidson, I. 1991. The archaeology of language origins: a review. *Antiquity,* **65,** 39–48.

Davidson, I. 1997a. The power of pictures. In: Beyond Art: *Pleistocene Image and Symbol* (Ed. by M. Conkey, O. Soffer, D. Stratmann, & N. Jablonski), pp. 125–58. San Francisco: Memoirs of the California Academy of Sciences, vol. 23.

Davidson, I. 1997b. Pervye liudi, stavshie avstraliitsami. In: *Chelovek saseliaet planeru Zemli: Global'noe rasselenie gominid* (Ed. by A. A. Velichko & O. Soffer), pp. 226–46. Moscow: Institute of Geography, Russian Academy of Sciences.

Davidson, I., & Noble, W. 1989. The archaeology of perception: traces of depiction and language. *Curr. Anthropol.,* **30,** 125–55.

Davidson, I., & Noble, W. 1992. Why the first colonization of the Australian region is the earliest evidence of modern human behavior. *Archaeol. in Oceania,* **27,** 135–42.

Davidson, I., & Noble, W. 1993a. Tools and language in human evolution. In: *Tools, Language and Cognition in Human Evolution* (Ed. by K. R. Gibson & T. Ingold), pp. 363–88. Cambridge: Cambridge University Press.

Davidson, I., & Noble, W. 1993b. On the evolution of language. *Curr. Anthropol.,* **34,** 165–66.

Davidson, I., & Noble, W. 1998. Two views on language origins. *Cambridge Archaeol. J.,* **8,** 82–88.

Davidson, I., & Noble, W. n.d. Changes in hominid brain sizes and argument about the evolutionary emergence of language. Ms. in preparation.

Dawkins, R. 1987. *The Blind Watchmaker.* New York: W. W. Norton.

Deacon, T. W. 1992. The neural circuitry underlying primate calls and human language. In: *Language Origin: A Multidisciplinary Approach* (Ed. by J. Wind, B. Chiarelli, B. Bichakjian, A. Nocentini, & A. Jonker), pp. 121–62. Boston: Kluwer Academic.

Deacon, T. W. 1997. *The Symbolic Species: The Co-evolution of Language and the Brain.* New York: W. W. Norton.

Deane, P. D. 1992. *Grammar in Mind and Brain: Explorations in Cognitive Syntax.* Berlin: Mouton de Gruyter.

de Boysson-Bardies, B., Vihman, M. M., Roug-Hellichius, L., Durand, C., Landberg, I., & Arao, F. 1992. Material evidence of infant selection from the target language: a cross-linguistic phonetic study. In: *Phonological Development: Models, Research, Implications* (Ed. by C. Ferguson, L. Menn, & C. Stoel–Gammon), pp. 369–91. Timonium, Maryland: York Press.

Defler, T. R. 1978. Allogrooming in two species of macaques (*Macaca nemestrina* and *Macaca radiata*). *Primates,* **19,** 153–67.

Denham, W. W. 1975. Population properties of physical groups among the Alyawara tribe of Central Australia. *Archaeol. & Phys. Anthropol. in Oceania,* **10,** 114–51.

Dennett, D. C. 1988. The intentional stance in theory and practice. In: *Machiavellian Intelligence* (Ed. by R. Byrne & A. Whiten), pp. 180–201. Oxford: Oxford University Press.

Dennett, D. C. 1995. *Darwin's Dangerous Idea.* London: Penguin Books.

Descartes, R. 1980 [1641]. *Discourse on Method and Meditations on First Philosophy.* Translated by D. A. Cress. Indianapolis: Hackett Publishing.

De Troyer, A., Kelly, S., Macklem, P. T., & Zin, W. A. 1985. Mechanics of intercostal space and actions of internal and external intercostal muscles. *J. Clin. Invest.,* **75,** 850–57.

de Waal, F. B. M. 1984. *Chimpanzee Politics: Power and Sex among Apes.* New York: Harper and Row.

de Waal, F. B. M. 1986. The brutal elimination of a rival among captive male chimpanzees. *Ethol. Sociobiol.,* **7,** 237–51.

de Waal, F. B. M. 1988. The communicative repertoire of captive bonobos (*Pan paniscus*) compared to that of chimpanzees. *Behaviour,* **106,** 183–251.

de Waal, F. B. M. 1989. *Peacemaking among Primates.* Cambridge, Massachusetts: Harvard University Press.

de Waal, F. B. M. 1996. *Good Natured: The Origins of Right and Wrong in Humans and Other Animals.* Cambridge, Massachusetts: Harvard University Press.

de Waal, F. B. M., & Ren, R. 1988. Comparison of the reconciliation behavior of stumptail and rhesus macaques. *Ethology,* **78,** 129–42.

Dewey, J. 1966 [1916]. *Democracy and Education.* New York: Free Press.

de Winter, W. 1988. Behavioral flexibility and the evolution of language. In: *The Genesis of Language: A Different Judgement of Evidence* (Ed. by M. Landsberg), pp. 247–69. Berlin: Mouton de Gruyter.

Dittus, W. J. 1984. Toque macaque food calls: semantic communication concerning food distribution in the environment. *Anim. Behav.,* **32,** 470–77.

Donald, M. 1991. *Origins of the Modern Mind: Three Stages in the Evolution of Culture and Cognition.* Cambridge, Masachusetts: Harvard University Press.

Donald, M. 1993. Precis of *Origins of the Modern Mind: Three Stages in the Evolution of Culture and Cognition. Behav. Brain Sci.,* **16,** 737–91.

Duchin, L. E. 1990. The evolution of articulate speech: comparative anatomy of the oral cavity in *Pan* and *Homo. J. Hum. Evol.,* 5, 285–90.

Dunbar, R. I. M. 1988. *Primate Social Systems.* London: Croom Helm.

Dunbar, R. I. M. 1991. Functional significance of social grooming in primates. *Folia Primatol.,* **57,** 121–31.

Dunbar, R. I. M. 1992. Neocortex size as a constraint on group size in primates. *J. Hum. Evol.,* **20,** 469–93.

Dunbar, R. I. M. 1993. Coevolution of neocortical size, group size, and language in humans. *Behav. Brain Sci.,* **16,** 681–735.

Dunbar, R. I. M. 1995. Neocortex size and group size in primates: a test of the hypothesis. *J. Hum. Evol.,* **28,** 287–96.

Dunbar, R. I. M. 1996. *Grooming, Gossip, and the Evolution of Language.* Cambridge, Massachusetts: Harvard University Press.

Eckerman, C. O. 1993. Imitation and toddlers' achievement of co-ordinated action with others. In: *New Perspectives on Early Communicative Development* (Ed. by J. Nadel & L. Camaoni), pp. 116–38. London: Routledge.

Edelman, G. M. 1987. *Neural Darwinism: The Theory of Neuronal Group Selection.* New York: Basic Books.

Ehret, G. 1987. Categorical perception of sound signals: facts and hypotheses from animal studies. In: *Categorical Perception* (Ed. by S. Harnad), pp. 301–31. New York: Cambridge University Press.

Eimas, P. D., Siqueland, P., Jusczyk, P., & Vigorito, J. 1971. Speech perception in infants. *Science,* **171,** 303–6.

Ekman, P. 1994. Strong evidence for universals in facial expressions: a reply to Russell's mistaken critique. *Psychological Bulletin,* **115,** 268–87.

Ekman, P., Friesen, W. V., & Ellsworth, P. 1972. *Emotion in the Human Face: Guidelines for Research and an Integration of Findings.* New York: Pergamon Press.

Elman, J. L., Bates, E. A., Johnson, M. H., Karmiloff-Smith, A., Parisi, D., & Plunkett, K. 1996. *Rethinking Innateness.* Cambridge, Massachusetts: MIT Press.

Elowson, A. M., & Snowdon, C. T. 1994. Pygmy marmosets, *Cebuella pygmaea,* modify vocal structure in response to changed social environment. *Anim. Behav.,* **47,** 1267–77.

Elowson, A. M., Snowdon, C. T., & Lazaro-Perea, C. 1998a. "Babbling" and social context in infant monkeys: parallel to human infants. *Trends in Cognitive Science,* **2,** 35–43.

Elowson, A. M., Snowdon, C. T., & Lazaro-Perea, C. 1998b. Infant "babbling" in a nonhuman primate: complex sequences of vocal behavior. *Behaviour,* **135,** 643–64.

REFERENCES

Elowson, A. M., Sweet, C. S., & Snowdon, C. T. 1992. Ontogeny of trill and J–call vocalizations in the pygmy marmoset, *Cebuella pygmaea. Anim. Behav.*, **42**, 703–15.

Elowson, A. M., Tannenbaum, P. L., & Snowdon, C. T. 1991. Food-associated calls correlate with food preferences in cotton-top tamarins. *Anim. Behav.*, **42**, 931–37.

Erdal, D., & Whiten, A. 1994. On human egalitarianism: an evolutionary product of Machiavellian status escalation? *Curr. Anthropol.*, **35**, 175–83.

Erdal, D., & Whiten, A. 1996. Egalitarianism and Machiavellian intelligence in human evolution. In: *Modelling the Early Human Mind* (Ed. by P. Mellars & K. Gibson), pp. 139–50. Cambridge: McDonald Institute for Archaeological Research.

Estrada, A., Estrada, R., & Ervin, F. 1977. Establishment of a free-ranging colony of stumptail macaques (*Macaca arctoides*), I: social relations. *Primates*, **18**, 647–76.

Evans, C. S., Evans, L., & Marler, P. 1993. On the meaning of alarm calls. *Anim. Behav.*, **46**, 23–38.

Evans, C. S., Macedonia, J. M., & Marler, P. 1993. Effects of apparent size and speed on the response of chickens, *Gallus gallus*, to computer-generated simulations of aerial predators. *Anim. Behav.*, **46**, 1–11.

Falk, D. 1975. Comparative anatomy of the larynx in man and the chimpanzee: implications for language in the Neandertal. *Am. J. Phys. Anthropol.*, **43**, 123–32.

Falk, D. 1983. Cerebral cortices of East African early hominids. *Science*, **221**, 1072–74.

Falk, D. 1986. Evolution of cranial blood drainage in hominids: enlarged occipital/marginal sinuses and emissary foramina. *Am. J. Phys. Anthropol.*, **70**, 311–24.

Farabaugh, S. M., Linzenbold, A., & Dooling, R. J. 1994. Vocal plasticity in budgerigars (*Melopsittacus undulatus*): evidence for social factors in the learning of contact calls. *J. Comp. Psychol.*, **108**, 81–92.

Farnell, B. 1995. *Do You See What I Mean: Plains Indian Sign Talk and the Embodiment of Action.* Austin: University of Texas Press.

Fauconnier, G. 1994. *Mental Spaces.* New York: Cambridge University Press.

Fauconnier, G., & Turner, M. 1996. Blending as a central process of grammar. In: *Conceptual Structure, Discourse, and Language* (Ed. by A. E. Goldberg), pp. 113–30. Stanford, California: Center for the Study of Language and Information Publications.

Fedigan, L. M. 1982. *Primate Paradigms: Sex Roles and Social Bonds.* Montreal: Eden Press.

Fernald, A. 1989. Intonation and communicative intent in mothers' speech to infants: is the melody the message? *Child Devel., 60,* 1497–1510.

Fernald, A. 1992. Human maternal vocalizations to infants as biologically relevant signals: an evolutionary perspective. In: *The Adapted Mind* (Ed. by J. Barkow, L. Cosmides, & J. Tooby), pp. 329–427. New York: Oxford University Press.

Fiez, J. A., Petersen, S. E., Cheney, M. K., and Raichle, M. E. 1992. Impaired non-motor learning and error detection associated with cerebellar damage. *Brain,* **115,** 155–78.

Filion, C. M., Washburn, D. A., & Gulledge, J. P. 1996. Can monkeys (*Macaca mulatta*) represent invisible displacement? *J. Compar. Psychol., 110,* 386–95.

Finlay, B. L., & Darlington, R. B. 1995. Linked regularities in the development and evolution of mammalian brains. *Science,* **268,** 1578–84.

Fischer, J. L. 1988. Grasping and the gesture theory of language origins. In: *The Genesis of Language: A Different Judgment of Evidence* (Ed. by M. Landsberg), pp. 67–77. Berlin: Mouton de Gruyter.

Fletcher, R. 1981. People and space: a case study on material behavior. In: *Pattern of the Past* (Ed. by I. Hodder, G. L. Isaac, & N. Hammond), pp. 97–128. Cambridge: Cambridge University Press.

Foley, R. A. 1990. The causes of brain enlargement in human evolution. *Behav. Brain Sci.,* **13,** 354–56.

Foley, R. A., & Lee, P. C. 1989. Finite social space, evolutionary pathways, and reconstructing hominid behavior. *Science,* **243,** 901–6.

Foley, R. A., & Lee, P. C. 1991. Ecology and energetics of encephalization in hominid evolution. *Phil. Trans. Royal Soc. Lond.,* series B, **334,** 223–32.

Fooden, J. 1980. Classification and distribution of living macaques (*Macaca* Lacépède, 1799). In: *The Macaques: Studies in Ecology, Behavior, and Evolution* (Ed. by D. G. Lindburg), pp. 1–9. New York: Van Nostrand Reinhold.

Fónagy, I. 1988. Live speech and preverbal development. In: *The Genesis of Language: A Different Judgment of Evidence* (Ed. by M. E. Landsberg), pp. 183–203. Berlin: Mouton de Gruyter.

Fossey, D. 1972. Vocalizations of the mountain gorilla. *Anim. Behav.,* **20,** 36–53.

Fouts, R. S. 1975. Capacities for language in great apes. In: *Sociology and Psychology of Primates* (Ed. by R. H. Tuttle), pp. 371–90. The Hague: Mouton.

Fouts, R. S., Hirsch, A. D., & Fouts, D. S. 1982. Cultural transmission of a human language in a chimpanzee mother-infant relationship. In: *Psychobiological Perspectives: Child Nurturance* (Ed. by H. E. Fitzgerald, J. A. Mullins, & P. Page), pp. 159–93. New York: Plenum.

Fowler, C. A. 1986. An event approach to the study of speech perception from a direct-realist perspective. *J. Phonetics,* **14,** 3–28.

Fowler, C. A. 1995. Access to phonological structure in listening to speech. Paper presented to the American Acoustical Association, Washington, D.C., May 1995.

Fowler, C. A., & Levy, E. T. 1995. Talker-listener attunements to speech events. *J. Contemp. Legal Issues,* **7,** 305–28.

Franco, F., & Butterworth, G. 1996. Pointing and social awareness: declaring and requesting in the second year. *J. Child Lang.,* **23,** 307–36.

Frayer, D. W., Wolpoff, M. H., Thorne, A. G., Smith, F. H., & Pope, G. G. 1993. Theories of modern human origins: the paleontological test. *Am. Anthropol.,* **95,** 14–50.

Fridlund, A. J. 1994. *Human Facial Expression: An Evolutionary View.* San Diego: Academic Press.

Frishberg, N. 1975. Arbitrariness and iconicity: historical change in American sign language. *Language,* **51,** 696–719.

Gallup, G. G., Jr. 1970. Chimpanzees: self-recognition. *Science,* **167,** 86–87.

Gallup, G. G., Jr. 1982. Self-awareness and the emergence of mind in primates. *Am. J. Primatol.,* **2,** 237–48.

Gardner, B. T., & Gardner, R. A. 1985. Signs of intelligence in cross-fostered chimpanzees. *Phil. Trans. Royal Soc. Lond.,* series B, **308,** 159–76.

Gardner, B. T., & Gardner, R. A. 1989. *Teaching Sign Language to Chimpanzees.* Albany: State University of New York Press.

Gardner, B. T., & Gardner, R. A. 1992. Prelinguistic development of children and chimpanzees. In: *Language Origin: A Multidisciplinary Approach* (Ed. by J. Wind, B. Chiarelli, B. Bichakjian, A. Nocentini, & A. Jonker), pp. 245–64. Boston: Kluwer Academic.

Gardner, R. A., & Gardner, B. T. 1969. Teaching sign language to a chimpanzee. *Science,* **165,** 664–72.

Gardner, R. A., & Gardner, B. T. 1975. Early signs of language in child and chimpanzee. *Science,* **187,** 752–53.

Gardner, R. A., Gardner, B. T., & Drumm, P. 1989. Voiced and signed responses of cross-fostered chimpanzees. In: *Teaching Sign Language to Chimpanzees* (Ed. by

R. A. Gardner, B. T. Gardner, & T. E. Van Cantfort). Albany: State University of New York Press.

Garner, R. L. 1896. *Gorillas and Chimpanzees*. London: Osgood, McIlvaine and Company.

Gautier, J-P., & Gautier-Hion, A. 1977. Vocal communication in Old World primates. In: *How Animals Communicate* (Ed. by T. A. Sebeok), pp. 890–964. Bloomington: Indiana University Press.

Geschwind, N., 1965. Disconnection syndromes in animals and man. *Brain,* **88,** 237–94, 585–644.

Gibson, K. R. 1983. Comparative neurobehavioral ontogeny: the constructionist perspective in the evolution of language, object manipulation and the brain. In: *Glossogenetics* (Ed. by E. de Grolier), pp. 52–82. New York: Harwood Academic.

Gibson, K. R. 1986. Cognition, brain size, and the extraction of embedded food resources. In: *Primate Ontogeny, Cognition and Social Behavior* (Ed. by J. Else & P. C. Lee), pp. 93–105. Cambridge: Cambridge University Press.

Gibson, K. R. 1988. Brain size and the evolution of language. In: *The Genesis of Language: A Different Judgment of Evidence* (Ed. by M. Landsberg), pp. 149–72. Berlin: Mouton de Gruyter.

Gibson, K. R. 1990. New perspectives on instincts and intelligence: brain size and the emergence of hierarchical mental constructional skills. In: *"Language" and Intelligence in Monkeys and Apes: Comparative Developmental Perspectives* (Ed. by S. T. Parker & K. R. Gibson), pp. 97–128. Cambridge: Cambridge University Press.

Gibson, K. R. 1993a. Animal minds, human minds. In: *Tools, Language and Cognition in Human Evolution* (Ed. by K. R. Gibson & T. Ingold), pp. 3–19. Cambridge: Cambridge University Press.

Gibson, K. R. 1993b. Generative interplay between technical capacities, social relations, imitation and cognition. In: *Tools, Language and Cognition in Human Evolution* (Ed. by K. R. Gibson & T. Ingold), pp. 131–37. Cambridge: Cambridge University Press.

Gibson, K. R. 1993c. Tool use, language and social behavior in relationship to information processing capacities. In: *Tools, Language and Cognition in Human Evolution* (Ed. by K. R. Gibson & T. Ingold), pp. 251–69. Cambridge: Cambridge University Press.

Gibson, K. R. 1994. Continuity theories of human language versus the Lieberman model. *Lang. & Comm.*, **14,** 97–114.

Gibson, K. R. 1996. The biocultural human brain, seasonal migrations, and the emergence of the Upper Paleolithic. In: *Modelling the Early Human Mind* (Ed. by P. Mellars & K. Gibson), pp. 33–47. Cambridge: McDonald Institute for Archaeological Research.

Gibson, K. R., & Ingold, T., eds. 1993. *Tools, Language and Cognition in Human Evolution.* Cambridge: Cambridge University Press.

Gibson, K. R., & Jessee, S. 1993. Commentary on Glottogenesis and anatomically modern *Homo sapiens*: the evidence for and implications of a later origin of vocal language. *Curr. Anthropol.*, **34,** 585.

Gibson, K. R., & Jessee, S. 1994. Cranial base shape and laryngeal position. *Am. J. Phys. Anthropol.*, Suppl., **18,** 93.

Giles, H., & Smith, P. 1979. Accommodation theory: optimal levels of convergence. In: *Language and Social Psychology* (Ed. by H. Giles & R. St. Clair), pp. 45–65. Oxford: Basil Blackwell.

Givón, T. 1989. *Mind Code and Context: Essays in Pragmatics.* Hillsdale, New Jersey: Lawrence Erlbaum.

Givón, T. 1995. *Functionalism and Grammar.* Amsterdam: John Benjamins.

Goldin-Meadow, S. 1993. When does a gesture become language? A study of gesture used as a primary communication system by deaf children of hearing parents. In: *Tools, Language and Cognition in Human Evolution* (Ed. by K. R. Gibson & T. Ingold), pp. 63–85. Cambridge: Cambridge University Press.

Goldin-Meadow, S. 1997. The resilience of language in humans. In: *Social Influences on Vocal Development* (Ed. by C. T. Snowdon & M. Hausberger), pp. 293–311. Cambridge: Cambridge University Press.

Goldin-Meadow, S., Butcher, C., Mylander, C., & Dodge, M. 1994. Nouns and verbs in a self-styled gesture system: what's in a name? *Cog. Psychol.*, **27,** 259–319.

Goldin-Meadow, S., & Mylander, C. 1983. Gestural communication in deaf children: noneffect of parental input on language development. *Science*, **221,** 372–74.

Gómez, J. C. 1997. The study of the evolution of communication as a meeting of disciplines. *Evol. of Comm.*, **1,** 101–32.

Goodall, J. 1964. Tool-use and aimed throwing in a community of free-ranging chimpanzees. *Nature*, **201,** 1264–66.

Goodall, J. 1968. A preliminary report on expressive movements and communication in the Gombe Stream chimpanzees. In: *Primates: Studies in Adaptation and Variability* (Ed. by P. C. Jay), pp. 313–74. New York: Holt, Rinehart and Winston.

Goodall, J. 1986. *The Chimpanzees of Gombe: Patterns of Behavior.* Cambridge, Massachusetts: Harvard University Press.

Goodwin, M. H. 1990. *He-Said–She-Said: Talk as Social Organization among Black Children.* Bloomington: Indiana University Press.

Goodwin, M. H. 1997. Crafting activities: building social organization through language in girls' and boys' groups. In: *Social Influences on Vocal Development* (Ed. by C. T. Snowdon & M. Hausberger), pp. 328–41. Cambridge: Cambridge University Press.

Gopnik, A., & Wellman, H. M. 1994. The theory theory. In: *Mapping the Mind: Domain Specificity in Cognition and Culture* (Ed. by L. A. Hirschfeld & S. A. Gelman), pp. 257–93. Cambridge: Cambridge University Press.

Gouzoules, H., & Gouzoules, S. 1989. Design features and developmental modification of pigtail macaque, *Macaca nemestrina,* agonistic screams. *Anim. Behav.,* **37,** 383–401.

Gouzoules, H., Gouzoules, S., & Ashley, J. 1995. Representational signaling in non-human primate vocal communication. In: *Current Topics in Primate Vocal Communication* (Ed. by E. Zimmerman, J. D. Newman, & U. Jurgens), pp. 235–51. New York: Plenum Press.

Gouzoules, S., Gouzoules, H., & Marler, P. 1984. Rhesus monkeys (*Macaca mulatta*) screams: representational signalling in the recruitment of agonistic aid. *Anim. Behav.,* **32,** 182–93.

Gowlett, J. A. J. 1996. Mental abilities of early *Homo:* elements of constraint and choice in early rule systems. In: *Modelling the Early Human Mind* (Ed. by P. Mellars & K. Gibson), pp. 191–216. Cambridge: McDonald Institute for Archaeological Research.

Green, S. 1975. Variation of vocal pattern with social situation in the Japanese monkey (*Macaca fuscata*): a field study. In: *Primate Behavior,* vol. 4 (Ed. by L. A. Rosenblum), pp. 1–104. New York: Academic Press.

Greenfield, L. 1997. *Growing Up in the Fast Lane.* New York: Knopf.

Greenfield, P. M. 1991. Language, tools, and the brain: the development and evolution of hierarchically organized sequential behavior. *Behav. Brain Sci.,* **14,** 531–95.

Greenfield, P. M., & Savage-Rumbaugh, E. S. 1990. Grammatical combination in

Pan paniscus: process of learning and invention in the evolution and development of language. In: *"Language" and Intelligence in Monkeys and Apes: Comparative Developmental Perspectives* (Ed. by S. T. Parker and K. R. Gibson), pp. 540–78. Cambridge: Cambridge University Press.

Greenfield, S. 1997. *The Human Brain: A Guided Tour.* London: Weidenfeld and Nicolson.

Gross, P. R., Levitt, N., & Lewis, M., eds. 1996. *The Flight from Science and Reason.* Annals of the New York Academy of Sciences, no. 775.

Groves, C. P. 1989. *A Theory of Human and Primate Evolution.* Oxford: Clarendon Press.

Hailman, J. P., Ficken, M. S., & Ficken, R. W. 1985. The "chick-a-dee" call of *Parus atricapillus:* a recombinant system of animal communication compared with written English. *Semiotica,* **56,** 191–224.

Haiman, J. 1985. *Natural Syntax.* Cambridge: Cambridge University Press.

Haiman, J., ed. 1985. *Iconicity in Syntax: Proceedings of a Symposium on Iconicity in Syntax, Stanford, June 24–26, 1983.* Amsterdam: John Benjamins.

Haiman, J. 1994. Ritualization and the development of language. In: *Perspectives on Grammaticalization* (Ed. by W. Pagliuca), pp. 3–28. Amsterdam: John Benjamins.

Haiman, J. 1998. *Talk Is Cheap: Sarcasm, Alienation, and the Evolution of Language.* Oxford: Oxford University Press.

Harcourt, A. H. 1993. Brains, grouping and language. *Behav. Brain Sci.,* **16,** 706.

Harcourt, A. H., Stewart, K. J., & Hauser, M. 1993. Functions of wild gorillas' close calls, I: repertoire, context, and interspecific comparison. *Behaviour,* **124,** 89–122.

Harding, R. S. O., & Teleki, G. 1981. *Omnivorous Primates: Gathering and Hunting in Human Evolution.* New York: Columbia University Press.

Harris, J. W. K., & Capaldo, S. D. 1993. The earliest stone tools: their implications for an understanding of the activities and behaviour of late Pliocene hominids. In: *The Use of Tools by Human and Non-human Primates* (Ed. by A. Berthelet & J. Chavaillon), pp. 196–220. Oxford: Clarendon Press.

Hasegawa, T., Hiraiwa, M., Nishida, T., & Takasaki, H. 1983. New evidence of scavenging behavior in wild chimpanzees. *Curr. Anthropol.,* **24,** 231–32.

Hausberger, M., Richard-Yris, M. A., Henry, L., Lepage, L., & Schmidt, I. 1995. Song sharing reflects the social organization in a captive group of European starlings (*Sturnus vulgaris*). *J. Comp. Psychol.,* **109,** 222–41.

Hauser, M. D. 1988. How infant vervet monkeys learn to recognize starling alarm calls. *Behaviour,* **105,** 187–201.

Hauser, M. D. 1989. Ontogenetic changes in the comprehension and production of vervet monkey (*Cercopithecus aethiops*) vocalizations. *J. Comp. Psychol.,* **103,** 149–58.

Hauser, M. D. 1996. *The Evolution of Communication.* Cambridge, Massachusetts: MIT Press.

Hauser, M. D., & Fowler, C. 1991. Declination in fundamental frequency is not unique to human speech: evidence from nonhuman primates. *J. Acoust. Soc. Amer.,* **91,** 363–69.

Hauser, M. D., Teixidor, P., Fields, L., & Flaherty, R. 1993. Food-elicited calls in chimpanzees: effects of food quantity and divisibility. *Anim. Behav.,* **45,** 817–19.

Hauser, M. D., & Wrangham, R. N. 1987. Manipulation of food calls in captive chimpanzees. *Folia Primatol.,* **48,** 207–10.

Hayden, B. 1993. The cultural capacities of the Neandertals: a review and re-evaluation. *J. Hum. Evol.,* **24,** 113–46.

Hayes, C. 1951. *The Ape in Our House.* New York: Harper Brothers.

Hayes, K. J., & Nissen, C. H. 1971. Higher mental functions of a home-raised chimpanzee. In: *Behavior of Nonhuman Primates* (Ed. by A. M. Schrier & F. Stollnitz), pp. 59–115. New York: Academic Press.

Heim, J. L. 1989. La nouvelle reconstitution de crane de la Capelle-aux-Saints: methode et resultats. *Bull. Mem. Soc. d'Anthropol. Paris,* **1,** 95–118.

Hemelrijk, C. K. 1996. Reciprocation in apes: from complex cognition to self-structuring. In: *Great Ape Societies* (Ed. by W. C. McGrew, L. F. Marchant, & T. Nishida), pp. 185–95. Cambridge: Cambridge University Press.

Herzog, M., & Hopf, S. 1984. Behavioral responses to species-specific warning calls in infant squirrel monkeys reared in social isolation. *Am. J. Primatol.,* **7,** 99–106.

Hewes, G. W. 1973. Primate communication and the gestural origin of language. *Curr. Anthropol.,* **14,** 5–12.

Heyes, C. M. 1994. Reflections on self-recognition in primates. *Anim. Behav.,* **47,** 909–19.

Hinde, R. A. 1976. Interactions, relationships and social structure. *Man,* **11,** 1–17.

Hinde, R. A. 1986. Can nonhuman primates help us understand human behavior? In: *Primate Societies* (Ed. by B. B. Smuts, D. L. Cheney, R. M. Seyfarth, R. W. Wrangham, & T. T. Struhsaker), pp. 413–20. Chicago: University of Chicago Press.

Hinde, R. A. 1987. *Individuals, Relationships, and Culture.* Cambridge: Cambridge University Press.

Hinton, G., McClelland, J. L., & Rumelhart, D. E. 1986. Distributed representations. In: *Parallel Distributed Processing* (Ed. by D. E. Rumelhart & J. L. McClelland), pp. 77–109. Cambridge, Massachusetts: MIT Press.

Hinton, L., Nichols, J., & Ohala, J. J., eds. 1944. *Sound Symbolism.* Cambridge: Cambridge University Press.

Hockett, C. F. 1960. The origin of speech. *Sci. Amer.,* **203,** 88–96.

Hockett, C. F. 1963. The problem of universals in language. In: *Universals of Language* (Ed. by J. H. Greenberg), pp. 1–29. Cambridge, Massachusetts: MIT Press.

Hockett, C. F., & Ascher, R. 1964. The human revolution. *Curr. Anthropol.,* **5,** 135–68.

Hofer, M. A., & Shair, H. N. 1978. Ultrasonic vocalizations during social interaction and isolation in two-week-old rats. *Dev. Psychobiol.,* **11,** 495–504.

Hofer, M. A., & Shair, H. N. 1993. Ultrasonic vocalization, laryngeal braking and thermogenesis in rat pups: a reappraisal. *Behav. Neurosci.,* **107,** 354–62.

Hohmann, G., & Fruth, B. 1995. Loud calls in great apes: sex difference and social correlates. In: *Current Topics in Primate Vocal Communication* (Ed. by E. Zimmerman, J. D. Newman, & U. Jurgens), pp. 161–84. New York: Plenum Press.

Holloway, R. L. 1983. Human paleontological evidence relevant to language behavior. *Human Neurobiol.,* **2,** 105–14.

Holloway, R. L. 1985. The poor brain of *Homo sapiens Neandertalensis:* see what you please. In: *Ancestors: The Hard Evidence* (Ed. by E. Delson), pp. 319–24. New York: Alan R. Liss.

Hooff, J. A. R. A. M. van. 1972. The phylogeny of laughter and smiling. In: *Non-Verbal Communication* (Ed. by R. A. Hinde), pp. 209–41. Cambridge: Cambridge University Press.

Hooff, J. A. R. A. M. van. 1976. The comparison of facial expression in man and higher primates. In: *Methods of Inference from Animal to Human Behavior* (Ed. by M. von Cranach), pp. 165–96. Chicago: Aldine.

Hopper, P. 1987. Emergent grammar. In: *General Session and Parasession on Grammar and Cognition* (Ed. by J. Aske, N. Beery, L. Michaelis, & H. Flip), pp. 139–57. Proceedings of the 13th annual meeting of the Berkeley Linguistics Society. Berkeley, California.

Humphrey, N. K. 1976. The social function of intellect. In: *Growing Points in Ethology* (Ed. by P. P. G. Bateson & R. A. Hinde), pp. 303–17. Cambridge:

Cambridge University Press.

Husler, M., & Schmid, P. 1995. Comparison of the pelves of STS 14 and AL 288–1: implications for birth and sexual dimorphism in Australopithecines. *J. Human Evol.*, 29, 363–83.

Hutchens, E. 1995. *Cognition in the Wild.* Cambridge, Massachusetts: MIT Press.

Huttenlocher, J., Haight, W., Bryk, A., Selzer, M., & Lyons, T. 1991. Early vocabulary growth: relation to language input and gender. *Devel. Psychol.*, **27**, 236–48.

Izard, C. E. 1994. Innate and universal facial expressions: evidence from developmental and cross-cultural research. *Psychological Bulletin*, **115**, 288–99.

Jakobson, R. 1965. Quest for the essence of language. *Diogenes*, **51**, 21–37.

Jacobson, R. 1966. Implications of language universals for linguistics. In: *Language Universals, with Special Reference to Feature Hierarchies* (Ed. by J. Greenberg), pp. 208–19. The Hague: Mouton.

Jakobson, R., & Halle, M. 1956. *Fundamentals of Language.* Gravenhage: Mouton.

Jensen, G. D., & Gordon, B. N. 1970. Sequences of mother-infant behavior following a facial communicative gesture of pigtail monkeys. *Biol. Psych.*, **2**, 267–72.

Jerison, H. J. 1973. *Evolution of the Brain and Intelligence.* New York: Academic Press.

Jerison, H. J. 1979. The evolution of diversity in brain size. In: *Development and Evolution of Brain Size: Behavioral Implications* (Ed. by M. Hahn, C. Jensen, & B. Dudek), pp. 29–57. New York: Academic Press.

Jerison, H. J. 1980. Allometry, brain size, cortical surface, and convolutedness. In: *Primate Brain Evolution: Methods and Concepts* (Ed. by E. Armstrong & D. Falk), pp. 77–84. New York: Plenum Press.

Johnson, G. 1995. Chimp talk debate: is it really language? *New York Times,* June 6, C-1.

Johnson, G. A. 1982. Organizational structure and scalar stress. In: *Theory and Explanation in Archaeology* (Ed. by C. Renfrew, M. J. Rowlands, & B. A. Seagraves), pp. 389–421. London: Academic Press.

Johnson, J. S., & Newport, E. L. 1989. Critical period effects in second language learning: the influence of maturational state on the acquisition of English as a second language. *Cog. Psychol.*, **21**, 60–99.

John-Steiner, V. 1985. *Notebooks of the Mind: Explorations of Thinking.* Albuquerque: University of New Mexico Press.

Jones, S., Martin, R., & Pilbeam, D. 1992. *The Cambridge Encyclopedia of Human*

Evolution. Cambridge: Cambridge University Press.

Jouanjean-l'Antoene, A. 1997. Reciprocal interactions and the development of communication and language between parents and children. In: *Social Influences on Vocal Development* (Ed. by C. T. Snowdon & M. Hausberger), pp. 312–27. Cambridge: Cambridge University Press.

Judge, P. G. 1991. Dyadic and triadic reconciliation in pigtail macaques (*Macaca nemestrina*). *Am. J. Primatol.,* **23,** 225–37.

Kaas, J. 1987. The organization of the neocortex in mammals: implications for theories of brain function. *An. Rev. Psychol.,* **38,** 129–51.

Kano, T. 1992. *The Last Ape: Pygmy Chimpanzee Behavior and Ecology.* Stanford, California: Stanford University Press.

Kaplan, J. R. 1977. Patterns of fight interference in free-ranging rhesus monkeys. *Am. J. Phys. Anthropol.,* **47,** 279–87.

Karmiloff-Smith, A. 1979. *A Functional Approach to Child Language.* Cambridge: Cambridge University Press.

Keeley, L. H., & Toth, N. 1981. Microwear polishes on early stone tools from Koobi Fora, Kenya. *Nature,* **293,** 464–65.

Kegl, J., Senghas, A., & Coppola, M. 1996. Creation through contact: sign language emergence and sign language change in Nicaragua. In: *Comparative Grammatical Change: The Intersection of Language Acquisition, Creole Genesis, and Diachronic Syntax* (Ed. by M. de Graff). Cambridge, Massachusetts: MIT Press.

Kellman, P. 1993. Kinematic foundations of infant visual perception. In: *Visual Perception and Cognition in Infancy* (Ed. by C. Granrud). Hillsdale, New Jersey: Lawrence Erlbaum.

Kelso, J. A. S., Saltzman, E. L., & Tuller, B. 1986. The dynamical perspective on speech production: data and theory. *J. Phonetics,* **14,** 29–59.

Kendon, A. 1988. How gestures can become like words. In: *Cross-Cultural Perspectives in Nonverbal Communication* (Ed. by F. Poyatos), pp. 131–41. Toronto: C. J. Hogrefe.

Kendon, A. 1991. Some considerations for a theory of language origins. *Man,* **26,** 199–221.

Kendon, A. 1992. Some recent work from Italy on quotable gestures (emblems). *J. Ling. Anthropol.,* **2,** 92–108.

Kendon, A. 1993. Human gesture. In: *Tools, Language and Cognition in Human Evolution* (Ed. by K. R. Gibson & T. Ingold), pp. 43–62. Cambridge: Cambridge University Press.

Kennedy, J. S. 1992. *The New Anthropomorphism*. Cambridge: Cambridge University Press.

Kessel, E. 1955. The mating activity of balloon flies. *J. Systematic Zool.*, **4**, 97–104.

Kimura, D. 1993. *Neuromotor Mechanisms in Human Communication*. New York: Oxford University Press.

King, B. J. 1994a. *The Information Continuum: Evolution of Social Information Transfer in Monkeys, Apes, and Hominids*. Santa Fe, New Mexico: School of American Research Press.

King, B. J. 1994b. Evolutionism, essentialism, and an evolutionary perspective on language: moving beyond a human standard. *Lang. & Comm.*, **14**, 1–13.

King, B. J. 1996. Syntax and the origins of language. *Lang. & Comm.*, **16**, 193–203.

King, B.J. n.d. Ape gestures and language origins. Unpublished manuscript.

King, B. J., & Shanker, S. G. 1997. The expulsion of primates from the garden of language. *Evol. Comm.*, **1**, 59–99.

Klima, E. S., & Bellugi, U. 1966. Syntactic regulation in the speech of children. In: *Psycholinguistic Papers* (Ed. by J. Lyons & R. J. Wales), pp. 183–203. Edinburgh: Edinburgh University Press.

Klima, E. S., & Bellugi, U. 1979. *The Signs of Language*. Cambridge, Massachusetts: Harvard University Press.

Kluender, K. R. 1994. Speech perception as a tractable problem in cognitive science. In: *Handbook of Psycholinguistics* (Ed. by M. A. Gernsbacher), pp. 173–217. San Diego: Academic Press.

Kluender, K. R., Diehl, R. L., & Killeen, P. R. 1987. Japanese quail can learn phonetic categories. *Science*, **237**, 1195–97.

Knauft, B. M. 1991. Violence and sociality in human evolution. *Curr. Anthropol.*, **32**, 391–428.

Kortland, A. 1962. Chimpanzees in the wild. *Sci. Amer.*, **206**, 128–38.

Kramer, M., & Schmidhammer, J. 1992. The chi-squared statistic in ethology: use and misuse. *Anim. Behav.*, **44**, 833–41.

Kramer, S. N. 1963. *The Sumerians: Their History, Culture, and Character*. Chicago: University of Chicago Press.

Kuczaj, S. A., & Kirkpatrick, V. M. 1993. Similarities and differences in human and animal language research: toward a comparative psychology of language. In: *Language and Communication: Comparative Perspectives* (Ed. by H. Roitblat, L. Herman, & P. Nachtigall), pp. 45–63. Hillsdale, New Jersey: Lawrence Erlbaum.

Kuhl, P. K., & Miller, J. D. 1975. Speech perception in the chinchilla: voiced-voiceless distinction in alveolar plosive consonants. *Science,* **190,** 69–72.

Kuhn, S. 1995. *Mousterian Lithic Technology.* Princeton, New Jersey: Princeton University Press.

Kummer, H. 1968. Social organization of hamadryas baboons: a field study. *Biblioteca Primatologica,* **6,** 1–189.

Kuper, A. 1994. *The Chosen Primate: Human Nature and Cultural Diversity.* Cambridge, Massachusetts: Harvard University Press.

Laitman, J., Heimbach, R. C., & Crelin, E. S. 1979. The basicranium of fossil hominids as an indicator of their upper respiratory systems. *Am. J. Phys. Anthropol.,* **51,** 15–34.

Lakoff, R. 1975. *Language and a Woman's Place.* New York: Harper and Row.

Lakoff, G. 1987. *Women, Fire, and Dangerous Things: What Categories Reveal about the Mind.* Chicago: University of Chicago Press.

Lane, H. 1976. *The Wild Boy of Aveyron.* Cambridge, Massachusetts: Harvard University Press.

Langacker, R. W. 1987. *Foundations of Cognitive Grammar, vol. 1: Theoretical Foundations.* Stanford, California: Stanford University Press.

Langacker, R. W. 1988. An overview of cognitive grammar. In: *Topics in Cognitive Linguistics* (Ed. by B. Rudzka-Ostyn), pp. 3–48. Amsterdam: John Benjamins.

Langacker, R. W. 1990. Subjectification. *Cog. Ling.,* **1,** 5–38.

Langacker, R. W. 1991a. *Concept, Image, and Symbol: The Cognitive Basis of Grammar.* Berlin: Mouton de Gruyter.

Langacker, R. W. 1991b. *Foundations of Cognitive Grammar, vol. 2: Descriptive Application.* Stanford, California: Stanford University Press.

Langacker, R. W. 1995. A dynamic usage-based model. Unpublished paper.

Leavens, D. A., Hopkins, W. D., & Bard, K. A. 1996. Indexical and referential pointing in chimpanzees (*Pan troglodytes*). *J. Compar. Psychol.,* **110,** 346–53.

Lee, R. B. 1979. *The !Kung San.* Cambridge: Cambridge University Press.

Leiner, H. C., Leiner, A. L., & Dow, R. S. 1986. Does the cerebellum contribute to mental skills? *Behav. Neurosci.,* **100,** 443–54.

Lenneberg, E. 1967. *The Biological Foundations of Language.* New York: Wiley.

Lennon, E. M. 1984. Exploration, communication, and symbolization: gestural development in infancy. Master's thesis, Rutgers University, New Brunswick, New Jersey.

Liberman, A. M., Cooper, F. S., Shankweiler, D. P., & Studdert-Kennedy, M. 1967.

Perception of the speech code. *Psychol. Rev.*, **74**, 431–61.

Lieberman, D. 1993. Variability in hunter-gatherer seasonal mobility in the southern Levant: from the Mousterian to the Natufian. In: *Hunting and Animal Exploitation in the Later Paleolithic and Mesolithic of Eurasia* (Ed. by G. L Peterkin, H. M. Bricker, & P. Mellars), pp. 207–19. Washington, D.C.: American Anthropological Association.

Lieberman, D. E., & Shea, J. J. 1994. Behavioral differences between archaic and modern humans in the Levantine Mousterian. *Am. Anthropol.*, **96**, 300–332.

Lieberman, P. 1975. *On the Origins of Language: An Introduction to the Evolution of Human Speech.* New York: Macmillan.

Lieberman, P. 1991. *Uniquely Human: The Evolution of Speech, Thought, and Selfless Behavior.* Cambridge, Massachusetts: Harvard University Press.

Lieberman, P. 1995. What primate calls tells us about human evolution. In: *Current Topics in Primate Vocal Communication* (Ed. by E. Zimmerman, J. D. Newman, & U. Jurgens), pp. 273–82. New York: Plenum Press.

Lieberman, P., Crelin, E. S., & Klatt, D. H. 1972. Phonetic ability and related anatomy of the newborn, adult human, Neandertal man, and the chimpanzee. *Am. Anthropol.*, **74**, 287–307.

Lieblich, A. K., Symmes, D., Newman, J. D., & Shapiro, M. 1980. Development of the isolation peep in laboratory-bred squirrel monkeys. *Anim. Behav.*, **28**, 1–9.

Lindburg, D. G. 1991. Ecological requirements of macaques. *Lab. Anim. Sci.*, **41**, 315–22.

Limongelli, L., Boysen, S. T., & Visalberghi, E. 1995. Comprehension of cause-effect relations by tool-using chimpanzees *(Pan troglodytes). J. Compar. Psychol.*, **109**, 18–26.

Lock, A. J. 1980. *The Guided Reinvention of Language.* London: Academic Press.

Locke, J. L. 1993. *The Child's Path to Spoken Language.* Cambridge, Massachusetts: Harvard University Press.

Locke, J. L., & Snow, C. 1997. Social influences on vocal learning in human and nonhuman primates. In: *Social Influences on Vocal Development* (Ed. by C. T. Snowdon & M. Hausberger), pp. 274–92. Cambridge: Cambridge University Press.

Lorenz, K. Z. 1937. The companion in the bird's world. *Auk*, **54**, 245–73.

Luria, A. 1966. *Higher Cortical Functions in Man.* New York: Basic Books.

MacArthur, R. H., & Wilson, E. O. 1967. *Island Biogeography.* Princeton, New Jersey: Princeton University Press.

Macedonia, J. M., & Evans, C. S. 1993. Variation among mammalian alarm call systems and the problem of meaning in animal signals. *Ethology*, **93**, 177–97.

MacLarnon, A. 1993. The vertebral canal. In: *The Nariokotome* Homo erectus *Skeleton* (Ed. by A. C. Walker & R. E. F. Leakey), pp. 359–90. Cambridge, Massachusetts: Harvard University Press.

Maddieson, I. 1984. *Patterns of Sound.* Cambridge: Cambridge University Press.

Maestripieri, D. 1994. Mother-infant relationships in three species of macaques (*Macaca mulatta, M. nemestrina, M. arctoides*), II: the social environment. *Behaviour*, **131**, 97–113.

Maestripieri, D. 1996a. Gestural communication and its cognitive implications in pigtail macaques *(Macaca nemestrina). Behaviour*, **133**, 997–1022.

Maestripieri, D. 1996b. Social communication among captive stumptail macaques (*Macaca arctoides). Int. J. Primatol.*, **17**, 785–802.

Maestripieri, D. 1996c. Maternal encouragement of infant locomotion in pigtail macaques, *Macaca nemestrina. Anim. Behav.*, **51**, 603–10.

Maestripieri, D. 1996d. Primate cognition and the bared-teeth display: a reevaluation of the concept of formal dominance. *J. Comp. Psychol.*, **110**, 402–5.

Maestripieri, D. 1997. Gestural communication in macaques: usage and meaning of nonvocal signals. *Evol. Comm.* **1**, 193–222.

Maestripieri, D., & Call, J. 1996. Mother-infant communication in primates. *Adv. Study Behav.*, **25**, 613–42.

Maestripieri, D., & Scucchi, S. 1989. Seasonal changes in social relationships in an all-female rhesus monkey (*Macaca mulatta*) group. *Behaviour*, **110**, 106–14.

Maestripieri, D., & Wallen, K. 1997. Affiliative and submissive communication in rhesus macaques. *Primates*, **38**, 127–38.

Mahler, M., Pine, F., & Bergman, E. 1975. *The Psychological Birth of the Human Infant.* New York: Basic Books.

Maki, S., Fritz, J., & England, N. 1993. An assessment of early differential rearing conditions on later behavioral development of captive chimpanzees. *Infant Behav. and Devel.*, **16**, 373–82.

Malmkjaer, K. 1991. Functional linguistics. In: *The Linguistics Encylopedia* (Ed. by K. Malmkjaer), pp. 158–61, London: Routledge.

Manning, A. 1967. *An Introduction to Animal Behavior.* New York: Addison-Wesley.

Marchman, V. A. 1993. Constraints on plasticity in a connectionist model of the English past tense. *J. Cog. Neurosci.*, **5**, 215–34.

Markova, I., Graumann, C., & Foppa, K. 1995. *Mutualities in Dialogue.* Cambridge: Cambridge University Press.

Marler, P. 1970. Birdsong and speech development: could there be parallels? *Am. Sci.*, **58**, 669–74.

Marler, P. 1976. An ethological theory of the origin of vocal learning. In: *Origins and Evolution of Language and Speech* (Ed. by S. R. Harnad, H. D. Steklis, & J. Lancaster), pp. 386–95. New York: New York Academy of Sciences.

Marler, P., Evans, C. S., & Hauser, M. D. 1992. Animal signals: motivational, referential, or both. In: *Nonverbal Vocal Communication* (Ed. by H. Papousek, J. Uwe, & M. Papousek), pp. 66–86. Cambridge: Cambridge University Press.

Marler, P., & Peters, S. 1982. Subsong and plastic song: their role in vocal learning processes. In: *Acoustic Communication in Birds, vol. 1: Song Learning and Its Development* (Ed. by D. E. Kroodsma & E. H. Miller), pp. 25–50. New York: Academic Press.

Marler, P., & Tenaza, R. 1977. Signaling behavior of wild apes with special reference to vocalization. In: *How Animals Communicate* (Ed. by T. Sebeok), pp. 965–1033. Bloomington: Indiana University Press.

Marshack, A. 1989. Evolution of the human capacity: the symbolic evidence. *Yearbk. Phys. Anthropol.*, **32**, 1–34.

Marshall, L. 1976. *The !Kung of the Nyae Nyae*. Cambridge, Massachusetts: Harvard University Press.

Martin, P., & Bateson, P. 1986. *Measuring Behaviour: An Introductory Guide.* Cambridge: Cambridge University Press.

Martin, R. D. 1981. Relative brain size and basal metabolic rate in terrestrial vertebrates. *Nature*, **293**, 57–60.

Masataka, N. 1983. Categorical responses to natural and synthesized alarm calls in Goeldi's monkeys (*Callimico goeldi*). *Primates*, **24**, 40–51.

Massey, A. 1977. Agonistic aids and kinship in a group of pigtail macaques. *Behav. Ecol. Sociobiol.*, **2**, 31–40.

Matsuzawa, T. 1996. Chimpanzee intelligence in nature and in captivity: isomorphism of symbol use and tool use. In: *Great Ape Societies* (Ed. by W. C. McGrew, L. F. Marchant, & T. Nishida), pp. 196–209. Cambridge: Cambridge University Press.

Matthews, P. H. 1991. *Morphology.* 2d ed. Cambridge: Cambridge University Press.

May, B., Moody, D., & Stebbins, W. 1989. Categorical perception of conspecific communication sounds by Japanese macaques. *J. Acoust. Soc. Amer.*, **85**, 837–47.

McClelland, J. L., & Rumelhart, D., eds. 1986. *Parallel Distributed Processing*, vol. 2. Cambridge, Massachusetts: MIT Press.

McCune, L. 1992. First words: a dynamic systems view. In: *Phonological Development: Models, Research, Implications* (Ed. by C. A. Ferguson, L. Menn, & C. Stoel-Gammon), pp. 313–36. Parkton, Maryland: York Press.

McCune, L. 1995. A normative study of representational play at the transition to language. *Devel. Psychol.,* **31,** 198–206.

McCune, L., & Vihman, M. M. 1987. Vocal motor schemes. *Papers and Reports in Child Language,* **26,** 72–79.

McCune, L., & Vihman, M. M. 1999. Relational words + motion events: a universal bootstrap to syntax? Poster presentation, biennial meeting of the Society for Research in Child Development, Albuquerque, New Mexico.

McCune, L., & Vihman, M. M. n.d. Phonetic skill predicts precocious language. Ms. submitted for publication.

McCune, L., Vihman, M. M., Roug-Hellichius, L., Delery, D. B., & Gogate, L. 1996. Grunt communication in human infants (*Homo sapiens*). *J. Comp. Psychol.,* **110,** 27–37.

McCune-Nicolich, L. 1981a. The cognitive basis of relational words. *J. Child Lang.,* **8,** 15–36.

McCune-Nicolich, L. 1981b. Toward symbolic functioning: structure of early pretend games and potential parallels with language. *Child Devel.,* **52,** 785–97.

McGrew, W. C. 1987. Tools to get food: the subsistants of the Tasmanian Aborigines and Tanzanian chimpanzees compared. *J. Anthropol. Res.,* **43,** 247–58.

McGrew, W. C. 1989. Why is ape tool use so confusing? In: *Comparative Socioecology: The Behavioural Ecology of Humans and Other Mammals* (Ed. by V. Standen & R. A. Foley), pp. 457–72. Oxford: Blackwell Scientific.

McGrew, W. C. 1992. *Chimpanzee Material Culture: Implications for Human Evolution.* Cambridge: Cambridge University Press.

McGrew, W. C. 1993. The intelligent use of tools: twenty propositions. In: *Tools, Language and Cognition in Human Evolution* (Ed. by K. R. Gibson & T. Ingold), pp. 151–70. Cambridge: Cambridge University Press.

McGrew, W. C., Marchant, L. F., & Nishida, T., eds. 1996. *Great Ape Societies.* Cambridge: Cambridge University Press.

McGrew, W. C., & Tutin, C. E. G. 1978. Evidence for a social custom in wild chimpanzees? *Man,* **13,** 234–51.

McGrew, W. C., Tutin, C. E. G., Baldwin, P. J., Sharman, M. J., & Whiten, A. 1978. Primates preying upon vertebrates: new records from West Africa. *Carnivore,* **1,**

41–45.

McNeill, D. 1992. *Hand and Mind: What Gestures Reveal about Thought*. Chicago: University of Chicago Press.

Mellars, P. A. 1992. Archaeology and the population dispersal hypothesis of modern human origins in Europe. *Phil. Trans. Royal Soc. Lond.*, series B, **337**, 225–334.

Mellars, P. A. 1995. *The Neandertals*. Princeton, New Jersey: Princeton University Press.

Mellars, P. 1996. *The Neanderthal Legacy: An Archaeological Perspective from Western Europe*. Princeton, New Jersey: Princeton University Press.

Mignault, C. 1985. Transition between sensorimotor and symbolic activities in nursery-reared chimpanzees. *J. Hum. Evol.*, **14**, 747–58.

Miles, H. L. 1990. The cognitive foundations for reference in a signing orangutan. In: *"Language" and Intelligence in Monkeys and Apes* (Ed. by S. T. Parker & K. R. Gibson), pp. 511–39. Cambridge. Cambridge University Press.

Miles, H. L., & Harper, S. E. 1994. "Ape language" studies and the study of human language origins. In: *Hominid Culture in Primate Perspective* (Ed. by D. Quiatt & J. Itani), pp. 253–78. Niwot, Colorado: University Press of Colorado.

Miller, L. C., Bard, K. A., Juno, C. J., & Nadler, R. D. 1986. Behavioral responsiveness of young chimpanzees *(Pan troglodytes)* to a novel environment. *Folia Primatol.*, **47**, 128–42.

Miller, L. C., Bard, K. A., Juno, C. J., & Nadler, R. D. 1990. Behavioral responsiveness to strangers in young chimpanzees (*Pan troglodytes*). *Folia Primatol.*, **55**, 142–55.

Milton, K. T. 1988. Foraging behaviour and the evolution of primate intelligence. In: *Machiavellian Intelligence* (Ed. by R. Byrne & A. Whiten), pp. 284–305. Oxford: Clarendon Press.

Mishkin, M. B., Malamut, B., & Bachevalier, J. 1984. Memories and habits: two neural systems. In: *Neurobiology of Learning and Memory* (Ed. by G. Lynch, J. L. McGaugh, & N. M. Weinberger), pp. 65–77. New York: Guilford Press.

Mitani, J. 1996. Comparative studies of African ape vocal behavior. In: *Great Ape Societies* (Ed. by W. C. McGrew, L. F. Marchant, & T. Nishida), pp. 241–54. Cambridge: Cambridge University Press.

Mitchell, J. C. 1996. Studying biface butchery at Boxgrove: red deer butchery with replica handaxes. *Lithics*, **16**, 64–69.

Mithen, S. 1990. *Thoughtful Foragers: A Study of Prehistoric Decision Making*.

Cambridge: Cambridge University Press.

Moore, J. 1996. Savanna chimpanzees, referential models and the last common ancestor. In: *Great Ape Societies* (Ed. by W. C. McGrew, L. F. Marchant, & T. Nishida), pp. 275–92. Cambridge: Cambridge University Press.

Morgan, C. L. 1894. *An Introduction to Comparative Psychology*. London: Walter Scott.

Morse, P. A., & Snowdon, C. T. 1975. An investigation of categorical speech discrimination by rhesus monkeys. *Percept. Psychophys.*, **17**, 9–16.

Mundinger, P. 1970. Vocal imitation and recognition of finch calls. *Science*, **168**, 480–82.

Natale, F. 1989a. Patterns of object manipulation. In: *Cognitive Structure and Development in Nonhuman Primates* (Ed. by F. Antinucci), pp. 145–62. Hillsdale, New Jersey: Lawrence Erlbaum.

Natale, F. 1989b. Stage 5 object concept. In: *Cognitive Structure and Development in Nonhuman Primates* (Ed. by F. Antinucci), pp. 89–96. Hillsdale, New Jersey: Lawrence Erlbaum.

Natale, F., & Antinucci, F. 1989. Stage 6 object-concept and representation. In: *Cognitive Structure and Development in Nonhuman Primates* (Ed. by F. Antinucci), pp. 97–112. Hillsdale, New Jersey: Lawrence Erlbaum.

Negus, V. E. 1949. *The Comparative Anatomy and Physiology of the Larynx*. New York: Hafner.

Neisser, U. 1967. *Cognitive Psychology*. New York: Appleton-Century-Crofts.

Nelson, D. A., & Marler, P. 1989. Categorical perception of a natural stimulus continuum: birdsong. *Science*, **244**, 976–78.

Nelson, K. 1985. *Making Sense: The Acquisition of Shared Meaning*. New York: Academic Press.

Newman, J. D. 1995. Vocal ontogeny in marmosets and macaques: convergent and divergent lines of development. In: *Current Topics in Primate Vocal Communication* (Ed. by E. Zimmermann, J. D. Newman, & U. Jurgens), pp. 73–97. New York: Plenum Publishing.

Newman, J. D., & Symmes, D. 1982. Inheritance and experience in the acquisition of primate acoustic behavior. In: *Primate Communication* (Ed. by C. T. Snowdon, C. H. Brown, & M. R. Petersen), pp. 259–78. New York: Cambridge University Press.

Nicolich, L. McC. 1977. Beyond sensorimotor intelligence: assessment of symbolic maturity through analysis of pretend play. *Merrill-Palmer Quarterly*, **23**, 89–101.

Nieuwenhuijsen, K., Slob, A. K., & van der Werff ten Bosch, J. J. 1988. Gender-related behaviors in group-living stumptail macaques. *Psychobiology*, **16**, 357–71.

Nishida, T. 1980. The leaf-clipping display: a newly discovered expressive gesture in wild chimpanzees. *J. Hum. Evol.*, **9**, 117–28.

Nishida, T., & Hiraiwa-Hasegawa, M. 1987. Chimpanzees and bononos: cooperative relationships among males. In: *Primate Societies* (Ed. by B. B. Smuts, D. L. Cheney, R. M. Seyfarth, R. W. Wrangham, & T. T. Struhsaker), pp. 165–77. Chicago: University of Chicago Press.

Noble, W., & Davidson, I. 1991. The evolutionary emergence of modern human behavior: language and its archaeology. *Man*, **26**, 223–53.

Noble, W., & Davidson, I. 1993. Tracing the emergence of modern human behavior: methodological pitfalls and a theoretical path. *J. Anthropol. Archaeol.*, **12**, 121–49.

Noble, W., & Davidson, I. 1996. *Human Evolution, Language, and Mind: A Psychological and Archaeological Inquiry*. Cambridge: Cambridge University Press.

Nowicki, S. 1989. Vocal plasticity in captive black-capped chickadees: the acoustic basis of call convergence. *Anim. Behav.*, **37**, 64–73.

Nudo, R. J., & Masterson, R. B. 1990. Descending pathways to the spinal cord, IV: some factors related to the amount of cortex devoted to the corticospinal tract. *J. Comp. Neurol.*, **296**, 584–97.

Oakley, K. P., Andrews, P., Keeley, L. H., & Clark, J. D. 1977. A reappraisal of the Clacton spearpoint. *Proc. Prehist. Soc.*, **43**, 13–30.

Oba, R., & Masataka, N. 1996. Interspecific responses of ringtailed lemurs to playback of antipredator alarm calls given by Verraux's sifakas. *Ethology*, **102**, 441–53.

Ohala, J. J. 1994. The frequency code underlies the sound-symbolic use of voice pitch. In: *Sound Symbolism* (Ed. by L. Hinton, J. Nichols, & J. J. Ohala), pp. 325–47. Cambridge: Cambridge University Press.

Oi, T. 1990. Patterns of dominance and affiliation in wild pig-tailed macaques (*Macaca nemestrina nemestrina*) in West Sumatra. *Int. J. Primatol.*, **11**, 339–56.

Oller, K., Weiman, L. A., Doyle, W. J., & Ross, C. 1992. Infant babbling and speech. *J. Child Lang.*, **3**, 1–11.

Olson, D. R. 1986. The cognitive consequences of literacy. *Canadian Psychol.*, **27**, 109–21.

Omedes, A. 1985. Ontogeny of social communication in silvery marmosets, *Callithrix argentata. Miscellanea Zool.*, **9**, 413–18.

Owren, M. J., Seyfarth, R. M., & Hopp, S. L. 1992. Categorical vocal signaling in non-human primates. In: *Nonverbal Vocal Communication: Comparative and Developmental Approaches* (Ed. by H. Papousek, U. Jurgens, & M. Papousek), pp. 102–22. New York: Cambridge University Press.

Parker, S. T. 1985. A social-technological model for the evolution of language. *Curr. Anthropol.*, **26**, 617–39.

Parker, S. T. 1990. Why big brains are so rare: energy costs of intelligence and brain size in anthropoid primates. In: *"Language" and Intelligence in Monkeys and Apes: Comparative Developmental Perspectives* (Ed. by S. T. Parker & K. R. Gibson), pp. 129–54. Cambridge: Cambridge University Press.

Parker, S. T. 1996. Apprenticeship in tool-mediated extractive foraging: the origins of imitation, teaching, and self-awareness in apes. In: *Reaching into Thought: The Minds of the Great Apes* (Ed. by A. E. Russon, K. Bard, & S. T. Parker), pp. 348–70. Cambridge: Cambridge University Press.

Parker, S. T., & Gibson, K. R. 1979. A model of the evolution of language and intelligence in early hominids. *Behav. Brain Sci.*, **2**, 367–407.

Parker, S. T., & Gibson, K. R., eds., 1990. *"Language" and Intelligence in Monkeys and Apes: Comparative Developmental Perspectives*. Cambridge: Cambridge University Press.

Parker, S. T., Mitchell, R. W., & Boccia, M. L., eds. 1994. *Self-Awareness in Animals and Humans: Developmental Perspectives*. Cambridge: Cambridge University Press.

Peirce, C. S. 1932. *Collected Papers.* (Ed. by C. Hartshorne & P. Weiss). Cambridge, Massachusetts: Harvard University Press.

Peirce, C. S. 1955 [1940]. Logic as semiotic: the theory of signs. In: *The Philosophical Writings of Peirce* (Ed. by J. Buchler), pp. 98–119. New York: Dover.

Pelaez, F. 1982. Greeting movements among adult males in a colony of baboons, *Papio hamadryas, P. cynocephalus* and their hybrids. *Primates, 22,* 233–244.

Pepperberg, I. M. 1997. Social influences on the acquisition of human-based codes in parrots and nonhuman primates. In: *Social Influences on Vocal Development* (Ed. by C. T. Snowdon & M. Hausberger), pp. 157–77. Cambridge: Cambridge University Press.

Peters, C. R. 1972. Evolution of the capacity for language: a new start on an old problem. *Man, 7,* 33–49.

Peters, C. R. 1974. On the possible contribution of ambiguity of expression to the development of protolinguistic performance. In: *Language Origins* (Ed. by R. W. Westcott), pp. 83–102. Silver Spring, Maryland: Linstock Press.

Peterson, S. E., Fox, P. T., Posner, M. I., Minitun, M. A., & Raichle, M. E. 1988. Positron emission tomographic studies of the processing of single words. *J. Cog. Neurosci.*, **1**, 153–70.

Petit, O., & Thierry, B. 1992. Affiliative function of the silent bared-teeth display in moor macaques *(Macaca maurus)*: further evidence for the particular status of Sulawesi macaques. *Int. J. Primatol.*, **13**, 97–105.

Petitto, L. A., & Martentette, P. F. 1991. Babbling in the manual mode: evidence for the ontogeny of language. *Science*, **251**, 1493–96.

Piaget, J. 1954. *The Construction of Reality in the Child*. New York: Basic Books.

Piaget, J. 1955. *The Language and Thought of the Child*. New York: World Publishing.

Piaget, J. 1962. *Play, Dreams and Imitation*. New York: Norton.

Pierce, J. D. 1985. A review of attempts to condition operantly alloprimate vocalizations. *Primates*, **26**, 202–13.

Pinker, S. 1991. Rules of language. *Science*, **253**, 530–35.

Pinker, S. 1994. *The Language Instinct: How the Mind Creates Language*. New York: William Morrow.

Pinker, S., & Bloom, P. 1990. Natural language and natural selection. *Behav. Brain Sci.*, **13**, 707–84.

Pisoni, D. B. 1977. Identification and discrimination of the relative onset of two component tones: implications for the perception of voicing in stops. *J. Acoust. Soc. Amer.*, **61**, 1352–61.

Pisoni, D. B., & Lazarus, J. H. 1974. Categorical and non-categorical modes of speech perception along the voicing continuum. *J. Acoust. Soc. Amer.*, **55**, 328–33.

Plooij, F. X. 1978. Some basic traits of language in wild chimpanzees? In: *Action, Gesture, and Symbol: The Emergence of Language* (Ed. by A. Lock), pp. 111–31. London: Academic Press.

Plooij, F. X. 1979. How wild chimpanzee babies trigger the onset of mother-infant play and what the mother makes of it. In: *Before Speech: The Beginning of Interpersonal Communication* (Ed. by M. Bullowa), pp. 223–43. Cambridge: Cambridge University Press.

Plooij, F. X. 1984. *The Behavior of Free-Living Chimpanzee Babies and Infants*. Norwood, New Jersey: Ablex.

Poizner, H., Klima, E. S., & Bellugi, U. 1987. *What the Hands Reveal about the Brain*. Cambridge, Massachusetts: Harvard University Press.

Pola, Y. V., & Snowdon, C. T. 1975. The vocalizations of pygmy marmosets,

Cebuella pygmaea. Anim. Behav., **23,** 823–46.

Poplack, S. 1987a. Language status and language accommodation along a linguistic border. In: *Language Spread and Language Policy: Issues, Implications, and Case Studies* (Ed. by P. H. Lowenberg), pp. 90–118. Washington, D.C.: Georgetown University Press.

Poplack, S. 1987b. Contrasting patterns of code switching in two communities. In: *Aspects of Multilingualism* (Ed. by E. Wande, J. Anward, B. Nordberg, L. Steensland, & M. Thelander), pp. 51–76. Uppsala: Borgstroms.

Porges, S. W., Doussard-Roosevelt, J. A., & Maiti, A. K. 1994. Vagal tone and the physiological regulation of attention. In: *Development of Emotion Regulation: Biological and Behavioral Considerations* (Ed. by N. A. Fox), pp. 167–86. Chicago: Monographs of the Society for Research in Child Development.

Potts, R., & Shipman, P. 1981. Cutmarks made by stone tools on bones from Olduvai Gorge, Tanzania. *Nature,* **291,** 577–80.

Povinelli, D. J., Nelson, K. E., & Boysen, S. T. 1992. Comprehension of role-reversal in chimpanzees: evidence of empathy. *Anim. Behav.,* **43,** 633–40.

Povinelli, D. J., Parks, K. J., & Novak, M. A. 1992. Role reversal by rhesus monkeys but no evidence of empathy. *Anim. Behav.,* **44,** 269–81.

Povinelli, D. T., Rulf, A. B., & Bierschwale, D. T. 1994. Absence of knowledge attribution and self-recognition in young chimpanzees (*Pan troglodytes*). *J. Compar. Psychol.,* **108,** 74–90.

Premack, D. 1986. *Gavagai! Or the Future History of the Animal Language Controversy.* Cambridge, Massachusetts: MIT Press.

Premack, D. 1988. Does the chimpanzee have a theory of mind? *Behav. Brain Sci.,* **4,** 515–26.

Premack, D., & Premack, A. J. 1983. *The Mind of an Ape.* New York: W. W. Norton.

Pubols, B. H., & Pubols, L. M. 1972. Neural organization of somatosensory information in the spider monkey. *Brain Behav. Evol.,* **5,** 342–66.

Ragir, S. 1992. Adaptationist and nativist positions on language origins: a critique. In: *Language Origin: A Multidisciplinary Approach* (Ed. by J. Wind, B. Chiarelli, B. Bichakjian, A. Nocentini, & A. Jonker), pp. 39–48. Boston: Kluwer Academic.

Randall, J. A. 1995. Modification of foot-drumming signatures by kangaroo rats: changing territories and gaining new neighbours. *Anim. Behav.,* **49,** 1227–37.

Redican, W. K. 1975. Facial expressions in nonhuman primates. In: *Primate Behavior: Development in Field and Laboratory Research* (Ed. by L. A. Rosenblum), pp. 103–94. New York: Academic Press.

Reed, E. S. 1995. The ecological approach to language development: a radical solution to Chomsky's and Quine's problems. *Lang. & Comm.*, **15**, 1–29.

Remmers, J. E. 1973. Extra-segmental reflexes derived from intercostal afferents: phrenic and laryngeal responses. *J. Physiol. Lond.*, **233**, 45–62.

Reynolds, P. C., 1983. Ape constructional ability and the origin of linguistic structure. In: *Glossogenetics: The Origin and Evolution of Language* (Ed. by E. de Grolier), pp. 185–200. New York: Harwood Academic Publishers.

Reynolds, P. C., 1993. The complementation theory of language and tool use. In: *Tools, Language and Cognition in Human Evolution* (Ed. by K. R. Gibson & T. Ingold), pp. 407–45. Cambridge: Cambridge University Press.

Rhine, R. J., Cox, R. L., & Costello, M. B. 1989. A twenty-year study of long-term and temporary dominance relations among stumptailed macaques (*Macaca arctoides*). *Am. J. Primatol.*, **19**, 69–82.

Richman, B. 1997. Common fallacies that plague most language origins stories. *LOS Forum*, **24**, 15–39.

Robinson, J. G. 1979. Vocal regulation of the use of space by groups of titi monkeys, *Callicebus moloch*. *Behav. Ecol. Sociobiol.*, **5**, 1–15.

Robinson, J. G. 1984. Syntactic structures in the vocalizations of wedge-capped capuchin monkeys, *Cebus olivaceus*. *Behaviour*, **90**, 46–79.

Romanes, G. J. 1882. *Animal Intelligence.* New York: Appleton.

Roug, L., Landberg, I., & Lundberg, L. 1989. Phonetic development in early infancy: a study of four Swedish children during the first 18 months of life. *J. Child Lang.*, **16**, 19–40.

Roug-Hellichius, L. 1998. Babble, grunts and words: a study of phonetic shape and functional use in the beginnings of language. Ph.D. diss., Department of Linguistics, University of Stockholm, Stockholm, Sweden.

Roush, R. S. 1996. Food-associated calling behavior in cotton-top tamarins (*Saguinus oedipus*): environmental and developmental factors. Ph.D. diss., University of Wisconsin, Madison.

Roush, R. S., & Snowdon, C. T. 1994. Ontogeny of food-associated calls in cotton-top tamarins. *Anim. Behav.*, **47**, 263–73.

Roush, R. S., & Snowdon, C. T. n.d. The effects of social status on food-associated calling behaviour in captive cotton-top tamarins. *Anim. Behav.* In press.

Rovee-Collier, C. K. 1995. Time windows in cognitive development. *Devel. Psychol.*, **31**, 147–69.

Rovee-Collier, C. K., Sullivan, M. W., Enright, M. K., Lucas, D., & Fagen, J. W.

1980. Reactivation of infant memory. *Science*, **208**, 1159–61.

Ruehlmann, T. E., Bernstein, I. S., Gordon, T. P., & Balcaen, P. 1988. Wounding patterns in three species of captive macaques. *Am. J. Primatol.*, **14**, 125–34.

Ruff, C. B., Trinkaus, E., & Holliday, T. W. 1997. Body mass and encephalization in Pleistocene *Homo*. *Nature*, **387**, 173–76.

Ruff, C. B., & Walker, A. 1993. Body size and body shape. In: *The Nariokotome Homo erectus Skeleton* (Ed. by A. C. Walker & R. E. F. Leakey), pp. 234–65. Cambridge, Massachusetts: Harvard University Press.

Ruff, H. A. 1984. Infants' manipulative exploration of objects: effects of early age and object characteristics. *Devel. Psychol.*, **20**, 9–20.

Rumbaugh, D. M., Savage-Rumbaugh, E. S., & Washburn, D. A. 1994. Learning, prediction, and control with an eye to the future. In: *The Development of Future-Oriented Processes* (Ed. by M. M. Haith, J. B. Benson, R. J. Roberts, Jr., & B. F. Pennington), pp. 119–38. Chicago: University of Chicago Press.

Rumelhart, D., & McClelland, J., eds. 1986. *Parallel Distributed Processing*, vol. 1. Cambridge, Massachusetts: MIT Press.

Russell, J. A. 1994. Is there universal recognition of emotion from facial expression? A review of the cross-cultural studies. *Psychological Bulletin*, **115**, 102–41.

Russell, J. A. 1995. Facial expressions of emotion: what lies beyond minimal universality? *Psychol. Bull.*, **118**, 379–91.

Russon, A. E., & Galdikas, B. M. F. 1995. Constraints on great apes' imitation: model and action selectivity in rehabilitant orangutan imitation. *J. Compar. Psychol.*, **109**, 5–17.

Rymer, R. 1992a. A silent childhood—I. *New Yorker*, April 13, 41–81.

Rymer, R. 1992b. A silent childhood—II. *New Yorker*, April 20, 43–77.

Rymer, R. 1993. *Genie: A Scientific Tragedy*. New York: HarperCollins.

Sacher, G. A., & Staffeldt, E. F. 1974. Relation of gestation time to brain weight for placental mammals. *Am. Natural.*, **108**, 593–615.

Sade, D. S. 1972. A longitudinal study of the social behavior of rhesus monkeys. In *Functional and Evolutionary Biology of Primates* (Ed. by R. H. Tuttle), pp. 378–98. Chicago: Aldine.

Saffran, J. R., Aslin, R. N., & Newport, E. L. 1996. Statistical learning in eight-month-old infants. *Science*, **274**, 1926–28.

Saussure, F. de. 1959 [1916]. *Course in General Linguistics*. New York: Philosophical Library.

Savage-Rumbaugh, E. S. 1979. Symbolic communication: its origin and early development in the chimpanzee. *New Directions for Child Development*, **3**, 1–15.

Savage-Rumbaugh, E. S. 1986. *Ape Language: From Conditioned Response to Symbol.* New York: Columbia University Press.

Savage-Rumbaugh, E. S., 1996. Paper presented at the 15th conference of the International Primatological Society and the 11th conference of the American Society of Primatologists, Madison, Wisconsin.

Savage-Rumbaugh, S., & Lewin, R. 1994. *Kanzi: The Ape at the Brink of the Human Mind.* New York: John Wiley and Sons.

Savage-Rumbaugh, E. S., McDonald, K., Sevcik, R. A., Hopkins, W. D., & Rubert, F. 1986. Spontaneous symbol acquisition and communicative use by pygmy chimpanzees *(Pan paniscus). J. Exp. Psychol.*, **115**, 211–35.

Savage-Rumbaugh, E. S., Murphy, J., Sevcik, R. A., Brakke, K. E., Williams, S. L., & Rumbaugh, D. M. 1993. *Language Comprehension in Ape and Child.* Monographs of the Society for Research in Child Development, **58**, nos. 3–4.

Savage-Rumbaugh, S., Romsky, M., Hopkins, W., & Sevcik, R. 1989. Symbol acquisition and use by *Pan troglodytes, Pan paniscus, Homo sapiens.* In: *Understanding Chimpanzees* (Ed. by P. Heltne & L. Marquardt), pp. 266–95. Cambridge, Massachusetts: Harvard University Press.

Savage-Rumbaugh, E. S., & Rumbaugh, D. M. 1993. The emergence of language. In: *Tools, Language and Cognition in Human Evolution* (Ed. by K. R. Gibson & T. Ingold), pp. 86–108. Cambridge: Cambridge University Press.

Savage-Rumbaugh, E. S., Rumbaugh, D. M., & McDonald, K. 1985. Language learning in two species of apes. *Neurosci. Biobehav. Rev.,* **9**, 653–65.

Savage-Rumbaugh, E. S., Shanker, S. G., & Taylor, T. J. 1996. Apes with language. *Critical Quarterly*, **38**, 45–57.

Savage-Rumbaugh, E. S., Shanker, S. G., & Taylor, T. J. 1998. *Apes, Language, and the Human Mind.* New York: Oxford University Press.

Savage-Rumbaugh, E. S., & Wilkerson, B. J. 1978. Socio-sexual behavior in *Pan paniscus* and *Pan troglodytes:* a comparative study. *J. Hum. Evol.,* **7**, 327–44.

Savage-Rumbaugh, E. S., Wilkerson, B. J., & Bakeman, R. 1977. Spontaneous gestural communication among conspecifics in the pygmy chimpanzee (*Pan paniscus*). In: *Progress in Ape Research* (Ed. by G. H. Bourne), pp. 97–116. New York: Academic Press.

Savage-Rumbaugh, E. S., Williams, S. L., Furuichi, T., & Kano, T. 1996. Language perceived: *Pan paniscus* branches out. In: *Great Ape Societies* (Ed. by W. C. McGrew, L. F. Marchant, & T. Nishida), pp. 173–84. Cambridge: Cambridge

University Press.

Schegloff, E. 1972. Sequencing in conversational openings. In: *Directions in Sociolinguistics* (Ed. by J. Gumperz & D. Hymes), pp. 346–80. New York: Holt, Rinehart and Winston.

Schepartz, L. A. 1993. Language and modern human origins. *Yrbk. Phys. Anthropol.*, **36**, 91–126.

Searle, J. 1969. *Speech Acts.* Cambridge: Cambridge University Press.

Searle, J. 1983. *Intentionality.* Cambridge: Cambridge University Press.

Searle, J. 1992. *The Rediscovery of the Mind.* Cambridge, Massachusetts: MIT Press.

Sebeok, T. A., & Rosenthal, R. 1981. *The Clever Hans Phenomenon: Communication with Horses, Whales, Apes, and People.* Annals of the New York Academy of Sciences, no. 364.

Seidenberg, M. S., & Pettito, L. A. 1979. Signing behavior in apes: a critical review. *Cognition*, **7**, 177–215.

Semaw, S., Renne, P., Harris, J. W. K., Feibel, C. S., Bernor, R. L., Fesseha, N., & Mowbray, K. 1997. 2.5-million-year-old stone tools from Gona, Ethiopia. *Nature*, **385**, 333–36.

Sereno, M. I. 1991a. Four analogies between biological and cultural/linguistic evolution. *J. Theor. Biol.*, **151**, 467–507.

Sereno, M. I. 1991b. Language and the primate brain. In: *Proceedings of the Thirteenth Annual Cognitive Science Conference*, pp. 79–84. Hillsdale, New Jersey: Lawrence Erlbaum.

Seyfarth, R., & Cheney, D. 1986. Vocal development in vervet monkeys. *Anim. Behav.*, **34**, 1640–58.

Seyfarth, R. L., & Cheney, D. L. 1997. Some general features of vocal development in nonhuman primates. In: *Social Influences on Vocal Development* (Ed. by C. T. Snowdon & M. Hausberger), pp. 249–73. Cambridge: Cambridge University Press.

Seyfarth, R., Cheney, D. L., Harcourt, A. H., & Stewart, K. J. 1994. The acoustic features of gorilla double grunts and their relation to behavior. *Am. J. Primatol.*, **33**, 31–50.

Seyfarth, R. M., Cheney, D. L., & Marler, P. 1980. Monkey response to three different alarm calls: evidence for predator classification and semantic communication. *Science*, **210**, 801–3.

Shea, J. 1989. A functional study of the lithic industries associated with hominid fossils in the Kebara and Qafzeh Caves, Israel. In: *The Human Revolution:*

Behavioural and Biological Perspectives on the Origins of Modern Humans (Ed. by P. Mellars & C. Stringer), pp. 610–25. Princeton, New Jersey: Princeton University Press.

Shea, J. 1993. Lithic use-wear evidence for hunting by Neandertals and early modern humans from the Levantine Mousterian. In: *Hunting and Animal Exploitation in the Later Paleolithic and Mesolithic of Eurasia* (Ed. by G. L Peterkin, H. M. Bricker, & P. Mellars), pp. 189–97. Washington, D.C.: American Anthropological Association.

Shephard, P. 1996. *The Others: How Animals Made Us Human.* Washington, D.C.: Island Press.

Silberbauer, G. B. 1981. *Hunter and Habitat in the Central Kalahari Desert.* Cambridge: Cambridge University Press.

Singleton, J. L., Morford, J. P., & Goldin-Meadow, S. 1993. Once is not enough: standards of well-formedness in manual communication created over three different timespans. *Lang.,* **69,** 683 715.

Sinha, C. 1988. *Language and Representation: A Socio-Naturalistic Approach to Human Development.* New York: Harvest-Wheatsheaf.

Sinha, C. 1989. Evolution, development and the social production of mind. *Cultural Dynamics,* **2,** 188–208.

Skinner, B. F. 1969. *Contingencies of Reinforcement: A Theoretical Analysis.* New York: Appleton-Century-Crofts.

Slade, A. 1987a. A longitudinal study of maternal involvement and symbolic play during the toddler period. *Child Devel.,* **58,** 367 75.

Slade, A. 1987b. Quality of attachment and early symbolic play during the toddler period. *Child Devel.,* **58,** 78–85.

Slobin, D. I. 1985. The child as a linguistic icon-maker. In: *Iconicity in Syntax: Proceedings of a Symposium on Iconicity in Syntax, Stanford, June 24–26, 1983* (Ed. by J. Haiman), pp. 221–48. Amsterdam: John Benjamins.

Smith, B. H. 1993. The physiological age of KNM-WT 15000. In: *The Nariokotome Homo* erectus *Skeleton* (Ed. by A. C. Walker & R. E. F. Leakey), pp. 195–220. Cambridge, Massachusetts: Harvard University Press.

Smith, E. A. 1981. The application of optimal foraging theory to the analysis of hunter-gatherer group size. In: *Hunter-Gatherer Foraging Strategies* (Ed. by B. Winterhalder & E. A. Smith), pp. 36–65. Chicago: University of Chicago Press.

Smith, H. L., Newman, J. D., & Symmes, D. 1982. Vocal concomitants of affiliative behavior in squirrel monkeys. In: *Primate Communication* (Ed. by C. T.

Snowdon, C. H. Brown, & M. R. Petersen), pp. 30–49. New York: Cambridge University Press.

Smith, W. J. 1996. Communication and expectations: a social process and the cognitive operation it depends upon and influences. In: *Readings in Animal Cognition* (Ed. by M. Beckoff & D. Jamieson), pp. 243–56. Cambridge, Massachusetts: MIT Press.

Smuts, B. B., Cheney, D. L., Seyfarth, R. M., Wrangham, R. W., & Struhsaker, T. T., eds. 1986. *Primate Societies*. Chicago: University of Chicago Press.

Smuts, B. B., & Watanabe, J. M. 1990. Social relationships and ritualized greetings in adult male baboons (*Papio cynocephalus anubis*). *Int. J. Primatol.*, **11**, 147–72.

Snowdon, C. T. 1987. A naturalistic view of categorical perception. In: *Categorical Perception* (Ed. by S. Harnad), pp. 332–54. New York: Cambridge University Press.

Snowdon, C. T. 1989. Vocal communication in New World monkeys. *J. Hum. Evol.*, **18**, 611–33.

Snowdon, C. T. 1990. Language capacities of nonhuman animals. *Yrbk. Phys. Anthropol.*, **33**, 215–43.

Snowdon, C. T. 1993a. A comparative approach to language parallels. In: *Tools, Language and Cognition in Human Evolution* (Ed. by K. R. Gibson & T. Ingold), pp. 109–28. Cambridge: Cambridge University Press.

Snowdon, C. T. 1993b. The rest of the story: grooming, group size and vocal exchanges in neotropical primates. *Behav. Brain Sci.*, **16**, 718.

Snowdon, C. T. 1993c. A vocal taxonomy of the Callitrichids. In: *Marmosets and Tamarins: Systematics, Behaviour and Ecology* (Ed. by A. B. Rylands), pp. 78–94. Oxford: Oxford University Press

Snowdon, C. T., & Cleveland, J. 1984. "Conversations" among pygmy marmosets. *Am. J. Primatol.*, **7**, 15–20.

Snowdon, C. T., & Elowson, A. M. 1992. Ontogeny of primate vocal communication. In: *Topics in Primatology, vol. 1: Human Origins* (Ed. by T. Nishida, W. C. McGrew, P. Marler, M. Pickford, & F. B. M. de Waal), pp. 279–90. Tokyo: Tokyo University Press.

Snowdon, C. T., & Hausberger, M. 1997. *Social Influences on Vocal Development*. Cambridge: Cambridge University Press.

Snowdon, C. T., & Hodun, A. 1981. Acoustic adaptations in pygmy marmoset contact calls: locational cues vary with distance between conspecifics. *Behav. Ecol. Sociobiol.*, **9**, 295–300.

Snowdon, C. T., & Pola, Y. V. 1978. Interspecific and intraspecific responses to synthesized marmoset vocalizations. *Anim. Behav.*, **26**, 192–206.

Sorensen, A. P., Jr. 1967. Multilingualism in the northwest Amazon. *Am. Anthropol.*, **69**, 670–85.

Squire, L. R., & Zola-Morgan, S. 1988. Memory: brain systems and behavior. *Trends in Neurosciences*, **11**, 170–75.

Stanford, C. B., Wallis, J., Matama, H., & Goodall, J. 1994. Patterns of predation by chimpanzees on red colobus monkeys in Gombe National Park, 1982–1991. *Am. J. Phys. Anthropol.*, **94**, 213–28.

Stanger, K. F. 1993. Structure and function of the vocalizations of nocturnal prosimians (Chcirogalcidac). Ph.D. diss., Eberhard-Karls-Universitat, Tubingen, Germany.

Stark, R. E. 1993. The coupling of comfort sound vocalization with early social interaction. Paper presented at the biennial meeting of the Society for Research in Child Development, New Orleans, Louisiana.

Stark, R. E., Bernstein, L. E., & Demorest, M. E. 1993. Vocal communication in the first 18 months of life. *J. Speech & Hearing Res.*, **36**, 548–58.

Steels, L. 1997. The synthetic modeling of language origins. *Evol. of Comm.*, **1**, 1–40.

Steklis, H. D. 1985. Primate communication, comparative neurology, and the origin of language re-examined. *J. Hum. Evol.*, **14**, 157–73.

Stephan, H., Frahm, H., & Baron, G. 1981. New and revised data on volumes of brain structures in insectivores and primates. *Folia Primatol.*, **35**, 1–39.

Stern, D. 1985. *The Interpersonal World of the Infant: A View from Psychoanalysis and Developmental Psychology*. New York: Basic Books.

Stewart, K. J., & Harcourt, A. H. 1994. Gorillas' vocalizations during rest periods: signals of impending departure? *Behaviour*, **130**, 29–40.

Stiner, M. C. 1994. *Honor among Thieves: A Zooarchaeological Study of Neandertal Ecology*. Princeton, New Jersey: Princeton University Press.

Stiner, M. C., & Kuhn, S. L. 1992. Subsistence, technology, and adaptive variation in Middle Palaeolithic Italy. *Am. Anthropol.*, **94**, 306–39.

Stoel-Gammon, C., & Otomo, K. 1986. Babbling development of hearing-impaired and normally hearing subjects. *J. Speech Hear. Disord.*, **51**, 33–41.

Stokoe, W. 1983. Apes who sign and critics who don't. *Springer Series in Language Communication*, **11**, 147–58.

Stringer, C. B. 1992. Replacement, continuity and the origin of *Homo sapiens*. In: *Continuity or Replacement: Controversies in* Homo sapiens *Evolution* (Ed. by

G. Bräuer & F. H. Smith), pp. 9–24. Rotterdam: A. A. Balkema.

Stringer, C. B., & Gamble, C. 1993. *In Search of the Neanderthals: Solving the Puzzle of Human Origins*. London: Thames and Hudson.

Stringer, C., & McKie, R. 1997. *African Exodus: The Origins of Modern Humanity*. London: Random House.

Struhsaker, T. T. 1967. Auditory communication among vervet monkeys (*Cercopithecus aethiops*). In: *Social Communication among Primates* (Ed. by S. Altmann), pp. 281–324. Chicago: University of Chicago Press.

Strum, S., Forster, D., & Hutchens, E. 1997. Why Machiavellian intelligence may not be Machiavellian. In: *Machiavellian Intelligence II: Extensions and Evaluations* (Ed. by A. Whiten and R. Byrne), pp. 50–85. Cambridge: Cambridge University Press.

Studdert-Kennedy, M. 1987. The phoneme as a perceptuomotor structure. In: *Language Perception and Production: Relationships between Listening, Speaking, Reading, and Writing* (Ed. by D. A. Allport), pp. 67–84. London: Academic Press.

Sundberg, M. L. 1996. Toward granting linguistic competence to apes: a review of Savage-Rumbaugh et al.'s *Language Comprehension in Ape and Child. J. Exp. Anal. of Behavior*, **65,** 477–92.

Symmes, D., & Biben, M. 1988. Conversational vocal exchanges in squirrel monkeys. In: *Primate Vocal Communication* (Ed. by D. Todt, P. Goedeking, & D. Symmes), pp. 123–32. Berlin: Springer-Verlag.

Talmage-Riggs, G., Winter, P., Ploog, D., & Mayer, W. 1972. Effect of deafening on the vocal behavior of the squirrel monkey (*Saimiri sciureus*). *Folia Primatol.,* **17,** 404–20.

Talmy, L. 1975. The semantics and syntax of motion. In: *Semantics and Syntax* (Ed. by J. Kimball), pp. 181–238. New York: Academic Press.

Tanner, J. E., & Byrne, R. W. 1996. Representation of action through iconic gesture in a captive lowland gorilla. *Curr. Anthropol.,* **37,** 162–73.

Tanner, N. M. 1981. *On Becoming Human*. Cambridge: Cambridge University Press.

Tattersall, I. 1995. *The Fossil Trail*. Oxford: Oxford University Press.

Tattersall, I. 1996. *The Last Neanderthal: The Rise, Success, and Mysterious Extinction of our Closest Human Relatives*. New York: Macmillan.

Taylor, T. J. 1994. The anthropomorphic and the skeptical. *Lang. & Comm.,* **14,** 115–27.

Taylor, T. J. 1996. The origin of language: why it never happened. *Lang. Sci.,* **19,** 67–77.

Teleki, G. 1973. *The Predatory Behavior of Wild Chimpanzees.* Lewisburg, Pennsylvania: Bucknell University Press.

Teleki, G. 1989. Population status of wild chimpanzees (*Pan troglodytes*) and threats to survival. In: *Understanding Chimpanzees* (Ed. by P. G. Heltne & L. A. Marquardt), pp. 312–53. Cambridge, Massachusetts: Harvard University Press.

Tenaza, R. 1985. Songs of hybrid gibbons (*Hylobates lar X H. muelleri*). *Am. J. Primatol.*, **8**, 249–53.

Terrace, H. S. 1979. *Nim: A Chimpanzee Who Learned Sign Language.* New York: Knopf.

Terrace, H. S. 1985. In the beginning was the "name." *Am. Psychol.*, **40**, 1011–28.

Terrace, H. S., Pettito, L. A., Sanders, R. J., & Bever, T. G. 1979. Can an ape create a sentence? *Science,* **206**, 891–900.

Thelen, E. 1981. Rythmical behavior in infancy: an ethological perspective. *Devel. Psychol.*, **17**, 237–57.

Thelen, E. 1991. Motor aspects of emergent speech. In: *Biological and Behavioral Determinants of Language Development* (Ed. by N. A. Krasnegor, D. M. Rumbaugh, R. L. Schiefelbusch, & M. Studdert-Kennedy), pp. 339–62. Hillsdale, New Jersey: Lawrence Erlbaum.

Thelen, E. 1993. Timing and developmental dynamics in the acquisition of early motor skills. In: *Developmental Time and Timing* (Ed. by G. Turkewitz & D. A. Devenny), pp. 85–104. Hillsdale, New Jersey: Lawrence Erlbaum.

Thieme, H. 1997. Lower palaeolithic hunting spears from Germany. *Nature,* **385**, 807–10.

Thieme, H., & Veil, S. 1985. Neue Untersuchungen zum eemzeitlichen Elefanten-Jagdplatz Lehringen, Ldkr. Verden. *Die Kunde* N.F., **36**, 11–58.

Thierry, B. 1984. Clasping behavior in *Macaca tonkeana. Behaviour,* **89**, 1–28.

Thierry, B. 1990. Feedback loop between kinship and dominance: the macaque model. *J. Theor. Biol.*, **145**, 511–21.

Thierry, B., Demaria, C., Preuschoft, S., & Desportes, C. 1989. Structural convergence between silent bared-teeth display and relaxed open-mouth display in the tonkean macaque (*Macaca tonkeana*). *Folia Primatol.*, **52**, 178–84.

Thorndike, E. L. 1889. Animal intelligence: an experimental study of the associative processes in animals. *Psychol. Rev.*, Monographs Supp. **28**, 1–109.

Tinbergen, N. 1951. *The Study of Instinct.* Oxford: Clarendon Press.

Tinbergen, N. 1952. Derived activities: their causation, biological significance, origin, and emancipation during evolution. *Q. Rev. Biol.*, **27**, 1–32.

Tobias, P. L. 1987. The brain of *Homo habilis:* a new level of organization in cerebral evolution. *J. Hum. Evol.,* **16,** 741–62.

Tomasello, M. 1990. Cultural transmission in the tool use and communicatory signaling of chimpanzees? In: *"Language" and Intelligence in Monkeys and Apes* (Ed. by S. T. Parker & K. R. Gibson), pp. 274–311. Cambridge: Cambridge University Press.

Tomasello, M. 1993. It's imitation, not mimesis. *Behav. Brain Sci.,* **16,** 771–72.

Tomasello, M. 1994. The question of chimpanzee culture. In: *Chimpanzee Cultures* (Ed. by R. W. Wrangham, W. C. McGrew, F. B. M. De Waal, & P. G. Heltne), pp. 301–17. Cambridge, Massachusetts: Harvard University Press.

Tomasello, M. 1995. Language is not an instinct. *Cognitive Develop.,* **10,** 131–56.

Tomasello, M. 1996. Do apes ape? In: *Social Learning in Animals: The Roots of Culture* (Ed. by C. Heyes & B. Golef), pp. 319–46. San Diego: Academic Press.

Tomasello, M., & Call, J. 1994. Social cognition of monkeys and apes. *Yearbk. Phys. Anthropol.,* **37,** 273–305.

Tomasello, M., & Call, J. 1997. *Primate Cognition.* New York: Oxford University Press.

Tomasello, M., Call, J., Nagell, K., Olguin, R., & Carpenter, M. 1994. The learning and use of gestural signals by young chimpanzees: a trans-generational study. *Primates,* **35,** 137–54.

Tomasello, M., & Camaioni, L. 1997. A comparison of the gestural communication of apes and human infants. *Hum. Devel.,* **40,** 7–24.

Tomasello, M., George, B. L., Kruger, A. C., Farrar, M. J., & Evans, A. 1985. The development of gestural communication in young chimpanzees. *J. Hum. Evol.,* **14,** 175–86.

Tomasello, M., Gust, D., & Frost, G. T. 1989. A longitudinal investigation of gestural communication in young chimpanzees. *Primates,* **30,** 35–50.

Tomasello, M., Kruger, A. C., & Ratner, H. H. 1993. Cultural learning. *Behav. Brain Sci.,* **16,** 495–552.

Tooby, J., & DeVore, I. 1987. The reconstruction of hominid behavioral evolution through strategic modeling. In: *The Evolution of Human Behavior: Primate Models* (Ed. by W. G. Kinzey), pp. 183–237. Albany: State University of New York Press.

Toth, N., & Schick, K. 1993. Early stone industries and inferences regarding language and cognition. In: *Tools, Language and Cognition in Human Evolution* (Ed. by K. R. Gibson & T. Ingold), pp. 346–62. Cambridge: Cambridge University Press.

Trevarthen, C. 1979. The function of emotions in early infant communication and development. In: *New Perspectives in Early Communicative Development* (Ed. by J. Nadel & L. Camaioni), pp. 48–81. London: Routledge.

Trinkaus, E., & Shipman, P. 1993. *The Neandertals: Of Skeletons, Scientists, and Scandal.* New York: Vintage Books.

Tyack, P. L., & Sayigh, L. S. 1997. Vocal learning in cetaceans. In: *Social Influences on Vocal Development* (Ed. by C. T. Snowdon & M. Hausberger), pp. 208–33. Cambridge: Cambridge University Press.

Ujhelyi, M. 1996. Is there any intermediate stage between animal communication and language? *J. Theor. Biol.*, **180,** 71–76.

van Hooff, J. A. R. A. M. 1967. The facial displays of the Catarrhine monkeys and apes. In: *Primate Ethology* (Ed. by D. Morris), pp. 7–68. London: Weidenfield.

Van Lawick, H., Marler, P., & Van Lawick-Goodall, J. 1971. *Vocalizations of Wild Chimpanzees.* 16-mm film. New York: Rockefeller University.

van Schaik, C. P. 1989. The ecology of social relationships amongst female primates. In: *Comparative Socioecology: The Behavioural Ecology of Humans and Other Mammals* (Ed. by V. Standen & R. Foley), pp. 195–218. Boston: Blackwell.

Vauclair, J. 1990. Primate cognition: from representation to language. In: *"Language" and Intelligence in Monkeys and Apes* (Ed. by S. T. Parker & K. R. Gibson), pp. 312–29. New York: Cambridge University Press.

Vehrencamp, S. 1983. A model for the evolution of despotic versus egalitarian societies. *Anim. Behav.*, **31,** 667–82.

Vihman, M. M. 1996. *Phonological Development: The Origin of Language in the Child.* Oxford: Blackwell.

Vihman, M. M., Macken, M. A., Miller, R., Simmons, H., & Miller, J. 1985. From babbling to speech: a reassessment of the continuity issue. *Language,* **61,** 395–443.

Vihman, M. M., & McCune, L. 1994. When is a word a word? *J. Child Lang.,* **21,** 517–42.

Vihman, M. M., & Miller, R. 1988. Words and babble at the threshold of language acquisition. In: *The Emergent Lexicon: The Child's Development of a Linguistic Vocabulary* (Ed. by M. D. Smith & J. Locke), pp. 151–84. New York: Academic Press.

Vihman, M. M., & Velleman, S. 1989. Phonological reorganization: a case study. *Lang. Speech,* **32,** 149–70.

Vihman, M. M., Velleman, S., & McCune, L. 1994. How abstract is child phonology? In: *First and Second Language Phonology* (Ed. by M. Yavas), pp. 9–44. San

Diego: Singular Publishing Group.

Visalberghi, E., & Fragaszy, D. M. 1990. Do monkeys ape? In: *"Language" and Intelligence in Monkeys and Apes* (Ed. by S. T. Parker & K. R. Gibson), pp. 247–75. Cambridge: Cambridge University Press.

Visalberghi, E., Fragaszy, D. M., & Savage-Rumbaugh, S. 1995. Performance in a tool-using task by common chimpanzees (*Pan troglodytes*), bonobos *(Pan paniscus)*, an orangutan *(Pongo pygmaeus)*, and capuchin monkeys *(Cebus apella)*. *J. Compar. Psychol.*, **109**, 52–60.

Visalberghi, E., & Limongelli, L. 1994. Lack of comprehension of cause-effect relationships in tool-using capuchin monkeys (*Cebus apella*). *J. Compar. Psychol.*, **108**, 15–22.

Volman, S. F., & Khanna, H. 1995. Convergence of untutored song in group-reared zebra finches. *J. Comp. Psych.*, **109**, 211–21.

Vygotsky, L. S. 1978. *Mind in Society: The Development of Higher Mental Processes.* Cambridge, Massachusetts: Harvard University Press.

Wade, T. D. 1979. Inbreeding, kin selection, and primate social evolution. *Primates*, **20**, 355–70.

Walker, A. C. 1993. Perspectives on the Nariokotome discovery. In: *The Nariokotome* Homo erectus *Skeleton* (Ed. by A. C. Walker & R. E. F. Leakey), pp. 411–30. Cambridge, Massachusetts: Harvard University Press.

Wallace, R. 1989. Cognitive mapping and the origin of language and mind. *Curr. Anthropol.*, **30**, 518–26.

Wallace, R. 1994. Spatial mapping and the origin of language: a paleoneurological model. In: *Studies in Language Origins*, vol. 3. (Ed. by J. Wind, A. Jonker, R. Alcott, & L. Rolfe), pp. 31–43. Philadelphia: John Benjamins.

Wallman, J. 1992. *Aping Language.* Cambridge: Cambridge University Press.

Waters, R. S., & Wilson, W. A., Jr. 1976. Speech perception by rhesus monkeys: the voicing distinction in synthesized labial and velar stop consonants. *Percept. Psychophys.*, **19**, 285–89.

Watson, J. B. 1919. *Psychology from the Standpoint of a Behaviorist.* Philadelphia: Lippincott.

Weigel, R. M. 1980. Dyadic spatial relationships in pigtail and stumptail macaques: a multiple regression analysis. *Int. J. Primatol.*, **1**, 287–321.

Weiner, J. 1995. *The Beak of the Finch.* New York: Vintage.

Weiner, L. F. 1984. The evolution of language: a primate perspective. *Word*, **35**, 255–69.

Welker, W. I., Adrian, H. O., Lifschutz, W., Kaulen, R., Caviedes, E., & Gutman, W. 1976. Somatosensory cortex of the llama (*Lama glama*). *Brain Behav. Evol.*, **13**, 184–93.

Welker, W. I., & Carlson, M. 1976. Somatic sensory cortex of hyrax *(Procavia)*. *Brain Behav. Evol.*, **13**, 294–301.

Welker, W. I., & Seidenstein, S. 1959. Somatic sensory representation in the cerebral cortex of the raccoon. *J. Comp. Neurol.*, **111**, 469–501.

Werner, H., & Kaplan, B. 1963. *Symbol Formation*. New York: Wiley.

Wertsch, J. 1985. *Vygotsky and the Social Formation of Mind*. Cambridge, Massachusetts: Harvard University Press.

Wertsch, J. 1991. *Voices of the Mind: A Sociocultural Approach to Mediated Action*. Cambridge, Massachusetts: Harvard University Press.

Whallon, R. 1989. Elements of cultural change in the later Paleolithic. In: *The Human Revolution: Behavioural and Biological Perspectives on the Origins of Modern Humans* (Ed. by P. Mellars & C. Stringer), pp. 433–54. Princeton, New Jersey. Princeton University Press,

Wheeler, P. E. 1985. The loss of functional body hair in man: the influence of thermal environment, body form and bipedality. *J. Human Evol.*, **14**, 23–28.

Whiten, A. 1991. *Natural Theories of Mind: Evolution, Development and Simulation of Everyday Mindreading*. Oxford: Basil Blackwell.

Whiten, A. 1993. Social complexity: the roles of primates' grooming and people's talking. *Behav. Brain Sci.*, **16**, 719.

Whiten, A., & Byrne, R. W. 1988. Tactical deception in primates. *Behav. Brain Sci.*, **11**, 233–74.

Wickelgren, I. 1997. Working memory linked to intelligence. *Science*, **275**, 1581.

Wiener, L. 1984. The evolution of language: a primate perspective. *Word*, **35**, 255–69.

Wilcox, S. 1996. Not from Jove's brow. *Lang & Comm.*, **16**, 179–92.

Wind, J. 1970. *On the Phylogeny and the Ontogeny of the Human Larynx*. Groningen, Netherlands: Wolters-Noordhoff.

Winterhalder, B. 1981. Foraging strategies in the boreal forest. In: *Hunter-Gatherer Strategies* (Ed. by B. Winterhalder & E. A. Smith), pp. 66–98. Chicago: University of Chicago Press.

Wood, B. A. 1992. Origin and evolution of the genus *Homo*. *Nature*, **355**, 783–90.

Wrangham, R. W. 1987. The significance of African apes for reconstructing human evolution. In: *The Evolution of Human Behavior: Primate Models* (Ed. by W.

G. Kinzey), pp. 51–71. Albany: State University of New York Press.

Wrangham, R. W., Chapman, C. A., Clark-Arcadi, A. P., & Isabirye-Basuta, G. 1996. Social ecology of Kanyawara chimpanzees: implications for understanding the costs of great ape groups. In: *Great Ape Societies* (Ed. by W. C. McGrew, L. F. Marchant, & T. Nishida), pp. 45–57. Cambridge: Cambridge University Press.

Wrangham, R. W., & Peterson, D. 1997. *Demonic Males: Apes and the Origins of Human Violence.* New York: Houghton Mifflin.

Wynn, T. G. 1979. The intelligence of later Acheulean hominids. *Man* (n.s.), **14,** 371–91.

Wynn, T. G. 1993. Layers of thinking in tool behavior. In: *Tools, Language and Cognition in Human Evolution* (Ed. by K. R. Gibson & T. Ingold), pp. 389–406. Cambridge: Cambridge University Press.

Yerkes, R. 1925. *Almost Human.* New York: Century.

Zeller, A. C. 1996. The interplay of kinship organisation and facial communication in the macaques. In: *Evolution and Ecology of Macaque Societies* (Ed. by J. E. Fa & D. G. Lindburg), pp. 527–50. New York: Cambridge University Press.

Ziegler, T. E., Snowdon, C. T., & Uno, H. 1990. Social interactions and determinants of ovulation in tamarins *(Saguinus).* In: *Primate Socioendocrinology* (Ed. by T. E. Ziegler & F. B. Bercovitch), pp. 113–33. New York: Alan R. Liss.

Zihlman, A. 1996. Reconstructions reconsidered: chimpanzee models and human evolution. In: *Great Ape Societies* (Ed. by W. C. McGrew, L. F. Marchant, & T. Nishida), pp. 293–304. Cambridge: Cambridge University Press.

Zimmerman, E., Newman, J. D., & Jurgens, U., eds. 1995. *Current Topics in Primate Vocal Communication.* New York: Plenum Press.

Zoloth, R. R., Petersen, M. R., Beecher, M. D., Green, S., Marler, P., Moody, D. B., & Stebbins, W. 1979. Species-specific perceptual processing of vocal sounds by monkeys. *Science,* **204,** 870–72.

Index

School of American Research
Advanced Seminar Series

PUBLISHED BY SAR PRESS

PUBLISHED BY CAMBRIDGE UNIVERSITY PRESS

DREAMING: ANTHROPOLOGICAL AND
PSYCHOLOGICAL INTERPRETATIONS
  Barbara Tedlock, ed.

THE ANASAZI IN A CHANGING
ENVIRONMENT
  George J. Gumerman, ed.

REGIONAL PERSPECTIVES ON THE OLMEC
  Robert J. Sharer & David C. Grove, eds.

THE CHEMISTRY OF PREHISTORIC
HUMAN BONE
  T. Douglas Price, ed.

THE EMERGENCE OF MODERN HUMANS:
BIOCULTURAL ADAPTATIONS IN THE
LATER PLEISTOCENE
  Erik Trinkaus, ed.

THE ANTHROPOLOGY OF WAR
  Jonathan Haas, ed.

THE EVOLUTION OF POLITICAL SYSTEMS
  Steadman Upham, ed.

CLASSIC MAYA POLITICAL HISTORY:
HIEROGLYPHIC AND ARCHAEOLOGICAL
EVIDENCE
  T. Patrick Culbert, ed.

TURKO-PERSIA IN HISTORICAL
PERSPECTIVE
  Robert L. Canfield, ed.

CHIEFDOMS: POWER, ECONOMY, AND
IDEOLOGY
  Timothy Earle, ed.

PUBLISHED BY UNIVERSITY OF CALIFORNIA PRESS

WRITING CULTURE: THE POETICS
AND POLITICS OF ETHNOGRAPHY
  James Clifford &
  George E. Marcus, eds.

RECONSTRUCTING PREHISTORIC PUEBLO
SOCIETIES
William A. Longacre, ed.

NEW PERSPECTIVES ON THE PUEBLOS
Alfonso Ortiz, ed.

STRUCTURE AND PROCESS IN LATIN
AMERICA
Arnold Strickon &
Sidney M. Greenfield, eds.

THE CLASSIC MAYA COLLAPSE
T. Patrick Culbert, ed.

METHODS AND THEORIES OF
ANTHROPOLOGICAL GENETICS
M. H. Crawford & P. L. Workman, eds.

SIXTEENTH-CENTURY MEXICO: THE
WORK OF SAHAGUN
Munro S. Edmonson, ed.

ANCIENT CIVILIZATION AND TRADE
Jeremy A. Sabloff &
C. C. Lamberg-Karlovsky, eds.

PHOTOGRAPHY IN ARCHAEOLOGICAL
RESEARCH
Elmer Harp, Jr. ed.

MEANING IN ANTHROPOLOGY
Keith H. Basso & Henry A. Selby, eds.

THE VALLEY OF MEXICO: STUDIES IN PRE-
HISPANIC ECOLOGY AND SOCIETY
Eric R. Wolf, ed.

DEMOGRAPHIC ANTHROPOLOGY:
QUANTITATIVE APPROACHES
Ezra B. W. Zubrow, ed.

THE ORIGINS OF MAYA CIVILIZATION
Richard E. W. Adams, ed.

EXPLANATION OF PREHISTORIC CHANGE
James N. Hill, ed.

EXPLORATIONS IN ETHNOARCHAEOLOGY
Richard A. Gould, ed.

ENTREPRENEURS IN CULTURAL CONTEXT
Sidney M. Greenfield, Arnold Strickon,
& Robert T. Aubey, eds.

THE DYING COMMUNITY
Art Gallaher, Jr., &
Harlan Padfield, eds.

SOUTHWESTERN INDIAN RITUAL DRAMA
Charlotte J. Frisbie, ed.

LOWLAND MAYA SETTLEMENT PATTERNS
Wendy Ashmore, ed.

SIMULATIONS IN ARCHAEOLOGY
Jeremy A. Sabloff, ed.

CHAN CHAN: ANDEAN DESERT CITY
Michael E. Moseley & Kent C. Day, eds.

SHIPWRECK ANTHROPOLOGY
Richard A. Gould, ed.

ELITES: ETHNOGRAPHIC ISSUES
George E. Marcus, ed.

THE ARCHAEOLOGY OF LOWER CENTRAL
AMERICA
Frederick W. Lange &
Doris Z. Stone, eds.

LATE LOWLAND MAYA CIVILIZATION:
CLASSIC TO POSTCLASSIC
Jeremy A. Sabloff &
E. Wyllys Andrews V, eds.

Photo by Katrina Lasko

Participants in the School of American Research advanced
seminar "The Evolution of Language: Assessing the Evidence
from Nonhuman Primates," Santa Fe, New Mexico, October
1996. Kneeling, from left: Talbot Taylor, Dario Maestripieri.
Standing, from left: Iain Davidson, Robbins Burling,
Sue Savage-Rumbaugh, Sherman Wilcox, Barbara King,
Lorraine McCune, Charles Snowdon, Kathleen Gibson.